Z 90 —

AF835566

Case-Law and the Development of International Law

Case-Law and the Development of International Law

Contributions by International Courts and Tribunals

Edited by

Patrícia Galvão Teles and Manuel Almeida Ribeiro

BRILL
NIJHOFF

LEIDEN | BOSTON

Library of Congress Cataloging-in-Publication Data

Names: International Law Association. Regional Conference (2019 : Universidade do Minho) | Teles, Patrícia Galvão, 1970- editor. | Ribeiro, Manuel de Almeida, editor. | Universidade do Minho, host institution. | International Law Association. Portuguese branch, sponsoring body.
Title: Case-law and the development of international law : contributions by international courts and tribunals / edited by Patrícia Galvão Teles and Manuel Almeida Ribeiro.
Description: Leiden ; Boston : Brill Nijhoff, [2022] | Includes index. | Summary: "This book explores recent contributions of the case-law of international courts and tribunals to the development of international law. It begins by looking at how such case-law has contributed to the development of the methodology of international law and to the development of procedural rules. It further examines recent contributions from three major players in the international judicial arena: the International Court of Justice, the International Tribunal for the Law of the Sea and the mechanisms for Investor-State Dispute Settlement"– Provided by publisher.
Identifiers: LCCN 2021038884 (print) | LCCN 2021038885 (ebook) | ISBN 9789004467651 (hardback) | ISBN 9789004467668 (ebook)
Subjects: LCSH: International courts–Influence–Congresses. | International law–Cases–Congresses.
Classification: LCC KZ6250 .I585 2022 (print) | LCC KZ6250 (ebook) | DDC 341.5/5–dc23
LC record available at https://lccn.loc.gov/2021038884
LC ebook record available at https://lccn.loc.gov/2021038885

Typeface for the Latin, Greek, and Cyrillic scripts: "Brill". See and download: brill.com/brill-typeface.

ISBN 978-90-04-46765-1 (hardback)
ISBN 978-90-04-46766-8 (e-book)

Copyright 2022 by Koninklijke Brill NV, Leiden, The Netherlands.
Koninklijke Brill NV incorporates the imprints Brill, Brill Nijhoff, Brill Hotei, Brill Schöningh, Brill Fink, Brill mentis, Vandenhoeck & Ruprecht, Böhlau Verlag and V&R Unipress.
All rights reserved. No part of this publication may be reproduced, translated, stored in a retrieval system, or transmitted in any form or by any means, electronic, mechanical, photocopying, recording or otherwise, without prior written permission from the publisher. Requests for re-use and/or translations must be addressed to Koninklijke Brill NV via brill.com or copyright.com.

This book is printed on acid-free paper and produced in a sustainable manner.

Printed by Printforce, United Kingdom

Contents

PART 4
The Contribution of the International Tribunal for the Law of the Sea (ITLOS) to the Developement of the Law of the Sea

PART 5
Investor-State Dispute Settlement and Its Impact on International Investment Law

PART 6
General Conclusions

Note from the Editors

This edited volume is based on the proceedings of the second regional conference of the International Law Association (ILA) that the Portuguese Society of International Law, its Portuguese Branch, has organized. The conference took place in the School of Law of the University of Minho, in Braga, on 18–19 September 2019, under the theme "The Contribution of the Case-Law of International Courts and Tribunals to the Development of International Law".

The first conference organized by the Portuguese Branch of the ILA had taken place in Lisbon in 2014 with the title "Towards a Universal Justice? Putting International Courts and Jurisdictions into Perspective." In its aftermath, a book was also published by Brill-Nijhoff, with the edited contributions of the presenters in the conference.[1]

The theme of the 2019 conference was a suitable follow-up to that of the previous event and one of increasing importance in view of the current state of play regarding the development of international law.

After the Second World War, the international order of the second half of the XX century, although in a context of a "divided world" – to use an expression coined by Antonio Cassese -, witnessed a golden age regarding the development of general international law, with the construction of an extended set of regimes, from international human rights law, to humanitarian law and the law of the sea, to mention just a few examples.

The end of the Cold War brought with it the hope that the new framework of international relations would allow further developments. So far, these hopes have not been confirmed and there are few reasons to believe that this will change in the near future.

This does not mean, of course, that international law froze. On the contrary, bilateral treaties have been concluded in many fields, as well as in treaties in regional frameworks. However, multilateral conventions with universal reach have less and less managed to find a favourable environment to develop. It is common, nowadays, to speak about States' "lack of appetite" for new multilateral conventions. In the last two decades, the Draft Articles prepared by the International Law Commission, including on the important topic of State Responsibility, have not been adopted as conventions in the framework of the United Nations. In particular, since 2015, with the Paris Agreement on Climate

---

1 D. Moura Vicente (ed.), *Towards a Universal Justice? Putting International Courts and Jurisdictions into Perspective* (Brill Nijhoff, 2016).

Change, very few or none have been the major universal treaties concluded or in perspective of being so in the near future.

In this context, the role of international courts and tribunals has had an enhanced relevance, and will continue to do so, in the building and the development of the legal foundations of the international legal order, such as for the identification of international customary law and regarding the interpretation of treaties.

International courts and tribunals, including the International Court of Justice and the International Tribunal for the Law of the Sea, have been busier than ever in the past decades. States have placed renovated trust in judicial instances to settle their disputes and such instances have also taken the opportunity in the cases they are seized of, in contentious and at times in advisory proceedings, to further contribute to the development of international law.

This book looks, thus, through different lenses, to the recent contribution of the case-law of international courts and tribunals to the development of international law. It starts by looking at how such case-law has contributed to the development of the methodology of international law and to the development of procedural rules.

It then examines recent contributions from three major players in the international judicial arena: the International Court of Justice, the International Tribunal for the Law of the Sea and the mechanisms for Investor-State Dispute Settlement.

Although the majority of the permanent members of the Security Council do not accept the compulsory jurisdiction of the International Court of Justice, its jurisprudence has been, in the same way as the one of its predecessor, the Permanent Court of International Justice, one way of building widely accepted paths regarding the development of international law.

The International Tribunal for the Law of the Sea, a more recent institution in the international order, is a means for the resolution of disputes concerning the common use of the sea, a space not yet fully explored that our planet still offers to all humankind, in the hope that it will contribute to the peaceful profit of its benefits by all nations.

Bilateral investment treaties have allowed for an increasing flow of foreign investment, indispensable for a fairer spread of the benefits of globalization. But this has also led to an increasing number of investor-State disputes, involving a multiplicity of actors, and the search for the best model for the mechanisms to resolve such disputes.

It is our sincere hope that the contributions of the distinguished participants in the conference, some of which are made available to the international legal community in this edited volume, will be of added value to the ongoing debates on the important matter of the role of international courts and tribunals in the development of international law.

We thank all the participants who attended the conference in Braga in September of 2019 and, in particular, the authors who have contributed to this book. It is with great pride that this book contains a mix of contributions from established scholars and practitioners and promising new voices from diverse regions of the world, ensuring also gender balance with regard to the contributors.

The editors are also very grateful to Brill-Nijhoff for supporting this publication and to António Varela Cid, who has greatly assisted in the editing of the book.

Patrícia Galvão Teles
Vice-President of the Portuguese Society of International Law

Manuel Almeida Ribeiro
President of the Portuguese Society of International Law
Lisbon, April 2021

Notes on Contributors

Manuel Almeida Ribeiro
has a degree in Law (1978) from UERJ – Universidade do Estado do Rio de Janeiro (Brazil), holds a PhD in Political Science (1992) from the Universidade Técnica de Lisboa and is aggregate professor since 2002 in political and juridical sciences of the Universidade Técnica de Lisboa. He was assistant professor in the Law School of the Universidade de Lisboa (1981–1984), assistant professor in the Social and Political Sciences of the Universidade de Lisboa (1983–1982), professor (1992–2003) and, since 2003, is a tenured professor. He is currently President of the Sociedade Portuguesa de Direito Internacional, the Portuguese Branch of the International Law Association.

Vasco Becker-Weinberg
is professor at NOVA School of Law, Lisbon, and is the co-coordinator of the LL.M program on The Law of the Sea and the Sea-Economy, ranked in 2018 and 2019, respectively, 3rd and 4th best in the world in the Eduniversal Best Masters Ranking. Professor Becker-Weinberg teaches law of the sea and ocean governance subjects, as well as public international law, and has researched at prominent academic institutions and written and published extensively. He has been on several delegations to international fora and advises on law of the sea matters and on policies and legislation on many ocean governance subjects. Professor Becker-Weinberg was previously Legal Advisor to the Portuguese Secretary of the Sea and a full-time scholar at the International Max Planck Research School for Maritime Affairs at the University of Hamburg.

Maria Emilynda Jeddahlyn Pia V. Benosa
is a Research Associate at the Centre for International Law of the National University of Singapore. Prior to this, she was a Law Reform Specialist for the University of the Philippines Law Centre's Institute for Maritime Affairs and Law of the Sea and has acted as Legal Adviser to key Philippine government offices on maritime security and the protection of marine biodiversity beyond national jurisdiction. She obtained her LL.M. in National Security Law, and a Certificate in International Arbitration and Dispute Resolution from Georgetown University Law Centre in 2018 under a Fulbright Foreign Student Program grant. In 2017, she held the Hamilton Shirley Amerasinghe Fellowship at the UN Division for Ocean Affairs and the Law of the Sea. She has also been

teaching Public International Law and Local Governments at the University of the Philippines College of Law since 2018.

Giulia Bernabei
is Senior Research Fellow at the Max Planck Foundation for International Peace and the Rule of Law in Heidelberg, Germany. She produced this publication prior to the beginning of her current position and her association with the Max Planck Foundation. She has previously researched and also taught public international law and international human rights law in various capacities. She holds a Dottorato di Ricerca in Discipline Giuridiche (PhD in Legal Disciplines) from Università degli Studi Roma Tre and a Master of Laws in Public International Law from Queen Mary University of London.

Pierre Bodeau-Livinec
holds a PhD (*summa cum laude*) in public international law. He is qualified as a Professor of public law in 2010 (*"agrégation"*). He currently teaches at University Paris Nanterre and serves as Director of the CEDIN. He also acts as director of the Diploma in Energy Law, Investment and International Arbitration and of the Nanterre International Law Summer School. Before entering an academic career, he held numerous positions, especially within the French Ministry of Foreign Affairs (2003–2006) and in the United Nations Office of Legal Affairs (2006–2010). His research focuses on the law of international organizations and on international responsibility. He is the Director of Studies of the International Law Association. He has been involved as counsel in numerous proceedings before international courts and tribunals, including the ICJ.

Laurence Boisson de Chazournes
has been professor in international law and international organization at the Faculty of Law of the University of Geneva since 1999. She is Director of the Geneva LL.M. in International Dispute Settlement (MIDS) and Co-director of the Geneva Centre for International Dispute Settlement (CIDS) since 2018. She is a Member of the Institute of International Law. She is an adviser to various international organizations (UN, ILO, WHO), governments and law firms. In the area of dispute settlement, she advises and litigates on a wide range of international law issues. She has served as chairperson of WTO arbitration panels, pleaded before the ICJ and been an arbitrator in investment arbitration (ICSID, ICC, PCA). She is a member of the PCA and of the CAS, in which she has also been appointed arbitrator.

Karem L. Cárdenas Ynfanzón
holds a law degree from the Pontifical Catholic University of Peru (PUCP), a Master in International Law from the Graduate Institute of International and Development Studies in Geneva, and is a PhD candidate in International Law at the same Institute, where she is also a Teaching Assistant. She has been legal assistant to Professor Dire Tladi, member of the United Nations International Law Commission, lawyer of the Office of Public International Law of the Ministry of Foreign Affairs of Peru, and international lawyer at the Office of Legal Affairs of the Peruvian Agency for Technical Cooperation of Peru (APCI).

Anna Czaplińska
is Assistant Professor at the Faculty of Law and Administration, University of Lodz, Poland. She is a member of the Council of the ILA Polish Branch, having been its Secretary-General between 2007–2017 and Communication Officer since 2017. She is a laureate of the Manfred Lachs Award for the best book on international law by a Polish author (2015). She also was scholar of the Association Heinrich Klebes pour la Promotion des Études sur l'Europe et la Démocratie at the Pierre-Mendès-France University (2003/2004).

Łukasz Dawid Dąbrowski
holds a PhD in Law and is attorney-at-law. He is currently an assistant professor at the Collegium of World Economy at Warsaw School of Economics. He is also Lecturer at the Faculty of Law and Administration at University Cardinal Stefan Wyszyński in Warsaw, in the Department of Human Rights Protection and International Humanitarian Law. He is a member of the Legislative Commission of the Polish Bar Council, of the International Law Association Polish branch, and of the Polish Association of European Studies. He provides legal services to telecommunications companies and represents legal entities in administrative and civil procedures in all types of courts.

Somesh Dutta
specializes in international dispute resolution, currently focusing on international investment law and investor-State dispute settlement at the Max Planck Institute Luxembourg for Procedural Law. His work experience includes working with the International Court of Justice and in the public international law and international arbitration practice of a leading international law firm. His research interests further include general public international law, international economic law and comparative constitutional law.

Patrícia Galvão Teles
is a member of the United Nations International Law Commission and Associate Professor of International Law at the Autonomous University of Lisbon. She is a member of the Permanent Court of Arbitration and is currently Vice-President of the Portuguese Society of International Law. She is also Senior Legal Adviser on International Law at the Legal Department of the Portuguese Ministry of Foreign Affairs and Co-Director of the Singapore eAcademy of International Law at the Centre for International Law of the Singapore National University. In 2004, she was a member of the Portuguese Delegation in the "Case concerning the Legality of the Use of Force" before the International Court of Justice, and in 1995 she assisted the Portuguese Delegation during the oral hearings in the "Case concerning East Timor" also before the International Court of Justice. She holds a PhD in International Law from the Graduate Institute for International and Development Studies in Geneva, a Master's in International Law from the same Institute and has a Law degree from the Faculty of Law of the University of Lisbon.

Stratis G. Georgilas
was called to the Athens' Bar in 1995. He is the Head of Chambers at G-H Law Chambers in Athens and the Secretary-General of ILA/Hellenic Section. He has pleaded cases before domestic Courts in Greece, the CJEU, the ECHR and other International Courts and Tribunals. He has rendered his services to several States on issues of international dispute settlement, international criminal law, law of armed conflict and aviation law. He holds a LL.M. from Cambridge University, where he studied at Hughes Hall and the Faculty of Law (1994). He read "Ptychion" in Law at Democritus University of Thrace – Faculty of Law (1992).

Joanna Gomula
has an LL.M from the University of Warsaw, an LL.M form the University of Michigan, and a PhD from the Polish Academy of Sciences. She is a Fellow at the Lauterpacht Centre for International Law, University of Cambridge. She has been associated for many years with Queen Mary College, University of London, where she has lectured WTO dispute settlement and international economic law and is the convener for the World Trade Law course of the External LL.M programme at University of London. She is also a professional lecturer at the Diplomatic Academy of Vienna, and a member of the ILA Committee on the Procedure of International Courts and Tribunals.

Claudio Grossman
is Professor of Law, Dean Emeritus, and the Raymond Geraldson Scholar for International and Humanitarian Law at American University Washington College of Law (WCL), where he served as Dean from 1995 until 2016. He is a member of the UN International Law Commission (ILC), former Chair of the UN Treaties Bodies (2013) and former member and chair of the UN Committee Against Torture. He was Member (1994–2000) and twice Chair of the Inter-American Commission on Human Rights (IACHR). His extensive litigation experience includes litigation before the International Court of Justice (ICJ) as Agent and Co-Agent of Chile (2013–2018) in the case Obligation to Negotiate Access to the Pacific Ocean, Bolivia v. Chile; and Advocate representing Chile (2008–2014) in the case Maritime Dispute (Peru v. Chile). He was awarded the 2020 Goler T. Butcher Medal by the American Society of International Law (ASIL), in recognition of his outstanding contributions to the development and effective realization of international human rights law.

Rita Guerreiro Teixeira
is a PhD researcher and teaching assistant at KU Leuven, Institute for International Law, and Junior Member of the Leuven Centre for Global Governance Studies. Her research focuses on recent developments in environmental lawmaking by international organizations. Additionally, she is a research assistant to Professor Galvão Teles at the International Law Commission and a guest researcher at CEDIS, the Research Centre on Law and Society of NOVA University, Lisbon. She holds a Bachelor's degree in Law from NOVA University, Lisbon and a LL.M in Public International Law (*cum laude*) from Leiden University. She worked as a legal intern at the Permanent Court of Arbitration and the European Commission, and is a qualified lawyer in Portugal.

Catherine Kessedjian
is Professor Emerita of the University Panthéon-Assas Paris II. She acts as arbitrator in a selected number of International Commercial and Investment Disputes. She also acts as mediator in French and English. She is a member of numerous professional organizations, notably the American Law Institute (ALI) and the Institut de droit international. For ALI, she presently acts as a member of the International Advisers Committee for the Restatement on Foreign Relations Law. She is the President of the French Branch of the International Law Association and Vice Chair of the global ILA. Until 2016, she was the Deputy Director of the European College of Paris and Director of Studies of the LL.M in European Law. In 2016, she was Visiting Professor at

Padova University (Italy) and in 2017 Wainwright Senior Fellow and Visiting Professor at McGill Faculty of Law. She was Hauser Global Visiting Professor at New York University School of Law in 2004, 2008 and 2011, and Visiting Professor at Yale Law School in January 2010.

Ioannis Konstantinidis
holds a PhD from the Sorbonne Law School/Université Paris 1 Panthéon-Sorbonne. He is an Assistant Professor of Public International Law at Qatar University – College of Law and Affiliate Member of the Centre for Law and Development. He is the Secretary of the Qatari Branch of the International Law Association. He regularly acts as counsel before the International Court of Justice and other international courts and tribunals. He is nominated on the List of Arbitrators under Annex VII of the United Nations Convention on the Law of the Sea. His research and practice focus on general international law, law of the sea, international litigation and arbitration, and human rights.

Fernando Loureiro Bastos
is an Associate Professor of Public Law at the Faculty of Law, University of Lisbon. He is also Head of Research Group (HRG) on International and European Law of the Lisbon Centre for Research in Public Law; Director of Studies of the SPDI – Sociedade Portuguesa de Direito Internacional (Portuguese Branch of the International Law Association); Member of the editorial committee of the *Enciclopédia Luso-Brasileira de Direito Internacional* (Portuguese-Brazilian Encyclopaedia of International Law), Member of the ILA Committee on International Law and Sea Level Rise and Member and of the ILA on Global Cultural Heritage Governance. He was Co-Agent and Counsel of the Republic of Guinea-Bissau, Case 19 – *M/V "Virginia G"*, International Tribunal for the Law of the Sea (2011–2014).

Nilüfer Oral
is Director of the Centre for International Law at the National University of Singapore. She is also a member of the law faculty at Istanbul Bilgi University and a member of the United Nations International Law Commission. She is co-chair of the ILC study group on sea-level rise in relation to international law. She has also worked as a legal advisor to the Turkish Foreign Ministry on matters related to the law of the sea. She was a climate change negotiator for the Turkish delegation to the UNFCCC between (2009 – 2016). She is a Distinguished Fellow of the Law of the Sea Institute at Berkeley Law (University of California Law Berkeley) and a Senior Fellow at the NUS Law School. She has been a Distinguished Lecturer at the Centre for International

Law at the National University of Singapore, the UN Regional Law Courses for International Law and the Rhodes Academy for the Law of the Sea. She was elected to the IUCN Council (2012–2016); served as Co-chair of the IUCN Specialist Group on Oceans, Coasts and Coral Reefs (2006–2018); Chair of the IUCN Academy of Environmental Law (2014–2017). She is currently a member of the IUCN World Commission on Environmental Law Steering Committee. She is also the series editor for the *International Straits of the World* publications (Brill); on the Board of Editors of the *European Journal of International Law*; Associate Editor of the *Research Perspectives in the Law of the Sea* (Brill); and the editorial board of the *International Journal of Marine and Coastal Law*.

Paula Wojcikiewicz Almeida
is an International Law Professor at Getulio Vargas Foundation Law School in Rio de Janeiro (since 2008); Director of the Jean Monnet Centre of Excellence on EU-South America Global Governance, sponsored by the European Commission; and an Associate Researcher at the Institute of International and European Law at the Sorbonne (IREDIES). She holds a Doctorate with honours *summa cum laude* in International and European Law from the *Université Paris 1 Panthéon-Sorbonne*. She has been a Researcher at the Centre for Studies and Research in International Law and International Relations of The Hague Academy of International Law (2010), Post-doctoral Visiting scholar at the Max Planck Institute for Comparative Public Law and International Law (2014) and Visiting professor at the École de droit de la Sorbonne (2019).

Michael Wood
is a member of the United Nations International Law Commission, and a Senior Fellow of the Lauterpacht Centre for International Law, University of Cambridge. He is a barrister at Twenty Essex, London, where he practises in the field of public international law, including before international courts and tribunals. He was Legal Adviser to the UK's Foreign and Commonwealth Office between 1999 and 2006, having joined as an Assistant Legal Adviser in 1970.

CHAPTER 1

Prologue – One Hundred Years of International Justice and Its Contribution to the Development of International Law

Patrícia Galvão Teles

1 One Hundred Years of International Justice

In an article published in the Harvard Law Review in 1922, Manley O. Hudson wrote, in the opening phrase, "a World Tribunal for the adjudication of international disputes is at last a reality!"[1]

For centuries, the traditional methods of international dispute settlement were either political or military. Disputes were settled by negotiation or through war, in many instances by peace treaties after conflict, such as the Treaty of Westphalia, to quote perhaps one of the most famous peace treaties in world history and that laid the foundations for modern international law and international relations.

It was only with the first international arbitrations, namely the *Alabama Claims* arbitration that took place in the late 19th Century, that the ideal of judicial means of international dispute settlements began to gain strength.

The Hague Peace Conferences of 1899 and 1907 were instrumental to that purpose, with the creation of the Permanent Court of Arbitration (PCA) and the affirmation of the fundamental importance of the peaceful settlement of international disputes as a principle of international law. Although the PCA was not – and is still not today – a fully permanent institution, since it is rather a list of arbitrators that can be called upon by the parties to a dispute to constitute an *ad hoc* arbitral tribunal, the choice of the word "Permanent" had particular meaning since it revealed a desire to move from *ad hoc* to more stable institutions of judicial dispute settlement.

"Permanent" was also the word to be included in the name of such first truly non *ad hoc* international judicial institution, the Permanent Court

1 M. O. Hudson, 'The Permanent Court of International Justice', 35/3 *Harvard Law Review* (1922) 245–275 at 245.

© KONINKLIJKE BRILL NV, LEIDEN, 2022 | DOI:10.1163/9789004467668_002

of International Justice (PCIJ), created under the auspices of the League of Nations, in the aftermath of the First World War.

Article 14 of the Covenant of the League of Nations gave the Council of the League the responsibility for formulating plans for the establishment of a Permanent Court of International Justice, which would be competent to settle international disputes submitted by States, but also to give advisory opinions on disputed or questions referred to it by the Council of the Assembly of the League of Nations. In 1920, the Council appointed an Advisory Committee of Jurists that submitted that year a report with the basic elements for a Permanent Court. The Statute of the PCIJ was adopted by the Assembly of the League of Nations in December 1920. After ratification by a majority of Member States, it entered into force in September 1921, and its inaugural sitting took place a few months later in early 1922.

The establishment of the Permanent Court of International Justice was, therefore, groundbreaking, since it was the first institution of its kind. Although it functioned only for 25 years, it has left enduring features that are still present in international justice today.

Of the peace architecture of the post First World War, the PCIJ was possibly one of the most successful pieces of such framework designed at the Treaty of Versailles and the League of Nations negotiations.

In its meagre 25 years of existence, and being a completely new institution, the PCIJ dealt with 29 contentious cases between States and issued 27 advisory opinions. At the same time, several hundred treaties, conventions and declarations conferred jurisdiction upon it over specified categories of disputes.

75 years ago in April 1946, the International Court of Justice (ICJ) held its opening session at the Peace Palace in The Hague, as the Assembly of the League of Nation passed a resolution dissolving the Permanent Court of International Justice. As current ICJ President Joan E. Donoghue stated in her address to mark the 75th Anniversary of the Court,[2] the 18th of April 1946 marked the "passing of the torch" of international adjudication to the new Court, which held great promise as the principal judicial organ of the United Nations.

The ICJ inherited much from the PCIJ, such as its Statute, a rich jurisprudence and the iconic seat of the Peace Palace in The Hague. It is certainly the case of greatest continuity between the League of Nations and the United Nations, making it quite appropriate to speak about one hundred years of

2 Joan E. Donoghue, "Reflections on the 75th Anniversary of the International Court of Justice", 16 April 2021, available at https://www.un.org/en/un-chronicle/reflections-75th-anniversary-international-court-justice.

international justice, since there was really no interruption in terms of form or substance between the two Courts.

The main features of the Statute of the PCIJ are also present in the ICJ Statute today: the composition of the bench and profile of the judges, a contentious and advisory function, the paramount importance of consent for the exercise of jurisdiction and the enumeration of the sources of international law to be applied by the court.

2 The International Court of Justice at the Centre of the International Justice System

As the International Court of Justice celebrates its 75th Anniversary, the fundamental role of the Court in the international legal order must be underlined and recalled. Being the principal judicial organ of the United Nations, it has one of the most important mandates in the international community which is the peaceful settlement of disputes and the strengthening of the international rule of law.

In the last decades, the volume of the Court's work has increased continuously. In April 2021, there were 14 cases pending before the Court and 1 of them has been introduced that year. Between 2019 and mid-2021, the Court rendered 1 advisory opinion and 5 decisions in contentious proceedings.

The continuous growing of the activities of the Court are a testimony to the fact that more and more States trust the ICJ with the settlement of their complex and sensitive disputes. It is important to note that these cases before the ICJ come from all over the world and relate to diverse areas of international law, such as the law of the sea, land and maritime delimitation, use of force, international humanitarian law, reparations, genocide, diplomatic law, racial discrimination, immunities, demonstrating not only the universality of the Court, but also the expansion of the scope of its work and its growing specialization.

This strengthens dramatically the contribution of the International Court of Justice to the development of international law, and therefore the Court should count on the full support of all members of the international community for the functions it performs on behalf of that community.

It is also to be recalled that, as it will be discussed below, although the International Court of Justice if a leading player in the international judicial arena, as the truly universal and world court in the exercise of general jurisdiction, there are other international courts and tribunals whose existence and importance should also be underlined. The continued contacts and cooperation between international courts and tribunals is a very positive development. As it will discussed below, all of them work together in the enhancement of the international legal order and must complement each other in the furtherance of this goal.

Moreover, though not the subject of this book, domestic court's decisions in matters of international law, which are also more and more frequent, are another building block in the international judicial architecture.[3]

As of April 2021, 193 States were parties to the Statute of the Court. Palestine, though not a party to the Statute of the Court, has deposited a declaration accepting the Court's competence with regard to certain disputes. 74 States have now deposited with the Secretary-General a declaration of acceptance of the Court's compulsory jurisdiction in accordance with Article 36 (2) of the Statute. Moreover, more than 300 bilateral or multilateral treaties provide for the Court to have jurisdiction in the resolution of disputes arising out of their application or interpretation. This highlights the role of the Court as the main judicial body in the interpretation and application of international law.

In the 2005 UN World Summit and in other occasions, the recommendation was made that States that have not yet done so consider accepting the jurisdiction of the Court, in accordance with the Statute. It would also be desirable that in multilateral or bilateral agreements more consideration should be given to accepting the jurisdiction of the Court, including on an optional basis.

While recognizing that in contemporary international law there is an intrinsic – but unavoidable – paradox between the obligation of States to settle their disputes in a peaceful manner and the paramount need for sovereign consent to put into practice such settlement mechanisms, it is our firm conviction that the International Court of Justice plays a crucial role in the upholding and development of the international legal order and that this role is more and more accepted by the international community as a whole.

3 The Other Components of the International Justice System Today

Until the end of the Cold War, there were only a handful of standing international courts and tribunals, in particular the International Court of Justice, the European Court of Justice, the European Court of Human Rights, the

3 Cf. A. Nollkaemper, A. Reinisch *et al* (eds.), *International Law in Domestic Courts – A Casebook* (Oxford University Press, 2018).

Inter-American Court of Human Rights and a few non-permanent of *ad hoc* ones such as the US-Iran Claims Tribunal.

It was since the mid-1990's that the international community witnessed the creation of an array of new international courts and tribunals, some with a permanent while others with an *ad hoc* character. To name some of the most relevant institutions: the International Criminal Tribunal for the Former Yugoslavia, the International Criminal Tribunal for Rwanda, the Special Court for Sierra Leone, the International Criminal Court, the African Court of Human and People's Rights/African Court of Justice and Human Rights, the International Tribunal for the Law of the Sea, the Word Trade Organization dispute settlement mechanism, several Investor-State Arbitral Tribunals, etc.

It is clear, thus, that today there exists a more complex and comprehensive international justice system with several components, to which both States, International Organizations and individuals, depending on the specific mandate and rules of each institution, can have access to.

This international justice system with its several components is not, however, an integrated one, each court and tribunal being created by its own legal instrument, having the power to determine its own competence and to develop its own case-law.

4 Proliferation of International Courts and Tribunals and Fragmentation International Law?

The multiplication of judicial institutions in the international arena just described, led to intense debates on the proliferation of international courts and tribunals and the possible impact on the fragmentation of international law.

In such debates, proposals were made for a more structured and hierarchical system, with the ICJ at the top of the center of the system. The International Law Commission was also seized with the issue of fragmentation and in 2006 produced an important study on "Fragmentation of International Law: Difficulties arising from the diversification and expansion of International Law".[4]

These debates, intense as they were in the last two decades,[5] have tended to vanish as international courts and tribunals, without being integrated in a

4 See A/CN.4/L.682, Corr.1 and Add.1; A/CN.4/L.702; and ILC Report A/61/10, 2006, chap. XII, paras. 237–251.

5 See, e.g., B. Kingsbury, 'Is the Proliferation of International Courts and Tribunals a Systemic Problem', 31 *NYU Journal of International Law and Politics* (1999); T. Buergenthal, 'Proliferation of International Courts and Tribunals: Is It Good or Bad?' 14/2 *Leiden Journal of International*

structured system, have shown by their very practice that the fears of a negative effect of their proliferation and the fragmentation of international law turned out not to be so problematic and, to the contrary, produced effects of positive reinforcement and synergies.

5 The Contribution of International Courts and Tribunals to the Development of International Law

International courts and tribunals are not "law-makers". As the Statute of the International Court of Justice states, in Article 38 (2), judicial decisions are subsidiary means for the determination of rules of law.

It is nevertheless undeniable that international courts and tribunals have contributed immensely to the development of international law in the last one hundred years,[6] by interpreting and applying the primary sources of international law: international conventions, customary international law and general principles of law.

Looking at the international judicial system as a whole, though an organic system rather than a tightly knit structure as in domestic jurisdictions, its contribution to the development of international law has been constant and varied.

Through their case-law, international courts and tribunals have contributed to the development of the fundamental principles of international law outlined in the UN Charter: sovereignty and non-interference in internal affairs, the prohibition of the use of force, self-determination and the promotion and protection of human rights.

In core and traditional areas of international law, the role of international courts and tribunals in the application and clarification of such areas has been fundamental. Key examples come to mind regarding issues of sovereignty and land delimitation, treaty law, law of State responsibility, diplomatic and

---

Law (2001), 267–275; K. Oellers-Frahm, 'Multiplication of International Courts and Tribunals and Conflicting Jurisdiction – Problems and Possible Solutions', 5 *Max Planck Yearbook of United Nations Law* (2001) 67–104. See also I. Buffard, J. Crawford, A. Pellet and S. Wittich (eds.), *International Law between Universalism and Fragmentation. Festschrift in Honour of Gerhard Hafner* (Brill, 2008).

6 See, *inter alia*, N. Boschiero *et al* (eds.), *International Courts and the Development of International Law: Essays in Honour of Tullio Treves* (Asser Press, 2013); C. J. Tams and J. Sloan (eds.), *The Development of International Law by the International Court of Justice* (Oxford University Press, 2013); and G. De Baere and J. Wouters (eds.), *The Contribution of International and Supranational Courts to the Rule of Law, Cheltenham* (Edward Elgar Publishing, 2015).

consular relations and the law of the sea.[7] In particular, the role of the international courts and tribunals, namely the ICJ and ITLOS but also arbitral tribunals, in maritime delimitation in application of the 1958 Geneva Conventions and then the 1982 UNCLOS merits to be highlighted.

In more recent years, international courts and tribunals have added their contribution to the development of international law in newer and more specialized fields such as international environmental law, human rights, international criminal law and trade and investment, to highlight some examples. Climate change is likely to be, in the near future, a new field to be added to this list.

In conclusion, international courts and tribunals are not only a cornerstone of the fundamental principle of international law contained in Articles 2 (3) and 33 of the UN Charter regarding the peaceful settlement of disputes, but they are also "developers" of international law in the sense that they contribute to its application and interpretation and through that to its better understanding and to the advancement of the rule of law.

To conclude with the words of Judge Cançado Trindade: "It has become clear today that contemporary international tribunals, rather than threatening the cohesion of international law, enrich and strengthen it, in asserting its aptitude to resolve disputes in distinct domains of international law, at both inter-State and intra-State levels (…). Contemporary international law has thereby become more responsive to the fulfilment of the basic needs of the international community, of human beings and of humankind as a whole, among which that of the realization of justice."[8]

7 See, for instance, P. Couvreur, *The International Court of Justice and the Effectiveness of International Law* (Brill, 2016).

8 A. A. Cançado Trindade, 'Reflections on a Century of International Justice: Developments, Current State and Perspectives' available at https://www.journals.vu.lt/teise/article/view/9834/7823.

PART 1

The Contribution of International Courts and Tribunals to the Methodology of International Law

Introduction

Manuel Almeida Ribeiro

The methodology of international law is a topic of the utmost importance for international lawyers. Education in law means essentially allowing the student to master the legal discourse – legal terminology and legal concepts. The lawyer, when reasoning *de lege lata*, is supposed to be able to interpret the law, which means to identify in a given system the relevant norms in order to decide the case at hand and to determine the content of each norm. On the other hand, if the lawyer reasons *de lege ferenda*, the goal is to devise and propose improvements to the existing body of law.

When working within his or her domestic legal order, knowledge of the law requires that the lawyer has access to the relevant written instruments, the case-law and legal scholarship, each of them dealing with the same normative material. When it comes to international law, the landscape is much more complex: legal scholarship is culturally plural, as it is the case-law and even the terminology used by international lawyers.

Nowadays, even in non-western States, where western law had an influence in the development of the legal system, similar rules often determine different outcomes.

How is this reflected in international law and its own method? It seems that the significance of its concepts and language must object of a common understanding by all its subjects, namely and most importantly States.

What is the role of international courts and tribunals in forging such a common understanding? It depends on their nature and jurisdiction. The concept of human rights that a regional court such as the European Court of Human Rights deals with must incorporate the common notion of what each one of those rights means to Europeans in a given time, and even in this restricted geographical jurisdiction it is not always easy to find that common notion.

If the jurisdiction of the court or tribunal is referred to a technical or economic field, the concepts and language may be determined in a significant measure by economic or trade terms which can facilitate the understanding of the underlying realities.

In a court, which has a unique role in the architecture of a specific international order, as the European Court of Justice, the build-up of a corpus of jurisprudence over decades of existence and its central role in the day-to-day life of the European institutions made it a central actor in the making of that legal order.

© KONINKLIJKE BRILL NV, LEIDEN, 2022 | DOI:10.1163/9789004467668_003

At the international level, the importance of the International Court of Justice (ICJ) cannot be compared with that of any other international judicial institution.

The ICJ and its predecessor, the Permanent Court of International Justice, had throughout the 20th and the 21st centuries a decisive importance in the formation of concepts, the identification of customary law and the refinement of legal terminology. In our view, the main reasons which explain the importance of the ICJ in international scholarship and in the practice of States stem from its nature as the principal judicial organ of the United Nations, the circumstance of integrating judges from all the legal traditions of the world and the institutional prestige it has. Moreover, the ICJ is the only international court whose jurisdiction is universal, along both geographical and substantive dimensions.

The contributions in the present Part deal with important features of the methodology in international law and how international courts and tribunals have contributed to it. In particular, they look into the role of a sound methodology in determining and applying international law and also to the importance of the precedent effect of the work of international courts and tribunals.

Firstly, *Michael Wood* explores the ways the word "methodology" is used by international lawyers, not always meaning the same. After mentioning some of those meanings, he endorses the notion proposed by Dire Tladi, according to which the methodology of international law is "the *manner* in which the rules are identified and the *manner* in which the content of such rules is determined". The author inquires whether practitioners should be concerned with methodology, concluding that, in his view, the only promising method for international lawyers is positivism. He addresses the importance of style and of being careful with words in the practice of international law, offering as examples the expression "general international law" and the word "legitimacy" of carelessly used language. Finally, the author analyses the methodology and style of the International Court of Justice and how it has consistently made clear that a sound methodology is important in determining and applying the law.

Secondly, *Karem L. Cárdenas Ynfanzón* addresses the importance of the precedents of international courts and tribunals, and why the decisions of the International Court of Justice have a special impact in the development of international law, which results both from the social deference towards some features associated with its precedents, such as stability, predictability, fairness, experience and expertise, and the institutional authority of the court as a judicial institution and an organ of the United Nations. The author refers to the use of ICJ precedents as "anchors" for international lawyers, "against which the vast majority of legal arguments in international law are contrasted, assessed, accepted and/or excluded", "bringing a certain degree of stability and predictability to an international law practice that is increasingly more indeterminant".

CHAPTER 2

Method and Style in International Law, and the International Court of Justice's Contribution

Michael Wood

1 Introduction

Method and style have particular importance in the practice of international law, not least because it is a worldwide legal system not rooted in any particular country, civilization or language. To play its role as a common language for the whole of the international community – and to be plausible, to persuade – international law should aspire to a common method and style. It needs to ensure that a certain result is not a matter of personal preference or policy. If an accepted methodology is followed, and the manner by which it has been applied is indicated clearly, the result is more likely to be viewed as correct and legitimate.

Concern about method in international law is nothing new. Writing well over a century ago, Oppenheim observed that the lack of a generally recognized method of the science of international law was perilous for the discipline: "It is on account of the disagreement as regards the right method that we disagree so much as regards certain rules of international law".[1] For him there had to be one "right" method – "[f]or the right method secures the best results, and it is these we are aiming at".[2]

International courts and tribunals are significant actors in shaping international law: Jennings suggested, some thirty years ago, that international law had become a case-law.[3] The choices of international courts and tribunals as

1 L. Oppenheim, 'The Science of International Law: Its Task and Method', 2 *American Journal of International Law* (1908) 313 at 326–327 (writing that "[t]he three schools of the Grotians, the Naturalists, and the Positivists [are all] still in the field, and their methods are naturally different", and adding that "besides these three schools there are to be mentioned the followers of Austin in England, who define international law as a part of the so-called positive morality …").

2 *Id.*, at 327 (also asking in this context: "How is it possible to offer a body of firm, distinct, and clear-cut rules of law, if rules of morality and of religion, if political aspirations and chimerical schemes for a better future, are constantly mixed up with what is really law?").

3 R.Y. Jennings, 'An International Lawyer Takes Stock', 39 *International & Comparative Law Quarterly* (1990) 513 at 519.

© KONINKLIJKE BRILL NV, LEIDEN, 2022 | DOI:10.1163/9789004467668_004

to method and style naturally invite close attention; they are important for the persuasiveness of the decision concerned and its impact on the relevant dispute and possibly beyond.

I will make three general points. First, the word 'methodology' is commonly used by international lawyers, but not always with the same meaning. Second, practitioners are for the most part unlikely to think much about different 'methodologies' in international law: they will usually be conscious of applying one, almost ingrained, methodology to any particular issue. Third, 'style' in international legal argument may be as important as 'methodology' (the two are not unrelated); one basic and obvious point is the need for clarity. I conclude with some remarks on the contribution of the International Court of Justice (ICJ) to the method and style of international law.

2 What Is Meant by 'Methodology'?

As a term, 'methodology' is more or less interchangeable with 'method'. The latter sounds less abstract (and is shorter); it is the term memorably used by Oppenheim in his 1908 article on the 'task and method of international law'.[4] The word 'method' was also used by Rosenne in his *Practice and Methods of International Law*,[5] and, more recently, by Capps in his piece on 'Lauterpacht's Method'[6] and by Alvarez-Jiménez in his article on 'Methods for the Identification of Customary International Law in the International Court of Justice's Jurisprudence'.[7] Authors who favoured 'methodology' include Maarten Bos in his 1984 volume *A Methodology of International Law*,[8] Olivier Corten in his *Méthodologie du droit international public* of 2009,[9] and Stefan

4 *Supra* note 1.

5 S. Rosenne, *Practice and Methods of International Law* (Oceana, 1984).

6 P. Capps, 'Lauterpacht's Method', 82 *British Yearbook of International Law* (2011) 248.

7 A. Alvarez-Jiménez, 'Methods for the Identification of Customary International Law in the International Court of Justice's Jurisprudence: 2000–2009', 60 *International & Comparative Law Quarterly* (2011) 681. For another example, see W.T. Worster, 'The Inductive and Deductive Methods in Customary International Law Analysis: Traditional and Modern Approaches' 45 *Georgetown Journal of International Law* (2014) 445.

8 M. Bos, *A Methodology of International Law* (Elsevier Science Publishers B.V., 1984).

9 O. Corten, *Méthologie du droit international public* (Editions de l'Université de Bruxelles, 2009), which includes a useful bibliography. While Corten's text is based on his course for those coming new to research in international law, it is of interest to all international lawyers. As Corten explains, research is not limited to academic endeavours, but is equally relevant for a practitioner advising a client. For an earlier work from the *Université Libre*

Talmon in 'Determining Customary International Law: The ICJ's Methodology between Induction, Deduction and Assertion'.[10]

Other good words – good because simple – are 'approach' and 'technique'. Sometimes we see references to 'tradition', 'school', or 'schools of thought'. The International Law Commission (ILC), in the commentary to its conclusions on 'Identification of customary international law', explained that the conclusions dealt with "*the way in which* rules of customary international law are to be determined, *that is, the legal methodology* for undertaking that exercise".[11] This seemingly straightforward wording was adopted after an extensive debate within the Commission, both in plenary and in the Drafting Committee, as to the most appropriate way to describe, in Conclusion 1, the function and purpose of the set of conclusions. As the Statement of the Chairperson of the Drafting Committee records,

> the proposed text for this draft conclusion [that originally referred to "the methodology for determining the existence and content of rules of customary international law"] gave rise to a number of comments during the debate in Plenary on the use of the word "methodology". The Drafting Committee considered that this term should be avoided, since some saw it as associated with science and as referring to a thought on the method, rather than to the method itself. Various alternative proposals were considered, such as "method", "process" or "rules". The Drafting Committee concluded that the chosen formulation would best convey that the main purpose of the draft conclusions was to identify the way in which rules of customary international law are to be determined, rather than to identify the content of customary international law itself. The formulation was

---

de Bruxelles (ULB), see J. Salmon and E. David, *Méthologie de la recherche en droit international public*, 3rd edition (PUB, 1994).

10 S. Talmon, 'Determining Customary International Law: The ICJ's Methodology between Induction, Deduction and Assertion', 26 *European Journal of International Law* (2015) 417. Yet another example is M. Koskenniemi, 'Methodology of International Law' (2007), in A. Peters (2021–) and R. Wolfrum (2004–2020) (eds.), *Max Planck Encyclopedia of Public International Law* (Oxford University Press, 2008–), available at http://www.mpepil.com/.

11 A/73/10: *Report of the International Law Commission on its Sixty-seventh session (30 April–1 June and 2 July–10 August 2018)*, Chapter V, paragraph 1 of the commentary to conclusion 1 (emphasis added). In resolution 73/203 of 20 December 2018, the UN General Assembly "[took] note of the conclusions on identification of customary international law … with the commentaries thereto, [brought] them to the attention of States and all who may be called upon to identify rules of customary international law, and encourage[d] their widest possible dissemination".

> also favoured as it captured the flexibility of the identification process and was thought to not be too prescriptive.[12]

This debate is but one indication that 'methodology' is a word with no single meaning in the discipline of international law.[13] Even if common ground was indeed reached within the ILC on this particular occasion, elsewhere the lack of clarity may have serious consequences. Klabbers points out, for example, that among writers on international law "international legal method is no longer about possible ways of finding out what the law says but, rather, about possible ways of doing academic research".[14] He suggests that writers "have lost touch with legal practice, and the discipline has become transfixed by methodological debates", and he warns that "[i]nstead of the fragmentation of international law being a concern, we should be worried about the fragmentation of international lawyers".[15]

In a recent article, Dire Tladi stressed the importance of "faithfulness to the methodology of international law", by which he meant "the *manner* in which the rules are identified and the *manner* in which the content of such rules [is] determined".[16] I shall use the words 'methodology' and 'method' with essentially that meaning (and very much endorse that plea). Any account of method in international law must, however, go beyond sources, even if they lie at its heart. Methodology refers to the approach taken in any legal inquiry – in short, to how to structure an argument and arrive at conclusions.

12 Statement of the Chairman of the Drafting Committee, Mr. Gilberto Saboia, 7 August 2014, pp. 2–3, available at https://legal.un.org/ilc/sessions/66/pdfs/english/dc_chairman_statement_identification_of_custom.pdf.

13 Another example may be found in the reply sent by Martti Koskenniemi in the late 1990s to the editors of the *American Journal of International Law* symposium on 'Method in International Law', in which he stated that it was "impossible for [him] to think about [his] – or indeed anybody's – 'method' in the way suggested by the symposium format": M. Koskenniemi, 'Letter to the Editors of the Symposium', 93 *American Journal of International Law* (1999) 351.

14 J. Klabbers, 'On Epistemic Universalism and the Melancholy of International Law', 29 *European Journal of International Law* (2018) 1057 at 1062.

15 *Ibidem.*

16 D. Tladi, 'The Constitutional Court's Judgment in the *SADC Tribunal* Case: International Law Continues to Befuddle', 10 *Constitutional Court Review* (2020) 129 at 130.

3 Should Practitioners Be Concerned with Methodology?

The question may be asked of an international lawyer, what is his or her 'approach' to a particular subject: positivist or naturalist? conservative or progressive? realist or idealist? British/European/American?[17] civil law or common law? North/South/East/West? first, second, or third world? nineteenth, twentieth, or twenty-first century? In fact, these terms do not make much sense, at least when applied to practising international lawyers, most of whom cannot be categorized so simplistically. Practising international lawyers inevitably need to take into account the tendencies and expectations of those they seek to convince (for example, a court), as well as the realities of international life and law.

When I joined the Legal Advisers at the United Kingdom's Foreign and Commonwealth Office in 1970, if we had to assess a legal question in depth (as opposed to answering on the spot, which was what we normally had to do), we would ask ourselves how the International Court of Justice would decide the matter. That was seen as an objective touchstone for determining the applicable rule of international law on the question at hand, which might, in theory at least, be decided by the ICJ. We were, in those days, chiefly dealing with questions such as privileges and immunities, diplomatic protection, or treaty interpretation. We would analyse the likely views of each of the 15 Members of the Court. I do not know how far this practice continues – I suspect much less so – or whether it would have ever applied to less technical matters, such as the law on the use of force – I suspect not. But anyone advising on European Union law will certainly need to take full account of the Luxembourg Court's methodology and track-record. The same is true of the Strasbourg Court. And no doubt it is the same in other areas subject to their own specialised courts and tribunals, such as the World Trade Organization.

While academic lawyers may choose to adopt various methodologies for their scholarly work, for practising international lawyers there is therefore *a* methodology, one with which they need to approach the concrete international legal question facing them in order to present in reply the most credible and sustainable argument. When interpreting a treaty, for example, they will invariably apply the Vienna Convention's rules on treaty interpretation. When seeking to ascertain whether a rule of customary international law exists, they

17 For a recent account of 'traditions', see P. Hilpold (ed.), *European International Law Traditions* (Springer, 2021).

will search for a general practice accepted as law in accordance with the two-element approach.

By way of example, a few years ago I had to investigate whether members of a special mission enjoyed immunity under customary international law.[18] This arose in 2010 in the *Khurts Bat* case, where the English High Court was called upon to address the matter for the first time.[19] To establish that there was such a rule it was necessary to present the Court with sufficient State practice and evidence of *opinio juris* (even though in this particular case the existence of the rule was not contested by the other party). The subsequent *Freedom and Justice Party* case in the High Court[20] and Court of Appeal[21] dealt at some length with the methodology for identifying rules of customary international law and in doing so clearly found the work of the International Law Commission helpful:

> Since the decision of the Divisional Court, the ILC has published a further version of its draft conclusions on its project on the *Identification of Customary International Law*. There are sixteen conclusions, which are set out in appendix 2 below, which must be read with the commentary published with them but not reproduced below (ILC Report, 68 GAOR Supp 10 (A/71/10) (2016)). They are subject to possible further, but likely to be minor, amendment before adoption. We are mindful of that, but also of the fact that they are the writings of some of the most qualified jurists drawn from across the world who have debated the matter most thoroughly between themselves over an extended period of time. We have found them a valuable source of the principles on this subject and, since they are not controversial between the parties, this judgment should be read on the basis that we have sought to follow them in our consideration of this appeal in view of their importance and scholarship. To do so does not appear to create any inconsistency between our approach and that

18 M. Wood, 'The Immunity of Official Visitors', 16 *Max Planck Yearbook of United Nations Law* (2012) 35; A. Sanger and M Wood, 'The Immunities of Members of Special Missions', in T. Ruys, N. Angelet and L. Ferro (eds.), *Cambridge Handbook on Immunities and International Law* (Cambridge University Press, 2019) 452; A. Sanger, M. Wood and Council of Europe, *Immunities of Special Missions* (Brill, 2019).

19 *Khurts Bat v Investigating Judge of the German Federal Court* [2011] EWHC 2029 (Admin); [2013] QB 349.

20 *R (on the application of the Freedom and Justice Party) v Secretary of State for Foreign and Commonwealth Affairs* [2016] EWHC 2010 (Admin).

21 *R (on the application of the Freedom and Justice Party) v Secretary of State for Foreign and Commonwealth Affairs* [2018] EWCA Civ 1719; [2018] WLR(D) 460.

> of the Divisional Court. The appellants accept that even in their present form, they carry great weight.[22]

I tend to believe that there is only one 'method' that affords and promotes legal certainly: positivism. It is much maligned in certain academic circles, but seen as essential by practitioners. I sat on a jury recently, where the doctoral candidate, who dealt with a question concerning existing international law, had proclaimed in his thesis that he was an unashamed positivist, but that he could equally have chosen some other methodology. I strongly disagreed with the last part of this statement.[23]

International law is under frequent challenge from some quarters, and it is therefore particularly important to adhere to a positivist method. It is necessary, for the authority of international law, to maintain a distinction between law and non-law.[24] And given the fact that the effect of the inquiry may be to 'impose' an obligation on a State reluctant to accept it, the juridical investigation and analysis must necessarily be rigorous and realistic in their application: "Anything less than that may seem to do for a time but will not survive the moment of truth when some government chooses to question, ignore or defy the alleged rule".[25]

Writings on international law, too, should follow a positivist method if they are intended to be useful in the real world. No doubt some writings following other methods can make an interesting read for practising lawyers,[26] but that

---

22 *Id.*, at para. 18.

23 This brings to mind the opening paragraph of an article by Schwarzenberger, in which he stated that "[a] wise man once said that scholars would do well to postpone the discussion of questions of method until they approached the end of their academic work". This statement, Schwarzenberger continued, "may imply that methodological problems require an amount of detachment and wisdom that is not likely to be acquired at an earlier stage. In any case, this judgment on youth should be heeded as a warning against dealing with such questions in an exclusive spirit": G. Schwarzenberger, 'The Inductive Approach to International Law', 60 *Harvard Law Review* (1947) 539.

24 See also R.Y. Jennings, 'The Discipline of International Law', 57 *International Law Association Rep. Conf.* (1976) 620 at 632 ("[u]nless the formal test of what is international law and what is not can be tightened, clarified and disciplined, we shall find international law becoming more and more a series of expressions in juridical guise of the ambitions of different political and economic pressure groupings. Too often already it comes near to an assertion that what I say three times is the *opinio juris*. Such expressions of particular interests can of course be very powerful – on occasion, and for a time, apparently more powerful than true law. But unless the line can be drawn more or less clearly between law and proposal, international law will be greatly weakened").

25 *Id*, at 631.

26 Slaughter and Ratner refer to "theoretical innovations leading to new ways of thinking" about the law (and also observe that "[m]any authors have used the term ["method"], but

is usually about it, and they contribute to an increasing – and highly regrettable – disconnect between academia and practice. Many young lawyers adopt for their doctoral dissertations a methodology detached from the real world. Is this the best way to commence research? For example, how can a young lawyer interested in 'critical legal studies' sensibly criticize without knowing the law and how it is applied in practice? The writer may of course offer an opinion *de lege ferenda*; but he or she must always do so openly.

4 Style and International Law

While style is largely a personal matter, in law style – the language used and manner of organizing argument – is an inherent and fundamental part of the trade, and there may well be certain widely shared guidelines and expectations. Style is also closely linked to methodology.[27]

One specific aspect of 'style' is the vocabulary of international law, to which the ILC has made a significant contribution. In some fields of international law, such as sources, international responsibility, the law of treaties, State succession, and even the law of the sea, the vocabulary has been largely standardized as a result of the painstaking work of the ILC and its careful consideration by States. It is important that this has happened on a multilingual basis – in the six UN languages and beyond. Except where there is good reason to depart from this widely accepted vocabulary, we should use the language as found in international conventions and ILC texts, to assist in mutual understanding around the world and advance the ability of international law to serve as a 'common language' among States.

The careful choice of words to convey meaning is essential, and here one thing is clear: to convince, language needs to be readily understood. Judges and clients – indeed any reader or listener – are unlikely to be impressed by

---

with the assumption that the reader would know what was meant"): A.-M. Slaughter and S.R. Ratner, 'Appraising the Methods of International Law: A Prospectus for Readers', 93 *American Journal of International Law* (1999) 291.

27 So much so that some even use the term 'style' to substitute for 'method'; see Koskenniemi, *supra* note 13, at 353 (writing to the editors of the *American Journal of International Law* symposium on 'Method in International Law' and referring to his previous work, *Tyyli Metodina* (Style as Method), he said that "in the course of my discussion [I] hope that my occasional substitution of the word 'style' for your chosen signifier – 'method' – in the above text was no slip of the pen"). On the relationship of the language of international law to method, see P. Allott, 'Language, Method and the Nature of International Law', 45 *British Yearbook of International Law* (1971) 79.

carelessness and imprecision. The words used should be simple; ambiguous terms should generally be avoided, as should any 'private language'; argument should be straightforward; brevity is a virtue. Minor but nonetheless distracting faults of style include the poor use of language (and not just by those not operating in their mother tongue), and citations that are taken out of context, or are just plain inaccurate (for example, all too frequently one sees attributed to the ILC what has been written by a Special Rapporteur or said by an individual ILC member).[28]

I shall take two examples of language that is often used carelessly or to disguise meaning, the term 'general international law' and the word 'legitimacy'; then I shall comment on the curious expression popular with politicians today, 'rules-based international order'.

General international law. States, the International Court of Justice and other international tribunals, writers, and even the ILC use the term 'general international law' in a variety of contexts and with a range of meanings. Its use to mean only customary international law, as is sometimes intended, can be confusing. At times the term seems to be used to mean something broader than general customary international law, such as customary international law together with general principles of law, and/or together with widely accepted international conventions. It is desirable that the specific meaning intended by the term 'general international law' is made clear whenever the context leaves the meaning unclear (which it often does), since otherwise the reader or listener is in the dark about the actual source of international law being relied upon. This may be deliberate; it is hardly transparent.

Legitimacy. Turning to the nebulous word 'legitimacy', I take by way of example the justifications offered for, and reactions to, the attack by American, French and British forces on Syria on 14 April 2018 following a use of chemical weapons by the Assad regime. In May 2018, the Security Council held a lengthy open debate on 'Upholding international law within the context of the maintenance of international peace and security'. To read the verbatim record is somewhat depressing. There were the usual empty phrases and mutual attacks. But the debate was enlivened by the representative of the Russian Federation, who said:

---

28 For an egregious example see the Swiss Federal Criminal Tribunal's judgment in the case concerning the immunity of a former Algerian Defence Minister: *A v Ministère public de la Confédération* (the Nezzar case), judgment of 25 July 2012, para. 5.4.2, available at https://ihl-databases.icrc.org/ applic/ihl/ihl-nat.nsf/caseLaw.xsp?documentId=A440E11391847AB8C1257C60005AE1B2&action=openDocument&xp_countrySelected=CH&xp_topicSelected=GVAL-992BU6&from =state&SessionID=DRLPNPW8L4.

> as for international law, the West long ago came up with a formula for that – "illegal but legitimate". This international legal nihilism culminated in the aggression against Syria on 14 April [2018]. … it is not surprising that we have not seen the United States, Britain and France make any special efforts to come up with some sort of justification for their actions on 14 April. Their illegality from the point of view of international law is so obvious that the people in those countries' capitals are themselves clearly aware of it all. … The only country that has attempted to explain anything is the Government of Great Britain. London could not come up with anything better than a reference to the concept of humanitarian intervention as essential to preventing the suffering of the Syrian people. But we all know that the world community has rejected that even as an abstract theory.[29]

Legality versus legitimacy is not a new debate among international lawyers.[30] It is twelve years since Anthea Roberts published her article entitled 'Legality vs. Legitimacy: Can Uses of Force be Illegal but Justified?',[31] and sixteen years since she wrote it. The article took particular aim at Bruno Simma and Tom Franck, who had each in their own different ways popularised the 'unlawful but legitimate' line. Tom Franck's book on *Recourse to Force*, written after the Kosovo intervention, concludes with a chapter entitled: 'What, eat the cabin boy? Uses of force that are illegal but justifiable.'[32] Simma's article on 'NATO, the UN and the Use of Force: Legal Aspects',[33] written just before the

29 S/PV.8262, 17 May 2018, p. 27.

30 T.M. Franck, 'Legitimacy in the International System', 82 *American Journal of International Law* (1988) 705; T.M. Franck, *The Power of Legitimacy among Nations* (Oxford University Press, 1990); R. Wolfrum and V. Röben (eds.), *Legitimacy in International Law* (Springer, 2008); R. Wolfrum, 'Legitimacy in International Law' (2011), in A. Peters (2021–) and R. Wolfrum (2004–2020) (eds.), *Max Planck Encyclopedia of Public International Law* (Oxford University Press, 2008–), available at http://www.mpepil.com.; J. Brunnée and S. Toope, *Legitimacy and Legality in International Law: An Interactional Account* (Cambridge University Press, 2010). The 2010 report of the Dutch Iraq Inquiry (the 'Davids Inquiry') seems to have touched on the question of legitimacy: N.J. Schrijver, 'The Dutch Committee of Inquiry on the War in Iraq and the Basis in International Law for the Military Intervention', 87 *British Yearbook of International Law* (2016) 125 at 129–130.

31 A. Roberts, 'Legality vs. Legitimacy: Can Uses of Force be Illegal but Justified?', in P. Alston and E. Macdonald (eds.), *Human Rights, Intervention, and the Use of Force* (Oxford University Press, 2008) 179. The piece was written in mid-2003, and was only slightly updated when it was published in 2008.

32 T.M. Franck, *Recourse to Force: State Action against Threats and Armed Attacks* (Cambridge University Press, 2002) 174.

33 B. Simma, 'NATO, the UN and the Use of Force: Legal Aspects', 10 *European Journal of International Law* (1999) 1.

intervention in Kosovo, took a somewhat different line, but the overall conclusion was quite similar.

As Roberts has written, "[t]he term 'legitimacy' is both overused and underdefined in international law'.[34] One thing should be clear, at least to international lawyers: "[l]egitimacy is to be distinguished from legality (lawfulness). ..."[35] The word 'legitimate' is used by politicians, and by some lawyers, in many ways, sometimes quite nuanced, not to say obscure. The word conveys something positive, though it is not always clear what. I agree with Anthea Robert's approach and with her conclusions, and need say no more.[36]

Rules-based international order. It seems that hardly any political figure (at least in 'the West') can resist referring these days to a 'rules-based international order'. As a favoured mantra, it seems to be replacing 'the rule of law in international affairs', but is even less clear. What rules? Whose order? It is often used alongside (or perhaps even in place of) respect for international law. In the Security Council debate just mentioned, many speakers referred to both.

While 'rules-based international order' may suggest general support for multilateralism, and must thus be 'a good thing', it sometimes seems to be used as little more than a convenient slogan to attack those with whom one disagrees. It may be another way of avoiding a straightforward commitment to compliance with international law.

As so often, our German colleagues have helpfully sought to clarify matters. It has been suggested that the German Government's use of the term 'rules-based international order' –

> ... is a dangerous development, because if an international order that bases itself on rules does not require consent to these rules, the question arises of who ultimately lays down these rules and determines their content. In practice, the "rules-based order" seems to be an attempt to establish law-making by majority at the international level. However, the will of a few (Western) States, or even the majority of States, cannot be equated to international or regional rules, or be the basis for a "rules-based order". While international law is based on the principle of sovereign equality of States, a "rules-based order" detached from the requirement of consent may become an order of the strong, or an order by dictate of the majority.

34 Roberts, *supra* note 31, at 205.

35 Wolfrum, 'Legitimacy in International Law', *supra* note 30, at para. 1.

36 See also M. Wood, 'International Law and the Use of Force: What Happens in Practice?', 53 *Indian Journal of International Law* (2013) 345 at 350.

> States may not act in compliance with this "rules-based order" because they do not consider themselves bound by the "rules" it consists of, and in fact they are not. This creates the added danger that the use of this new term will come to undermine the credibility of international law.[37]

On 6 March 2020, the Legal Adviser to the Federal Foreign Office explained the difference between "international law" and "the rules-based international order" as follows:

> International law refers to the legally binding rules on the relations between subjects of international law such as states. The political term rules-based order encompasses the legally binding rules of international law, but extends also to non-binding norms, standards and procedures in various international fora and negotiating processes.[38]

5 The Methodology and Style of the International Court of Justice

The ICJ (in the tradition of its predecessor, the PCIJ) has consistently made clear that a sound methodology is important in determining and applying the law. Its insistence or guidance on method may be as important as (if not more important than) its pronouncements expounding the content of the law.

The Court, which of course has to apply the *lex lata* and for the most part seeks to avoid entering into purely theoretical matters, does not always provide doctrinal explanations. To the extent that it does explain the methodology it is employing, it may provide guidance on determining international law, essentially offering a route-map for practitioners. This has been the case particularly with regard to treaties, including the rules for interpretation;[39] with regard to

---

37 S. Talmon, 'Rules-based order v. international law?', in GPIL – *German Practice in International Law*, 20 January 2019, available at https://gpil.jura.uni-bonn.de/2019/01/rules-based-order-v-international-law/.

38 S. Talmon, 'Notable statements on international law during March 2020', in *GPIL – German Practice in International Law*, 12 May 2020, available at https://gpil.jura.uni-bonn.de/2020/05/notable-statements-on-international-law-during-march-2020/.

39 See, for example, G. Guillaume, 'Methods and Practice of Treaty Interpretation by the International Court of Justice', in G. Sacerdoti, A. Yanovich and J. Bohanes (eds.), *The WTO at Ten: The Contribution of the Dispute Settlement System* (Cambridge University Press, 2006) 465.

the identification of customary international law;[40] and with regard to many other secondary rules of international law.[41] It is where there is little guidance from the Court that real difficulties may arise, such as in relation to the general principles of law within the meaning of Article 38 (1) (*c*) of its Statute.

To develop a sound methodology, a study of the ICJ's approach is thus helpful. That was precisely what the ILC did throughout its work on the topic *Identification of customary international law*. First the Commission looked at State practice, which was quite sparse; then at the case-law of courts and tribunals, which was much richer; then at the work of other bodies and at writings, which were of varying utility.[42] By far the most useful material was to be found in the ICJ's judgments and opinions.[43]

It is sometimes remarked that the Court does not always follow its own prescriptions. I do not, however, agree with the criticism of those who conclude that its 'method' (in determining customary international law) is mainly by way of assertion.[44] Even if, for quite understandable reasons, the Court does not always seem explicitly to apply the rigour it demands in principle, it has most probably assessed the materials and in any event at the end of the day is entitled to rely upon the principle *jura novit curia*. At least the judges will have carefully considered the written and oral pleadings.

The Court's tendency not to enter into legal issues that do not need to be answered came up starkly in the ICJ's *Oil Platforms* case,[45] discussed by

---

40 See, for example, P. Tomka, 'Customary International Law in the Jurisprudence of the World Court: The Increasing Relevance of Codification', in L. Lijnzaad and Council of Europe (eds.), *The Judge and International Custom* (Brill Nijhoff, 2016) 2.

41 Such as those concerning unilateral declarations of States.

42 For the Special Rapporteur's guidance as to this methodology, see A/CN.4/653, paras. 18, in *Yearbook of the International Law Commission 2012*, Vol. II, Part One, p. 55; and A/CN.4/663, paras. 54–65, in *Yearbook of the International Law Commission 2013*, Vol. II, Part One, pp. 127–130.

43 See also M. Wood, 'The UN International Law Commission and Customary International Law', in E. Cannizzaro (ed.), *Gaetano Morelli Lectures Series (Vol. 3 – 2020), Discourses on Methods in International Law: An Anthology* (International and European Papers Publishing, 2020) 65 at 84.

44 O. Sender and M. Wood, 'The International Court of Justice and Customary International Law: A Reply to Stefan Talmon', *EJIL: Talk!*, 30 November 2015, available at https://www.ejiltalk.org/the-international-court-of-justice-and-customary-international-law-a-reply-to-stefan-talmon/.

45 *Oil Platforms (Islamic Republic of Iran v. United States of America), Preliminary Objection, Judgment, ICJ Reports 1996*, p. 803; *Oil Platforms (Islamic Republic of Iran v. United States of America), Judgment, ICJ Reports 2003*, p. 161.

Dominic Raab in an article in the *Leiden Journal*.[46] Raab contrasted Judge Simma's policy-inspired view of the Court's role with the cautious approach of Judge Kooijmans. Kooijmans observed in his Separate Opinion that the approach of the Court, in making a finding in the *dispositif* which was neither necessary nor relevant for deciding the claim, was unprecedented in the history of the Court (and the PCIJ before it). The Court set a "hazardous" precedent and raised questions about "the scope of a judgment of the Court".[47] Raab concluded with a word of warning –

> The Court in the *Oil Platforms* case, notwithstanding its narrow basis of jurisdiction, went out of its way to address the legal issues arising in relation to the US claim to be exercising the right of self-defence during the so-called tanker war. The uncertainty generated by such a conception of the judicial function is unlikely to strengthen the Court's appeal to states.[48]

Another consideration to be borne in mind in assessing the style of the ICJ's decisions is that the Court consists of quite a large group of lawyers, who have to strive to reach agreement on particular wording. And they do so in the context of deciding the specific case before them. (This contrasts with the ILC, an even larger body of lawyers, who need to come up with general statements of the law.) The Court's style is thus inevitably impacted by the need to reach agreement on the text by many judges coming from various traditions and sometimes holding nuanced positions. At the same time, one should perhaps not always be distracted by particular wording. For example, one member of the Court, when asked about its use of the term "general international law" as opposed to "customary international law", implied that it might be simply to avoid repetition and to make the text read better.[49]

•••

46 D. Raab, "Armed Attack' after the *Oil Platforms* Case', 17 *Leiden Journal of International Law* (2004) 719.

47 *Oil Platforms (Islamic Republic of Iran v. United States of America), Judgment, ICJ Reports 2003*, p. 161, at p. 247, para. 3.

48 *Supra* note 46, at 734.

49 See also A/CN.4/SR.3317: Provisional summary record of the International Law Commission's 3317th meeting (8 July 2016), p. 5, where the ICJ President, Judge Abraham, addressed the Commission saying that "[i]n respect of terminology, it might be noted that, in its judgment of 16 December 2015, the Court had referred to obligations resulting from both customary international law and general international law, without drawing any clear distinction between the two. However, it should not be deduced from that language that the Court considered the terms to be synonymous. It might – or might

One concluding remark: it should be recalled that method and style are often influenced by one's teachers; in my case, by Professor Clive Parry, who perhaps accounts for a practical, positivist outlook and perhaps for a certain humour, not I hope cynicism, on my part. A heavy responsibility is placed therefore upon teachers of international law, though of course the students, too, have a responsibility to question what they are taught. We are told that Hersch Lauterpacht began as Kelsen's pupil; but being Lauterpacht he quickly developed his own method.[50] So, if necessary, there is always the possibility that we may escape from those who taught us.

Postscript

In an article dated 28 June 2021, the Russian Foreign Minister criticized the invocation of the 'rules-based world order' in no uncertain terms:

> The documents adopted at the Cornwall and Brussels summits cemented the rules-based world order concept as a counterweight to the universal principles of international law with the UN Charter as its primary source.
>
> In doing so, the West deliberately shies away from spelling out the rules it purports to follow, just as it refrains from explaining why they are needed. .... [51]

---

not – be the case that the concepts overlapped to a certain extent, but nothing more than that should be deduced in that respect from the language of the judgment, and any over-interpretation, to which writers were often inclined, should be resisted"; see also at p. 7, where he added that "[a] decision was what was written down on paper and what could be inferred logically and necessarily therefrom. The inferences which could be logically drawn from the text of a judgment bound the Court, even though the judges might not have realized the implications of a given sentence, since what was implicit was inherent in what was explicit. Logical reasoning was what was called for, not an attempt to guess the potential intentions behind the Court's position; any such attempt was no more than worthless speculation or supposition".

50 See Capps, *supra* note 6.

51 Article by Sergey Lavrov, Russian Minister of Foreign Affairs, "The Law, the Rights and the Rules", Moscow, June 28, 2021, available at https://www.mid.ru/en/foreign_policy/news//asset_publisher/cKNonkJE02Bw/content/id/4801890.

CHAPTER 3

The Authority of the Precedents of the International Court of Justice in the Argumentative Practice in International Law

Karem L. Cárdenas Ynfanzón

1 Introduction

The importance that individuals assign to past events or precedents when making decisions can be evidenced in their daily and professional life, regardless of their field of work. Without any coercion or threat, very often individuals feel compelled to follow the same path as in past decisions, granting a certain type of *authority* upon them. In international law, this is not different. It is a discipline whose development has been boosted by the precedents of courts and tribunals, and their influence on international lawyers' practice, particularly those of the International Court of Justice (ICJ).

Most international lawyers have likely *experienced* the authority of precedents in their daily work. However important that "practical experience" is, it is worth very little without the appropriate theoretical lens to make sense of it.[1] Indeed, as Bianchi points out, every practitioner –consciously or unconsciously– presupposes a theory, a set of presuppositions and beliefs that constitute the background that defines how their practice is carried out.[2] Hence, just as two sides of the same coin, neither practice nor theory can be disconnected from one another,[3] even more so if we consider that the underlying theory does have practical consequences.[4]

1 As Jamin and Xifaras emphasise, "il ne suffit pas de pratiquer pour sortir du sommeil dogmatique, encore faut-il pouvoir décrire et penser son expérience. Faire de la théorie de ce que font vraiment les juristes est une des tâches les plus difficiles (…)." C. Jamin and M. Xifaras, 'De la vocation des facultés de droit (françaises) de notre temps pour la science et l'enseignement', 72 *Revue interdisciplinaire d'etudes juridiques* (2014) 107, 129.

2 A. Bianchi, *International Law Theories: An Inquiry into Different Ways of Thinking* (Oxford University Press, 2016) 8.

3 *Ibid.*, 9.

4 *Ibid.*, 19.

© KONINKLIJKE BRILL NV, LEIDEN, 2022 | DOI:10.1163/9789004467668_005

Such diversity of insights is clearly exposed in the different theoretical lenses used thus far to address the concepts of authority[5] and precedents.[6] This contribution provides an account of the authority of precedents in international law acknowledging such diversity to explain more accurately the kind of authority that precedents have in international law, one that allowed such diversity in the first place, and its impact on the field. To that end, it builds upon a nuanced thesis of the indeterminacy of international law,[7] along with a broad theoretical toolkit solidly grounded in practice.

This perspective will allow us to pay attention not only to legal elements (i.e. rules, formal sources, etc.) but also to social, structural, epistemic, and behavioural factors, which make sense and shape the first ones. Thereby, it will consider international law as a system of argumentative practice that is embedded in a pre-existing argumentative structure, against which the validity (or plausibility) of legal arguments is assessed,[8] a system of production of

---

5 J. Raz, *The Authority of Law* (Clarendon Press, 1997) 11–12. H.G. Gadamer, *Truth and Method* (Continuum, 2004) 281. R.S. Peters, P.G. Winch and A.E. Duncan-Jones, 'Symposium: Authority', 32 *Proceedings of the Aristotelian Society*, Supplementary Volumes (1958) 207, 213–214. R. Cotterrell, 'Transnational Legal Authority: A Socio-Legal Perspective', in R. Cotterrell and M. Del Mar (eds.), *Authority in Transnational Legal Theory. Theorising Across Disciplines* (Edward Elgar Publishing, 2016) 265. R.B. Friedman, 'On the Concept of Authority in Political Philosophy', in J. Raz (ed.), *Authority* (New York University Press, 1990) 60. M. Del Mar, 'Imaginaries of Authority: Towards an Archaeology of Disagreement', in R. Cotterrell and M. Del Mar (eds.), *Authority in Transnational Legal Theory. Theorising Across Disciplines* (Edward Elgar Publishing, 2016) 248. O. J. Sending, 'Recognition and Liquid Authority', 9 *International Theory* (2017) 311, 316–317. F. Zarbiyev, 'Saying Credibly What the Law Is: On Marks of Authority in International Law', 9 *Journal of International Dispute Settlement* (2018) 291, 295–298.

6 M. M. Mbengue, 'Precedent', in J. d'Aspremont and S. Singh (eds.), *Concepts for International Law* (Edward Elgar Publishing, 2019) 711. G. Guillaume, 'The Use of Precedent by International Judges and Arbitrators', 2 *Journal of International Dispute Settlement* (2011) 5, 23. G. Sacerdoti, 'The Authority of "Precedent" in International Adjudication: The Contentious Case of the WTO Appellate Body's Practice', 19 *The Law & Practice of International Courts and Tribunals* (2020) 497, 502. K. J. Pelc, 'The Welfare Implications of Precedent in International Law', in J. Jemielniak, L. Nielsen and H. P. Olsen (eds.), *Establishing Judicial Authority* in *International Economic Law* (Cambridge University Press, 2016) 175. K. L. Scheppele and K. E. Soltan, 'The Authority of Alternatives', 29 *Nomos* (1987) 169, 178. I. Venzke, 'Between Power and Persuasion: On International Institutions' Authority in Making Law', 4 *Transnational Legal Theory* (2013) 354, 368. F. Schauer, 'Precedent', 39 *Stanford Law Review* (1987) 571, 571.

7 M. Koskenniemi, *From Apology to Utopia: The Structure of International Legal Argument* (Cambridge University Press, 2006) 568. B. S. Chimni, *International Law and World Order. A Critique of Contemporary Approaches* (Cambridge University Press, 2017) 2.

8 J. d'Aspremont, 'The International Court of Justice and the Irony of System-Design', 8 *Journal of International Dispute Settlement* (2016) 366, 368.

good legal arguments.[9] And despite the fact that such a system is indeterminate (which allows it to be approached from different perspectives), the degree of indeterminacy is not such that makes it impossible for international lawyers to interact with each other. Some common notions make it possible to have shared understandings within a group, providing certain predictability and homogeneity to international law. One of these common elements is the authority of ICJ precedents.

2 Authority of ICJ Precedents as a Social Deference

The context in which international law is embedded is a complex structure, where the members of a group interact with each other, transmitting and reinforcing certain practices and ideas creating common "background knowledge"[10] and "cognitive frames."[11] Those elements inform their subsequent practices and create expectations that others will act alike. Thereby, actions and ideas aligned with that common background are accepted and recognized as valid, while excluding those that are not.[12] In that sense, common background knowledge and cognitive frames, along with the expectations triggered by them, serve as tools to discipline others' behaviour, signalling them how their choices and actions should be.[13]

This social dynamic can be evidenced in international lawyers' practice. When we make an argument, most of the time we feel constrained to take into consideration certain aspects highly valued among the international law community, practices, and ideas that are part of our common background. This is because we give importance to the reaction of the targeted audience (which we aim to convince), to the consequences of our argument, and most importantly to be coherent with the common background. All those factors influence how

9 F. Zarbiyev, 'The "Cash Value" of the Rules of Treaty Interpretation', 32/1 *Leiden Journal of International Law* (2019) 1, 7; Koskenniemi (note 7) 568.

10 Referring to shared understandings that emerge, evolve, or fade through processes of social interaction and social learning. J. Brunnée and S. J. Toope, 'Interactional International Law: An Introduction', 3 *International Theory* (2011) 307, 310.

11 M. Wählisch, 'Cognitive Frames of Interpretation in International Law', in A. Bianchi, D. Peat and M. Windsor (eds.), *Interpretation in International Law* (Oxford University Press, 2015) 333.

12 P. Bourdieu, *Outline of a Theory of Practice* (Cambridge University Press, 2005) 78.

13 T. Lemke, *Foucault's Analysis of Modern Governmentality: A Critique of Political Reason* (Verso Books, 2019) 152.

our peers recognize us as credible,[14] which in turn render our arguments (and practice in general) more effective. One aspect of that common background is the weight we grant to relying on or referring to precedents, regardless of their formal binding character and their content, and despite the rejection of a "stare decisis" doctrine in international law. Among the different examples, an important case in point are the ICJ precedents, whose advisory opinions are not binding, while its judgments are but only for the parties to the case.

With that in mind, more than by virtue of a formal instrument or a right of a person or entity to command, ICJ precedents seem to have "authority" based on the collective deference granted by international lawyers to them, in their belief that they should be followed, or at least taken into consideration in their practice. Indeed, such belief inducing deference towards ICJ precedents is based on features associated with them, positively valued by the international law community (i.e. stability, predictability, fairness, experience, expertise, etc.). It is a broader notion of authority of a social character that is present in the argumentative practice of international lawyers, as a subspecies of power-relations, experienced differently by them. On the one hand, their authority is used by international lawyers to induce others to accept their claims by supporting (or justifying) them with ICJ precedents. It is what Venzke calls the ability to make others believe that they must defer.[15] Whereas, on the other hand, it is an authority constraining their decision-making process, foreseeing the effects or reactions to their arguments: for ICJ judges, being aware that their decisions would be taken as precedents and whether the consequences thereof are desirable; and for others, the consequences of their arguments if not aligned or even refer to ICJ precedents, and whether they could bear the costs. This includes the case of departing therefrom, as international lawyers very often also feel compelled to explain the reasons for doing so without challenging their authority.

In that sense, regardless of their formal bindingness and whether agreeing or disagreeing with their content, the authority of ICJ precedents resides in their power to be constraining points of reference in the argumentative practice of international lawyers. Be it as a past-based constraint (to follow similar paths already used by ICJ) or as a future-determinative constraint (awareness of being able to create precedents or consequences for not being aligned with ICJ precedents). Yet, as Sending remarks, as an authority of a social character,

14 R. B. Brandom, 'Some Pragmatist Themes in Hegel's Idealism: Negotiation and Administration in Hegel's Account of the Structure and Content of Conceptual Norms,' 7 *European Journal of Philosophy* (1999) 164, 169–170.

15 Venzke (note 6) 362–363.

it is not fixed but constantly negotiated and contested.[16] In that sense, it is contingent on international lawyers' ability to reinforce the aspects supporting ICJ precedents' authority through *institutional* and *discursive* resources.[17] In the following lines, these two aspects will be further developed: (i) the "institutional" side of their authority, which refers to the authority of ICJ as an institution with expertise (epistemic authority), and (ii) the "discursive constraints" of ICJ precedents.

3 The Institutional Authority of the ICJ

Within a context of non-hierarchical relations, and even though there is no international rule endowing the ICJ with authority over international lawyers, it is considered by a significant number of them as having authority to say what the law is. For instance, it is quite telling that the members of the UN International Law Commission (ILC) usually base their statements on determinations made by the ICJ. At the end of the 2018 discussions of the ILC Drafting Committee on peremptory norms of general international law (*jus cogens*), the Report of the Chair of the Drafting Committee asserted that "[i]t should be recalled that, in its judgment in the *Gabčíkovo-Nagymaros Project* (Hungary/Slovakia) case, the International Court of Justice noted that Articles 65 and 67 [of the 1969 Vienna Convention] reflect customary international law."[18]

But why do international lawyers grant the ICJ such authority? The explanation might lay in the features that the ICJ possesses: (a) being a *judicial institution*; and b) an organ of the UN, a universal international organization that *represents the international community* of States. From the first feature, the ICJ may evoke objectivity, technical expertise or credentials in law, impartiality, and independence. Whereas from the second feature, it may have gained good or moral motivations and the representation of the international community.[19] For instance, in the Third Report on Peremptory Norms of General

16 Sending (note 5) 315.

17 M. Barnett and M. Finnemore, *Rules for the World: International Organizations in Global Politics* (Cornell University Press, 2004) 5. M. Finnemore, 'Norms, Culture, and World Politics: Insights from Sociology's Institutionalism', 50 *International Organization* (1996) 325, 325.

18 ILC, 'Interim Report by the Chair of the Drafting Committee. Seventieth Session New York, 30 April – 1 June, and Geneva, 2 July – 10 August 2018' (2018) 9.

19 An interesting view of these features is Fuad Zarbiyev's "marks of authority". He suggests that those marks of authority may be found in the process (that brings objectivity, impartiality and independence of the outcome), in the superior knowledge of the institution

International Law (*jus cogens*), due to the decentralized system that international law is, the ILC Special Rapporteur suggested to recommend the practice to submit the cases of nullity of treaties to an impartial body such as the ICJ which would "declare" the nullity for conflicting with jus cogens rules:

> 48. ... The decision by the International Court of Justice or an arbitral tribunal under article 66 (a) [of the 1969 Vienna Convention] does not create the nullity [of treaties], it merely declares or confirms it. While it is correct, as has been pointed out that "it would be difficult to claim authoritatively that a treaty is void" on the basis of "unilateral statements" under article 53, this is not as a result of a consequence flowing from jus cogens. Rather, it is a general problem of international law that arises from auto-interpretation resulting from a decentralized legal system without a compulsory system of adjudication.
>
> 52. In the light of this, the Special Rapporteur proposes that the Commission recommends, as a practice, that, even in cases where the Vienna Convention does not apply because one or both of the States are not party to the Vienna Convention, the procedure in article 66 (a) should be applicable. ...[20]

Be that as it may, the ICJ is seen as an institution socially recognized as having the necessary professional credentials (the entitlement) to know and speak what the law is. As Zarbiyev highlighted, "an authoritative utterance determines behaviour not because of a threat of sanctions (or promise of a reward), or through persuasion, but because it emanates from a particular person."[21] In this case, it is an epistemic authority that is socially sanctioned and enforced, as international lawyers learn to accept that within the community the ICJ is "an authority" in the topic.[22] It relies on a collective belief that international lawyers can place their cognitive trust in its judgments,[23] renouncing to follow their own assessments.[24]

(more technical, specialized body), the reputation, and the authorship. Zarbiyev (note 5) 298–308.

20 ILC, 'Third Report on Peremptory Norms of General International Law (Jus Cogens)' by D. Tladi, Special Rapporteur' (2018), A/CN.4/714, paras 48, 52.

21 Zarbiyev (note 5) 295.

22 It has also been called sign, symbol, certificate, credentials. Friedman (note 5) 70.

23 Zarbiyev (note 5) 297.

24 Friedman (note 5) 73.

A case in point is also the sanctions episode between Qatar and the United Arab Emirates (UAE). The imposition of sanctions by the UAE over Qatar triggered a series of actions from both sides in different contexts. With both having an overall goal in the background (to discredit the other part and justify/lift the sanctions), they presented their claims within institutional contexts (i.e. ICJ, Human Rights Committee, Human Rights Council, ICAO, UNGA, Arab League) to obtain therefrom authoritative precedents in their favour. Yet, the focus was mainly on the proceedings before ICJ, where the UAE appealed an ICAO decision.[25] It sought that the ICJ asserted its exclusive authority on a specific subject ("countermeasures"), and with it to get a precedent that constrained other bodies like ICAO to align accordingly or to refrain from assessing it.[26]

Likewise, we can refer to the use of ICJ's opinions in institutions such as the WTO. In the case *United States – Standards for Reformulated and Conventional Gasoline*, in order to assert the customary status of the general rule of interpretation set out in Article 31 of the Vienna Convention, the WTO Appellate Body relied, first, on the *Territorial Dispute Case* (*Libyan Arab Jamahiriya v. Chad*) from the ICJ, and then added references from the European Court of Human Rights (ECHR), and the Inter-American Court of Human Rights.[27] That assertion served as a basis for the Appellate Body to apply such a rule to interpret 'the General Agreement and the other "covered agreements" of the Marrakesh Agreement Establishing the World Trade Organization',[28] under Article 3 (2) of the *Understanding on Rules and Procedures Governing the Settlement of Disputes* that refers to "customary rules of interpretation of public international law". However, the Appellate Body gave a step further and stated that a consequence of the general rule of interpretation was that "[a]n interpreter is not free to adopt a reading that would result in reducing whole clauses or paragraphs of a treaty to redundancy or inutility."[29] To make such a statement

---

25 UAE, 'Joint Application Instituting Proceedings. Appeal against a Decision of the ICAO Council Dated 29 June 2018 on Preliminary Objections (Application A) (*Kingdom of Bahrain, Arab Republic of Egypt, Kingdom of Saudi Arabia, and the United Arab Emirates v. State of Qatar*)', https://www.icj-cij.org/files/case-related/173/173-20180704-APP-01-00-EN.pdf.

26 A similar concept could be "comity", as a would-be procedural law principle to avoid conflict of jurisdictions. T. Schultz and N. Ridi, 'Comity and International Courts and Tribunals', 50 *Cornell International Law Journal* (2017) 577, 579.

27 WTO Appellate Body, 'United States–Standards for Reformulated and Conventional Gasoline' (WTO 1996) WT/DS2/AB/R 17, available at https://docs.wto.org/dol2fe/Pages/FE_Search/FE_S_S009-DP.aspx?language=E&CatalogueIdList=14573&CurrentCatalogueIdIndex=0&FullTextHash= (accessed 30 July 2019).

28 *Ibid.*

29 *Ibid.*, 23.

encroaching the interpreter's freedom, it cited the *Corfu Channel Case* and the *Territorial Dispute Case* (*Libyan Arab Jamahiriya v. Chad*) from the ICJ.

This kind of authority entails the institution or person endowed with it, in asserting such authority, to make others believe and to behave as "an authority". Concerning the *Tadić* case, the ICJ asserted its authority in the *Application of the Convention on the Prevention and Punishment of the Crime of Genocide* (*Bosnia and Herzegovina v. Serbia and Montenegro*) case. There, the ICJ expressed that it had carefully considered the ICTY Appeals Chamber reasoning in the *Tadić* case about the "overall control" necessary to trigger a State's responsibility; however, it could not subscribe to its view.[30] It affirmed its authority to establish the parameters to assess state responsibility, a topic over which it had primary competence.

More recently, Judge Yusuf (while he was President of the ICJ) delivered a speech during the ILC 2019 session on "general principles of law", where he stated that "legitimate expectations" was a notion coming from investment arbitration that could not be transposed to a general international law forum as the ICJ. With that statement, he aimed not only at limiting the reach of that concept to investment arbitration but also to discourage international lawyers from bringing up such a concept before other courts with general competences or other than investment law.

It is worthwhile stressing the content-independence of the authority of ICJ precedents. An ICJ decision – as any other text – can be read and interpreted in different or even opposite manners depending on the interests and cognitive frames of the reader. The reader can even – at first – criticize and even reject a decision. A case in point is the *Jurisdictional Immunities* decision, which was initially strongly criticized.[31] However, given the strong positioning of the ICJ as "an authority" with the right to say the law, eventually, those aspects initially considered as not in accordance with standards were accepted or normalized. Thereby, we can see that the dynamic within the international law community provokes that eventually resistant behaviours get aligned with the standards or get excluded.

30 *Application of the Convention on the Prevention and Punishment of the Crime of Genocide (Bosnia and Herzegovina v Serbia and Montenegro), Judgment, ICJ Reports 2007, p. 43*, para. 403.

31 For instance, the Italian constitutional court declared that judgment as unconstitutional, specifically preventing the exercise of the right to access to courts. R. Pavoni, '*Simoncioni v. Germany*', 109 *American Journal of International Law* (2015) 400. See also Judge Cançado Trindade's dissenting opinion.

4 The "Discursive Constraints" of the ICJ Precedents

Particularly interesting is to observe the ICJ precedents being used as "anchors" for international lawyers' arguments, even with supporting opposite views. Indeed, the indeterminacy of the content of international rules may explain why international legal operators with opposite arguments can refer to the same ICJ reasonings or assertions (or even its omissions) to support their opposing arguments. This is particularly evident in the arguments of the parties to a case before the ICJ, where they usually present their own reading of the ICJ precedents, in a manner compatible with their arguments. That can be seen, for instance, during the public hearings before the ICJ on provisional measures in the case *Alleged violations of the 1955 Treaty*,[32] wherein both Iran and the U.S. referred and relied on the ICJ precedents to support their arguments on why or why not the sanctions imposed by the U.S. upon Iran violated the 1955 Treaty. Each had foreseen in advance the cases that the other party would refer to in their arguments, which is why both sides cited almost the same cases, although interpreting them in favour of their main arguments and goals.

At the same time, those precedents were deemed authoritative enough to induce the ICJ itself to grant deference to them and decide alike (or what the parties considered to be "alike" under each's own interpretation). The outcome of these provisional measures hearings reveals such effect upon the court, if we consider that in its order of 3 October 2018 it granted provisional measures to Iran but in a limited manner, since it upheld most of U.S. claims.[33] This reveals that precedents constrain international lawyers (in different roles, i.e. advocates, judges, etc.) when performing in two capacities: (i) as *recipients* of precedents (when making decisions or arguments); and (ii) as *authors* of would-be precedents (being conscious that their decisions may become precedents for

32 ICJ, Public sitting in the case concerning Alleged violations of the 1955 Treaty of Amity, Economic Relations, and Consular Rights (*Islamic Republic of Iran v. United States of America*) 2018 [CR 2018/16] 77; ICJ, Public sitting in the case concerning Alleged violations of the 1955 Treaty of Amity, Economic Relations, and Consular Rights (*Islamic Republic of Iran v. United States of America*) 2018 [CR 2018/17] 68; ICJ, Public sitting in the case concerning Alleged violations of the 1955 Treaty of Amity, Economic Relations, and Consular Rights (*Islamic Republic of Iran v. United States of America*) 2018 [CR 2018/18] 46; ICJ, Public sitting in the case concerning Alleged violations of the 1955 Treaty of Amity, Economic Relations, and Consular Rights (*Islamic Republic of Iran v. United States of America*) 2018 [CR 2018/19] 41.

33 *Alleged Violations of the 1955 Treaty of Amity, Economic Relations, and Consular Rights (Islamic Republic of Iran v United States of America), Order, Provisional Measures* [2018].

themselves or others). These two sides of precedents' authority complement each other, which when combined with the authority of the ICJ as an institution, its precedents can act–using Çali's words– as a recourse of international law that makes it a tool of governance.[34] Or, as Jean d'Aspremont put forward about precedents in general, they work like "a system of argumentative constraints meant to build past-based and future-determinative coherence."[35]

Bearing the above in mind, it may be tempting to think that the legal operators are absolutely free to invoke any past event as precedent. All precedents can indeed be past events, yet not all past events might be considered as authoritative precedents for a specific situation. It would depend on the characterization of a prior decision in plausible terms so that it could be deemed by the targeted audience as "relevant" and applicable to a specific situation. Such characterization is carried out not only based on legal factors (i.e. interpretation, backgrounds, approaches, legal reasoning) but also on *underlying* social factors (i.e. identities, collective beliefs, epistemic communities, a community of practice,[36] etc.). Such factors inform the plausibility standards that need to be considered to effectively compel the audience to defer in favour of the alleged precedent. For instance, the U.S. reliance on the legal reasoning used in the *Legality of Nuclear Weapons* advisory opinion to justify its use of drones did not convince many about its legality.[37]

Notwithstanding, be it effectively or ineffectively used – it should be pinpointed that the ICJ precedents usually remain the focal points or anchors[38] of international lawyers' reasoning when building and/or justifying their arguments. In the case *Land and Maritime Boundary between Cameroon and Nigeria*, for example, the Court stated that the legal reasoning used in the *Right of Passage over Indian Territory* had no direct effect on the case; however, "[t]he real question is whether, in this case, there is cause not to follow the reasoning

34 B. Çalı, 'Authority', in Jean d'Aspremont and Sahib Singh (eds.), *Concepts for International Law* (Edward Elgar Publishing, 2019) 49.

35 J. d'Aspremont (note 8) 368.

36 E. Adler, 'The Spread of Security Communities: Communities of Practice, Self-Restraint, and NATO's Post – Cold War Transformation', 14 *European Journal of International Relations* (2008) 195.

37 For more about the debates on the legality of use of drones, see: J. Pejic, 'Extraterritorial Targeting by Means of Armed Drones: Some Legal Implications', 96 *International Review of the Red Cross* (2014) 67.; M. J. Boyle, 'The Legal and Ethical Implications of Drone Warfare', 19 *The International Journal of Human Rights* (2015) 105.

38 On the role of anchors, see D. Ariely, 'The Fallacy of Supply and Demand', *Predictably Irrational. The Hidden Forces that Shape Our Decisions* (Harper Perennial, 2010) 41.

and conclusions of earlier cases."[39] With that, it shifted the argumentative burden to those alleging a different path. Indeed, it might be true that – as former ICJ judge Guillaume asserted – precedents as "the starting point of judges' reflections".[40] Yet, the reason for that could be not only an unconscious constraint but rather the awareness of the rhetorical advantages of relying on precedents from a highly valued institution within the community. Especially, when we deal with highly controversial cases, appeals to the law and particularly to the ICJ legal reasoning in prior cases developing that law could be a legitimate refuge to justify certain decisions.[41]

But their authority is manifested in other ways too. Not only they are anchors influencing opinions, decisions and behaviour of international lawyers and institutions where they operate as a measure to assess the plausibility of their content (i.e. the ECJ, WTO Appellate Body, ILC,[42] etc.). They are also anchors or focal points for critics, providing the discursive tools to depart therefrom, openly (challenging their coherence) or strategically (alleging their inapplicability to a specific situation). That is the case of the *Tadić* judgment, where the ICTY Appeals Chamber took the ICJ *Nicaragua* decision as a reference to depart from its notion of "effective control",[43] and to affirm – regarding criminal responsibility – that "The Appeals Chamber fails to see why in each and every circumstance international law should require a high threshold for the test of control."[44] Whereas to interpret its own statute, the ICTY relied on the ICJ reasoning on treaty interpretation set forth in *Competence of the General Assembly* advisory opinion.[45]

These discursive constraints of the authority of ICJ's precedents have not only contributed to understanding international law as an argumentative practice, but also have brought to it an air of stability and predictability amidst the diverse lenses through which international lawyers' approach international

39 *Land and Maritime Boundary between Cameroon and Nigeria, Preliminary Objections, Judgment, ICJ Reports 1998*, p. 275, para. 28.

40 G. Guillaume, 'The Use of Precedent by International Judges and Arbitrators', 2 *Journal of International Dispute Settlement* (2011) 5, at 2.

41 I. Venzke, 'Judicial Authority and Styles of Reasoning: Self-Presentation between Legalism and Deliberation', in J. Jemielniak, L. Nielsen and H.P. Olsen (eds.), *Establishing Judicial Authority in International Economic Law* (Cambridge University Press, 2016) 246.

42 During the 2019 Sessions of the ILC, the deliberations about the peremptory norms of general international law (*jus cogens*) touched upon – among others – the issue of which norms had been recognized by the ICJ, even indirectly (acknowledging the same effects) as having attained the *jus cogens* status.

43 *Tadić (IT-94-1-A), Appeals Chamber, 15 July 1999*, 115.

44 *Ibid.*, 117.

45 *Ibid.*, 282–283.

law. Indeed, by way of reclaiming for itself a privileged place in the field, the ICJ has positioned its precedents as *unavoidable* anchors for international lawyers when making arguments, either to agree or disagree, if they want to be taken seriously by their peers.[46]

5 Conclusions

The reliance on precedents to support arguments is something common in the practice of international lawyers, a consolidated standard of professional performance. It is based on a collective belief that – when building arguments – one should show deference to prior judgments to which one assigns or attributes certain authoritative marks or features. This belief is socially sanctioned and enforced by international lawyers in their interactions, through the expectations they share as peers which are used to determine whether others are peers or not. This dynamic compels international lawyers to behave alike in this respect: relying on precedents in their argumentative practice, specifically those assigned with authoritative features. Thereby, the more features a precedent has, the more authoritative will be. It is in this way that international lawyers grant authority to precedents upon them, an authority of a social character, and as such it is not immutable but gradual, for it is constantly shaped, contested, and reinforced among them.

In the particular case of ICJ precedents, their authority gets intertwined with the authority that international lawyers give to the ICJ as an institution. Such confluence makes that the ICJ precedents are granted a higher degree of authority among the wide spectrum of precedents in international law. Usually associated with features like objectivity, impartiality, technical expertise in general public international law, ICJ precedents exercise discursive constraints over international lawyers, regardless of the subject-matter where they perform, the theoretical approaches they may use, or the arguments they may raise. Their authority, though, not only depends on international lawyers' performance but also on the Court's assertion of its authority (acting as "an authority"), reinforcing the belief that to rely on its precedents is important for the correct performance of the profession, to be taken seriously, and therefore for a more effective argumentative practice.

In sum, one of the major contributions of the ICJ to international law is the fact that its precedents are unavoidable anchors against which the vast majority

46 Brandom (note 14) 170.

of legal arguments in international law are contrasted, assessed, accepted, and/or excluded. Thereby, despite the different approaches, cognitive frames, and other constraints impacting international lawyers' argumentative practice and making it increasingly diverse, the authority of ICJ precedents brings a certain degree of stability and predictability (or at least an appearance thereof) to the international law practice.

PART 2

The Contribution of International Courts and Tribunals to the Development of Procedural Rules

Introduction

Laurence Boisson de Chazournes

The interest in procedural law among international lawyers has grown in recent years, and this is especially the case in the field of international dispute settlement. Procedural rules play a central role in ensuring the sound administration of justice as well as contributing to respect for the rule of law.

The establishment of international tribunals during the 18th and 19th centuries led to the creation and identification of a number of procedural rules necessary for their proper functioning. Building on these early experiences, an effort to systematise procedural rules was undertaken at the beginning of the 20th century, an effort which took shape in the Hague Conventions of 1899 and 1907 for the Pacific Settlement of International Disputes. It was then the creation of new courts, particularly permanent ones, that enabled the development of procedural law. One may think of the adoption of the Statute of the Permanent Court of International Justice in 1920 and that of its successor, the International Court of Justice (ICJ) in 1945. The latter, together with the Rules adopted by the ICJ in 1946 and revised several times thereafter, including a wholesale revision in 1978, have played a major role in influencing and guiding other courts, tribunals and dispute settlement mechanisms.

In addition to the creation of these courts and tribunals, it is also their practice that has given rise to a number of procedural rules and principles. Confronted with a vacuum in their procedural instruments, the courts and tribunals have then established the missing rule or principle. In doing so, they often draw inspiration from the procedural rules and principles of national legal systems. However, they are not imported "lock, stock and barrel",[1] but rather adapted to the specificities of the international judicial context in which they are to find application.

Procedural rules are manifold, as exemplified in the Final Report of the International Law Association's (ILA) Committee on the Procedure of International Courts and Tribunals submitted to the 79th Biennial Conference of the ILA in 2020.[2] In some instances, there is a need to refine their application and to reform them in the future, as was recommended by the ILA Committee.

1 To use the words of Lord McNair in his separate opinion to the advisory opinion of the ICJ in *International Status of South-West Africa, Advisory Opinion, ICJ Reports 1950*, p. 128, at 148.

2 See International Law Association, 79th Biennial Conference, https://ila2020kyoto.org/welcome.html.

© KONINKLIJKE BRILL NV, LEIDEN, 2022 | DOI:10.1163/9789004467668_006

The three Chapters of Part 2 of the present volume deal with key procedural rules and principles, i.e. provisional measures, *compétence de la compétence* and the intervention of third States. The authors offer stimulating perspectives on their application and interplay, as well as the potential ways in which their various contours could be reformed.

Stratis G. Georgilas, reflecting on the recent case-law of the ICJ related to provisional measures, makes observations about the manner in which the Court understands and discusses the "plausibility test" as well as the link between the rights claimed and the provisional measures requested. The author suggests that while taking into account the discretion the Court enjoys when indicating this type of measures, the judicial organ should expand its legal reasoning to ensure "the proper function of the rule of law in the international arena" and "the convincing force of a Court's Order well beyond the litigants' sphere and needs".

Anna Czaplińska analyses, in light of two examples, the way in which international courts and tribunals can shape procedural rules. Noting the existence of various interpretative attitudes that international courts and tribunals may adopt, the author focuses more especially on the phenomenon of "interpretive activism aimed to justify limitation or lack of competence" and on its impact on the procedural norms regarding the assessment of a court's competence to resolve a given case. Looking at the *Monetary Gold* principle as conceived in the 1954 judgment of the ICJ and the way it was taken into account in the *East Timor* case, the author considers that in the latter case, "the judgment is a model example of activist interpretation of the admissibility criteria in order to justify lack of the Court's competence". The other example which is explored is the "pilot judgment" procedure developed by the European Court of Human Rights.

Paula Wojcikiewicz Almeida considers that the ICJ has, up to now, been too modest in utilising its powers to expand procedural rules so that global public goods may be better protected. In this context, the author emphasises that there is a need to expand rules permitting the standing and participation of third States in bilateral proceedings. Looking at the rules governing intervention, a call is made for removing obstacles to intervention under Articles 62 and 63 of the ICJ Statute through a modification of the Rules of the Court. The issue of *amicus curiae* briefs is also addressed in this contribution.

While dealing with provisional measures, *compétence de la compétence* and intervention, the three contributions shed light on other procedural principles of great importance for the sound administration of justice, be it *jura novit curia*, the distinction between jurisdiction and admissibility or the contours of the legal right to bring a claim. The constitutive instruments of international courts and tribunals as well as their rules may find application in addressing these procedural issues. Another way in which international courts and tribunals can act despite the silence of their constitutive instruments is through the exercise of their general power to regulate their own procedures. By virtue of these inherent powers, international courts and tribunals have, for example, suspended proceedings,[3] prevented participation of a lawyer[4] or interpreted and revised judgments.[5] Notably, the ICJ has used its inherent powers to confer jurisdiction on itself to decide whether an order indicating measures has been complied with.[6] As a consequence, it is reasonable to predict that international courts and tribunals will continue to play an important part in future developments regarding their own procedural rules.

3 PCA, *MOX Plant Case* (*Ireland v. United Kingdom*), Order no. 3 Suspension, 24 June 2003, PCA Case No. 2002-01, para. 3.

4 *Hrvatska Elektroprivreda v. Slovenia, ICSID Case No ARB/05/24, Order Concerning the Participation of Counsel, 6 May 2008,* para. 34.

5 *United States-United Kingdom Arbitration concerning Heathrow Airport User Charges* (*United States-United Kingdom*), *Supplementary Decision, 1 November 1993*, 24 *Reports of International Arbitral Awards* 1, pp. 352–354, paras. 2.23–2.32.

6 *LaGrand* (*Germany v. United States of America*), *Judgment, ICJ Reports 2001*, p. 466. at 484, para. 45.

CHAPTER 4

The "Sparse Axiomatic Statement of Article 41" of the Statute of the International Court of Justice and the Court's Latest Orders: *Pathemata Mathemata*

Stratis G. Georgilas

1 Prolegomena

We have seen, and there is no doubt whatsoever about it, that diversity is a prominent characteristic of the current docket of the International Court of Justice (henceforth, the Court). One can easily identify all sorts of disputes pending before the principal judicial organ of the UN. Notwithstanding the obvious, namely an ever-growing number of States trusting, sometimes unreservedly, the institution, a long-awaited maturity of State practice became crystal-clear. While the freedom of choosing the means for the settlement of international disputes remains unimpaired, some took a significant decision to entrust the vindication of their rights to a judicial forum.[1]

Alas, other States consider themselves all-powerful, if not all-mighty. Since the time element runs usually against the aggrieved State's legal interests and rights, the latter is more or less forced to ask the Court to indicate provisional measures of protection. In most cases, the requesting party usually seeks the clear imposition of Right over Might, as unilaterally understood. Therefore, its litigation strategy corresponds to a swift military manoeuvre, mainly for its own benefit and, presumably, for the stability of international society, too.

When asking for provisional measures of protection, the primary goal, from a requesting State's viewpoint, is to try and keep feasible the option of returning to the *status quo ante*, before any irreversible change of State affairs takes place, or, at the very least, to preserve fully the exercise of its rights that are to be adjudged finally during the merits phase. To paraphrase Shigeru Oda, indicating provisional measures is deemed to be an almost essential instrument

1 A. Yusuf, 'Compulsory Jurisdiction of the Court under the Optional Clause', in S. van Hoogstraten (ed.), *New Challenges to International Law* (Brill, 2018) 8, 10.

© KONINKLIJKE BRILL NV, LEIDEN, 2022 | DOI:10.1163/9789004467668_007

in the panoply of any judicial process.[2] Moving to the greater picture, international society is concerned to "box" the particular dispute, avoid any unpleasant spill-over and contain any aggravation to a serious animosity that could threaten international peace and security, destroying unavoidably and practically any notion of international justice.[3]

To get back to my original point, although judicialization of all international affairs and disputes remains far from becoming a reality, the judgements of the Court are

> a repository of legal experience to which it is convenient to adhere; because they embody what the Court has considered to be good law; because respect for decisions given in the past makes for certainty and stability, which are of the essence of the good administration of justice. …[4]

It is well known that Article 41 of the Statute was the result of a proposal by the Brazilian jurist Raul Fernandes.[5] By the way, since in the conference where this article was presented, we enjoyed the excellent Portuguese hospitality, one should be particularly mindful of the Portuguese contribution in international justice. Due to time restraints, it remains impossible to venture into deep details on the overreaching case-law produced when Judge da Matta, Judge Fernandes and Judge Ferrer-Correia were serving at the Bench.[6]

It has to be acknowledged, though, that the depth of the Separate Opinions rendered by Judge Cançado Trindade in the *Application of the International Convention on the Elimination of all Forms of Racial Discrimination* (*Qatar v United Arab Emirates,* Provisional Measures) and Judge *ad hoc* Kateka in the *Immunities and Criminal Proceedings* (*Equatorial Guinea v. France,* Provisional Measures) ignited my interest for a closer examination. What I propose to share with you is not how the Court construes the so-called "*plausibility test*" and the

2 'Provisional measures – the practice of the International Court of Justice' in V. Lowe and M. Fitzmaurice (eds.), *Fifty Years of the International Court of Justice* (CUP, 1996), 541.

3 P. Couvreur, *The International Court of Justice and the Effectiveness of International Law* (Brill, 2017) 119.

4 H. Lauterpacht, *The Development of International Law by the International Court* (CUP, 2010) 14.

5 *Procès-Verbaux* of the Proceedings of the Committee of Jurists (1920) 608–9. S. Rosenne, *Provisional Measures in International Law* (OUP, 2005) 22–29.

6 A. Eyefinger, *The International Court of Justice 1946–1996* (Kluwer, 1996) and the official site of the ICJ, available at http://www.icj-cij.org/en/members (accessed 14 January 2021). C. Miles, *Provisional Measures before International Courts and Tribunals* (CUP, 2017) 1–6, 42–58.

link between the rights claimed and the provisional measures requested in its recent case-law. I shall rather try to articulate what, in my view, constitutes a substantial lack of reasoning, given the discretion the Court enjoys when indicating provisional measures. My concluding remarks will try to envisage a novel *modus operandi* between judicial propriety and the imperative need for judicial reasoning, the latter being utterly needed for the proper function of the rule of law in the international arena.

2 The 'Plausibility' Test

It breaks no novel ground to underline the identical, if not *verbatim*, reasoning of the Court, namely

> The power of the Court to indicate provisional measures under Article 41 of the Statute has as its object the preservation of the respective rights claimed by the parties in a case, pending its decision on the merits thereof. It follows that the Court must be concerned to preserve by such measures the rights which may subsequently be adjudged by it to belong to either party. Therefore, the Court may exercise this power only if it is satisfied that the rights asserted by the requesting party are at least plausible.[7]

---

7 *Application of the International Convention on the Elimination of All Forms of Racial Discrimination* (*Georgia v. Russian Federation*), Provisional Measures, Order of 15 October 2008, *ICJ Reports 2008*, pp. 388–389, para. 118; *Certain Activities Carried Out by Nicaragua in the Border Area* (*Costa Rica v. Nicaragua*), *Provisional Measures, Order of 8 March 2011*, *ICJ Reports* 2011 (I), p. 18, para. 53; *Questions relating to the Seizure and Detention of Certain Documents and Data* (*Timor-Leste v. Australia*), *Provisional Measures, Order of 3 March 2014*, *ICJ Reports 2014*, p. 153, para. 26; *Immunities and Criminal Proceedings* (*Equatorial Guinea v. France*), *Provisional Measures, Order of 7 December 2016*, *ICJ Reports 2016* (II), p. 1165, para. 78; *Jadhav* (*India v. Pakistan*), *Provisional Measures, Order of 18 May 2017*, *ICJ Reports 2017*, p. 240, para. 35; *Application of the International Convention for the Suppression of the Financing of Terrorism and of the International Convention on the Elimination of All Forms of Racial Discrimination* (*Ukraine v. Russian Federation*), *Provisional Measures, Order of 19 April 2017*, *ICJ Reports 2017*, p. 104, para. 63; *Application of the International Convention on the Elimination of all Forms of Racial Discrimination* (*Qatar v United Arab Emirates*), Order of 23 July 2018, para. 43, available at https://www.icj-cij.org/files/case-related/172/172-20180723-ORD-01-00-EN.pdf (accessed 14 January 2021); *Alleged Violations of the 1955 Treaty of Amity, Economic Relations and Consular Rights* (*Islamic Republic of Iran v. USA*), Order of 3 October 2018, para. 53, available at https://www.icj-cij.org/files/case-related/175/175-20181003-ORD-01-00-EN.pdf (accessed 14 January 2021); *Application of the Convention on the Prevention and Punishment of the Crime of Genocide* (*The Gambia

Taking into consideration that the Court resolves concrete international disputes and does not operate similarly to an academic institution articulating abstract theories, the "plausibility" test raises a few issues, namely its precise definition, the ability to distinguish it properly and the exact framework of "employing a possible interpretation" as its tool, to name only but a few.[8]

Indeed, the requesting party bears the burden of being accurate, relying on clear-cut instruments and norms, presenting in fullness its rights and the way it exercises them as opposed to the alleged misconduct of the defendant vis-à-vis these very same rights. All claims presented by the requesting party have to be clear and precise.[9] Should the respondent State choose not to contest them, thus acquiescing that the requesting party does indeed hold the rights under examination,[10] the Court will usually draw an inference to this effect and adjudge it on the face of its Order.[11] On the contrary, should the respondent

---

v. Myanmar), Order of 23 January 2020, para. 43, available at https://www.icj-cij.org/public/files/case-related/178/178-20200123-ORD-01-00-EN.pdf (accessed 14 January 2021).

8 Judge Koroma maintained convincingly that the threshold of plausibility is not immediately apparent: *Separate Opinion, Certain Activities Carried Out by Nicaragua in the Border Area (Costa Rica v. Nicaragua), Order of 8 March 2011, ICJ Reports 2011*, p. 6, 31–32. An excellent overview of case-law on "plausibility" can be traced in J. Quintana, *Litigation at the International Court of Justice* (Brill, 2015) 659–669 and C. Miles (*supra* note 6), 198–201 and 'Provisional Measures and the 'New' Plausibility in the Jurisprudence of the International Court of Justice', 88 *BYIL* (2018) 1–46. Recent case-law and a full academic analysis on the plausibility criterion is thoroughly presented in R. Kolb, 'Digging Deeper into the "Plausibility of Rights"- Criterion in the Provisional Measures Jurisprudence of the ICJ', 19 *The Law and Practice of International Courts and Tribunals* (2020) 365.

9 *Application of the International Convention for the Suppression of the Financing of Terrorism and of the International Convention on the Elimination of All Forms of Racial Discrimination (Ukraine v. Russian Federation), Provisional Measures, Order of 19 April 2017, ICJ Reports 2017*, p. 104, para. 72. "(...) for the purposes of its Request for the indication of provisional measures, Ukraine invokes its rights and the respective obligations of the Russian Federation solely under Article 18 of the Convention". Also, *Alleged Violations of the 1955 Treaty of Amity, Economic Relations and Consular Rights (Islamic Republic of Iran v. USA)*, Order of 3 October 2018, para. 64, as per the legal basis of Iran's claims.

10 *Ibid*, at para. 65. Also, *Questions relating to the Seizure and Detention of Certain Documents and Data (Timor-Leste v. Australia), Provisional Measures, Order of 3 March 2014, ICJ Reports 2014*, p. 153, para. 27. For a partial acknowledgement, see the practice of France, *Immunities and Criminal Proceedings (Equatorial Guinea v. France), Provisional Measures, Order of 7 December 2016, ICJ Reports 2016* (II), p. 1165, para. 79.

11 E.g. para. 47 of the Court's Order in *Application of the Convention on the Prevention and Punishment of the Crime of Genocide (The Gambia v. Myanmar)*, Order of 23 January 2020. Myanmar did not specifically address the question whether the rights asserted by the Gambia were at least plausible. It merely argued that a "plausible claim", under the Genocide Convention, must include sufficient and reliable evidence of the required specific genocidal intent.

State contest the rights of the requesting State, the former needs additionally to provide specific and detailed factual and legal analysis, otherwise its argument will not provide a sufficient basis to exclude the plausibility of the right claimed.[12]

Although a full and detailed assessment is neither mandatory nor necessary,[13] the Court held that evidence to support the plausibility test, deriving from a report of a UN body or organ (in the *Application of the International Convention on the Elimination of all Forms of Racial Discrimination, Qatar v United Arab Emirates*) or a Report of a Fact–Finding Mission (in the *Application of the Convention on the Prevention and Punishment of the Crime of Genocide, The Gambia v. Myanmar*) is valuable for assessing the effect of the measure under consideration.[14] In the *Application of the International Convention for the Suppression of the Financing of Terrorism and of the International Convention on the Elimination of All Forms of Racial Discrimination* (*Ukraine v. Russian Federation*), the Court indicated its inclination to ascertain whether there are sufficient reasons for considering that other elements set out in the instrument invoked, such as the elements of intention or knowledge and the element of application of the legal instrument's purpose, as specified authentically, are present. In that particular case, Ukraine did not put before the Court any evidence which afforded a sufficient basis to find it plausible that these elements were present.[15]

Quite differently, in the *Questions relating to the Seizure and Detention of Certain Documents and Data* (*Timor-Leste v. Australia*) the Court identified the principal claim of Timor-Leste, namely the violation of its right to communicate with its counsel and lawyers in a confidential manner with regard to issues forming the subject-matter of pending arbitral proceedings and future negotiations between the Parties. In such a situation, the Court held that a State

---

12 *Jadhav* (*India v. Pakistan*), *Provisional Measures, Order of 18 May 2017, ICJ Reports 2017*, p. 240, para. 43.

13 The Court is adamant on this aspect. Given this approach, I cannot share Kolb's fear (*supra* note 8, 369, 387) about "strategic abuse and merits contamination" during the incidental procedure of provisional measures, for a prudent applicant would not choose to disclose at an early stage the fullness of its arguments and the supporting facts/evidence.

14 *Application of the International Convention on the Elimination of all Forms of Racial Discrimination* (*Qatar v United Arab Emirates*), Order of 23 July 2018, para. 47. Also in *Application of the Convention on the Prevention and Punishment of the Crime of Genocide* (*The Gambia v. Myanmar*), Order of 23 January 2020, paras 53–55, 65.

15 *Application of the International Convention for the Suppression of the Financing of Terrorism and of the International Convention on the Elimination of All Forms of Racial Discrimination* (*Ukraine v. Russian Federation*), *Provisional Measures, Order of 19 April 2017, ICJ Reports 2017*, p. 104, para. 74.

enjoys a plausible right to the protection of its communications with counsel relating to an arbitration or to negotiations, in particular, to the protection of the correspondence between them, as well as to the protection of confidentiality of any documents and data prepared by counsel to advise that State in such a context.

Finally, in the *Application of the Convention on the Prevention and Punishment of the Crime of Genocide* (*The Gambia v. Myanmar*) the Court declined to accept that the exceptional gravity of the allegations is a decisive factor warranting the determination of the existence of a genocidal intent.[16]

Does the plausibility test encompass evidentiary issues?[17] One has to differentiate clearly, if not distinguish, between the low standard of proof required and the existence of an elliptic, defective and sometimes contradictory reasoning of an Order. In Judge Greenwood's vivid description, it is for the applicant/requesting State to convince the Court by advancing

> something more than assertion but less than proof; in other words, the party must show that there is at least a reasonable possibility that the right which it claims exists as a matter of law and will be adjudged to apply to that party's case.[18]

The Court opts usually for three tools, namely the so-called possible interpretation of the legal instrument, the natural reading and the capability of affecting the exercise of the right invoked. Out of the three, only the last one may offer an indeed measurable (and therefore more objective) indicator. As per the first and second, this is an open-ended discussion, for their precise scope and content remain far from being clear. In my view, there is ample room for improving legal certainty on this particular aspect.

The Court usually follows a rather strict, if not black letter, approach. In the *Application of the International Convention for the Suppression of the Financing of Terrorism and of the International Convention on the Elimination of All Forms of Racial Discrimination* (*Ukraine v. Russian Federation*), the Court considered it imperative to clarify that

16 *Application of the Convention on the Prevention and Punishment of the Crime of Genocide* (*The Gambia v. Myanmar*), Order of 23 January 2020, para. 56.

17 Oellers-Fram and A. Zimmermann in A. Zimmermann, C. Tams *et al.* (eds.), *The Statute of the International Court of Justice: A Commentary* (OUP, 2019) 1157.

18 *Declaration, Certain Activities Carried Out by Nicaragua in the Border Area* (*Costa Rica v. Nicaragua*), *Order of 8 March 2011, ICJ Reports 2011*, p. 6, 47.

> corresponding rights are premised on the acts identified in Article 2, namely the provision or collection of funds with the intention that they should be used or in the knowledge that they are to be used in order to carry out acts set out in paragraphs 1 (a) and 1 (b) of this Article. Consequently, in the context of a request for the indication of provisional measures, a State party to the Convention may rely on Article 18 to require another State party to cooperate with it in the prevention of certain types of acts only if it is plausible that such acts constitute offences under Article 2 of the ICSFT.[...] it is necessary to ascertain whether there are sufficient reasons for considering that the other elements set out in Article 2, paragraph 1, such as the elements of intention or knowledge and the element of application of the ICSFT and CERD purpose specified in Article 2, paragraph 1 (b), are present.[19]

Interestingly enough, the very same was applied when the Court indicated that CERD

> imposes a number of obligations on States parties with regard to the elimination of racial discrimination in all its forms and manifestations. For the purposes of CERD, the term "racial discrimination" includes discrimination on the basis of ethnic origin [...] evidence presented before the Court by the Parties, it appears that some of the acts complained of by Ukraine fulfil this condition of plausibility. This is the case with respect to the banning of the Mejlis and the alleged restrictions on the educational rights of ethnic Ukrainians.[20]

That said, there are times when a broad interpretation is employed. For example, the Court was provisionally convinced that

> there is a correlation between respect for individual rights, the obligations of States parties under CERD and the right of States parties to seek compliance therewith [...] in the context of a request for the indication of provisional measures, a State party to CERD may avail itself of the rights under the above-mentioned Articles only if the acts complained of appear to constitute acts of racial discrimination as defined in Article 1 of the Convention [...] It appears that some of the acts of which Qatar

19 *Op. cit.*, paras. 74–5.
20 *Ibid.*, paras. 80 and 82.

> complains may constitute acts of racial discrimination as defined by the Convention. Consequently, the Court finds that at least some of the rights asserted by Qatar under Article 5 of CERD are plausible. This is the case, for example, with respect to the alleged racial discrimination in the enjoyment of rights such as the right to marriage and the choice of spouse, the right to education, as well as freedom of movement, and access to justice.[21]

The same cannot be maintained when examining the Court's interpretation in the *Application of the Convention on the Prevention and Punishment of the Crime of Genocide* (*The Gambia v. Myanmar*) case. Following a concise determination of a State's rights and duties under that Convention, the Court's reasoning seems to follow a rather *doric* order: the intention behind the Convention's provisions was briefly articulated; the correlation between the rights of the members of groups protected under the Genocide Convention, the obligations incumbent on States Parties thereto, and the (individual) right of any State party to seek compliance therewith by another State party fitted in less than a paragraph of the Order.[22]

Bearing in mind these provisional findings, one cannot but agree that it is quite difficult 'to formulate a general and precise rule as to the degree of closeness between the measures requested and the subject of the dispute'.[23]

Indeed, it is for the Court, whose methodology and reasoning need to be fully and clearly illustrated, to amplify its findings and support them with a more detailed analysis.

3 The 'Link' between the Rights Claimed and the Provisional Measures Requested

It has already been emphasized the onus falls upon the requesting party; it has to put forward and maintain that the exercise of the allegedly impaired rights

---

21 *Application of the International Convention on the Elimination of all Forms of Racial Discrimination* (*Qatar v United Arab Emirates*), Order of 23 July 2018, at paras. 51, 52 and 54, with reference to the *Application of the International Convention on the Elimination of All Forms of Racial Discrimination* (*Georgia v. Russian Federation*), *Provisional Measures, Order of 15 October 2008, ICJ Reports 2008*, pp. 391–392, para. 126.

22 *Application of the Convention on the Prevention and Punishment of the Crime of Genocide* (*The Gambia v. Myanmar*), Order of 23 January 2020, para. 52.

23 R. Kolb, *The International Court of Justice* (Hart, 2013) 627.

it seeks to protect is connected with the rights to be upheld on the merits. The applicant bears the procedural burden of precision and accuracy, as per both factual and legal elements of its application for the indication of provisional measures of protection. In most instances, both elements are clearly identifiable and complete. If this is not the case and not all necessary factual elements are put before the Court, I hold the opinion that the Bench must act *proprio motu* and seek to establish a more complete picture of all crucial details. At this incidental stage of proceedings, the adversarial system must yield to the proper administration of justice.

There are instances when a defendant may not choose to dispute the existence of a link.[24] It goes without saying that this practice may indicate a valuable admission. The Court needs to identify this admission, for it sometimes leads to the proper understanding of a case's particularities. As a result, it may also contribute to the proper administration of justice and emphasize the role of the Court as the guardian of international legality.

Case-law demands the existence of a direct connection between the rights claimed and the provisional measures requested. The Court insists that it is imperative to examine the aim of the measure requested, which is mostly, if not at all times, none other than preservation (and protection) of the rights invoked.[25] The Court usually considers that "by their very nature, these measures are aimed at protecting the right" under examination and concludes that

24 *Application of the Convention on the Prevention and Punishment of the Crime of Genocide (The Gambia v. Myanmar)*, Order of 23 January 2020, para. 59. M. Lando argues that the link emerges as an unnecessary and not helpful requirement in requests for provisional measures under article 41 of the Court's Statute, *The Law and Practice of International Courts and Tribunals* 19 (2020) 177, 179, 195, 199.

25 *Questions relating to the Seizure and Detention of Certain Documents and Data (Timor-Leste v. Australia), Provisional Measures, Order of 3 March 2014, ICJ Reports 2014*, p. 153, para. 31; *Immunities and Criminal Proceedings (Equatorial Guinea v. France), Provisional Measures, Order of 7 December 2016, ICJ Reports 2016* (II), p. 1165, para. 81; *Application of the International Convention for the Suppression of the Financing of Terrorism and of the International Convention on the Elimination of All Forms of Racial Discrimination (Ukraine v. Russian Federation), Provisional Measures, Order of 19 April 2017, ICJ Reports 2017*, p. 104, para. 86; *Jadhav (India v. Pakistan), Provisional Measures, Order of 18 May 2017, ICJ Reports 2017*, p. 240, para. 48; *Alleged Violations of the 1955 Treaty of Amity, Economic Relations and Consular Rights (Islamic Republic of Iran v. USA)*, Order of 3 October 2018, para. 75. In *Application of the International Convention on the Elimination of all Forms of Racial Discrimination (Qatar v United Arab Emirates)*, Order of 23 July 2018, paras. 58–9, the Court underlined that the requesting State was not asking only to put an end to collective expulsion but also at protecting other rights. *Application of the Convention on the Prevention and Punishment of the Crime of Genocide (The Gambia v. Myanmar)*, Order of 23 January 2020, para 61.

"a link exists between the right claimed by the requesting State and the provisional measures being sought".

This phrase is identical in all Orders, whether indicating or not, provisional measures and appears to be sufficient for the Court's reasoning. With the greatest of respect, I find this line of reasoning quite thin. As the case-law stands, it appears that this, seemingly independent, prerequisite for the indication of provisional measures of protection is treated usually by reference to, if not in essence absorbed by, plausibility. No serious effort has been made to clarify and articulate the bond between the link and the subject–matter of a pending case.

Surely, *jura novit curia* and there are instances where there is no need to state the obvious. This is not always the case, *ergo* the need to adopt a more elaborate reasoning. This, I believe, shall increase the convincing force of a Court's Order well beyond the litigants' sphere and needs. Conversely, its convincing force is seriously downgraded, and its application appears to be more of an art than a rigid science, for no trace of a detailed judicial reasoning, within the context of provisional measures, has been found.

4 Trends and Prospects

The docket speaks for itself. It is obvious that provisional measures of protection have changed in nature over the past 40 years.[26] The Court, is extremely cautious, for, as Shabtai Rosenne described it,

> the inherent nature of provisional measures proceedings and the factor of urgency supply an element of drama which fits in well with modern practices of diplomacy by television and the internet.[27]

It has silently followed a 'rule of law' approach, when indicating provisional measures of protection. First, the alleged breach of the applicant's rights ought

26 It has been argued that an increase of the number of cases does not necessarily entail a strengthening of international courts and consequently of the international rule of law. H. Krieger and G. Nolte, 'The International Rule of Law-Rise or Decline? Approaching Current Foundational Challenges' in H. Krieger, G. Nolte and A. Zimmermann (Eds.), *The International Rule of Law-Rise or Decline? Foundational Challenges* (OUP, 2019) 3, 14. Practice has shown otherwise.

27 S. Rosenne, *The Law and Practice of the International Court*, Volume III, 4th Edition (Martinus Nijhoff, 2006) 1416.

to be one that cannot be erased by mere financial means provided by the respondent. Secondly, it is well-accepted that a weak jurisdictional basis leads to an abuse of the applicant's right. Thirdly, the Court decides and indicates provisional measures on the basis of what is really put and argued before it. It renders orders and judgments, not lengthy essays and treatises.

International justice is served well when a prompt, transparent and efficient judicial machinery of the utmost standard upholds legal principles using a detailed and well-reasoned approach. In any case, the Court must find solutions most conducive to the necessity of stable and effective legal relations between the parties as well as to the benefit of the community as a whole.[28]

The Court enjoys latitude in its procedural assessments. Although consistency is evident in its case-law on provisional measures, its flexibility is sometimes minimal. A possible explanation would be that facts are sometimes presented *en masse* before the Court in an effort to somehow pre-empt its final judgement.

The Court has to shed away the ghost of *La Grand* (*Germany v. USA*), when its Order indicating provisional measures of protection was treated as if it was not empowered with a (provisionally) mandatory effect upon the litigants. By the way, what is the underlying reason that at the end of all orders the very same paragraph is repeated *verbatim?*

Everyone agrees that the proper administration of justice requires effectiveness. Therefore, the adoption of a novel procedure for monitoring the implementation of provisional measures indicated by the Court is more than welcome. Article 11 of the Resolution concerning the Internal Judicial Practice of the Court provides for the establishment of an *ad hoc* committee. It is composed of three judges and will assist the Court in monitoring the implementation of the provisional measures indicated. The committee will examine the information supplied by the litigants in this regard, report periodically to the Court, and recommend potential options for it.[29]

It is my firm belief that the time is ripe for the Court to fine-tune its approach on the reasoning of its Orders, especially when indicating provisional measures of protection. Stating extensively the views of the litigants and incorporating only but a minimal approach as per its own (provisional) findings makes one feel quite uncomfortable. I fear this approach does not serve international justice well. The reasoning has to be more convincing, given the time frame until a final judgement on the merits is rendered. The doors of the temple of

28 H. Lauterpacht, *The Function of Law in the International Community* (OUP, 2011) 131.

29 Available at https://www.icj-cij.org/public/files/press-releases/0/000-20201221-PRE-01-00-EN.pdf (accessed 14 January 2021).

peace remain open to States even when they are active belligerents.[30] That much, States and the international society expect.

30 H. Thirlway, 'Peace Justice, and Provisional Measures' in G. Gaja and J. Stoutenburg (eds.), *Enhancing the Rule of Law through the International Court of Justice* (Brill, 2014) 75.

CHAPTER 5

How International Courts Avoid the Exercise of Their Jurisdiction – the Competence of Competence and "Inverted Judicial Activism"

Anna Czaplińska

1 Introduction

The norms governing the competence of international courts and tribunals seem to constitute the most natural limits of their judicial discretion. They determine what type of matters (of contentious or other character) each given judicial institution can deal with, what conditions must be met in order to consider a case and to issue a decision on the merits.

However, the assessment of whether, in a specific case, the conditions set by competence norms are fulfilled falls under the responsibility of the very court or tribunal to which the case is referred. This power of international courts and tribunals is called "competence of competence" (in French *compétence de la compétence*, and in German *Kompetenz-Kompetenz*) and has the status of a principle arising from the core of performance of the judicial function.[1] Accordingly, each international judicial body is solely competent to resolve any dispute or doubt regarding the existence and scope of its competence in relation to a given case. Otherwise, as D. Shelton rightly stressed, international courts would have to either accept all cases addressed to them, regardless of any allegations of lack of jurisdiction, or automatically reject any matter in which such allegations would be raised.[2]

As a consequence, international courts themselves determine their jurisdiction on the basis of binding international law norms regulating their competences. These rules, in a formal way, do not differ from other norms of international law. They are created in the same way, in most cases enshrined

1 See D. Shelton, 'Form, Function and the Powers of International Courts', 9 *Chicago Journal of International Law* (2009), 456–457; C. F. Amerasinghe, *Jurisdiction of the International Tribunals* (Brill, 2003) p. 127; T. T. Koncewicz, *Zasada jurysdykcji powierzonej Trybunału Sprawiedliwości Wspólnot Europejskich* (Oficyna, 2009) p. 160. See also the ICJ judgment in the *Nottebohm* case (*Liechtenstein v. Guatemala*), *ICJ Reports 1953*, pp. 111, 119–120.

2 D. Shelton (note 1), p. 457.

© KONINKLIJKE BRILL NV, LEIDEN, 2022 | DOI:10.1163/9789004467668_008

in international agreements or other instruments establishing the courts or tribunals (e.g. resolutions of international organizations); some of them qualify as customary norms or even general principles of law (e.g. as the principle *compétence de la compétence*). In the same vein, as other norms, they acquire and lose binding force. Therefore, international courts, in order to apply norms regulating their competences, must interpret them by using the same recognized methods and subject to the same rules of interpretation as in the case of substantive norms.

The research I have conducted in this matter has led me to distinguish between four types of interpretative attitudes that international courts and tribunals may adopt: 1) an attitude of concealing or ignoring competence issues; 2) an attitude of interpretative restraint; 3) an attitude of interpretive activism aimed to justify their own competence; and 4) an attitude of interpretive activism aimed to justify a limitation or lack of competence – which I call "inverted judicial activism".[3] The adoption of a given approach by a judicial body in the interpretation of its competences may be of an incidental character, conditioned only by the circumstances of a given case, or systemic, when the court consistently adopts the same approach in every case in which similar elements appear. In this way, courts may shape certain concepts or even develop their own policies regarding issues related to the interpretation of competence norms.

The present paper focuses on the last of these approaches – the phenomenon of "inverted judicial activism" of international courts and tribunals in the interpretation of their competence norms and its consequences for the development (or decline) of procedural norms regarding the assessment of a court's competence to resolve a given case.

2 Reflections on the "Competent" Terminology

A precise definition of the subject of the present study requires, at the beginning, a clarification of some terminological questions. In legal texts, as well as in academic writings regarding the international judiciary, various notions are used regarding the capacity of a court or tribunal to address or dismiss a case. In English: jurisdiction, competence, admissibility. In French: *jurisdiction, compétence, recevabilité, saisine*. In German: *Zuständigkeit, Kompetenz Zulässigkeit*.

3 A. Czaplińska, 'Określanie własnej kompetencji przez sądy międzynarodowe – granica czy przejaw swobody orzeczniczej?', in A. Wyrozumska (ed.) *Granice swobody orzekania sądów międzynarodowych* (Lodz, 2014) p. 83 ff.

In Polish: *właściwość, jurysdykcja, kompetencja, dopuszczalność.* These notions are neither consistently used, even by the same entity or subject, nor consistently translated into other languages. In a given context, they may be treated as synonyms, while in another their respective scopes may be considered as subsidiary, interfering or even excluding each other. Both doctrine and courts recognize the existence of these terminological discrepancies and the possible difficulties resulting thereof.[4] An attempt to explain the relationship between the terms used, is made just for the purpose of the present study.

Prima facie, the term jurisdiction seems to have the broadest meaning, as it is used not only in reference to the exercise of the courts' function but also to define the State authority in general (as the power of creating, applying and enforcing the law) or the legal order established by it.[5] However, considering its etymological origin – the Latin proverb *iudicis est ius dicere, non dare* – and contrary to what Amerasinghe and Koncewicz have written,[6] it is rather the narrower understanding of the term "jurisdiction", expressing the essence of the function of the judiciary – that should be recognized as determinant for our purposes. Without calling into question the correctness of its use in the broader sense, in the present study the term jurisdiction is used primarily in the narrower sense, referring to courts, in particular – to international courts and tribunals.

Thus, the concept of jurisdiction in its original meaning defines the basic function of the judiciary. At the same time, it is used also in other contexts, for the determination of the kind and the scope of issues which a court can deal with, and which is determined by reference to the same criteria for any international court or tribunal. The first criterion is a personal one and refers to the circle of subjects authorized to effectively bring a case before the court (in respect of both contentious and non-contentious proceedings), as well as to the subjects against which it may be brought. The second criterion is the subject-matter of the cases. The third criterion is the temporal one. From the perspective of internal law, the issue of time is not only vital for assessing

4 See C. F. Amerasinghe (*supra* note 1), p. 58 ff; T.T. Koncewicz (note 1), p. 71 and ff; S. Rosenne, *International Courts and Tribunals, Jurisdiction and Admissibility of Inter-State Applications* (2008), in A. Peters (2021–) and R. Wolfrum (2004–2020) (eds.), *Max Planck Encyclopedia of Public International Law* (Oxford University Press, 2008–), available at http://www.mpepil.com/ (14 January 2021), paras. 1–2. See for example *Maritime Delimitation and Territorial Questions between Qatar and Bahrain (Jurisdiction and Admissibility) (Qatar v. Bahrain), ICJ Reports 1995,* paras. 16 ff and 45 ff; *Oil Platforms (Islamic Republic of Iran v. United States of America), ICJ Reports 2003,* para. 29.

5 E.g. C.F. Amerasinghe (note 1), p. 52 ff.

6 *Ibidem*; T. T. Koncewicz (note 1), p. 72.

the compliance with procedural deadlines. In the international legal order, where the basis of the court's competence is, in principle, the consent of the parties concerned,[7] it is also important to determine whether the circumstances of the case occurred during the period covered by this consent. The jurisdiction of international courts and tribunals must therefore be examined in these three dimensions: *ratione personae*, *ratione materiae* and *ratione temporis*.

A different meaning should be attributed to the notion of admissibility/inadmissibility of a case. In fact, admissibility refers to another aspect or even more precisely another and subsequent stage of performing the judicial function by an international court. The term admissibility (inadmissibility) determines the consequence of the occurrence (or not) of a fact, impact (or not) of some factor, the fulfilment (or not) of an event with which the norms regulating the functioning of a given court or tribunal connect the possibility (right, duty) to consider the case.[8] The consequence of the lack of jurisdiction is therefore the inadmissibility of a case – i.e. the inability to conduct the proceedings and to adjudicate on the substance of the case by the court. In practice, however, international courts and tribunals have a twofold approach to the relationship of jurisdiction and admissibility issues. Some (as the International Court of Justice and the International Tribunal for the Law of the Sea) take the view that these notions represent separate issues and admissibility refers to the factors which determine that the court, despite the fact that the matter falls within the scope of its jurisdiction, cannot rule on the case.[9] The conditions of admissibility are therefore, within this approach, something else than the premise of jurisdiction. Other courts (such as the Court of Justice of the European Union or the European Court of Human Rights) recognize that the examination of the jurisdiction of the court is one of the elements of the assessment of admissibility of the case.[10] Factors determining the scope of a court's jurisdiction are, from this point of view, one of the categories of admissibility criteria. Apart from them, the norms governing the functioning of the court may specify also other conditions for admissibility (inadmissibility), e.g. exhaustion of internal

7 Practice shows that, for example, in international criminal judiciary in specific cases, solutions deviating from this principle may be adopted, e.g. the creation of the International Criminal Tribunal for the former Yugoslavia by the resolution of the UN Security Council or the establishment of jurisdiction of the International Criminal Court in cases brought to it by Security Council.

8 The concept of admissibility may refer not only to litigation/proceedings in general, but also e.g. to individual acts of court, to evidence, etc.

9 See e.g. *Oil Platforms* case (note 4), para. 29. See also C. F. Amerasinghe (note 1), pp. 241 ff.

10 With reference to the CJEU, see also T. T. Koncewicz (note 1), p. 202 ff.

remedies, abuse of the right of complaint, *res iudicata*, etc. Whether and why such additional conditions are adopted, depends on the nature and purpose of the specific judicial body, as well as the nature of the matters within its jurisdiction and the kind of procedures under which it performs its functions. Thus, they can be regulated differently for each court or tribunal.[11] Accordingly, it would be difficult to compare the manner of their interpretation in the jurisprudence of various international courts since, for example, a given factor would appear as a premise of admissibility in the statute of only one of them.

For the above-mentioned reasons, the present paper focuses on jurisdiction in the strict sense and in its three dimensions: personal, material and temporal. It is by reference to these criteria, that the scope of the jurisdiction of each international court can be determined. Therefore, it is possible to analyse and compare what interpretation courts adopt regarding their own jurisdiction and its individual aspects. At the same time, because both the lack of jurisdiction of the court in a particular case as well as the occurrence of any other circumstances excluding its admissibility result in the inability to resolve the case by that court, I do not consider necessary narrowing the meaning of "admissibility" only to factors other than the criteria of jurisdiction. Thus, a broad understanding of the concept of admissibility is preferred, including also regarding the premises shaping the scope of jurisdiction of the court as one of the categories of admissibility conditions. It is bearing in mind this meaning that the term is used in this study.

Moreover, the terms admissibility/inadmissibility describe what is happening before the court from the perspective of the interested parties, especially those who file the case, and in contentious proceedings of those against whom it is filed, rather than from the perspective of the court itself.

From the point of view of the court or tribunal, it is possible to define the same situation by referring to the concept and notion of competence, as the

11 For example, exhaustion of domestic remedies constitutes a condition for the admissibility in individual complaint procedure before the ECHR, but no longer for the admissibility of an interstate complaint before the same court. As a rule, this is also a criterion for the state to take up diplomatic protection and submit a claim to protect its own citizens against another state. However, in the case of the specific type of proceedings as the prompt release procedure for immediate release of a vessel (under Article 292 of UNCLOS), although it derives from classical diplomatic protection, the condition of exhausting the internal remedies is not applicable – cf. ITLOS judgment of 7 February 2000 in case *No. 5 Camouco* (*Panama v. France*) para. 55 ff. Finally, with regard to international criminal courts, although the subject of their jurisdiction is the individual's responsibility, the condition of early exhaustion of the internal remedies is excluded, because these courts perform their functions as if in substitution for the domestic justice system.

institution being (or not) the competent organ to resolve the case. Within such an approach, both "competence" and "admissibility" refer therefore to the two sides of the same coin – the possibility to settle the case by the court. The term competence shall, thus, be understood as denoting a right – and, in principle, at the same time an obligation – of an international court or tribunal to rule on the case. Accordingly, the terms competence and jurisdiction may be used interchangeably in contexts in which the lack of distinction between them is not substantively significant.

3 "Inverted Judicial Activism" to Justify the Self-Limitation of the Court's Competence: Two Notable Examples

3.1 *The ICJ's Reinterpretation of the* Monetary Gold *Principle in the* East Timor *Judgment*

At first sight, refusal or avoidance by an international court from adjudicating a case may seem a manifestation of an attitude of judicial restraint. However, nothing could be more misleading: in the context of a research on the issue of the "competence of competence" the judicial restraint attitude is neutral in relation to the result of the process of interpretation. Activism, on the other hand, is a targeted approach characterized by the court's striving to achieve a certain result: confirmation or denial of one's own jurisdiction.[12] Regardless of whether in the interpretation of their competences, international courts and tribunals adopt an attitude of restraint or one of the variants of judicial activism, this interpretation is usually made in a dynamic manner, taking into account legal and non-legal factors affecting the perception of the role of courts in the international legal order and changes occurring in the real world. Meanwhile, the practice of international courts shows that they may be equally creative in justifying the possession of competence to consider a case, as well as the lack thereof.

The glaring example (at least in the legacy of the ICJ) of such an interpretation of jurisdictional rules, is the ICJ ruling in the *East Timor* case.[13] East Timor was a former Portuguese colony, and after 1960 a non-self-governing territory under the administration of Portugal. As a consequence of the Indonesian invasion in 1975 and subsequent occupation, Portugal lost the actual control over East Timor, but under international law it remained the only subject

12 A. Czaplińska (note 3) pp. 95–96.

13 *East Timor case (Portugal v. Australia)*, *ICJ Reports 1995*, p. 90 ff.

responsible for the affairs of East Timor and its population.[14] Over the years, Portugal's attitude towards its former colony has shifted from the absolute "metropolitan sovereign" to the "administering power" strongly advocating the completion of the decolonization process and the right to self-determination of the people of East Timor.[15]

Although the international community, in particular through the resolutions of the UN General Assembly and the Security Council, initially condemned Indonesia's aggression as a flagrant violation of international law,[16] as time passed, a number of States began to come to terms with Indonesia over the status quo.[17] One of the manifestations of this tendency was the conclusion in 1989 of an agreement between Australia and Indonesia on the delimitation and exploitation of the continental shelf between Australia and East Timor (the so-called Timor Gap Treaty).

In consequence thereof, Portugal brought a case against Australia before the ICJ, claiming that by entering into the treaty with Indonesia, Australia had violated Portugal's rights as administering power and the rights of the people of East Timor, including their right to self-determination. The ICJ, however, refused to decide the case, after having found that issuing of a judgment on the merits in the case would entail the necessity to rule on the rights and obligations of a third country – Indonesia – which did not participate in the dispute and did not agree to the jurisdiction of the Court, and would thus affect its legal interests.[18] To justify this finding, the ICJ developed a "creative" interpretation of the principle expressed in its judgment in the *Monetary Gold* case,[19] regardless of the fundamental differences between the circumstances of one and the other case.

The *Monetary Gold* case was submitted by Italy against France, the United Kingdom and the United States of America. The claim concerned a certain quantity of monetary gold reserves, originally belonging to the National Bank of Albania, which before the Second World War had been deposited in Rome

14 For a more detailed presentation of circumstances of the case see e.g. P. Hilpold, 'Krzysztof Skubiszewski and the right to self-determination', 39 *Polish Yearbook of International Law* (2019), p. 23 ff and the literature quoted there.

15 I fully agree with P. Hilpold on this point – see *ibidem*, p. 24.

16 Starting with UN General Assembly resolution 3485 (XXX) of 12 December 1975 and UN Security Council resolution 384 (1975) of 22 December 1975. For an exhaustive list see P. Hilpold (note 14) p. 24, note 10.

17 *Ibidem*.

18 *East Timor case* (note 13), paras. 28 ff.

19 *Monetary Gold Removed from Rome in 1943 (Italy v. France, United Kingdom of Great Britain and Northern Ireland and United States of America)*, *ICJ Reports 1954*.

(Italian banks had shares therein). In 1943, the gold had been seized and brought to Germany where it remained until the end of the war. After the surrender of Germany in 1945, it became subject to the rules of the peace agreements, according to which gold found in German territory was to be distributed among States as part of reparations due from Germany for war damages; France, the UK and the USA were responsible for the execution of these provisions.[20] Albania claimed its title to the gold, but it was contested by Italy and the UK, which claimed a share of the gold for themselves, respectively, as compensation for the damages arising from violations of international law that Albania allegedly had committed against them.[21] The case was submitted to arbitration, which resulted in a decision in favour of Albania. Italy, though, decided to contest this before the ICJ, instituting proceedings against the States responsible for enforcement of this decision and requesting the Court to rule that the gold should be given to Italy as partial satisfaction for the damages caused thereto by the Albanian law on nationalization of 1945.[22] However, no previous settlement, award or judgement ever confirmed that violation and damage.

Accordingly, the Court in *Monetary Gold* case would indeed had first to rule on Albania's possible liability vis-à-vis Italy in order to decide whether Italy really had a right to claim the gold. Therefore, the true subject-matter of that case was the legal relationship between Italy and Albania, which did not participate in the dispute and over which the ICJ indeed had no (personal) jurisdiction.

The Court extrapolated the argumentation from *Monetary Gold* to the circumstances of the *East Timor* case to make the principle also applicable to the latter. It claimed that, in order to assess whether Australia actually violated international law by concluding an agreement with the occupying power, it would have to rule on the illegality of the Indonesian occupation of East Timor, and it was not empowered to do so due to the lack of Indonesia's consent. It must be stressed, though, that from the point of view of international law, the ICJ was not the sole entity entitled to decide on the legality of States'

20 A. J. Grotto, 'Monetary Gold Arbitration and Case' (2008), in A. Peters (2021–) and R. Wolfrum (2004–2020) (eds.), *Max Planck Encyclopedia of Public International Law* (Oxford University Press, 2008–), available at http://www.mpepil.com/ (14 January 2021).

21 In the case of Italy, it was the nationalization of the Central Bank of Albania and expropriation of the Italian shareholders; in case of the UK it was the compensation for damage stemming from the *Corfu Channel case* (*United Kingdom of Great Britain and Northern Ireland v. Albania*), *ICJ Reports 1949*.

22 *Monetary Gold case* (note 19) p. 22.

actions. At that time, the illegality of the Indonesian occupation was a fact confirmed by the practice of States, especially within the UN (as mentioned above), which constantly confirmed Portugal's authority to represent East Timor. Additionally, it must be noted that a dispute resolution process under UN auspices, involving Portugal, Indonesia and the East Timorese people was already going on at that time. In the light of all this, such finding of the Court seems a bit odd, at least.

Portugal's position was based on the assumption that, since the rights infringed were effective *erga omnes*, for the establishment of the responsibility of Australia it did not matter whether another country also acted unlawfully. None of the pleadings submitted by Portugal referred to Indonesia. Actually, for confirming Australia's violation of international law it did not even matter with whom Australia concluded an agreement concerning East Timor – the decisive point would be that it did not conclude such agreement with Portugal, the only subject authorized under international law to represent the interests of East Timor and its population. This line of argumentation was developed in depth in the dissenting opinion by Judge Skubiszewski, *Ad Hoc* Judge appointed by Portugal, who actually deconstructed the Court's reasoning.[23] In respect of the applicability of *Monetary Gold* principle to the *East Timor* case, he pointed out that the basic condition thereof was that the third state's rights and/or obligations would constitute the very subject-matter of the case, and not just that it was likely to affect third state's interests, as it happened in *East Timor* case.[24] Judge Skubiszewski noticed that there were many bilateral disputes (and even types thereof, like territorial disputes) with great potential of involving interests of a third state, where the ICJ did not decline its jurisdiction.[25] Moreover, there were also disputes where rights and obligations of non-party States to the dispute were directly at stake, like in the *Certain Phosphate Lands in Nauru* case,[26] where the Court accepted jurisdiction despite the fact that Nauru's application was filed only against Australia, although the latter constituted the Administering Authority of Nauru jointly with New Zealand and the United Kingdom, and the subject-matter of the dispute concerned the activities of the Administering Authority as such.[27] These examples show that

23 *East Timor case* (note 13), dissenting opinion of Judge Skubiszewski, p. 224 ff; this opinion constitutes one of the most significant examples of the potential of individual judges' opinions to influence the development of international law. See also, in this context, the dissenting opinion of Judge Weeramantry, *East Timor case* (note 13), p. 139.

24 *East Timor case* (note 13), dissenting opinion of Judge Skubiszewski, paras. 59 ff.

25 *Ibidem*, para. 64.

26 *Certain Phosphate Lands in Nauru case* (*Nauru v. Australia*), *ICJ Reports 1992*, p. 240 ff.

27 *Ibidem*, paras. 48 ff.

the interpretation and application of the *Monetary Gold* principle in the *East Timor* case was neither consequent nor consistent with the ICJ jurisprudence.

The ICJ ruling was widely criticized on the point that there was too much judicial restraint (merely because the result was declination of jurisdiction).[28] However, in my opinion, this judgment is a model example of an activist interpretation of the admissibility criteria in order to justify the lack of the Court's competence, which in the effect made an obligation not to recognize an illegal situation non-challengeable and unenforceable.

3.2 *Introducing New Procedural Arrangements by Interpretation: The ECHR Invents the "Pilot Judgment"*

An activist attitude seeking to exclude or limit a court's own jurisdiction may also take the form of a systemic solution. An exceptional example thereof was developed in the practice of the European Court of Human Rights and it is the procedure of a "pilot judgment".[29]

At the end of the 1990s, the Court started to identify the so-called systemic problems – repeated allegations of similar, well-justified violations of the European Convention on Human Rights in complaints against the same State. Simultaneously, due to the rapid increase in the number of States Parties to the ECHR, applications began to overflow the Court. To address this problem, during the preparatory work on Protocol No. 14, the Court itself proposed a solution consisting of "freezing" such cases of systemic violations (withholding the proceedings at the very beginning), and signalling the existence of such a problem to the State concerned along with setting a deadline for adopting a systemic solution under national law.

This proposal was dropped, as allegedly too controversial for States Parties to agree on in the normal course of negotiating of the Protocol. However, at the same time, it was suggested to the Court that such a solution could be adopted within the existing ECHR regulations, if the ECHR used its judicial discretion to the limits in the interpretation of Article 46 (1) of the ECHR (the obligation of the States-Parties to abide by the final judgment of the Court in any case to which they are parties).[30] In 2004, the Committee of Ministers adopted

28 See, e.g., P. Kooijmans, 'The ICJ in the 21st Century: Judicial Restraint, Judicial Activism or Proactive Policy?', 56 *International and Comparative Law Quarterly* (2007), pp. 744–745.

29 L. Wildhaber, 'Pilot Judgment in cases of Structural or Systemic Problems on the National Level', in R. Wolfrum and U. Deutsch (ed.), *The European Court of Human Rights Overwhelmed by Applications: The Problems and Possible Solutions* (Springer 2009), p. 69 and ff. For an exhaustive analysis see D. Haider, *The pilot-judgement procedure of the European Court of Human Rights* (Brill, 2013).

30 L. Wildhaber (note 29), p. 70.

a resolution allowing for cooperation with the Court as part of the planned procedure.[31]

The first pilot judgment was given in the case *Broniowski v. Poland*, concerning the reparations for the property left by the applicants (or their ancestors) on the territory beyond the Bug River which after the Second World War was incorporated by the USSR.[32] Although the notion "pilot judgment" did not appear therein, it contained all the elements previously proposed by the ECHR: 1) finding a systemic problem in national order, 2) which may be the cause of the growing number of violations of the ECHR, 3) advice on the measures to be taken (including their retroactive character) and 4) postponement of consideration of other complaints having the same source for a prescribed period of time. The Committee of Ministers was also informed about the verdict.

The pilot judgment procedure was accepted by the States Parties without controversy and has already been used many times.[33] Currently, it is even codified in Article 61 of the Rules of Procedure of the Court. The pilot judgment owes wide acceptance to the fact that it is essentially a solution adopted in the interests of the States Parties and the Court itself, and not that of the individual applicants. The right of complaint to the ECHR of the latter is thus limited by this procedure in a manner not explicitly provided for by the provisions of the Convention – it is doubtful whether this is fully consistent with its object and purpose.

The pilot judgment procedure is the most extreme case of judicial activism regarding competence issues: the ECHR, without a proper legal basis, only through the interpretation of Article 46 of the ECHR, created a completely new type of conduct, regulating by its case-law also its procedural complexities. This example shows that the limits of the international courts' jurisdiction lie where the possibility of accepting their actions by States and other entities under their jurisdiction ends.

---

31 Committee of Ministers Resolution of 12 May 2004 (DH Res. (2004) 3) on "Judgments revealing an underlying systemic problem".

32 Judgment of the ECHR of 22 June 2004. Appl. No. 31443/96, *Broniowski v. Poland* (Merits), paras. 188 and ff.

33 See, e.g., judgment of the ECHR of 6 October 2005. Appl. No. 23032/02, *Lukenda v. Slovenia*; judgment of the ECHR of 15 January 2009. Appl. No. 33509/04, *Burdová v. Russia*; judgment of the ECHR of 23 November 2010, Appl. Nos. 60041/08 and 60054/08 *Greens and M.T. v. the United Kingdom*; judgment of the ECHR of 6 September 2016. Appl. No 73548/13 *W.D. v. Belgium*.

4 Conclusions

Although often seen as "natural limits" of judicial discretion, the norms regulating the competence of international courts and tribunals are also subject to the process of adjudication, in which the courts enjoy extensive interpretative freedom. The limits of this freedom are determined by the courts themselves, but within this process they take into account the rationality of the results of the interpretation and the possibility of acceptance thereof by the entities concerned.

The phenomenon of inverted judicial activism may be defined as progressive interpretation and application of competence rules aimed at demonstrating the lack of court's competence or its limitation. Although the refusal of an international court to recognise its jurisdiction in a given case has so far been regarded rather as an expression of judicial restraint, the examples provided from the practice of international courts and tribunals show that they can be equally creative in justifying their competence to deal with the case as well as lack thereof.

Such practices are capable, in particular, of affecting the shaping of procedural rules. Foremost, they contribute to the development of certain concepts and standards concerning the interpretation and application of competence norms decisive for the institution of proceedings as in the *Monetary Gold* case and in the *East Timor* case. But they may also result in the creation – by sole means of interpretation seeking to limit or exclude the court's own jurisdiction – of a completely new systemic procedural solution without a formal legal basis, as was the case with the "pilot judgment" procedure in the ECHR.

However, the phenomenon of "inverted activism" as a type of attitude of international courts and tribunals towards the interpretation of rules governing their competence should be of concern, both for its causes and for its consequences. The two significant examples, discussed above, indicate that the reasons behind the court's reluctance to deal with the case in question may be related rather to the mere convenience of the court than to the interest of the general public. The ICJ appears to have been driven by a desire to avoid certain discomfort in handling a politically sensitive case with the prospect of having to rule on the merits against an influential state. The ECHR had been striving to cope with the constantly increasing caseload by limiting the right of individual complaint through introducing an admissibility criterion not expressly provided for in the Convention. Both Courts then used the inverted activist interpretation in order to justify their refusal to fulfil their judicial function. Thus, the phenomenon of inverted judicial activism deserves a more profound examination, as it may impair the proper administration of justice and enforcement of the rule of law on international level.

CHAPTER 6

Enhancing the International Court of Justice Procedures in Order to Promote Community Interests

The Role of Third-Party Intervention

Paula Wojcikiewicz Almeida

1 Introduction

International law is not only a tool for coexistence among States, but also, and ultimately, a mechanism for the production and protection of global public goods (GPG).[1] The 'recognition of community interest in positive law' reflects this trend.[2] In the words of Judge Simma, 'international law has been moving in this direction for some decades now'.[3] If this reflects the current reality, one cannot deny that the realization of community interests also depends on the existence of an institutional structure for the promotion and protection of such interests.[4] However, in the current scenario, there is no supranational authority or appropriate public institution on a global level capable of compelling States to accomplish global achievements related to community interests.[5] As a component of the international governance structure, international courts and tribunals (ICTs) can be considered a key element to the promotion of the international rule of

1 GPG are also known for their properties of non-rivalry and non-excludability that result in the production of benefits to which everyone is entitled, or which affect all countries. These features, however, create a tension that ultimately leads to underinvestment and undersupply as free-rider and collective action problems arise. See D. Bodansky, 'What's in a Concept? Global Public Goods, International Law and Legitimacy', 23 *European Journal of International Law* (2012) 3, 658–659.

2 M. Benzing, 'Community Interests in the Procedure of International Courts and Tribunals', 5 *The Law and Practice of International Courts and Tribunals* (2006) 370.

3 B. Simma, 'From Bilateralism to Community Interest in International Law', 250 *Recueil des Cours de l'Académie de Droit International* (1994) 217, 234.

4 *Ibid.*, 285.

5 M. Benzing, *supra* note 2, 372; F. Cafaggi and D. D. Caron, 'Global Public Goods amidst a Plurality of Legal Orders: A Symposium', 23 *European Journal of International Law* (2012) 3, 645.

© KONINKLIJKE BRILL NV, LEIDEN, 2022 | DOI:10.1163/9789004467668_009

law,[6] including the provision of GPGs.[7] ICTs are equipped to protect, express and shape values that reflect GPG by the power granted in international treaties.[8] By developing international law, ICTs can be qualified as both 'intermediate GPG' and contributors to the protection and promotion of final GPG.[9]

Broadly, the rules of substantive international law that protect community interests are considered GPG, whereas the rules guiding international adjudication are of a procedural nature. Common to all international courts is a set of rules governing the process of adjudication, generally labelled as procedural. While procedure may guide and shape the application of substantive law,[10] it should itself be guided and shaped in a manner to ensure the protection of community interests. In other words, in cases involving *erga omnes* obligations, community interests should arguably guide the interpretation and development of procedural rules. This supposed positive relationship, in which procedure allows for an 'efficient application of substantive law that embodies public goods',[11] is not without difficulties. One may wonder whether procedural law could be used as an obstacle for the achievement of substantive rights, in particular, for the protection of GPG. Backlashes include situations where international adjudication prioritises procedures to the detriment of community interests.

As far as the ICJ is concerned, the tension between the multilateral nature of the conflicting substantive law and the bilateral nature of its own proceedings may generate significant negative reactions. Within the ICJ, procedures often act as a barrier to the achievement of GPG. There were lost opportunities in which the Court could have opted for the protection of community interests, but preferred, instead, to rely on procedure.[12] Such a stance can be perceived through its ruling on the *Application of the Convention on the Prevention and*

---

6 G. Ulfstein, 'International Courts and Judges: Independence, Interaction and Legitimacy', 46 *NYU Journal of International Law and Politics* (2014) 859–860.

7 A. Nollkamper, 'International Adjudication of Global Public Goods: The Intersection of Substance and Procedure', 23 *European Journal of International Law* (2012) 3, 769–770.

8 M. Benzing, *supra* note 2, 377.

9 A. Nollkamper, *supra* note 7, 783; G. Shaffer, 'International Law and Global Public Goods in a Legal Pluralist World', 23 *European Journal of International Law* (2012) 3674, 691.

10 A. Nollkaemper, *supra* note 7, 772.

11 *Ibid.*, 770.

12 For an analysis of other lost opportunities in which the ICJ did not further elaborate on the mechanisms provided for protecting community interests, see R. Wolfrum, 'Enforcing Community Interests Through International Dispute Settlement: Reality or Utopia?' in R. Geiger, D. Khan, A. Paulus, S. von Schorlemer and C. Vedder (eds.), *From Bilaterism to Community Interest: essays in Honour of Judge Bruno Simma* (OUP, 2011) p. 1132 at 1137–1138.

Punishment of the Crime of Genocide (Bosnia-Herzegovina v. Serbia),[13] where the Court refused to acknowledge Serbia's responsibility as a genocide perpetrator, despite evidence in the form of witnesses' testimonies along with previous ICTY decisions.[14] Furthermore, the Court took a somewhat similar stance on the *Obligations Concerning Negotiations Relating to Cessation of the Nuclear Arms Race and to Nuclear Disarmament* case,[15] when it adjudged that it could not proceed to the merits of the case on the grounds that a dispute was non-existent at the time of the filing of the application. The *Nuclear Arms Race* case represents a flagrant example of a formalistic decision made by the Court.[16]

These examples demonstrate that the International Court of Justice can sometimes be overly attached to procedure, resting on technicalities, so as to avoid deciding on the merits of high profile and politically charged cases. In order for the goal of protecting procedure to not prevail over the protection of community interests, one should expect that procedural law follows substantive law and *vice versa*. As a consequence, ICT's procedural law should allow for the adjudication of claims involving GPG, otherwise procedural law should be adjusted.[17] This is because the ICJ does not apply differentiated rules of procedure based on the prominent bilateral or multilateral interest in a dispute-settlement.[18] The idea is that 'the more the generation of legal normativity in the practice of international adjudication becomes visible, the more traditionally prevailing requirements for judicial procedures need to be supplemented by further considerations'.[19]

---

13 *Application of the Convention on the Prevention and Punishment of the Crime of Genocide (Bosnia and Herzegovina v. Serbia and Montenegro), Judgment, ICJ Reports 2007*, p. 43, at 403.

14 See, in particular, the Court's treatment of documentary evidence and the issue of disclosure of evidence and the possibility of drawing negative inferences, as discussed below in this article.

15 In 2016, the Marshall Islands brought to the ICJ three cases against India, Pakistan and the UK, as nuclear weapon States, in which it invoked the 1968 Treaty on the Non-Proliferation of Nuclear Weapons (NPT) as well as customary international law in the proceedings. *Obligations concerning Negotiations relating to Cessation of the Nuclear Arms Race and to Nuclear Disarmament (Marshall Islands v. United Kingdom)* (Preliminary Objections: Memorial of the Marshall Islands) (2016), 51–59.

16 I. Venzke, 'Public interests in the International Court of Justice – a comparison between Nuclear Arms Race (2016) and South West Africa (1966)', in 'Symposium on the Marshall Islands Case', 111 *American Journal of International Law* (2017) 68.

17 A. Nollkaemper, *supra* note 7, 770.

18 M. Benzing, *supra* note 2, 385; R. Wolfrum, *supra* note 12, 1138–9.

19 A. von Bogdandy, I. Venzke, 'On the Democratic Legitimation of International Judicial Lawmaking', 12 *German Law Journal* (2011) 5, 1362. C. Chinkin, 'Article 62' in A. Zimmermann, C. Tomuschat, K. Oellers-Frahm, C. Tams and T. Thienel (eds), *The*

This paper argues that there is a disconnection between community interests and procedure, which has not been attuned to reflect contemporary international law challenges deriving from GPG.[20] Independently from consent, Courts can adjust and tailor their own rules for multiparty aspects.[21] Indeed, the procedural law of international judicial institutions is largely a product of their own making.[22] International tribunals are endowed with an inherent competence not only with regard to their own jurisdiction (*compétence de la competénce*), but also with regard to the interpretation of the provisions of their respective jurisdictional instruments. As clearly put by Judge Cançado Trindade, 'it is an "inherent power" of an international tribunal such as the ICJ to see to it that the procedure operates in a balanced way, ensuring procedural equality and the guarantees of due process, so as to preserve the integrity of its judicial function'.[23] Therefore, self-regulation is considered as the prevailing system and an important source of independence of an ICT, being 'one of the ways in which such a creature may escape its makers'.[24]

However, it appears that the ICJ has been very modest in utilizing its powers to expand procedural rules beyond its mandate to ensure application of substantive law embodied in GPG.[25] If changes in substantive law, notably when

Statute of the International Court of Justice: A Commentary (OUP, 2006), 1331, 1366; P. Palchetti, 'Opening the International Court of Justice to Third States: Intervention and Beyond' 6 *Max Planck UNYB* (2002), 139; R. Wolfrum, 'Intervention in the Proceedings before the International Court of Justice and the International Tribunal for the Law of the Sea', in P. C. Rao and R. Khan (eds.), *The International Tribunal for the Law of the Sea: Law and Practice* (Kluwer Law International, 2001).

20 See, generally, E. Cannizzaro and B. I. Bonafé, 'Of Rights and Remedies: Sovereign Immunity and Fundamental Human Rights', in U. Fastenrath, R. Geiger, D. Khan, A. Paulus, S. von Schorlemer and C. Vedder (eds.), *From Bilateralism to Community Interest: Essays in Honour of Judge Bruno Simma* (OUP, 2011).

21 A. Nollkamper, *supra* note 7, 787–788.

22 A. von Bogdandy, I. Venzke, 'On the Democratic Legitimation ...', 1362; R. Kolb, 'General Principles of Procedural Law', in A. Zimmermann, C. Tomuschat, K. Oellers-Frahm, C. Tams and Tobias Thienel (eds.), *The Statute of the International Court of Justice: A Commentary* (OUP, 2006), 793, 795.

23 *Certain Activities carried out by Nicaragua in the Border Area* (*Costa Rica v. Nicaragua*) *Proceedings joined with Construction of a Road in Costa Rica along the San Juan River* (*Nicaragua v. Costa Rica*), Order: joinder of proceedings, Separate Opinion of Judge Cançado Trindade) (2013) para. 14.

24 J.M. Sorel, 'International Courts and Tribunals, Procedure' (2019), available at http://opil.ouplaw.com/view/10.1093/law:epil/9780199231690/law-9780199231690-e40?rskey=urzeEi&result=1&prd=EPIL.

25 E. McWhinney, 'The International Court of Justice and International Law-Making: The Judicial Activism/Self-Restraint Antinomy', 5 *Chinese Journal of International Law* (2006) 1, 3.

GPG are at stake, are not reflected in the procedure of contentious inter-State judicial dispute settlement, there is indeed a need to expand rules permitting the standing and participation of the international community in bilateral proceedings. In the same vein, judicial procedures could be expanded in a way to strengthen the democratic legitimation of judicial decisions; procedural rules providing for greater transparency and opportunities of participation would reflect this trend.[26] Therefore, in cases involving litigation in the 'common interest', a diverse range of procedural issues may raise particular concerns,[27] notably regarding intervention of third parties.[28]

2 Broadening the Scope of Third-Party Intervention

According to Article 62 of the Statute, a third State may request to intervene whenever it has an interest of a legal nature which may be affected by the decision in the case; whereas the right of a third State to intervene on a question of interpretation of a treaty of which it is party is recognized by Article 63 of the Statute.[29] As clarified by the Court in the *Whaling in the Antarctic* case, intervention under Article 63 ('as of right') possesses a limited object, which 'is to allow a third State not party to the proceedings, but party to a convention whose construction is in question in those proceedings, to present to the Court its observations on the construction of that convention'.[30] In the sections below, we will focus on the controversial aspects of third-party intervention as provided for by the Rules of Court, before identifying concrete amendment proposals in order to ensure greater participation by the international community in ICJ proceedings.

26 A. von Bogdandy, I. Venzke, 'On the Democratic Legitimation ...', 1362; J. Crawford and A. Keene, 'Editorial' 7 *Journal of International Dispute Settlement* (2016), 225.

27 See A. Nollkamper, *supra* note 7, 778.

28 P. Palchetti, 'Opening ...', 139.

29 For a general assessment, see Y. Iwasawa, 'Third Parties Before Internationals Tribunals: The ICJ and the WTO', in N. Ando, E. McWhinney and R. Wolfrum (eds.), *Liber Amicorum Judge Shigeru Oda* (Kluwer Law International, 2002); and A.J.J. de Hoogh, 'Intervention Under Article 62 of The Statute and the Quest for Incidental Jurisdiction without the Consent of the Principal Parties', 6 *Leiden Journal of International Law* (1993) 17.

30 *Whaling in the Antarctic* (*Australia v. Japan*) (Declaration of Intervention: Order) (2013) *ICJ Rep* 3, para. 7.

2.1 *Discretional Intervention (Article 62 of the ICJ Statute)*

The rules governing the so-called 'discretional' intervention are historically unclear. This is maybe due to the prevailing tension between private – bilateral – and collective interests – community interests – in dispute settlement. Article 62 of the ICJ Statute reflects this ambiguity, being intentionally drafted in very general terms so that requirements for intervention would have to be decided case by case and *au fur et à mesure.*[31]

This uncertainty regarding criteria for intervention has made States reluctant to ask permission to intervene in cases brought before the Court. The Court has granted permission to intervene in only 3 out of 11 cases so far.[32] Despite the Court's effort 'to dispel some of the doubts and uncertainties which surround the exercise of the procedural faculty of intervention under Article 62 of its Statute',[33] most requirements for discretional intervention remain unsettled. Overall, the jurisprudence of the Court has been reluctant to further detail the requirements of intervention and, as equally important, has been unable to provide the necessary transparency of the proceedings, making it difficult for potential interveners to identify their legal interest.

2.1.1 Ensuring Greater Transparency and Non-Confidentiality of Proceedings

Since intervention is an incidental proceeding, third States wishing to intervene must file an application before the closure of the written proceedings in the principal case (Article 81 (1)). The term 'no later than the closure of the

31 See *Continental Shelf (Tunisia v. Libyan Jamahiriya) (Application for Intervention: Judgment) ICJ Reports 1981*, 3 para. 23.

32 *Nuclear Tests (New Zealand v. France) (Application for Intervention) ICJ Reports 1973; Continental Shelf (Tunisia v. Libyan Jamahiriya) (Application for Intervention) ICJ Reports 1981; Continental Shelf (Malta v. Libyan Jamahiriya) (Application for Intervention) ICJ Reports 1984; Land, Island and Maritime Frontier Dispute (El Salvador v. Honduras) (Application for Intervention) ICJ Reports 1990; Request for an Examination of the Situation in Accordance with Paragraph 63 of the Court's Judgment of 20 December 1974 in the Nuclear Tests (New Zealand v. France) (Applications for Intervention) ICJ Reports 1995; Land and Maritime Boundary between Cameroon and Nigeria (Cameroon v. Nigeria) (Application Intervention: Order) ICJ Reports 1999; Sovereignty over Pulau Ligitan and Pulau Sipadan (Indonesia v. Malaysia) (Application for Intervention), ICJ Reports 2001; Territorial and Maritime Dispute (Nicaragua v. Colombia) (Applications for Intervention) ICJ Reports 2011; Jurisdictional Immunities of the State (Germany v. Italy) (Application for Intervention) ICJ Reports 2011.* The Court admitted the applications of Nicaragua in the *Land, Island and Maritime Frontier Dispute* case, of Equatorial Guinea in the *Land and Maritime Boundary* case, and that of Greece in the *Jurisdictional Immunities of the State* case.

33 *Continental Shelf (Malta v. Libyan Jamahiriya) (Application for Intervention: Judgment), supra*, para. 46.

written proceedings', or as in the French version 'le plus tôt possible avant la clôture de la procedure écrite' has been interpreted by the Court as by the closure of the written phase.[34] However, an intervener may apply to be provided with the written pleadings and documents filed by the parties prior to filing its application to intervene.[35]

The question of the extent to which the Court's records should be open to third States has been hotly debated.[36] Article 85 (1) of the Rules of Court determines that only a State that has had its request to intervene accepted by the Court shall have access to the pleadings in the case. However, this has not been so construed in practice.[37] Potential interveners may consult written arguments of the parties in advance by invoking Article 53 (1) of the Rules of Court. The referred article reiterates that the Court must 'ascertain' the views of the parties before taking any decision regarding the access to the written documents of the case by third States. A joint interpretation of Article 85 (1) and 53 (1) of the Rules of Court indicates that a potential intervener may apply to be furnished with the written pleadings and documents prior to filing its application to intervene only if there is no objection by the parties to the main proceedings.

There was much doubt on the meaning of 'ascertain', i.e., whether this means that the parties' views are determinative or not. As the rules did not define its meaning, the Court, according to its *jurisprudence constante*, does not grant access to the pleadings where one of the parties objects.[38] Practice then indicates that the parties' views are determinant. For e.g. Malta's,[39] Italy's[40] and

34 The Philippines' request for permission to intervene in the *Ligitan and Sipadan* case is an example of the duration of proceedings as far as intervention is concerned (*Sovereignty over Pulau Ligitan and Pulau Sipadan* (*Indonesia v. Malaysia*) (*Application for Intervention: Judgment*) *ICJ Reports 2001*, 575, paras. 19–26). The Application was only filed in March 2001, more than 2 years after the registrar had sent notifications to all States, following the procedure provided for by Article 40 of the Statute. Although both parties objected the unduly timing of this application, the Court accepted the request for intervention since it was still within the prescribed deadline (*Sovereignty over Pulau Ligitan and Pulau Sipadan* (*Indonesia v. Malaysia*) (Application for Intervention: Judgment), *supra*, para. 23).

35 *Sovereignty over Pulau Ligitan and Pulau Sipadan* (*Indonesia v. Malaysia*) (Application for Intervention: Judgment), *supra*, para. 22); C. Chinkin, 'Article 62', 1539–1541.

36 C. Chinkin, 'Article 62', 1340.

37 *Territorial and Maritime Dispute* (*Nicaragua v. Colombia*) (*Application for Intervention by Costa Rica: Judgment*) *ICJ Reports 2011*, 348, paras. 7, 10 and 12.

38 C. Chinkin, 'Article 62', 1341.

39 *Continental Shelf* (*Tunisia v. Libyan Jamahiriya*) (*Application for Intervention: Judgment*), *supra*.

40 *Ibid.*

the Philippines'[41] requests for pleadings were rejected after the Court had ascertained that one of the parties objected. Conversely, Honduras and Costa Rica's requests in the *Territorial and Maritime Dispute case* were granted since no party objected.[42]

As a consequence, transparency and non-confidentiality of proceedings is only guaranteed if no party objects. It is evident that the 'lack of access to the parties' pleadings makes it difficult for a State requesting intervention to frame its application'.[43] Potential interveners would have to demonstrate a qualified legal interest, as restrictively interpreted by the Court, without having viewed either parties' pleadings or documentation. This argument was advanced by Malta for justifying its lack of precision in specifying the purpose for intervention.[44] Unable to be furnished with pleadings and having to meet the initial burden of proof of its legal interest, Malta's application was denied for it had 'said too little' to convince the Court of its pertinent 'legal interest'.[45] Philippines was also handicapped for not having access to the parties' pleadings.[46]

For the Court, there is no provision in its Rules establishing 'an inextricable link' between the access to pleadings and the filing of an application for permission to intervene.[47] However, how can the Court impose such a burden of proof to potential interveners if they are, in practice, handicapped by their ignorance of the exact scope of the claims?[48] Even though the Court never specified the exact standard of proof required, since intervention is an incidental proceeding it would seem that only *prima facie* evidence would be needed.[49]

---

41 *Sovereignty over Pulau Ligitan and Putau Sipadan* (*Indonesia v. Malaysia*) (*Application for Intervention: Judgment*), *supra.*

42 *Territorial and Maritime Dispute* (*Nicaragua v. Colombia*) (*Application for Intervention by Costa Rica: Judgment*) *ICJ Reports 2011*, 348, paras. 7 and 10.

43 C. Chinkin, 'Article 62', 1342.

44 *Continental Shelf* (*Tunisia v. Libyan Jamahiriya*) (*Application for Intervention: Judgment*), *supra.* See Separate Opinion of Judge Oda, *ICJ Reports 1981*, p. 23; Separate Opinion of Judge Schwebel, p. 35

45 See C. Chinkin, 'Third Party Intervention Before the International Court of Justice', 80 *American Journal of International Law* (1986) 3, 505. See *Continental Shelf* (*Tunisia v. Libyan Jamahiriya*) (*Application for Intervention: Judgment*), *supra*, para. 31, 34.

46 *Sovereignty over Pulau Ligitan and Putau Sipadan* (*Indonesia v. Malaysia*) (*Application for Intervention: Judgment*), *supra.*

47 *Sovereignty over Pulau Ligitan and Putau Sipadan* (*Indonesi v. Malaysia*) (*Application for Intervention: Judgment*), *supra*, para. 22.

48 C. Chinkin, 'Article 62', 1342.

49 I. Uchkunova, 'The Minotaur's Labyrinth: Third State Intervention before the International Court of Justice', 13 *The Law and Practice of International Courts and Tribunals* (2014) 2, 184.

Therefore, an amendment to the Rules of Court could envisage a bifurcated choice depending on the assumed prevalence of community interests in the detriment of bilateralism: (i) an amendment to Article 81 (1) in order to soften the burden of proof regarding the interest of a legal nature so that would be interveners would not be handicapped for not having access to the parties' pleadings; or (ii) an amendment to Article 85 (1) to allow potential interveners to be supplied with copies of the pleadings and documents annexed regardless of having their application previously granted by the Court; and/or an amendment to Article 53 (1) to allow the Court to, at any time, furnish copies of the pleadings and documents as requested, regardless of the parties' views.

A State seeking to intervene that has had access to the pleadings is in a better position to comply with the requirements of intervention as prescribed by Article 81 of the Rules, namely, to demonstrate a qualified legal interest.[50] This inevitably reflects the prevailing tension between bilateralism and community of interest.

2.1.2 Ensuring Flexibility in the Interpretation of the Requirements of Intervention

The main condition of intervention is set out in Article 62 of the Statute and in Article 81 (2) (a) of the Rules of Court: the existence of an 'interest of a legal nature' which may be affected by a decision in a specific case. The Court has been interpreting this criterion in a restrictive way, limiting the scope of discretional intervention to 'specific interests' or 'qualified legal interests' of third States capable of being affected and not only to interests in the legal rules and principles dealt with by the decision.[51] However, there is no definition of 'legal interest' for the purposes of discretional intervention.

As emphasized by the Court, a potential intervener would have to show that its 'interests' may be affected; that the referred 'interest' is the object of a real and concrete claim, based on law, to be decided by the Court; that it is connected to the subject matter of the particular dispute; and that it could possibly be affected – in its content and scope – by the Court's decision in the main proceedings – which is in practice difficult to prove.[52] In any case, such

50 C. Chinkin, 'Article 62', 1342.

51 See *Continental Shelf (Tunisia v. Libyan Jamahiriya) (Application for Intervention: Judgment)*, *supra*, para. 29–30; *Land, Island and Maritime Frontier Dispute (El Salvador v. Honduras) (Application for Intervention: Judgment)* ICJ *Reports 1990*, 92, para. 76; *Sovereignty over Pulau Ligitan and Putau Sipadan (Indonesia v. Malaysia) (Application for Intervention: Judgment)*, *supra*, paras. 52, 80, 83, 93.

52 See *Land, Island and Maritime Frontier Dispute (El Salvador v. Honduras) (Application for Intervention: Judgment)*, *supra*, 116, para. 58). *Territorial and Maritime Dispute (Application*

clarification on the requirements for intervention could be made clear in the wording of Article 81 (2) of the Rules.

If the Court reiterates the importance of fulfilling the condition laid down by Article 62 (1) and Article 81 (2) (a) of the Rules of Court, it recognizes that the aforementioned criterion – legal interest that may be affected – is applicable to both States seeking to intervene as a 'non-party'[53] and as a 'party'.[54] It is therefore a common requirement for all forms of intervention under Article 62.

Article 62 of the Statute only contains the first requirement as provided for by the Rules, i.e., the 'interest of a legal nature'. Other requirements for States wishing to intervene are complemented by Article 81 (2) (b) and (c) of the Rules of Court. According to Article 81 (2) (b), potential interveners would have to specify in their request the 'object of the intervention'. This definition has been proved extremely difficult for third States to justify intervention – be they parties or not.

Neither Article 62 of the Statute nor Article 81 of the Rules of Court further details the capacity or status according to which a State may seek to intervene. This is necessarily linked to the object of intervention, which is to be defined according to the status of the intervener State, whether as non-party or as a party.

2.1.2.1 *Intervention as Non-Party*

The *Land Island and Maritime Frontier Dispute* (El Salvador/Honduras) case gave the Court the opportunity to clarify intervention requirements according to the status of the parties. The Chamber stated that "to inform the Court of the nature of the legal rights of Nicaragua which are in issue in the dispute" could be considered a proper object of intervention.[55] Intervention cannot be used in order to submit new claims.

The extent of the object of intervention has also been subject to much controversy. The Court has already clarified that the intervening State is not required 'to give an exhaustive account of these interests in its application for permission to intervene, or at the hearings held to consider whether

for Intervention by Costa Rica: Judgment), *supra*, paras. 23–26. See for further details, B. I. Bonafé, 'Interests of a Legal Nature Justifying Intervention before the ICJ', 25 *Leiden Journal of International Law* (2012), 739.

53 *Territorial and Maritime Dispute* (*Application for Intervention by Costa Rica: Judgment*), *supra*, para. 26.

54 *Territorial and Maritime Dispute* (*Nicaragua v. Colombia*) (*Application for Intervention by Honduras: Judgment*) *ICJ Reports 2011*, 420, para. 30.

55 *Land, Island and Maritime Frontier Dispute* (*El Salvador v. Honduras*), *supra*, para. 90.

permission to intervene should be granted (...)', otherwise intervention would be pointless.[56] Potential interveners are, however, asked to show 'convincingly' that their legal interest can possibly be affected by the Court's decision – a mere interest in the applicable legal rule is not regarded as sufficient interest under discretional intervention proceedings.[57]

The Chamber took a restrictive approach and set a high standard of proof regarding the requirement of the legal interest that may be affected.[58] This has been adopted in subsequent case law, such as in the 2011 judgment on the application of Costa Rica to intervene in the maritime dispute between Nicaragua and Colombia.[59] All three requirements were apparently met in the case – object, absence of a jurisdictional link, legal interest – however, permission to intervene was denied because, in the Court's view, Costa Rica's interests could not be affected.[60]

As far as intervention by non-party is concerned, an amendment to Article 81 (2) (b) could clarify 'the object of intervention' by defining its proper purpose, which is to precisely inform the Court of one's rights or claims capable of being affected.

The high threshold imposed by the Court demotivates potential intervening States.[61] If the object of the intervention is to inform the Court of legal rights which are in issue in the dispute, the only way for a third State to submit such information would be to make use of a sort of *amicus curiae* mechanism.[62]

2.1.2.2 *Intervention as a 'Party'*

For many years it was understood that intervention under Article 62 was presumed to be a 'non-party' status intervention, as was reaffirmed by the Court in its Judgment in the first *Continental Shelf* case where there was a request

56 *Ibid.*, para. 89.

57 *Ibid.*, para. 76.

58 *Ibid.*, para. 61.

59 *Territorial and Maritime Dispute* (*Application for Intervention by Honduras: Judgment*), *supra*, 1029.

60 *Territorial and Maritime Dispute* (*Application for Intervention by Costa Rica: Judgment*), *supra*, para. 87.

61 *Territorial and Maritime Dispute,* (*Application for Intervention by Costa Rica: Judgment*), *supra*, Dissenting opinion of Judge Abraham, para. 27.

62 *Territorial and Maritime Dispute,* (*Application for Intervention by Costa Rica: Judgment*), *supra*, Declaration of Judge Gaja, para. 5. See also Hugh Thirlway, 'The Law and Procedure of the International Court of Justice 1960–1989. Supplement 2011: Parts Eleven, Twelve and Thirteen', 82 *British Yearbook of International Law* (2012) 1, 135–137, and 148.

for intervention.[63] This is because intervention was designed to enable participation of a third State whose interests are not central to the proceedings.[64] Dissenting opinions on Malta's request and on Italy's request to intervene in the *Continental Shelf* cases, opened the ICJ's path to recognise two forms of intervention deriving from Article 62.[65]

In the Chambers decision of 1990, it was 'accepted that a State may be permitted to intervene under Article 62 of the Statute either as a non-party or as a party'.[66] Among other requirements, a State seeking to intervene as a party 'may ask for rights of its own to be recognised by the Court in its future decision, which would be binding for that State in respect of those aspects for which intervention was granted, pursuant to Article 59 of the Statute'.[67] As opposed to 'non-party' intervention, the object of 'party' intervention is to allow the third State to ask for its own rights to be recognised by the Court.[68]

Therefore, an amendment to the Rules of Court could envisage a bifurcated choice for third States: (i) split the two forms of intervention into separate articles and define specific rules – i.e., Article 81 *bis* – applicable to 'party' intervention alongside with its particular criteria, such as the existence of a

---

63 The Court recalled the drafts of its Statute, implying that the misconception that an intervener under Article 62 could have party status may have originated from the English version of the text (containing the phrase 'as a third party'), which was later amended for it was deemed misleading (*Continental Shelf* (*Tunisia v. Libyan Jamahiriya*) (*Application for Intervention: Judgment*), *supra*, para. 24–25).

64 A. Sarvarian *et al.*, *Interim Report of the Committe on Procedure of International Courts and Tribunals*, International Law Association (2018), available at https://www.ila-hq.org/images/ILA/DraftReports/DraftReport_InternationalCourts.pdf; See, e.g. *Sovereignty over Pulau Ligitan and Putau Sipadan* (*Indonesia v. Malaysia*) (*Application for Intervention: Judgment*), *supra*, Separate Opinion of Judge *ad hoc* Weeramantry 643–647 (paras. 24–29); *Jurisdictional Immunities of the State* (*Germany v. Italy*) (*Application for Intervention: Judgment*) *ICJ Reports 2011*, 494, 501–502 (paras. 24–26).

65 *Continental Shelf* (*Tunisia v. Libyan Jamahiriya*) (Application for Intervention: Dissenting Opinion of Judge Oda), *supra*, p. 26; *Continental Shelf* (*Malta v. Libyan Jamahiriya*) (*Application for Intervention: Judgment*), *supra*, p. 91.

66 *Territorial and Maritime Dispute*, (*Application for Intervention by Honduras: Judgment*), *supra*, para. 27. The Court mentioned a passage of its judgment on Nicaragua's Application for permission to intervene in the case concerning Land, Island and Maritime Frontier Dispute to confirm its approach. However, as pointed out by B. I. Bonafé, the referred passage is rather ambiguous (B. I. Bonafé, 'Discretional Intervention (Article 62, Statute of the Court)', in P. W Almeida and J.M. Sorel (eds.), *Latin America and the International Court of Justice: Contributions to International Law* (Routledge, 2017), 106).

67 *Territorial and Maritime Dispute* (*Application for Intervention by Honduras: Judgment*), *supra*, para. 29.

68 *Continental Shelf* (*Malta v. Libyan Jamahiriya*) (*Application for Intervention: Judgment*), *supra*, para. 17–26.

jurisdictional link; or (ii) clarify the possibility for a third State to join as a new party with all its related consequences ('joinder of parties').

The 'jurisdictional link', i.e., the requirement of an agreement between the parties to the case and the third State seeking to intervene, is one of the factors that has most contributed to the confusion surrounding intervention.[69] This is because requiring a jurisdictional link could imply that intervention would be dependent on the consent of the parties to the main proceedings.

The Court has been historically unable to define its standards, thereby rendering the process of discretional intervention somewhat unpredictable.[70] The judgment on Nicaragua's Application to intervene in the *Land, Island and Maritime Frontier Dispute* case gave the Court the opportunity to State that no jurisdictional link was required for States seeking to intervene as 'non-parties'.[71] Indeed, the parameters of 'non-party' intervention, as established in the 1990 Chamber's decision, were confirmed by the full Court when it ruled that no jurisdictional link was required to grant permission to intervene.[72] The Court has observed that Article 62 of the Statute does not require, as a condition for intervention, the existence of a basis of jurisdiction between the parties to the main proceedings and the potential intervener.[73]

For the ICJ, such a requirement is only applicable to States seeking to intervene as a 'party' to the case.[74] Although Article 62 was not meant to cover party status intervention, the Court has affirmed that a State may intervene in a manner which would assert a right of its own before the parties, provided that the general title of jurisdiction (under Article 62 of the Statute) is reinforced by a specific jurisdictional link between the intervener and the parties to the case.[75] Although rejecting Honduras' Application for Permission to Intervene

---

69 There has been much doubt regarding whether Article 62 of the Statute is enough to provide this jurisdictional link or whether another article from another convention would be needed, and, consequently, how tight should this other link be.

70 See I. Uchkunova, *supra* note 49, 179.

71 *Land, Island and Maritime Frontier Dispute, supra*, para. 100.

72 *Land and Maritime Boundary between Cameroon and Nigeria* (*Cameroon v. Nigeria*) (*Application Intervention: Order*) *ICJ Reports 1999*, 1029, and *Jurisdictional Immunities of the State, supra*.

73 *Territorial and Maritime Dispute,* (*Application for Intervention by Costa Rica: Judgment*), *supra*, para. 38.

74 *Territorial and Maritime Dispute,* (*Application for Intervention by Costa Rica: Judgment*), *supra*, para. 39; *Sovereignty over Pulau Ligitan and Pulau Sipadan, supra*, para. 35.

75 *Continental Shelf* (*Malta/Libyan Jamahiriya*) (*Application for Intervention. Judgment*), *supra*, para. 18. See also *Land, Island and Maritime Frontier Dispute, supra*, para. 99; and *Sovereignty over Pulau Ligitan and Pulau Sipadan, supra*, para. 35.

due to the lack of a legal interest that may be affected by its decision,[76] the Court clearly reasserted this reasoning in its Judgment.[77]

Therefore, the requirement of a 'jurisdictional link' and the party or non-party status are intimately intertwined. This should be made clear in the Rules of Court by splitting the two forms of intervention into separate articles, thereby clarifying that a 'jurisdictional link' is only applicable to 'party' intervention. Moreover, the precise definition of a 'jurisdictional link' remains unclear and currently represents a significant obstacle for a third State wishing to intervene as a party.[78] If intervention as a party is to be maintained in the practice of the ICJ, the Rules of Court could be amended in order to ensure flexibility in the interpretation of such criteria.[79]

2.2 *Intervention 'as of Right' (Article 63 of the ICJ Statute)*

The filing of a declaration under Article 63 is qualified as intervention 'as of right', referring to the State's inherent right to be part of proceedings due to its membership of a convention whose interpretation is the object of a controversy.[80] However, as highlighted in the Judgment concerning the admissibility of the Cuban intervention in the *Haya de la Torre case*, it is for the Court to decide whether the conditions set forth in Article 63 are satisfied or not.[81] The Court exercised such a competence in the *Nicaragua v. United States case*,[82] and emphasized, more recently, in the *Whaling in the Antarctic case*, that 'the fact that intervention under Article 63 of the Statute is of right is not sufficient for the submission of a "declaration" to that end to confer *ipso facto* on the declarant State the status of intervener'.[83]

---

76 *Territorial and Maritime Dispute (Application for Intervention by Honduras: Judgment), supra, para. 68.*

77 *Territorial and Maritime Dispute (Application for Intervention by Honduras: Judgment), supra*, para. 28.

78 B. I. Bonafé, 'Discretional Intervention (Article 62, Statute of the Court)', *supra*, 106–107.

79 *Ibid.*, 107.

80 *Territorial and Maritime Dispute (Nicaragua v. Colombia) (Application for Intervention by Honduras: Judgment), supra*, 434, para. 36; *Continental Shelf (Tunisia v. Libyan Jamahiriya)* (Application for Intervention: Judgment), *supra*, 15, para. 26; *Haya de La Torre (Colombia v. Peru) (Application for Intervention: Judgment) ICJ Reports 1951*, 71, 76; *SS 'Wimbledon'* (United Kingdom and others *v.* Germany, Poland intervening) (Declaration for Intervention: Judgment) (1923) PCIJ Series A No. 1, 12.

81 *Haya de La Torre, supra*, 76–77.

82 *Military and Paramilitary Activities in and against Nicaragua (Nicaragua v. United States of America) (Declaration of Intervention:* Order) *ICJ Reports 1984*, 215.

83 *Whaling in the Antarctic (Declaration of Intervention: Order), supra*, para. 8. See also Gerald Fitzmaurice, 'The Law and Procedure of the International Court of Justice 1951–1954', 33 *British Yearbook of International Law* (1958) 203.

The interest for a third State to submit observations concerning the interpretation of multilateral treaties invoked in judicial proceedings between other States responds to the logic that ICJ judgments reach far beyond the States Parties to a case, as opposed to Article 59 of the Statute – which denies the binding effect of a decision of the Court on any State except the parties to the particular case – and produce impacts on the international community. Article 63 seems to constitute an exception to Article 59 since the construction of the convention given by the judgment will also bind the intervening State.[84]

In any case, the Court's judgments may be applied as precedents to other case law. The ICJ's interpretation of a rule of law may guide decision-makers when interpreting the same provision; also, the Court itself is likely to follow its own *jurisprudence constante* and not to depart from an earlier pronouncement.[85] Therefore, if States which are not parties to a case can be directly or indirectly affected by a judgment to be rendered by the Court, they may submit their views on questions relating to the existence or content of a rule of international law. This could be positive in order to facilitate the Court's task when interpreting relevant provisions of a convention, such as in the *Territorial and Maritime Dispute case*, involving Nicaragua and Colombia.[86]

As opposed to discretional intervention, intervention 'as of right' has been rarely used by third States. There were only five declarations of intervention filed on the Court's docket: Poland in the case concerning the S.S. "Wimbledon" (PCIJ);[87] Cuba in the *Haya de la Torre* case;[88] El Salvador in the case concerning *Military and Paramilitary Activities in and against Nicaragua*;[89] Samoa, the Solomon Islands, the Marshall Islands and the Federated States of Micronesia with respect to the *Request for an Examination of the Situation in Accordance with Paragraph 63 of the Court's Judgment of 20 December 1974 in the Nuclear Tests (New Zealand v. France)* case;[90] and New Zealand in the case concerning

84 C. Chinkin, 'Article 63', in A. Zimmermann, C. Tomuschat, K. Oellers-Frahm, C. Tams and T. Thienel (eds.) *'The Statute of the International Court of Justice: A Commentary'* (OUP, 2006), 1390.

85 See, in this sense, C. Chinkin, 'Article 63', *supra* note 84, 1391.

86 G. Gaja, 'A New Way for Submitting Observations on the Construction of Multilateral Treaties to the international Court of Justice', in U. Fastenrath, R. Geiger, D.E. Khan, A. Paulus, S. von Schorlemer and C. Vedder (eds.), *From Bilateralism to Community Interest: Essays in Honour of Judge Bruno Simma* (OUP, 2011), 666.

87 *SS 'Wimbledon', supra.*

88 *Haya de La Torre, supra.*

89 *Military and Paramilitary Activities in and against Nicaragua, supra.*

90 *Request for an Examination of the Situation in Accordance with Paragraph 63 of the Court's Judgment of 20 December 1974 in the Nuclear Tests (New Zealand v. France) (Declarations for*

Whaling in the Antarctic (Australia v. Japan).[91] Intervention was only admitted in the first two cases and in the last case.[92]

The resistance from third States to making use of intervention under Article 63 of the Statute is maybe due to the binding character of the construction given by the judgment on the intervening State.[93] In other words, the interpretation of the multilateral treaty that is given by the Court in its judgment will be binding upon any party that has intervened.[94] The binding character of the Court's interpretation is implicitly derived from the consent given by States when becoming parties to its Statute.[95] As pointed out by Judge Gaja, this 'represents a significant drawback for States potentially interested in submitting observations',[96] as it carries political implications. In order to make intervention 'as of right' more attractive to third States and to balance bilateralism and community interests, the following challenges are worth revisiting: the need to grant a hearing in all phases of proceedings (2.2.1); and the expansion of the possibilities for intervention by broadening its scope and rendering its requirements more flexible.

Intervention by the Governments of the Solomon Islands, the Federated States of Micronesia, Marshall Islands, Samoa Islands: Order) ICJ *Reports 1995*, 288.

91 *Whaling in the Antarctic, supra.*

92 *Haya de La Torre, supra*; and *Military and Paramilitary Activities in and against Nicaragua, supra*; and *Request for an Examination of the Situation in Accordance with Paragraph 63 of the Court's Judgment of 20 December 1974 in the Nuclear Tests, supra; and Whaling in the Antarctic, supra.*

93 The Court reiterated the binding character of the construction of the Convention in its judgment in *Whaling in the Antarctic, supra*, para. 20: 'in exercising its right to intervene in the case, New Zealand will be bound, under Article 63, paragraph 2, of the Statute, by the construction of the Convention given by the Court in its judgment'.

94 In the Whaling case, New Zealand intervened under Article 63 of the Statute due its membership to the *International Convention for the Regulation of Whaling* (1946), to which Japan and Australia are both members. New Zealand requested intervention as a non-party, but still acknowledging to be bound by the Court's decision: "In that regard, New Zealand emphasizes that it does not seek to be a party to the proceedings. But, in accordance with Article 63 of the Statute, New Zealand confirms that, by availing itself of its right to intervene, it accepts that the construction given by the judgment in the case will be equally binding upon it." *Whaling in the Antarctic, supra*, para. 9.

95 *Land, Island and Maritime Frontier Dispute, supra*, para. 96.

96 G. Gaja, 'A New Way for Submitting…', 669. See also H. Thirlway, 'Intervention', *The International Court of Justice* (OUP, 2016), 178 and S. Forlati, *The International Court of Justice: An Arbitral Tribunal or a Judicial Body?* (Springer, 2014), 187.

2.2.1 Ensuring the Need for a Hearing in All Phases of Proceedings

An important issue is linked to phase of the proceedings in which a declaration of intervention may be filed.[97] In the *Military and Paramilitary Activities* case,[98] the Republic of El Salvador filed a declaration of intervention[99] during the jurisdictional phase. It intended to be accepted as a party "with the sole purpose" of challenging the Court's jurisdiction.[100]

Nicaragua presented its written observations about the declaration of intervention by El Salvador.[101] After pointing out inconsistencies of both procedural and material nature, Nicaragua stated it did not wish to 'formally' object to El Salvador's intervention.[102] Pursuant to Article 84 (2) of the Rules, a hearing pertaining to the admissibility of a declaration of intervention will only be held if a party objects to it.[103] With Nicaragua adopting such a strategy, El Salvador was deprived of its rightful hearing under the Rules of Court.

In an unconventional stance, the Court rejected the declaration without a hearing and without providing the reasons for such denial.[104] In the words of judge Schwebel, 'considerations of judicial propriety, of the sovereign equality of States before the law, and of fair play, required a hearing'.[105] The most substantial indication for such a dismissal is maybe linked to the fact that El Salvador intervened in the jurisdictional phase,[106] while intervention under

97 Luis González García, 'Intervention by third parties under Article 63 of the Statute', in P. W. Almeida and J.M. Sorel (eds.), *Latin America and the International Court of Justice: Contributions to International Law* (Routledge, 2017), 111.

98 *Military and Paramilitary Activities in and against Nicaragua, supra.*

99 *Military and Paramilitary Activities in and against Nicaragua* (*Nicaragua v. United States of America*) (Declaration of Intervention) (1984) General List No. 70 ICJ 2.

100 *Military and Paramilitary Activities in and against Nicaragua* (*Nicaragua v. United States of America*) (Declaration of Intervention), *supra.*

101 *Military and Paramilitary Activities in and against Nicaragua* (*Nicaragua v. United States of America*) (Declaration of Intervention: Written Observations of Nicaragua) [1984] General List No. 70 ICJ 465.

102 *Military and Paramilitary Activities in and against Nicaragua* (*Nicaragua v. United States of America*) (Declaration of Intervention: Written Observations of Nicaragua), *supra*, 466.

103 See, for example, hearings granted by the Court in intervention proceedings under Article 63: Poland was granted a hearing in the SS *Wimbledon* case and Cuba was granted a hearing after Peru objected to the declaration of intervention in the *Haya de la Torre* case.

104 L. G. García, *supra* note 97, 115. See also J. Sztucki, 'Intervention under Article 63 of the ICJ Statute in the Phase of Preliminary Proceedings: The Salvadoran Incident', 79 *American Journal of International Law* (1985), 1012.

105 *Military and Paramilitary Activities in and against Nicaragua, supra*, Dissenting Opinion of Judge Schwebel, 231.

106 *Military and Paramilitary Activities in and against Nicaragua* (*Nicaragua v. United States of America*) (*Jurisdiction and Admissibility: Judgment*) *ICJ Reports 1984*, 392, 396 para. 6.

Article 63 would implicate that the Court has jurisdiction, therefore, pertaining to the merits of the case.[107]

Insofar as the jurisdictional link is not required for third States seeking to intervene under Article 63 of the Statute (Article 82 of the Rules of Court), 'it would seem reasonable that a State party to the treaty may intervene before the Court gives its interpretation of the treaty even if this occurs at the stage of establishing its jurisdiction or the admissibility of the case'.[108] Indeed, there appears to be no reason why intervention should not be allowed on issues of jurisdiction and admissibility of a case'.[109] The wording of Article 63 is broad enough to cover all phases of a case, which could be made clearer in the Rules of Court.

Also, observations by the main parties regarding the declaration of intervention might be interpreted more broadly and be considered as 'objections' for the purposes of Article 84 (2) of the Rules so as to avoid the Nicaragua case scenario. It would be unrealistic to think solely in terms of the integrity of the parties' in dispute to the detriment of third parties rights.[110]

2.2.2 Expanding Possibilities for Intervention

Article 63 of the Statute requires only that 'the construction of a convention to which States other than those concerned in the case are parties is in question'. Article 82 of the Rules of Court further details the need for a third State to be party to the referred convention and to identify its related provisions. It is required that the construction of the convention be determinative of the outcome of the case,[111] and be genuine without constituting an attempt to reopen an earlier case.[112] However, neither the wording of Article 63 nor the Court's jurisprudence indicate that the treaty in question must constitute the object of the dispute or that there is a dispute between the parties to the case over the construction of the treaty.[113]

---

107 W. D. Rogers, J. A. Beat, and C. Wolf, 'Application of El Salvador to Intervene in the Jurisdiction and Admissibility Phase of Nicaragua v. United States', 78 *American Journal of International Law* (1984) 4, 936.

108 G. Gaja, 'A New Way for Submitting…', 667; see also J. Sztucki, *supra* note 104, 1015; S. Rosenne, *Intervention in the International Court of Justice* (Martinus Nijhoff, 1993) 35–6.

109 C. Chinkin, 'Article 63', 1376; L. G. García, *supra* note 97, 117.

110 C. Chinkin, 'Third Party Intervention Before the International Court of Justice', 511. See also D. W. Greig, 'Third Party Rights and Intervention Before the International Court' 32 *Virginia Journal of International Law* (1992), 317.

111 C. Chinkin, 'Article 63', 1379.

112 See *Haya de la Torre, supra*, 71, 73–74. See also C. Chinkin, 'Article 63', 1385.

113 *Haya de la Torre, supra*, 76; *S.S. Wimbledon, supra*, 12.

Article 82 (3) of the Rules further clarifies that a State may file a declaration of intervention even if it has not received notification by the Registry, who has the task of identifying the States entitled to receive such a notification, as indicated by Article 63 of the statute. The question of the notification having caused difficulties in several cases,[114] this provision alleviates the burden imposed on the Registrar.

States wishing to intervene under Article 63 generally possess an individual interest regarding the convention in question. However, such an interest may not be limited to the construction of multilateral conventions, being also directed to rules of general international law. An expansion of the scope of intervention should be followed by the necessary transparency so that potential interveners will be able to identify the provisions of the convention at issue or the content of the rule of law invoked, even if the Court does not alleviate the burden of proof.

2.2.2.1 *Broadening the Scope by Including General International Law*

Article 63 of the Statute only refers to the construction of multilateral conventions, not to other sources of international law such as customary international law. This is similar to Article 56 of the 1899 Hague Convention for the Peaceful Settlement of International Disputes[115] and Article 84 of the 1907 Hague Convention for the Peaceful Settlement of International Disputes.[116] The term 'convention', although not defined by the Statute nor Rules of Court, must be given the same meaning as provided for by Article 38 of the Statute, being understood as a treaty (Article 2, para 1 (a) VCLT.[117] Therefore, 'convention' designates a multilateral treaty in force between the principal parties and the intervening State.[118]

114 H. Thirlway, 'Intervention', *The International Court of Justice* (OUP, 2016), 178.

115 Article 56 of the 1899 Hague Convention for the Peaceful Settlement of International Disputes reads as follows: 'When there is a question of interpreting a Convention to which Powers other than those concerned in the dispute are parties, the latter notify to the former the *compromis* they have concluded. Each of these Powers has the right to intervene in the case. If one or more of them avail themselves of this right, the interpretation contained in the award is equally binding on them' (highlighted by the author).

116 Article 84 of the 1907 Hague Convention for the Peaceful Settlement of International Disputes reads as follows: 'The Award is not binding except on the parties in dispute. When it concerns the interpretation of a **Convention** to which Powers other than those in dispute are parties, they shall inform all the Signatory Powers in good time. Each of these Powers is entitled to intervene in the case. If one or more avail themselves of this right, the interpretation contained in the Award is equally binding on them' (highlighted by the author).

117 C, Chinkin, 'Article 63', 1379.

118 See S. Forlati, *supra* note 96, 184; H. Thirlway, 'Intervention', 178.

It is undeniable that Court's statements on questions related to general international law may affect States that are not parties to the judicial proceedings. If a State's individual interest is in question, one could also argue that the international community is also concerned by the interpretation of the rule of international law.[119] This means that 'common interests of the international community' comes into play.[120]

As highlighted by Judge Oda, 'there seems to be no convincing reason why the Court's interpretation of the principles and rules of international law should be of less concern to a State'.[121] Indeed, non-party States could also supply information on State practice that may be 'helpful for the assessment of the rule of general international law'.[122]

In this context, an amendment could envisage either the expansion of the scope of 'convention' in order to include general international law or the inclusion of a separate provision to cover the principles and rules of international law. However, being aware that any extensive interpretation of Article 63 may encounter obstacles due to the clarity of its wording, two alternative solutions could be envisaged: either the use of the *amicus curiae* mechanism by States with the aim of defining rules of general international law;[123] or the adoption of a new rule or practice direction allowing the ICJ to consider brief statements to assist the Court in the correct interpretation of any legal rule involved in the case, regardless from its source.

2.2.2.2 *Alleviating the Burden of Proof and Providing Transparency for the Identification of the Particular Provisions of the Convention*

Once the Court declares the intervention admissible, the intervening State shall be supplied with copies of the pleadings and related documents and shall be entitled to submit its written observations on the subject-matter of the intervention, as well as to submit observations in the course of the oral proceedings. Information will only be available for third States after intervention is granted.

However, in order to fulfil the requirements provided for by Article 82 of the Rules, the would-be intervener would have to indicate the 'particular provisions

119 G. Gaja, 'A New Way ...', 666.

120 B. Simma, *supra* note 3, 234.

121 S. Oda, 'Intervention in the International Court of Justice: Articles 62 and 63 of the Statute', in R. Bernhardt et al (eds.), *Völkerrecht als Rechtsordnung, Internationale Gerichtsbarkeit, Menschenrechte: Festschrift für Hermann Mosler* (Springer Verlag, 1983), 646–647.

122 G. Gaja, 'A New Way ...', 672.

123 G. Gaja, 'A New Way ...', 672.

of the convention the construction of which it considers to be in question'. Considering the limited amount of information on the judicial proceedings available for third States, how can one identify precisely the provisions related to the interpretation of a multilateral treaty that are at issue?

Arguably, the Rules of Procedure should not be contemplated as providing additional obstacles for intervention.[124] If the parties were required to identify particular provisions of a convention (Article 82 (2) (b) of the Rules of Court), there would remain no clear distinction between Articles 63 and 62 of the Statute – the latter requiring the third State to demonstrate its legal interest.[125] Therefore, the Rules of Court could be modified in order to alleviate the burden of proof imposed on a State wishing to intervene, by allowing it not to identify the specific provisions of the convention in question.

Alternatively, the Court should ensure more transparency in its proceedings in a way to make information promptly available for would-be interveners. According to Article 53 of the Rules, the Court may, 'at any time, decide to make copies of the pleadings and related documents available to third States only after ascertaining the views of the parties. The Court may also decide to make such copies available to the public 'on or after the opening of the oral proceedings'. In any case, the Court's decision would be dependent upon the consent of the parties. If applications under Article 63 are filed no later than the opening of the oral proceedings (Article 82 of the Rules), 'it is possible that the would-be intervener would not have access to the pleadings and documents thereof at the time of its application.[126]

In this context, an amendment to the Rules of Court could provide a third State with the possibility of filing its request at a later stage.[127] The need for

124 D. W. Greig, *supra*, 313.

125 D. W. Greig, *supra*, 313; see L. G. García, *supra* note 97, 117.

126 G. Gaja, 'A New Way ...', 671.

127 Conversely, it has been argued that depending on when the declaration is filed it can stretch the overall length of the case. Indeed, an example of this extended duration is the *Whaling in the Antarctic* case (*Whaling in the Antarctic* (note 30), in which New Zealand filed its declaration to intervene under Article 63 of the Statute eight months after the closure of the written phase but before entering the oral phase. Yet New Zealand complied with the time limit imposed by Article 63 by filing a declaration no later than the date fixed for the beginning of the oral phase. In order to ensure efficiency it has been proposed that declarations of intervention under Article 63 should be filed in the same time-limit as those applications under Article 62 of the Statute, *soit* by the closure of the written proceedings. See Arman Sarvarian, *supra* note 64, 21. However, such a proposal would not take into account the need to safeguard transparency and access to pleadings and documents thereof by the intervening State. The latter would be obliged to file a declaration being 'handicapped' by the lack of information in order to properly identify 'the

an extended time limit, i.e. by the beginning of the oral proceedings – would also be necessary if a third State was allowed to submit its observations as *amicus curiae* by applying the procedure provided for Article 43 of the Rules applicable to international organizations,[128] as will be discussed below in this paper. Even if the referred deadline was extended, potential interveners would still suffer with restricted access and knowledge of the pleadings. A potential remedy could be the application of Article 43 para 1 of the Rules: the Court could furnish directions to the Registrar concerning notifications to the States Parties to a multilateral treaty in order to ensure they have sufficient information on the issues concerning the treaty at issue.[129] Also, the Court could use its website to ensure more transparency.[130]

3 Conclusions

There is no doubt that international adjudication contributes to the achievement of community interests embodied in GPG. Considering that procedure may undermine the protection of GPG, this paper has addressed concrete procedural challenges and identified possible solutions so that the Court can be attuned to this new era of international adjudication, as highlighted by dissenting Judge Weeramantry in the *Gabčíkovo-Nagymaros* case.[131] The proposed amendments on topics such as third-party intervention and *amicus curiae* briefs were also identified among specific reform proposals by the Counsel Survey conducted in preparation for the Seminar held on the 70th Anniversary of the Court's first inaugural sitting.[132] There were calls for 'greater transparency, a more interactive and less formalistic bench and increased openness to the practices and jurisprudence of other international tribunals, both on matters of substance and procedure'.[133]

particular provisions of the convention the construction of which it considers to be in question'.

128 According to Artcile 69 (2) of the Rules, the time limit for an international organization to submit information relevant to a case before the Court is fixed 'before the closure of the written proceedings'. See G. Gaja, 'A New Way …', 671 and J. Crawford and A. Keene, 'Editorial' 7 *Journal of International Dispute Settlement* (2016), 229.

129 G. Gaja, 'A New Way …', 671.

130 J. Crawford and A. Keene, *supra* note 128, 230.

131 *Gabčíkovo-Nagymaros Project* (*Hungary/Slovakia*) (*Judgment: Separate Opinion of Judge Weeramantry*) *ICJ Reports 1997*, 7, 118.

132 J. Crawford and A. Keene, *supra* note 128, 225–30.

133 *Ibid.*, 225.

There is indeed a tendency towards further 'multilateralisation' of procedural law whenever community interests are at stake.[134] As pointed out by Judge Simma, 'international law is finally overcoming the legal as well as moral deficiencies of bilateralism and maturing into a much more socially conscious legal order'.[135] This would enhance both the Court's 'normative' and 'democratic' legitimacy.[136] On the one hand, the normative conception of legitimacy deals with 'the rightness of an institutions' exertion of power within a society' by defining 'a set of moral standards by which an institution or regime is judged or justified'.[137] It is linked to 'legal legitimacy', which supposes the 'institution's observance of its legally constrained mandate' and includes 'the process by which rules, decisions, and actions are made, applied, or interpreted'.[138] If ICT s fulfil certain criteria such as transparency, accountability and due process, they may be viewed as legitimate. On the other hand, aspects of normative' legitimacy are also taken into consideration when assessing the 'democratic legitimacy' of global institutions. Indeed, transparency, the participation of those affected and deliberation are of particular significance in building up the 'democratic legitimacy' of ICT s.[139]

Transparent procedure also implies the participation of affected or interested parties in proceedings, including a dialogue between the court and the parties, third parties and *amicus curiae* briefs; while transparent reasoning

134 M. Benzing, *supra* note 2, 408.

135 B. Simma, *supra* note 3, 234. According to Judge Simma, 'classic bilateralist international law has fallen far behind the present State of consciousness of international society'.

136 There is no authoritative or generally accepted definition of 'legitimacy' (A. Follesdal, 'The Legitimacy Deficits of the Human Rights Judiciary: Elements and Implications of a Normative Theory', 14 *Theoretical Inquiries in Law* (2013) 2, 345). See also D. Behn, O. K. Fauchald and M. Langford, 'How to approach "legitimacy"', for the book project *Empirical Perspectives on the Legitimacy of International Investment Tribunals* (2015). For an application of the concepts of 'normative' and 'democratic' legitimacy to analyse the Mercosur's dispute settlement mechanism, see P. W. Almeida, 'The Legitimacy of International Trade Tribunals: the case of Mercosur' in G. Ulfstein, H. Ruiz-Fabri, R. House (eds.), *The Legitimacy of International Trade Courts and Tribunals* (Cambridge University Press, 2017).

137 D. Behn, O. K. Fauchald and M. Langford, *supra* note 136. For a definition of normative legitimacy, see A. Buchanan and R. O. Keohane, 'The Legitimacy of Global Governance Institutions' in R. Wolfrum and V. Röben (eds.), *Legitimacy in International Law* (Springer, 2008), 25; A. Follesdal, *supra* note 136, 345; and L. R. Helfer and K. J. Alter, 'Legitimacy and Lawmaking: A Tale of Three International Courts', 14 *Theoretical Inquiries in Law* (2013) 2, 479.

138 D. Behn, O. K. Fauchald and M. Langford, *supra* note 136.

139 A. von Bogdandy, 'The Democratic Legitimacy of International Courts: A Conceptual Framework' 14 *Theoretical Inquiries in Law* (2013) 2, 375.

concerns the decision-making process and tools according to which international courts and tribunals discuss and treat precedents.[140] Therefore, rules on third party intervention and *amicus curiae* briefs are all of the utmost importance not only for protecting community interests, but also for ensuring the normative and democratic legitimation of ICTs, and in particular of the ICJ.

The institute of *amici curiae* is among the possibilities of expanding procedural rules. *Amici curiae* 'are those actors who do not themselves have a legally protected interest in the particular case and yet want to intervene',[141] thereby opening bilateral litigation to issues of public or general interest.[142] Their goal is to 'introduce public interest considerations into the decision – and, indirectly, to impact on the development of international law'.[143] Despite being accepted and regulated by many courts and tribunals,[144] there remains considerable disagreement within the ICJ in this regard, which appears still reluctant to expand the dispute beyond the limits initially prescribed by the parties to the proceedings[145] so as to cover State submissions, as well as those by non-State actors, nongovernmental organizations and individuals, notably in cases where *erga omnes* obligations are at issue.

---

140 A. von Bogdandy, 'The Democratic Legitimacy of International Courts…', p. 376–7.

141 A. von Bogdandy, I. Venzke, 'On the Democratic Legitimation …', 1366–7. See also P. Sands, R. Mackenzie, 'International Courts and Tribunals, *Amicus Curiae*' in R. Wolfrum (ed.), *MPEPIL* (OUPIL, 2009); H. Ascensio, 'L'*Amicus Curiae* devant les Juridictions Internationales' 105 *Revue Générale de Droit International Public* (2001), 897.

142 D. Shelton, 'The Participation of Nongovernmental Organizations in International Judicial Proceedings,' 88 *American Journal of International Law* (1994) 4, 612.

143 Y. Ronen and Y. Naggan, 'Chapter 37: Third Parties' in C. P. R. Romano, K. Alter and Y. Shany (eds.), *The Oxford Handbook of International Adjudication* (OUP, 2013), 821.

144 See, e.g. ITLOS Statute, Arts. 84.1, 84.2; WTO DSU Artcile 13; ICSID Arbitration Rule 37.2.a; ECHR Article 36 (2); IACtHR Rules, Article 2 (3), 44; ICC Rules 103, 149; ICTY Rule 74; ICTR Rule 74, among others. For more details on *amicus curiae* before tribunals other than the ICJ, see J. Razzaque, 'Changing role of friends of the court in the International Courts and Tribunals', 1 *Journal on Non-State Actors in International Law* (2002), 169–200; L. Bartholomeusz, 'The *Amicus Curiae* before International Courts and Tribunals', 5 *Journal on Non-State Actors in International Law* (2005), 209–286; D. Shelton, *supra* note 142, 611–642; E. Brabandere, 'NGOs and the "Public Interest": The Legality and Rationale of *Amicus Curiae* Interventions in International Economic and Investment Disputes' 12 *Chicago Journal of International Law* (2011–2012) 85–113.

145 See Y. Ronen and Y. Naggan *supra* note 143, 823. Former President Gilbert Guillaume stated that governments and intergovernmental institutions should 'retain sufficient independence of decision to resist the powerful pressure groups which besiege them today with the support of the mass media' (see *Legality of the Threat or Use of Nuclear Weapons (Advisory Opinion: Separate Opinion of Judge Guillaume) ICJ Reports 1996*, 287, para. 5).

The plurilateral nature of international adjudication requires not only the expansion of the active legitimacy of submitting *amicus curiae* briefs but also the enlargement of its scope, notably when global public goods are at stake. If the goal is to 'introduce public interest considerations', the 'friends of court' could also contribute to upholding rules aimed at protecting fundamental values of the international community, such as *erga omnes* obligations. Indeed, *amicus curiae* briefs would be more suitable than intervention proceedings for cases in which an *erga omnes* obligation is at issue.[146] The third State's aim would be to affirm the collective character of the obligation in question, which would be an adequate and sufficient means for presenting its views to the Court. In such a case, the referred State would not have to demonstrate a legal interest of its own which would be directly in issue in the case.[147]

However, one may wonder how far ICTs should go in accommodating the function of protecting the interests of the international community without losing their legitimacy in the broader picture of dispute settlement.[148] There is indeed a fear that any expansion of procedural rules would open the floodgates and expose the ICJ to an uncontrolled number of subjects, which could compromise its function of settling bilateral disputes by undermining party equality and the efficient management of proceedings. This could demotivate states from choosing the Court as a legitimate dispute settlement *forum*, thereby generating political friction or backlashes.[149] The tension between the bilateral nature of ICJ proceedings and the necessary protection of community interests would also justify the overall internal reluctance to adapt ICJ Rules for 'multiparty litigation'. ICT Judges, notably from the ICJ, could fear that states could present lesser willingness to choose a *forum* considered not to fully guarantee their procedural autonomy.[150]

---

146 P. Palchetti, 'Opening...', 179.

147 In this sense, see P. Palchetti, 'Opening ...', 178–80. See, i.e., the Court's considerations with regards to the application by Malta for permission to intervene (*Continental Shelf* (*Tunisia v. Libyan Jamahiriya*) (*Application for Intervention*) *ICJ Reports 1981*, para. 19). For other authors arguing that in cases involving *erga omnes* obligations, the protection of community interests should be a sufficient interest for the purpose of discretional intervention (under Article 62 of the Statute), see Rudolf Bernhardt, *supra* note 121, 57; M. Benzing, *supra* note 2, 369; and S. D. Murphy, 'Amplifying the World Court's Jurisdiction through Counter-Claims and Third-Party Intervention', 33 *The George Washington Journal of International Law and Economics* (2000), 27.

148 G. Ulfstein, *supra* note 137, 865–866.

149 L. R. Helfer and K. J. Alter, 'Legitimacy and Lawmaking: A Tale of Three International Courts', 14 *Theoretical Inquiries in Law* (2013) 2, 484.

150 M. Benzing, *supra* note 2, 408.

The identification and protection of GPG by international courts therefore reflects a policy choice[151] that must be guided by good governance and be endowed with legitimacy[152] in order to avoid the potential risk of incurring in 'rhetorical function'[153] and/or abuse.[154] Such policy choice has to take into account the intertemporal dimension, which is also applicable to the formation, development and interpretation of international law.[155]

151 A. Nollkamper, *supra* note 7, 772.

152 F. Cafaggi and D. D. Caron, *supra* note 5, 645.

153 D. Bodansky, *supra* note 1, 655.

154 G. Shaffer, *supra* note 9, 674.

155 P. W. Almeida, 'Imunidades Jurisdicionais do Estado perante a Corte Internacional de Justiça…', 526–7.

PART 3

Recent Case-Law of the International Court of Justice (ICJ) and Its Significance for International Law

Introduction

Joanna Gomula

The first three chapters in this Part focus on selected case-law of the International Court of Justice in the years 2018–19. Although this is just a carve-out of the Court's jurisprudence in this brief period, the plethora of factual and legal issues before the Court is extensive. These range from 'classical' questions of international law, such as a State's obligation to negotiate its neighbour's access to the ocean or the legal implications of self-determination and territorial integrity, to more specialized questions, such as the interpretation of terms used to define racial discrimination. This jurisprudential abundance is further enriched by the fact that the Court's activity in this period included not only contentious cases, but also the exercise of its advisory function.

Although the fourth chapter reaches out to the Court's older jurisprudence, it clasps together the narrative on 'recent' case law by demonstrating the impact of the Court's rulings on the current state of the law, in this case, that of international organizations.

All four chapters thus share an important theme: the making of history of international law through the Court's jurisprudence.

In the first chapter of this Part, *Claudio Grossman* presents what he emphasizes to be a 'historic' judgment, issued by the Court on 1 October 2018, in the dispute between Bolivia and Chile, concerning the latter's alleged obligation to negotiate Bolivia's access to the Pacific Ocean. Although the Court's jurisdiction did not cover Bolivia's rights to obtain sovereign access to the sea, but concerned solely Chile's obligation to negotiate such access, its judgement is a fine lecture on the history, sources and important concepts of international law. In line with the Court's judgment, Professor Grossman reviews the possible sources of Chile's obligation to negotiate, among them treaties and customary international law, acquiescence, estoppel, and legitimate expectations (the latter rejected by the Court as a principle of general public international law), as well as the distinction between obligations of conduct and result. The chapter goes beyond the analysis of the Court's reasoning. The author, who served as Chile's Agent in the dispute, also provides a unique insight into the strategy of Chile's defence, shedding light on various practical issues that the defence team had to consider, including the assurance of gender diversity of the Chilean team's composition. As a result, the chapter serves not only a valuable first-hand assessment of the judgment, but also makes the reader realize

© KONINKLIJKE BRILL NV, LEIDEN, 2022 | DOI:10.1163/9789004467668_010

that beyond the formal text of the Court's decision there are anxieties and expectations of real people, and communities, affected by the dispute.

Of no less importance, from a legal and historical perspective, is the case discussed by *Giulia Bernabei* in the next chapter: the advisory opinion on the 'Legal Consequences of the Separation of the Chagos Archipelago from Mauritius in 1965', issued on 25 February 2019. The UN General Assembly's request for this advisory opinion was surrounded by controversy from the outset because at the heart of the matter was a *de facto* dispute between Mauritius and the United Kingdom. Dr Bernabei reviews the Court's analysis of the right to self-determination and its conclusion that the process of decolonization had not been 'lawfully completed' at the time of Mauritius' independence, thus placing an obligation on the United Kingdom to end its administration of the Chagos Archipelago 'as rapidly as possibly'. The significance of this case is bolstered by the contradiction between the seriousness of the ruling that the United Kingdom (a permanent member of the UN Security Council) had engaged in a 'wrongful act entailing international responsibility' and the non-binding nature of this pronouncement. This contradiction is central to the chapter's main objective: the exploration of the law-making capacity of the Court's advisory opinions and their impact on international law. The Chagos Archipelago case is significant also in light of its possible systemic implications. It has created a precedent that may leave States tempted to use advisory proceedings to bring disputes before the Court, in circumvention of the requirement of the parties' consent. In this respect, although a State's reluctance to cease the wrongful conduct confirmed in an advisory opinion is regrettable, the non-binding nature of advisory opinions may be a buffer against a more frequent use of this route.

The next chapter, authored by *Ioannis Konstantinidis*, again strikes an interesting historical note, providing another example of how parties may explore various routes to bring their grievances to the Court's attention. Dr Konstantinidis scrutinizes the Court's relatively novel jurisprudence relating to the 1965 International Convention on the Elimination of All Forms of Racial Discrimination. As many as three disputes have been referred to the Court in recent years under the Convention's Article 22, a dispute settlement clause previously (for almost four decades) dormant in inter-State practice. In all three cases – involving Georgia and Russia, Ukraine and Russia, and Qatar and the United Arab Emirates, respectively – there were underlying conflicts, which went beyond racial discrimination concerns. One may therefore speculate that, in the above cases, accessing the Court via the Convention's Article 22 was more symbolic than designed to resolve all differences between the parties. Dr Konstantinidis focuses on the dispute between Qatar and the United

Arab Emirates, providing an illuminating account of the interpretative issues arising in the dispute. The main question, answered by the Court in the negative, was whether the concept of 'national origin', as used in Article 1 of the Convention, should be understood to include 'current nationality'. Based on the Court's jurisprudence in all three cases, the author also analyses important procedural questions arising in connection with Article 22, above all, whether its preconditions should be cumulative or alternative (the Court having opted for the latter interpretation) and the extent to which the local remedies rule applies to disputes under the Convention.

While the previous three chapters may be said to reflect international law history *in statu nascendi*, for the last chapter in this Part history is of the essence. *Rita Guerreiro Teixeira* recalls one of the Court's first advisory opinions, that on 'Reparation for Injuries Suffered in the Service of the United Nations', and skilfully transposes its timeless conclusions on the current law of international organizations. The author considers the development of the concept of an international organization as a legal person in international law, reminding the reader – through a recollection of historical sources – that there was a time when what is obvious today (that international organizations possess such personality) was highly contested. The author also discusses the doctrine of implied powers, as developed by the Court in its advisory jurisprudence. It is interesting to note that the Court has both 'broadened and limited the scope of implied powers', displaying a shift from a broad perception of the powers of international organizations to a more limited one, based on functional limitations of these powers. This may be a reflection of similar trends in other areas of international law where conceptual stimuli are often provided as institutions develop, only to result in a quest for boundaries after such development begins to escape accountability.

The 'glimpse' of the Court's jurisprudence offered by the chapters in this Part confirms the position of the Court as a truly 'World Court'. It is evidence of the continuing trust placed with it by States for the fair and just resolution of international disputes.

CHAPTER 7

Obligation to Negotiate Access to the Pacific Ocean (*Bolivia v. Chile*) before the ICJ

The Obligation to Negotiate under International Law and Chile's Strategy

Claudio Grossman

1 Introduction

On 1 October 2018, the International Court of Justice (ICJ) delivered a historic verdict for Chile, which rejected all claims submitted by Bolivia and denied the existence of any *"obligation to negotiate"* a sovereign access (whether an obligation of means or an obligation of result) to the Pacific Ocean in favour of Bolivia through Chilean territory. The ICJ adopted the decision with 12 votes in favour of Chile, and 3 votes in dissent – including that of the Bolivian-appointed *ad hoc* judge.

The purpose of this article is, after a brief presentation of the case, to analyse its significance in terms of the obligation to negotiate in international law, and then to present the strategy pursued by Chile to defend its position that there were no obligations pending between Chile and Bolivia to negotiate sovereign access to the Pacific Ocean.

For the successful conduct of a case, it is essential to have a solid legal basis – including refuting the claims presented by the other party. However, conducting a case before the Court has many components beyond the simple articulation of legal arguments. For example, in this case, in a State like Chile with an inquisitive press and an assertive political opposition, it was important to design a litigation strategy that would address the need for information within a democratic society. This is particularly important in disputes that could have serious consequences concerning, for example, the territorial integrity of a State affecting the populations who are living in areas that could be impacted by the decision.

It is not unusual, as it was the case here, that the legal claims pursued by a State are accompanied by an international publicity campaign. In this case, Bolivia portrayed Chile as an unreliable State that violated its commitment to solve the problem of Bolivia's landlocked nature, to which it attributed its underdevelopment. Bolivia became a landlocked State after the War of the

© KONINKLIJKE BRILL NV, LEIDEN, 2022 | DOI:10.1163/9789004467668_011

Pacific,[1] which took place from 1879–1884 and resulted in the sovereignty in perpetuity in favour of Chile of territories that Bolivia had claimed as its own. The conclusion of the War of the Pacific, in accordance with the Treaty of 1904 between Chile and Bolivia, also gave Bolivia access to the Pacific Ocean in perpetuity through the Chilean harbours of the Pacific – among other benefits.[2]

Bolivia's political campaign created political pressure in Chile to respond to the assertions, as internally important sectors of the population resented the portrayal of Chile as a State that did not respect the rule of law or was deemed an aggressor. Important forces in Chile wanted the legal team to denounce Bolivia's assertions not only before international public opinion but also before the ICJ, a forum where Bolivia did not restrict itself to purely legal arguments but also political arguments. The need to balance the utilization of legal arguments and political accusations required Chile to make choices, including to what extent it needed to restrict itself to legal arguments.

This contribution will analyse the strategy pursued by the Chilean legal defence. Sharing this experience could be of value to other disputes, considering, however, that particular circumstances could create different contexts and challenges, like the nature and relevance of a dispute or the internal structure of a State. First, this article will present a brief description of the case and its development. Second, it will refer to the Court's decision and the *obligation to negotiate* in international law. Third, it will address the strategy pursued by Chile. Lastly, it will provide final observations on the impact of the judgment.

2 Description and Development of the Case

This case began on 24 April 2013 with the filing of Bolivia's lawsuit with the International Court of Justice,[3] requesting that Chile be forced to negotiate sovereign access to the Pacific Ocean. In response, Chile filed a preliminary objection, claiming that the Court lacked jurisdiction to decide the case. On 25 September 2015, the Court rejected the Chilean preliminary objection but decided, at the same time, that this case was not about determining if Bolivia

1 War of the Pacific, Encyclopedia Britannica, https://www.britannica.com/event/War-of-the-Pacific.

2 Tratado de Paz y Amistad de 20 de octubre de 1904 ("Treaty of Peace and Friendship of October 20, 1904"), https://www.aspb.gob.bo/wp-content/uploads/2015/10/Tratado-de-Paz-y-Amistad-de-20-de-octubre-de-1904.pdf.

3 Obligation to Negotiate Access to The Pacific Ocean (*Bolivia v. Chile*), Application instituting proceedings (24 April 2013).

had a right to obtain sovereign access to the sea, but only on whether there was an obligation to negotiate.[4] The Court determined that it would address the content of the latter obligation at the merits stage.[5]

After the Court's decision on its jurisdiction, the procedure, which had been suspended with the preliminary objection, continued. Chile presented its Counter-Memorial, which was followed by the Reply of Bolivia and, finally, the Rejoinder of Chile, ending the written phase of the procedure. Oral arguments took place between 19 and 28 March 2018.

On 1 October 2018, the Court delivered its ruling, rejecting every Bolivian claim and determining that – in accordance with international law – Chile was fully justified in its position that there was no obligation to negotiate sovereign access to the Pacific Ocean between Chile and Bolivia.[6]

The Court determined that all the legal sources invoked by Bolivia failed to prove the existence of an obligation owed by Chile to negotiate sovereign access to the Pacific Ocean. Accordingly, the Court rejected as grounds for an obligation: the existence of one or more bilateral agreements that would impose on Chile an obligation to negotiate; declarations and other unilateral acts; acquiescence; estoppel; legitimate expectations; Article 2 (3) of the UN Charter; Article 3 (i) of the Charter of the Organization for American States (OAS) and resolutions of the General Assembly of that regional organization; and the cumulative effect of numerous acts by Chile.

In respect to **bilateral agreements** as sources of an obligation to negotiate, the Court determined that agreements to generate a legal obligation require "an intention of the parties to be bound by legal obligations". Resorting to the norms of interpretation laid down in the Vienna Convention on the Law of Treaties and in an extensive analysis of the bilateral agreements invoked by Bolivia, the Court concluded that such intention had not been proven, rejecting Bolivia's claim.[7]

---

4 *Obligation to Negotiate Access to The Pacific Ocean* (*Bolivia v. Chile*), *Preliminary Objection, Judgment, ICJ Reports 2015*, 592, 610–11.

5 *Id.* at 605.

6 *Obligation to Negotiate Access to The Pacific Ocean* (*Bolivia v. Chile*), *Judgment, ICJ Reports 2018*, 507, para. 139 (hereinafter *Bolivia v. Chile*) ("On the basis of an examination of the arguments of the Parties and the evidence produced by them, the Court concludes, with regard to bilateral instruments invoked by Bolivia, that these instruments do not establish an obligation on Chile to negotiate Bolivia's sovereign access to the Pacific Ocean.").

7 *Id.*, para. 139. ("On the basis of an examination of the arguments of the Parties and the evidence produced by them, the Court concludes, with regard to bilateral instruments invoked by Bolivia, that these instruments do not establish an obligation on Chile to negotiate Bolivia's sovereign access to the Pacific Ocean.").

Equally, to reject Bolivia's claim based on Chile's **declarations and other unilateral acts**, the Court, resorting to the interpretation rules of the Vienna Convention on the Law of Treaties, determined that the wording of the texts did not prove the Bolivian claim for an obligation to negotiate.[8] Additionally, since the circumstances of the Chilean declaration and statements did not prove any intention to assume an obligation by Chile to negotiate sovereign access, the Court rejected the idea that unilateral acts by Chile generated any obligation.[9]

Concerning Bolivia's argument that an obligation to negotiate resulted from Chile's acquiescence to engage in negotiations on sovereign access in favour of Bolivia, the Court determined that Bolivia failed to identify any declaration by Chile "which required a response or reaction on the part of Chile in order to prevent an obligation from arising."[10]

---

8 *Id.*, para. 147 ("The Court notes that Chile's declarations and other unilateral acts on which Bolivia relies are expressed, not in terms of undertaking a legal obligation, but of willingness to enter into negotiations on the issue of Bolivia's sovereign access to the Pacific Ocean. For instance, Chile declared that it was willing 'to seek that Bolivia acquire its own outlet to the sea' and 'to give an ear to any Bolivian proposal aimed at solving its landlocked condition' (see paragraphs 142 and 143 above). On another occasion, Chile stated its 'unchanging purpose of studying, together with that brother country, within the framework of a frank and friendly negotiation, the obstacles that limit Bolivia's development on account of its landlocked condition' (see paragraph 143 above). The wording of these texts does not suggest that Chile has undertaken a legal obligation to negotiate Bolivia's sovereign access to the Pacific Ocean.").

9 *Id.*, para. 148 ("With regard to the circumstances of Chile's declarations and statements, the Court further observes that there is no evidence of an intention on the part of Chile to assume an obligation to negotiate. The Court therefore concludes that an obligation to negotiate Bolivia's sovereign access to the sea cannot rest on any of Chile's unilateral acts referred to by Bolivia.").

10 *Id.*, para. 152 ("The Court observes that 'acquiescence is equivalent to tacit recognition manifested by unilateral conduct which the other party may interpret as consent' (*Delimitation of the Maritime Boundary in the Gulf of Maine Area* (*Canada v. United States of America*), *Judgment, ICJ Reports 1984*, p. 305, para. 130) and that 'silence may also speak, but only if the conduct of the other State calls for a response' (*Sovereignty over Pedra Branca v. Pulau Batu Puteh, Middle Rocks and South Ledge* (*Malaysia v. Singapore*), *Judgment, ICJ Reports 2008*, p. 51, para. 121). The Court notes that Bolivia has not identified any declaration which required a response or reaction on the part of Chile in order to prevent an obligation from arising. In particular, the statement by Bolivia, when signing UNCLOS, that referred to 'negotiations on the restoration to Bolivia of its own sovereign outlet to the Pacific Ocean' did not imply the allegation of the existence of any obligation for Chile in that regard. Thus, acquiescence cannot be considered a legal basis of an obligation to negotiate Bolivia's sovereign access to the sea.").

Equally, the Court rejected Bolivia's claim that an obligation had been generated by estoppel, concluding that the "essential conditions required for estoppel are not fulfilled." In fact, Bolivia could not demonstrate that it had changed its position to its own "detriment or to Chile's advantage in reliance on Chile's representations."[11]

Legitimate expectations, another ground Bolivia invoked, was rejected by the Court. The Court determined that public international law did not include this principle since this principle has only been found in arbitral awards concerning "disputes between a foreign investor and the host State."[12]

As to the applicability of Article 2 (3) of the UN Charter as a source for Chile's obligation, the Court rejected Bolivia's argument, finding that the general duty prescribed by Article 2(3) to settle disputes in ways that preserve international peace and security, and justice did not require an obligation to engage in negotiations. The paragraphs of Article 2 leave "the choice of peaceful means of settlement to the parties concerned."[13] Additionally, the Court stated that the "principle of free choice of means" was confirmed by Resolution 2625 (XXV) of the General Assembly ("Declaration on Principles of International Law concerning Friendly Relations and Co-operation among States in accordance with

11 *Id.*, para. 159 ("The Court finds that in the present case the essential conditions required for estoppel are not fulfilled. Although there have been repeated representations by Chile of its willingness to negotiate Bolivia's sovereign access to the Pacific Ocean, such representations do not point to an obligation to negotiate. Bolivia has not demonstrated that it changed its position to its own detriment or to Chile's advantage, in reliance on Chile's representations. Therefore, estoppel cannot provide a legal basis for Chile's obligation to negotiate Bolivia's sovereign access to the sea.").

12 *Id.*, para. 162 ("The Court notes that references to legitimate expectations may be found in arbitral awards concerning disputes between a foreign investor and the host State that apply treaty clauses providing for fair and equitable treatment. It does not follow from such references that there exists in general international law a principle that would give rise to an obligation on the basis of what could be considered a legitimate expectation. Bolivia's argument based on legitimate expectations thus cannot be sustained.").

13 *Id.*, para. 165 ("The Court recalls that, according to Article 2, paragraph 3, of the Charter of the United Nations, '[a]ll Members shall settle their international disputes by peaceful means in such a manner that international peace and security, and justice, are not endangered.' This paragraph sets forth a general duty to settle disputes in a manner that preserves international peace and security, and justice, but there is no indication in this provision that the parties to a dispute are required to resort to a specific method of settlement, such as negotiation. Negotiation is mentioned in Article 33 of the Charter, alongside 'enquiry, mediation, conciliation, arbitration, judicial settlement, resort to regional agencies or arrangements' and 'other peaceful means' of the parties' choice. However, this latter provision also leaves the choice of peaceful means of settlement to the parties concerned and does not single out any specific method, including negotiation. Thus, the parties to a dispute will often resort to negotiation, but have no obligation to do so.").

the Charter of the United Nations") and Resolution 37/10 ("Manila Declaration on the Peaceful Settlement of International Disputes").[14]

The Court also rejected Bolivia's argument that invoked Article 3 (i) of the Charter of the OAS, concluding that "resort[ing] to a specific procedure such as "direct negotiation" is not an obligation under the Charter, which therefore cannot be the legal basis of an obligation to negotiate sovereign access to the Pacific Ocean between Bolivia and Chile."[15]

Concerning the Organization of American States resolutions adopted by its General Assembly as proving the existence of an obligation to negotiate sovereign access by Chile, the Court determined that those resolutions were merely recommendations and that both parties acknowledged that "resolutions of the General Assembly of the OAS are not per se binding and cannot be the source of an international obligation. Chile's participation in the consensus for adopting some resolutions therefore does not imply that Chile has accepted to be bound under international law by the content of these resolutions."[16]

---

14 *Id.*, para. 166 (the same approach was taken by resolution 2625 (XXV) of the General Assembly ("Declaration on Principles of International Law concerning Friendly Relations and Co-operation among States in accordance with the Charter of the United Nations"). Resolution 37/10 ("Manila Declaration on the Peaceful Settlement of International Disputes") also followed the same approach and proclaimed the "principle of free choice of means" for the settlement of disputes (para. 3). All this leads the Court to the conclusion that no obligation to negotiate Bolivia's sovereign access to the Pacific Ocean arises for Chile under the provisions of the Charter on the peaceful settlement of disputes.").

15 *Id.*, para. 167 ("Article 3(i) of the Charter of the OAS sets forth that '[c]ontroversies of an international character arising between two or more American States shall be settled by peaceful procedures.' Article 24 provides that international disputes between Member States 'shall be submitted to the peaceful procedures set forth' in the Charter, while Article 25 lists these 'peaceful procedures' as follows: 'direct negotiation, good offices, mediation, investigation and conciliation, judicial settlement, arbitration, and those which the parties to the dispute may especially agree upon at any time.' Resort to a specific procedure such as 'direct negotiation' is not an obligation under the Charter, which therefore cannot be the legal basis of an obligation to negotiate sovereign access to the Pacific Ocean between Bolivia and Chile.").

16 *Id.*, para. 171 ("The Court notes that none of the relevant resolutions of the General Assembly of the OAS indicates that Chile is under an obligation to negotiate Bolivia's sovereign access to the Pacific Ocean. These resolutions merely recommend to Bolivia and Chile that they enter into negotiations over the issue. Also, UNGA RES. 686, to which Bolivia calls special attention, only urges the Parties "to begin a process of rapprochement and strengthening of friendship of the Bolivian and Chilean peoples, directed toward normalizing their relations and overcoming the difficulties that separate them – including, especially, a formula for giving Bolivia a sovereign outlet to the Pacific Ocean, on bases that take into account mutual conveniences, rights and interests of all parties involved". Moreover, as both Parties acknowledge, resolutions of the General Assembly of the OAS are not per se binding and cannot be the source of an international obligation. Chile's

Finally, the Court rejected Bolivia's argument that an obligation to negotiate sovereign access by Chile resulted from the cumulative effect of numerous acts by Chile in a period covering 100 years of exchanges between both countries. The Court noted, however, that since all the alleged bases invoked by Bolivia did not generate a legal obligation to negotiate, "a cumulative consideration of the various bases cannot add to the overall result ... cumulative effect of successive acts by Chile is predicated on the assumption that an obligation may arise through the cumulative effect of a series of acts even if it does not rest on a specific legal basis."[17]

Having rejected all legal bases for an obligation to negotiate,[18] the Court determined that nothing prevented the parties from "continuing the dialogue and exchanges, in a spirit of good neighbourliness."[19]

---

participation in the consensus for adopting some resolutions therefore does not imply that Chile has accepted to be bound under international law by the content of these resolutions. Thus, the Court cannot infer from the content of these resolutions nor from Chile's position with respect to their adoption that Chile has accepted an obligation to negotiate Bolivia's sovereign access to the Pacific Ocean.").

17 *Id.*, para. 174 ("the Court notes that Bolivia's argument of a cumulative effect of successive acts by Chile is predicated on the assumption that an obligation may arise through the cumulative effect of a series of acts even if it does not rest on a specific legal basis. However, given that the preceding analysis shows that no obligation to negotiate Bolivia's sovereign access to the Pacific Ocean has arisen for Chile from any of the invoked legal bases taken individually, a cumulative consideration of the various bases cannot add to the overall result. It is not necessary for the Court to consider whether continuity existed in the exchanges between the Parties since that fact, if proven, would not in any event establish the existence of an obligation to negotiate Bolivia's sovereign access to the Pacific Ocean.").

18 *Bolivia v. Chile, ICJ Reports 2018*, 507, para. 175 ("In light of the historical and factual background above (see paragraphs 26–83), the Court observes that Bolivia and Chile have a long history of dialogue, exchanges and negotiations aimed at identifying an appropriate solution to the landlocked situation of Bolivia following the War of the Pacific and the 1904 Peace Treaty. The Court is however unable to conclude, on the basis of the material submitted to it, that Chile has "the obligation to negotiate with Bolivia in order to reach an agreement granting Bolivia a fully sovereign access to the Pacific Ocean" (Bolivia's submissions, see paragraphs 13, 14 and 15 above). Accordingly, the Court cannot accept the other final submissions presented by Bolivia, which are premised on the existence of such an obligation (Bolivia's submissions, see paragraphs 13, 14 and 15 above).").

19 *Bolivia v. Chile, ICJ Reports 2018*, 507, para. 176 ("Nevertheless, the Court's finding should not be understood as precluding the Parties from continuing their dialogue and exchanges, in a spirit of good neighborliness, to address the issues relating to the landlocked situation of Bolivia, the solution to which they have both recognized to be a matter of mutual interest. With willingness on the part of the Parties, meaningful negotiations can be undertaken.").

3 The Decision of the Court and the Obligation to Negotiate in International Law[20]

The Court's decision contributed to the confirmation of important concepts in international law, including: the content of the obligation to negotiate in international law, the difference of obligation of conduct and obligation of result, good faith as a requirement for negotiations, the extent of the obligation to negotiate in cases of obligation of conduct, and the inapplicability of legitimate expectations in public international law. Additionally, if an obligation to negotiate would have resulted from the diplomatic and political exchanges that had taken place over a long period of time, that could have had a very negative impact on diplomatic relations. Moreover, diplomatic relations are precisely what is needed in an interconnected world. If repeated exchanges among countries, including neighbouring countries, result in legal obligations *per se* without finding a source, diplomacy will suffer.

3.1 *Content of the Obligation to Negotiate*

The Court's decision confirmed the content of the obligation to negotiate in international law, establishing that there is no general obligation to negotiate under international law. The rule governing the settlement of interstate disputes comes from Articles 2 (3) and 33 of the UN Charter, which establish an obligation to settle such disputes by peaceful means. This customary norm[21] precludes resorting to forceful means but does not oblige States to definitively settle their disputes.[22] Article 33 does not prescribe a preferred method of resolution but requires States to resolve disputes by any peaceful method of their choice. The Manila Declaration on the Peaceful Settlement of International Disputes provides that disputes may only be submitted to a certain method

20 The content of the present section is based upon the answers presented in a panel before the American Society of International Law.

21 *Military and Paramilitary Activities in and Against Nicaragua* (*Nicaragua v. United States*), *Judgment*, ICJ *Reports 1986*, 14, para. 290 (June 27).

22 See A. Pellet, 'Peaceful Settlement of International Disputes', in R. Wolfrum (ed.), 8 *Max Plank Encyclopedia of International Law* (2013) 201, 205 ("In fact, the obligation to peacefully settle international disputes is limited to those 'the continuance of which is likely to endanger the maintenance of international peace and security.' … Even in that case, there is no real obligation to positively 'settle' the dispute as shown by the verb 'seek' in that same provision ('The parties to any dispute…shall, first of all, seek a solution …' [emphasis added]): the only real obligation is not to resort to armed force to settle disputes. Such a wording clearly implies an obligation of conduct or of behaviour, not of result….").

of resolution if both States agree.[23] No State may be compelled to employ a method it has not consented to; therefore, a method of settlement may not be selected unilaterally. There is also no obligation to resort to negotiations as a "default" method to resolve disputes, as they are just one of the peaceful means mentioned in Article 33. This conclusion was explicitly endorsed by the ICJ in the case concerning an *Obligation to Negotiate Access to the Pacific Ocean,* where it stated that "no obligation to negotiate Bolivia's sovereign access to the Pacific Ocean arises for Chile under the provisions of the Charter on the peaceful settlement of disputes."[24]

Although the ICJ rejected a general obligation to negotiate, States may be bound by customary law to negotiate in certain cases. For instance, in the *North Sea Continental Shelf* cases, the ICJ recognized a customary obligation to negotiate concerning the continental shelf, finding "delimitation must be the object of agreement between the States concerned, and that such agreement must be arrived at in accordance with equitable principles."[25]

There is also an obligation to negotiate in situations where the rights of one State necessarily overlap with the rights of another. In the *Fisheries Jurisdiction* case, the Court determined negotiations are necessary when the rights of a State may only be determined by reference to the rights of other States.[26] However, situations like this should be interpreted narrowly because otherwise the obligation could apply to any dispute, which would be inconsistent with the principle of free choice. The nature of the specific rights concerned will be decisive in establishing whether an obligation to negotiate exists. Additionally, a treaty may establish an obligation to negotiate expressly[27] or establish an obligation to conclude a subsequent instrument, which will require pursuing negotiations to that effect.[28] An example of the latter is the arbitration on the *Tacna-Arica Question,* where the arbitrator found that the States undertook an

---

23 G.A. Res. 37/10, annex, Manila Declaration on the Peaceful Settlement of International Disputes, (November 15, 1982).

24 *Bolivia v. Chile, ICJ Reports 2018,* 507, para. 166.

25 *North Sea Continental Shelf Cases (Federal Republic of Germany v. Denmark; Federal Republic of Germany v. Netherlands),* Judgment, *ICJ Reports 1969,* 3, para. 85 (20 Feb.).

26 See *Fisheries Jurisdiction (United Kingdom v. Iceland), Judgment (Merits), ICJ Reports 1974,* 3, paras. 74–75 (stating that it "is implicit in the concept of preferential rights that negotiations are required in order to define or delimit the extent of those rights" and adding "[t]he obligation to negotiate thus flows from the very nature of the respective rights of the Parties").

27 See, e.g., Treaty on the Non-Proliferation of Nuclear Weapons, Article 6, 729 UNTS 161.

28 See, e.g., Treaty of Ancón, Chile-Peru, Article 3.

obligation to negotiate an additional protocol resolving the remaining details of their dispute.[29]

A treaty may also establish negotiations as a precondition before resorting to other means. Here, there is no actual obligation to negotiate a solution, but the States may not resort to other means unless they have attempted negotiation. For instance, in *Georgia v. Russia*, the ICJ concluded that Article 22 of the Convention on the Elimination of All Forms of Racial Discrimination (CERD) required the States to pursue negotiation before submitting an application.[30] Because the Court concluded that no negotiations were undertaken before submitting the application, the conditions for exercising jurisdiction were not fulfilled.[31] Any alternative interpretation would leave the Article's terms devoid of any practical effect.[32] Similarly, the Pact of Bogotá does not establish an obligation to negotiate, but requires attempting negotiations before employing other means.[33] An obligation to negotiate may also be established by any other source of legal obligations. The parties to a dispute may choose to negotiate final details after reaching substantial agreement on major issues, set parameters for future negotiations, or commit pre-emptively to negotiate settlement of future conflicts. It is important to understand that these "pre-negotiations" live in the domain of diplomacy rather than the domain of law.

3.2 *Obligations of Conduct and Obligations of Result*

The distinction between obligations of conduct and obligations of result is clear.[34] Obligations of conduct require States "to strive to realize a certain

---

29 See *Tacna-Arica Question*, Chile-Peru, 2 R.I.A.A. 921, 927 (PCA. 1925) ("Finally, the Article provides for the negotiation by the two countries of 'a special protocol' which will prescribe, first, 'the manner in which the plebiscite is to be carried out' and second 'the terms and time for the payment of the ten million.' ").

30 International Convention on the elimination of All Forms of Racial Discrimination, Article 22, December 21, 1965, 660 UNTS. 195; See Case Concerning *Application of the International Convention on the Elimination of All Forms of Racial Discrimination* (*Georgia v. Russian Federation*), *Judgment, ICJ Reports 2011*, 70, para. 141 ("in their ordinary meaning, the terms of Article 22 of CERD, namely '[a]ny dispute…which is not settled by negotiation or by the procedures expressly provided for in this Convention' establish preconditions to be fulfilled before the seizing of the Court").

31 *Id.*, paras. 181–84.

32 *Id.* at para. 134.

33 See Pact of Bogotá, Article 2 (2) ("in the event that a controversy arises between two or more signatory States which, in the opinion of the Parties, cannot be settled by direct negotiations … the Parties bind themselves to use the procedures established in the present Treaty …").

34 See P.M. Dupuy, 'Reviewing the Difficulties of Codification: On Ago's Classification of Obligations of Means and Obligations of Result in Relation to State Responsibility', 10

result."[35] Alternatively, obligations of result require States to achieve a particular outcome.[36] I believe the distinction between obligations of conduct and result is useful for two main purposes: first, for determining the exact content of the obligation concerned; and second, for determining whether a given obligation has been extinguished. Since obligations of result are only fulfilled when the result is attained, a State will breach such obligations if it does not attain the result. In contrast, an obligation of conduct is fulfilled if the State has employed all the means reasonably available to it to comply with the relevant objective.[37] The general rule with obligations to negotiate is that they are obligations of conduct, imposing on the parties an obligation to conduct meaningful negotiations that are not frustrated by either party's absolute insistence on its own position.[38] In general, obligations to negotiate do not require reaching an agreement. For instance, Article 83 of UNCLOS[39] establishes an obligation of conduct, pronouncing a course of action rather than requiring

European Journal of International Law (1999) 371, 375 (expressing that Ago's understanding of the distinction is almost opposite to the classical approach).

35 See e.g., *Certain Questions of Mutual Assistance in Criminal Matters (Djibouti v. France), Judgment, ICJ Reports 2008*, 177, para. 104 (stating that obligations of conduct may establish broad objectives as well as a duty to attempt to attain those objectives through certain means: "The respective obligations of the Treaty are obligations of law, articulated as obligations of conduct or, in this case, of cooperation, of a broad and general nature, committing the Parties to work towards the attainment of certain objectives defined as progress in a variety of fields, as well as in matters relating to peace and security. These goals are to be achieved by the employment of certain procedures and institutional arrangements.").

36 Dupuy, *supra* note 34, at 375.

37 Therefore, in obligations of conduct, a breach will not occur if the result in question is not attained, as long as the standard of due diligence was duly observed. See *Application of the Convention on the Prevention and Punishment of the Crime of Genocide (Bosnia-Herzegovina v. Serbia), Judgment, ICJ Reports 2007*, 43, para. 430 (determining the relevant obligation was one of conduct and recognizing due diligence as a further requirement: "a State cannot be under an obligation to succeed, whatever the circumstances, in preventing the commission of genocide: the obligation of States Parties is rather to employ all means reasonably available to them, so as to prevent genocide so far as possible").

38 See *North Sea Continental Shelf*, para. 85 ("an obligation to conduct themselves so that the negotiations are meaningful, which will not be the case when either of them insists upon its own position without contemplating any modification of it"); *see also Railway Traffic Between Lithuania and Poland*, Advisory opinion, 1931 PCIJ. (ser. A/B) No. 42, at 116 ("an obligation to negotiate does not imply an obligation to reach an agreement").

39 See United Nations Convention on the Law of the Sea, Article 83, December. 10, 1982, 1833 UNTS. 397 ("1. The delimitation of the continental shelf between States with opposite or adjacent coasts shall be effected by agreement on the basis of international law, as referred to in Article 38 of the Statute of the International Court of Justice, in order to achieve an equitable solution.").

a predetermined result. This Article does not require the parties to reach an agreement through delimitation negotiations, and even specifically provides for further procedures if an agreement cannot be reached.

However, the parties may also define obligations to negotiate as obligations of result. In these cases, the parties would be committing to reach a precise result, and the obligation would only be fulfilled when an agreement is reached. Article VI of the Treaty of Non-Proliferation[40] establishes an obligation to negotiate, defining it as one of result. The ICJ held that this Article goes beyond requiring the parties to negotiate by requiring them to achieve total nuclear disarmament, specifically through good faith negotiations.[41]

3.3 *Good Faith as a Requirement When There Is an Obligation to Negotiate*

Good faith requires States to engage in negotiations with the sincere intention of reaching an agreement and to conduct themselves consistently with that intention. In the *Fisheries Jurisdiction* case, the ICJ held that in negotiations, States should reasonably respect the legal rights of the other State, since doing otherwise would frustrate the prospect of achieving an amicable solution.[42] In the *North Sea Continental Shelf* cases, the Court reaffirmed that States are obliged to enter negotiations with the intent of reaching an agreement and to conduct themselves so that such negotiations are meaningful.[43] Good faith demands States refrain from causing injury to the legal rights or interests of

40 See Treaty on the Non-Proliferation of Nuclear Weapons, Article 6, July 1, 1968, 729 UNTS 161 ("Each of the Parties to the Treaty undertakes to pursue negotiations in good faith on effective measures relating to cessation of the nuclear arms race at an early date and to nuclear disarmament, and on a treaty on general and complete disarmament under strict and effective international control.").

41 See *Legality of the Threat or Use of Nuclear Weapons, Advisory opinion, ICJ Reports 1996*, 226, para. 99 ("The legal import of that obligation goes beyond that of a mere obligation of conduct; the obligation involved here is an obligation to achieve a precise result – nuclear disarmament in all its aspects – by adopting a particular course of conduct, namely, the pursuit of negotiations on the matter in good faith.").

42 See *Fisheries Jurisdiction*, para. 78 (stating that the Parties should aim to "conduct their negotiations on the basis that each must in good faith pay reasonable regard to the legal rights of the other").

43 See *North Sea Continental Shelf*, para. 85 ("The parties are under an obligation to enter into negotiations with a view to arriving at an agreement, and not merely to go through a formal process of negotiation as a sort of prior condition for the automatic application of a certain method of delimitation in the absence of agreement; they are under an obligation so to conduct themselves that the negotiations are meaningful, which will not be the case when either of them insists upon its own position without contemplating any modification of it.").

another State while negotiations are taking place, and obliges them not to take actions that would frustrate negotiations.

Other cases have shed light on the contours of the obligation of good faith. For instance, the *Lake Lanoux* arbitration offered examples of potential infringements of good faith, including unjustified breaking off of discussion, abnormal delay, disregard of the agreed procedures, and systematic refusals to consider adverse proposals or interests.[44] Alternatively, the *Tacna-Arica Question* arbitration provided examples of actions that do not violate good faith, such as proposing conditions the party deems to be reasonable and appropriate or opposing inadvisable conditions proposed by the other party.[45] The arbitral tribunal further determined that since States are expected to act in accordance with their own constitutional principles, it does not violate good faith for a ratifying authority to refuse to ratify a protocol it deems unsatisfactory.[46] Instead, bad faith requires an intent to frustrate negotiations.[47] It is important to remember the words of Judge Fitzmaurice, who said in his lecture at The Hague Academy, that treaties answer the question of "what" needs to be done, while the principle of good faith answers the question of "why."[48]

3.4 *Extent of the Obligation of Conduct*

Obligations to negotiate are generally obligations of conduct, imposing on States the duty to pursue negotiations as far as possible.[49] However, nothing prevents States from binding themselves to an obligation of result. As recognized by the ICJ in the case concerning an *Obligation to Negotiate Access to*

---

44 *Lake Lanoux*, France-Spain, 12 R.I.A.A. 281, para. 11 (PCA, 1957).

45 See *Tacna-Arica Question*, at 929 (determining that each state had "the right to propose conditions which it deemed to be reasonable and appropriate to the holding of the plebiscite, or to oppose conditions proposed by the other Party which it deemed inadvisable").

46 *Id.* (deciding that "bad faith is not to be predicated upon the refusal of ratification of a particular proposed protocol deemed by the ratifying authority to be unsatisfactory" since states were expected to act in accordance with constitutional principles).

47 *Id.* at 930 (requiring for bad faith "an intent to frustrate the carrying out of the provisions...with respect to the plebiscite," and placing the burden of proof on the party alleging bad faith in the conduct of negotiations).

48 G. Fitzmaurice, 'The General Principles of International Law considered from the Standpoint of the Rule of Law', 92 *Recueil des Cours de l'Academie de Droit International* (1957) 7. This is an inspiring principle that needs to be concretized. I have already mentioned some examples of that concretization. Other manifestations of the concretization of this principle can be found in the law of treaties, including *pacta sunt servanda*.

49 Application of the Interim Accord of 13 September 1995 (*Macedonia v. Greece*), *Judgment*, *ICJ Reports 2011*, 644, para. 132 (explaining that, generally, obligations to negotiate are obligations that impose a duty on States to pursue negotiations "as far as possible").

the Pacific Ocean, the parties may establish an obligation to achieve a precise result.[50] In such cases, the wording employed by the parties must be unequivocal, since a commitment of this nature certainly reduces the wide margin of discretion usually granted to States involved in negotiations. In addition, it will be difficult to establish the existence of an obligation of result if the wording of the agreement is unclear.

3.5 *Negotiations, the Rule of Law and Diplomacy*

In international relations, it is essential that States feel free to negotiate without the danger that sheer negotiations could be construed as creating a legal obligation, in the absence of the intent of parties to generate one. It seems from the point of view of world order, there is an interest in encouraging States to enter into negotiations, particularly in the current context of growing interconnectedness in nearly all fields of human endeavour. "Legalizing" negotiations could have, as a result, less disposition from States to engage in meaningful exchanges. It is also difficult to deny that the word "legal" will not add much to the resolution of a conflict. Diplomacy and politics should also have a place in the toolkit of international mechanisms addressing conflict.

4 Strategic Elements

To defend its interest before the ICJ, Chile needed to develop a strategy that would refute the case that Bolivia brought.

4.1 *Ensuring the Best Defence for Chile*

Needless to say, the purpose of the defence was to ensure that Chile prevailed in this case, stressing that there was nothing pending that would force Chile to negotiate with Bolivia. This obvious purpose, in light of internal political considerations including Chile's self-perception as a State capable of defending its own interests, required not only the political direction but also the legal direction of the case to remain in Chilean hands. Accordingly, Chile's recruitment of a team of well-known jurists of the highest level and of different nationalities did not mean that Chile was delegating the defence of its

50 See *Bolivia v. Chile, ICJ Reports 2018*, 507, para. 87 ("When setting forth an obligation to negotiate, the parties may, as they did for instance in Article VI of the Treaty on the Non-Proliferation of Nuclear Weapons, establish an 'obligation to achieve a precise result.' ").

national sovereignty.[51] The legal defence of the State was not "outsourced" and accordingly was always subject to Chilean leadership and guidance. This was ensured by the appointment of agents and co-agents with a well-known expertise and knowledge in international law, as well as a team of Chilean jurists, also experts in international law, that worked full-time on the case.

A case always has components related to how a State positions itself in the field of international relations, even beyond the specific issues at stake. There are national political components (e.g., the need for national unity) and relevant historical issues that show a State's vision of itself and its international image. Also, there might be different options in a defence of a State, for example, in this particular case, if it was legally necessary to base the case for public opinion mostly in international law (as it was done) or to seek to give more relevance to the political issues involved. Because this case could have had a territorial impact on Chile, a constant process of exchange and communications between the legal team and the political leadership of the State was established to address different options and the complexities involved, including the regular presence of the Minister of Foreign Affairs in the meetings of the international and Chilean teams, and access to the President of the State as needed, which took place on different occasions.

4.2 *National Unity as a Fundamental Value*

Bolivia based its case on two premises: (1) the existence of alleged unfulfilled promises by Chile to engage in negotiations that will result in sovereign access to the Pacific Ocean for Bolivia, and (2) the existence of obligations emanating from resolutions of the OAS and the UN Charter.

For Chile, the OAS resolutions were only political in nature, and Chile never voted in favour of the existence of an obligation to negotiate with Bolivia when eleven consecutive OAS resolutions had been adopted concerning both countries. Moreover, these eleven yearly resolutions ended in 1989 when Chile was in the process of regaining its democracy, showing, in Chile's view, that the resolutions had been politically motivated by the international community's rejection of the Pinochet dictatorship. Never again did the OAS adopt a resolution asking for negotiations between Chile and Bolivia.

If there had been national division in Chile over the existence of an obligation to negotiate with Bolivia during the case pending before the ICJ, conditions could have been created for Bolivia to resume its initiatives before the

---

51 The international lawyers of the team were Sir D. Bethlehem, P.M. Dupuy, B. Juratowitch, H. Koh, K. Parlett, M. Pinto, J.M. Thouvenin and S. Wordsworth.

OAS calling for negotiations between Chile and Bolivia. This could have given greater support to Bolivia's arguments before the Court. *Mutatis mutandis*, a national division in Chile also could have given space for Bolivia's initiatives before the UN that had always proved unsuccessful.

The interpretation of the history of the international relations between Chile and Bolivia is another relevant example of the need for national unity. Incorporating the opinions of academics and historians could be important to support legal arguments before an international court, particularly in a case like this where the arguments of Bolivia were based, to a great extent, in unfulfilled promises by Chile dating back over 100 years. The existence of deep divisions interpreting historical fact can provide persuasive foundations that would weaken a national position. It was very important in this case that in the Chilean academic and historian communities there was consensus as to the nature of the negotiations that had taken place between Chile and Bolivia concerning access to the Pacific Ocean. For Chile, those negotiations, when they existed, were diplomatic in nature and did not have a legal character, as Bolivia wrongfully claimed.

It is important to note, however, that unity is not unanimity, and there can always be dissenting voices in a democracy. These voices should not be ignored and must certainly be seriously considered. They are not proof of lack of national unity, but part of the normal life of an open and democratic society.

National unity is not achieved, however, only by pointing out its desirability, but should reflect a reality. The desire for national unity was reflected in the composition of a national team and was pursued during all the proceedings of the case, creating a participatory process that included information, visits to the congress, reports to the public, and so forth. The national team must be diverse and satisfy needs that will be alluded to later.

4.3 *National and International Team of the Highest Level*

Needless to say, the composition of national and international teams of the highest level is essential, with jurists and historians of different legal traditions (common law vs. civil law) that also dominate the languages of the Court (English and French) and are then able to "speak" to a diverse Court.

There is a theoretical discussion about whether a proper defence consists only of articulating well-founded legal arguments. However, an important criterion of legitimacy includes the ability to be convincing, and that includes who is presenting an argument.[52] From this perspective, for example, Chile

52 It is obvious that the Court as a court of law will decide on the basis of the soundness of legal argument, and it is legitimate to ask whether these factors of legitimacy are relevant.

considered it essential to include in its defence team a prestigious Argentine jurist, Professor Monica Pinto, to rebut Bolivian claims about the value of OAS resolutions. Bolivia, for its part, which sought to present a strong Latin American component to its case, argued *inter alia* the value of OAS resolutions and had no Latin American jurists on its international team. It was also important to incorporate Kate Parlett, a prestigious Australian jurist, into the Chilean team, and have her argue during the oral phase, showing the gender diversity of the composition of the Chilean delegation in front of the Court, which was also diverse in its composition. Chile also considered the importance of combining lawyers whose specialty was the articulation of the general narrative of the case with others who tackled each Bolivian argument by deconstructing them to the smallest detail.

In the management of a national and international team of the highest level, it is essential to create a proper atmosphere for free discussion that would allow for the consistent challenging of ideas in order to ensure that all possibilities would be analysed. This requires continuous attention and care to ensure that everyone is heard with full respect for all ideas.

The composition and contributions of the national and international Chilean team incorporated the input of the Chilean Agents who exercised leadership in the different phases of the proceedings before the Court.[53] The author of this contribution, who had been already the co-Agent in the preceding phases of the case, became the Agent and was in charge, *inter alia*, of the preparation of the Rejoinder, the oral proceedings, of all matters related to the legal components of the case in its final phase, and participated in the process of political decisions and publicity related to the proceedings (e.g., appearance

What is undeniable is that Chile, in the public articulation of its legal grounds, thought it was important to satisfy criteria of legitimacy, including the different legal and demographic backgrounds, of its defense.

53 Felipe Bulnes, during the first stage of the process, was in charge of implementing the national decision to challenge the Court's jurisdiction. While the Court rejected the Chilean position that it lacked jurisdiction, to win this stage of the proceedings Bolivia was forced to present arguments that weakened its original request for the existence of an obligation of result to negotiate sovereign access by Chile to the Pacific Ocean. The existence of an obligation of result could have been seen as a violation of the Treaty of 1904 that established in perpetuity Chilean sovereignty on the disputed territories between Chile and Bolivia during the War of the Pacific between 1879–1884. For his part, José Miguel Insulza, who followed Bulnes as Agent, was key in the articulation of the Chilean Counter-Memorial that contained an important legal and historical analysis debunking Bolivian claims. These contributions required Bolivia to make very important efforts to reformulate, to a great extent, its case in its Reply, opening a space for Chile to argue that the Bolivian claims lacked coherence and consistency.

before Congress, press conferences, addressing public opinion, replacing an *ad hoc* judge, and so forth).[54]

The leadership contributions of the Ministers and former Ministers of Foreign Affairs of Chile, acting on behalf of the Presidents of Chile (who also met regularly with the Agents), the Supreme Court, the Foreign Relations Committees of the Senate and the Chamber of Deputies, the Bolivia-Chile Working Group on Bilateral Affairs and the historians who participated in the case greatly contributed to Chile's defence. The expertise and knowledge provided to the defence also gave political coverage in the conduct of the case by showing real participation of all sectors of Chilean society in the Chilean defence.

The defence of Chile required constant interaction with the press as it was necessary to keep the citizens informed of all events throughout the case. This required constant and planned meetings with the press, including visits to the newspapers, tv channels, and radio stations by members of the Chilean defence team. Additionally, a special policy was developed to present the Chilean position in social media.

4.4 *Organization and Anticipation of Different Scenarios*

The organization and assessment of possible scenarios allowed the Chilean team to anticipate possible arguments of Bolivia prior to the deadlines set by the Court. An example of this was that, since November 2016, the Chilean teams analysed the possible arguments that Bolivia would make in its Reply to the Chilean Counter-Memory. When Bolivia submitted its Reply in March 2017, Chile had more than twenty extensive papers on the possible Bolivian arguments, which were submitted and analysed at numerous meetings.

This previous work greatly facilitated the Chilean Rejoinder that was presented in September 2017 before the deadline established by the court. It is noteworthy that a State submits its Rejoinder before the deadline, as it was in this case, thereby giving a sense of solidity, security, and trust, that might be particularly relevant for national and international public opinion.

---

54 Also, during the proceedings, the Chilean legal defense team included Ambassadors María Teresa Infante, in the Hague, and Alfonso Silva, an experienced Chilean diplomat, who in their roles as co-agents contributed to all aspects of the case, including its strategic definitions. To address organizational topics, the definition of the issues and the assignment of responsibilities, among other subjects, the Agent had the valuable support of Alberto van Klaveren (who had been the Agent of Chile in the case between Chile and Peru), and of the executive coordinator of the team, Carolina Valdivia, a position held previously by Ximena Fuentes and Mariana Durney.

Similarly, the planning and incorporation of political sectors in the Chilean defence was essential to deal with the announcement by the Court that the oral arguments would take place in March 2018. It was previously expected that, at the soonest, those oral arguments would take place after May. Additionally, the Chilean transfer of presidential power had only taken place in February. When the Court's announcement took place at the end of January 2018, Chile had already assigned, in November 2017, possible topics for the oral arguments, and possible lawyers that would present to the Court. Additionally, it had scheduled a meeting in February to review the topics and presenters to the Court, with the national and international teams working since November on analysing and criticizing the presentations sent for review. Accordingly, it was not necessary to ask for any delay for the oral proceedings, in spite of the appointment of a new government in Chile. A change of government in Chile could have given an excuse for postponement of the oral proceedings, but it was unnecessary because of the preparation and composition of the teams, sending a strong message of continuity and solidity of the Chilean position.

As part of the process of national unity, the Agent, author of this contribution, and his co-Agents had met already with the candidates for the presidency, including President Piñera, who was elected and then already fully informed of the strategic direction of the case. Even before assuming power, the President-elect indicated his intention to ratify the team in charge of the Chilean defence.

Organization and foresight were also essential from another point of view. Unforeseen events always occur, and in the absence of organization there are no spaces to deal with them properly. This was the case on several occasions, which caused two important replacements: that of the *ad hoc* judge of Chile, Ms. Louise Arbour, who took an important position in the UN; and Pierre-Marie Dupuy, the lead French lawyer and an important authority in international law. Wrong replacement decisions could have serious implications for the case. The *ad hoc* judge must have the qualities and prestige needed to participate in the Court. If Chile had appointed an *ad hoc* judge that would vote against Chile (which happened in several cases), the repercussions could have been significant. Additionally, the need to replace Pierre-Marie Dupuy was essential for the Chilean defence since it considered the presence of a French lawyer required to address the Court from the point of view of the continental tradition. Also, the addition of a lawyer into a team could impact the internal dynamics and consensus necessary for a team effort. These appointments required multiple meetings, interviews, and evaluations of high-profile topics. When judging by the result of the case, the appointments of Donald McRae (as *ad hoc* judge), and Jean-Marc Thouvenin (as an authority in international law and the continental tradition) were successful.

It should also be noted the need to stand firm once a decision has been made. In a State like Chile, with a free press and numerous people with an interest in international issues, there was a strong critique of these decisions. However, the vast majority of the authoritative opinion gave Chile's defence the necessary space to make these decisions.

4.5 *Strategic Driving with the State's Political Authorities*

Chile's decision to focus the case on international law before the ICJ was not the result of a purely formalistic view on international law but was a strategic choice, considering the opposition was a Bolivian team that regularly referenced the "injustice" of its State's Mediterranean status or Chile's alleged "abusive" treatment by presenting a distorted view of history and appealing to feelings of "decolonization".

In various international fora and in the face of public opinion, the Chilean authorities responded to Bolivia's political arguments, but before the Court Chile's argument focused on international law. Under international law there were no bases to claim that Chile was obliged to enter into negotiations concerning sovereign access to the Pacific Ocean in favour of Bolivia – no obligation of conduct and no obligation of result existed.

Chile's position – which was consistent and soundly based on law – contrasted with Bolivia's position which, in addition to appealing to political arguments, diminished credibility in its case by presenting a proliferation of arguments that contradicted or led to mixed conclusions. Examples of this were Bolivia's arguments to oppose Chile's preliminary objection and the reasoning in its Reply and oral arguments on the definition of sovereign access or the value of the failed 1895 Treaties.

Needless to say, coordination with the political authorities was essential as well and took place at the highest level with the Ministers of Foreign Affairs of Chile, Alfredo Moreno, in the initial phase, Heraldo Muñoz, for much of the trial, and Roberto Ampuero, in the final phase. The presence, participation, and political responsibility of the chancellors was an essential element in ensuring Chile's proper defence.

The direct role of the chancellors was joined by an important participation of the Presidents of Chile, Michelle Bachelet and Sebastián Pinera. Both, the chancellors and presidents of Chile, constantly required detailed information on the case in their substantive and procedural aspects. The action of the State's authorities was essential to the achievement of national unity and gave political cover to the defence.

4.6 *Building an Alternative Narrative*

Bolivia resorted to every possible source of law to claim the existence of an international obligation of Chile to negotiate sovereign access to the Pacific Ocean. Conversely, Chile's position included demonstrating that this multiplicity and proliferation of arguments, instead of revealing strength, was a recognition of the weakness of Bolivia's case.

One mistake that many trial lawyers make, however, is to believe that their role is just to reply to the arguments presented by the opposing party. A purely defensive position has great risks, as it might allow for a single argument from the opposition to be credible and result in losing a case. Instead, it is crucial to redefine the themes at stake and present them in a different light, generating an alternative narrative.

Accordingly, it was important for Chile to show that its interactions with Bolivia not only denied the existence of an obligation, but rather were the result of a different dynamic, reshaping the issue. For example, Chile-Bolivia's negotiations on transit to the Pacific Ocean, and even talks on sovereign access, always took place in the field of diplomacy and were grounded both in the specific interests of both countries at some point in their history and the motivation of good-neighbour policies.

Indeed, both countries sought to maintain a mutually beneficial relationship but always took into account that the 1904 Treaty[55] that settled the issue of sovereignty was not disputed and continues to govern the relations among them. There was no outstanding issue of sovereignty.

Chile's defence emphasized, as its alternative narrative, in addition to the good-neighbour policy of always seeking to discuss matters of concern, that both countries were in a constant political, diplomatic dialogue. Changing the nature of these dialogues, distorting them, and attributing to them a legal value they lacked would seriously jeopardize diplomacy in an interconnected world. To the contrary, the Bolivian thesis that those diplomatic exchanges created legal obligations would have created serious barriers to dialogue when it is necessary to do the opposite: to promote diplomacy and generate dialogue without legal obligations.

4.7 *The Scope of the Case in International Law*

International law is the common narrative of sovereign States that interact in the field of international relations. It is not strange that there are different

55 Treaty of Peace and Friendship between Chile and Bolivia (1904), published in Chile's "Diario Oficial" No. 8.169, March 27, 1905.

interpretations of what is fair, and governments usually do not doubt the fairness of their positions. In the face of different views of fairness by the parties to a case, the law establishes a common space for discussion and decision.

Chile was not afraid of the fairness of its case and the morality of its positions. This included Bolivia's interpretations of the war between Chile and Bolivia in the 19th century. But these interpretations – by themselves – did not constitute an objective basis for a decision for the Court.

This does not mean, however, that Chile refrained from resorting to historical arguments. Indeed, the Vienna Convention on the Law of Treaties recognizes the role of historical arguments in the context of the rules of interpretation of treaty law. Accordingly, Chile restricted the use of historical material to the legal needs of demonstrating the scope and nature of the diplomatic exchanges with Bolivia, basically refusing to engage in arguments that would not fit a legal purpose. This contrasted with Bolivia's position, which made constant allusions to the conflict that existed between Chile and Bolivia that were not relevant to the case.

As noted above, in a comprehensive defence, the political components could have a role, especially in international organizations and in communication campaigns aimed towards national and international public opinion. Accordingly, it is valuable for a legal defence team to contribute with solid legal arguments to the decision-making process of the national political authorities to ensure a full understanding of the elements of the case that may be at stake.

4.8 *Staying on Course*

Chile's objectives, however, did not exclude addressing inappropriate historical allusions or exaggerations before the ICJ. This was particularly important in the closing arguments transmitted in real time to Chile and Bolivia.

Chile had to respond to Bolivia's assertions, presenting Chile as a State that "imprisoned" Bolivia and was "guilty" of Bolivia's problems. As mentioned before, the public nature of the proceedings, the standing of a State before international public opinion, and the internal political needs of a defence required straightening the record and preserving Chile's legitimacy as a reliable actor who acted in good faith in its exchanges with Bolivia throughout history.

5 Conclusions: The Judgment and Its Impact

As has been said, the Court rejected Bolivia's lawsuit in its entirety, by 12 votes against 3. The majority included: President Yusuf, Vice-President Xue, Judges

Tomka, Abraham, Bennouna, Cançado Trinidade, Donoghue, Gaja, Sebutinde, Bhandari, Gevorgian; and *ad hoc* Judge McRae. The minority, in dissent, included: Judges Robinson, Salam and *ad hoc* Judge Daudet.[56]

The ICJ's decision produces *res judicata* and is unappealable. Specifically, in the Chile-Bolivia relationship, it has enormous transcendental impact. As a result of the ruling, there is no legally pending issue between Chile and Bolivia concerning sovereign access for that State. There is no obligation to negotiate of any kind and there is also no basis for questioning the value of the 1904 Treaty.

From the point of view of international relations, the value of international law has been reiterated, as well as the content of the obligation to negotiate, reaffirming and creating a valuable space to preserve diplomacy. The ruling has also demonstrated the valuable role of the International Court of Justice in interpreting the law.

It is hoped that, as a result of this ruling, the relationship of Chile and Bolivia will be centred on the satisfaction of the common interests of both peoples in all possible areas, without question to the territorial integrity and sovereignty of both countries, which is a necessary basis to develop a relationship of friendship and brotherhood.

56 On the dissents of Judges Robinson, Salam, and Ad Hoc Judge Daudet, See *Bolivia v. Chile, ICJ Reports 2018,* 507, 569–621.

CHAPTER 8

The Law-Making Effect of ICJ Advisory Opinions

A Survey of the Chagos Opinion

Giulia Bernabei

1 Introduction

On 25 February 2019, the International Court of Justice ("ICJ" or "the Court") delivered its advisory opinion on 'Legal Consequences of the Separation of the Chagos Archipelago from Mauritius in 1965'[1] ("*Chagos Opinion*"). Multiple legal issues came into play, including questions of self-determination and State responsibility. This chapter considers the *Chagos Opinion*, and other selected ICJ advisory opinions, for their law-making significance.

The assumption that advisory opinions lack a binding character is correct,[2] as they are designed to provide guidance to the requesting UN organ or specialised agency, not compelling judgments.[3] But it would be oversimplifying matters to infer from this that advisory opinions do not have authoritative force,[4] a '*de facto* authority',[5] which enables them to inform the advancement of the international legal order. A law-making activity should be interpreted in an expansive way, as to include also instruments which, despite not being formal procedures as such, do in fact contribute to the substantive evolution of law.[6] Even though the advisory activity of the ICJ is lower, in terms of number, compared to its predecessor, the Permanent Court of International Justice

---

1 *Legal Consequences of the Separation of the Chagos Archipelago from Mauritius in 1965, Advisory Opinion of 25 February 2019, ICJ Reports 2019*, 95. Unless otherwise stated, sources were up-to-date until 16 December 2020. The author has however updated some case-law and materials until March 2021.

2 See K. Oellers-Frahm, 'Lawmaking through Advisory Opinions', 12 *German Law Journal* (2011)1033, at 1047–1050.

3 E.g. *Legality of the Threat or Use of Nuclear Weapons, Advisory Opinion of 8 July 1996, ICJ Reports 1996*, 226, para 15.

4 Oellers-Frahm, *supra* note 2, at 1050–1052.

5 *South West Africa (Ethiopia v. South Africa; Liberia v. South Africa), Second Phase, Judgment of 18 July 1966, ICJ Reports 1996*, 6, Dissenting Opinion of Judge Tanaka at 261; see also: *Interpretation of Peace Treaties, First Phase, Advisory Opinion of 30 March 1950, ICJ Reports 1950*, 65, Dissenting Opinion of Judge Winiarski, at 91.

6 See Oellers-Frahm, *supra* note 2, at 1052–1054.

© KONINKLIJKE BRILL NV, LEIDEN, 2022 | DOI:10.1163/9789004467668_012

(PCIJ),[7] its advisory function remains conceived so as to promote respect for international law.[8]

Through an analysis of literature,[9] this contribution explores the extent to which these opinions impact international law. The approach is chronological and teleological at the same time: what considerations can arise from the *Chagos Opinion* and from the developments it ensued?

2 The Law-Making Effect of Advisory Opinions

The law-making role of the ICJ is nowadays widely accepted.[10] Despite the suggestion of a dichotomy between *legal development* (the advancement of already existing international rules – acceptable) and *law-making* (the creation of new international norms – not acceptable), the author concurs with C. J. Tams' view[11] that in practice it is very difficult to distinguish the two.[12] A court is not a legislator[13] but it does assist the development of international law. In light of this, the *law-making* effect includes every way in which a court can possibly enhance the advancement of international law.

7 E.g. Oellers-Frahm, *supra* note 2, at 1035, with two more advisory opinions delivered after the publication of the article by Oellers-Frahm in 2011.

8 L. Boisson de Chazournes, 'Advisory Opinions and the Furtherance of the Common Interest of Mankind', in L. Boisson de Chazournes, C. P. R. Romano, *et al.* (eds.), *International Organization and International Dispute Settlement – Trends and Prospects* (2002), 105 and throughout the whole chapter.

9 Oellers-Frahm, *supra* note 2, at 1035; J. A. Frowein and K. Oellers-Frahm, 'Article 65' in A. Zimmermann, K. Oellers-Frahm, C. Tomuschat, *et al.* (eds.), The Statute of the International Court of Justice. A Commentary (2012), 1606, at 1621–1623; P. d'Argent, 'Article 65' in A. Zimmermann,, C. J. Tams, K. Oellers-Frahm, *et al.* (eds.), *The Statute of the International Court of Justice. A Commentary* (2019), 1783 at 1808–1810; L. Boisson de Chazournes, *supra* note 8, 105; Y. Shany, 'No Longer a Weak Department of Power? Reflections on the Enforcement of a New International Judiciary', 20 *European Journal of International Law* (2009) 73 at 77; T. F. Mayr and J. Mayr-Singer, 'Keep the Wheels Spinning: The Contributions of Advisory Opinions of the International Court of Justice to the Development of International Law', 76 ZaöRV (2016) 425 at 426.

10 E.g. A. Pellet and D. Müller, 'Article 38', in A. Zimmermann, C. J. Tams, K. Oellers-Frahm, *et al.* (eds.), *The Statute of the International Court of Justice. A Commentary* (2019), 819 at 954–961, who also mention the contribution of the Court to the evolution of international law through its advisory function, particularly at 958.

11 C. J. Tams, 'The Development of International Law by the International Court of Justice', in *Decisions of the ICJ as Sources of International Law? Gaetano Morelli Lectures Series (Vol. 2-2018)* (International and European Papers Publishing, 2018), 63 at 67-69.

12 See also Mayr and Mayr-Singer, *supra* note 9, at 431–434.

13 *Ibid.*, at 434–436.

The normative framework of the ICJ advisory function is set out in Article 96 of the UN Charter,[14] Articles 102–109 of the Rules of the Court[15] and Articles 65–68 of the ICJ Statute.[16] However, none of these provisions concern the effects that those opinions have on the international legal order. To some extent, these rules inherited the approach set out by Article 14 of the Covenant of the League of Nations[17] for the PCIJ, albeit they restricted their field of application to legal questions only.

The role of advisory opinions has attracted the attention of international jurists since the PCIJ was entitled to deliver them.[18] Albeit those opinions not being binding and not having *res judicata* effects,[19] with the doctrine of *stare decisis* being inapplicable,[20] academics and judges acknowledged that they carry some weight for the international system.[21] The legal effects of advisory opinions can be placed in two categories. On the one hand, advisory opinions can guide the action of the UN organs requesting them and also affect the subsequent decision-making power and activity of State entities.[22] The UN

14 1945 Charter of the United Nations 1 UNTS XVI, Article 96.

15 1978 Rules of Court (amendment entered into force 14 April 2005) ICJ Acts and Documents No. 6 (2007), 91.

16 1945 Statute of the International Court of Justice, annexed to the UN Charter, Ch XIV, 33 UNTS 933.

17 1919 Treaty of Peace concluded at Versailles, Covenant of the League of Nations, 225 CTS 188.

18 E.g. E. Hambro, 'The Authority of the Advisory Opinions of the International Court of Justice', 3 *ICLQ* (1954) 2; see also: P. Benvenuti, *L'accertamento del diritto mediante i pareri consultivi della Corte Internazionale di Giustizia* (Giuffrè, 1985); Sir F. Berman, 'The International Court of Justice as an 'Agent' of Legal Development?', in C. J. Tams and J. Sloan (eds.), *The Development of International Law by the International Court of Justice* (OUP, 2013), 7 at 13–16. On the 'Precedential value of advisory opinions', e.g. M. Shahabuddeen, *Precedent in the World Court* (CUP, 1996), at 165–171; for a discussion on whether advisory opinions can have *res judicata* effects, e.g. I. Scobbie, '*Res Judicata*, Precedent and the International Court: A Preliminary Sketch' (1999) 20 *Aust YBIL* 299, particularly at 312–314.

19 Mayr and Mayr-Singer, *supra* note 9, at 429.

20 M. M. Aljaghoub, *The Advisory Function of the International Court of Justice 1946 – 2005* (Springer, 2006) 117.

21 Frowein and Oellers-Frahm, *supra* note 9, at 1621–1622; d'Argent, *supra* note 9, at 1808–1811; see also: *Interpretation of Peace Treaties Opinion*, *supra* note 5, Separate Opinion of Judge Azevedo, para. 3.

22 Frowein and Oellers-Frahm, *supra* note 9, at 1621–1622 and 1628; for example, *Reparation for Injuries Suffered in the Service of the United Nations, Advisory Opinion of 11 April 1949, ICJ Reports 1949*, 174; *Certain Expenses of the United Nations (Article 17, para. 2, of the Charter), Advisory Opinion of 20 July 1962, ICJ Reports 1962*, 151.

General Assembly ("UNGA") is especially responsive to advisory opinions that it requests to the Court and tends to adopt resolutions in compliance with the Court's directions.[23] On the other hand, advisory opinions can in fact contribute to the development of international legal norms, where they make direct pronouncements on international legal questions.[24] The utility of this distinction remains, however, a mere theoretical exercise, as some opinions, e.g. the *Certain Expenses Opinion*,[25] might fall under both categories.

Additional effects may be found in some specific treaties or acts of international organizations which refer to the authority of advisory opinions in the settlement of legal disputes before their own judicial tribunals.[26] The abovementioned legal effects do not involve those that were once produced by opinions rendered pursuant to Article XII of the Statute of the Administrative Tribunal of the International Labour Organization, which has now been removed from the text of the Statute.[27]

---

23 Frowein and Oellers-Frahm, *supra* note 9, at 1621–1622; see: UNGA, Admission of New Members, Res. 197 (A) (III) (1948); UNGA, Advisory opinion of the International Court of Justice on the legality of the threat or use of nuclear weapons, Res. A/RES/51/45 M (1996); UNGA, Advisory opinion of the International Court of Justice on the legal consequences of the construction of a wall in the occupied Palestinian territory, including in and around East Jerusalem, Res. A/RES/ES-10/15 (2004); UNGA, Request for an advisory opinion of the International Court of Justice on whether the unilateral declaration of independence of Kosovo is in accordance with international law, Res. A/RES/64/298 (2010).

24 Frowein and Oellers-Frahm, *supra* note 9, at 1622 and 1628; ee: *Reservations to the Convention on the Prevention and Punishment of the Crime of Genocide, Advisory Opinion of 28 May 1951, ICJ Reports 1951*, 15; *Reparation for Injuries Opinion, supra* note 22; *Certain Expenses Opinion, supra* note 22; *Legal Consequences for States of the Continued Presence of South Africa in Namibia (South West Africa) notwithstanding Security Council Resolution 276 (1970), Advisory Opinion of 21 June 1971, ICJ Reports 1971*, 16; *Nuclear Weapons Opinion, supra* note 3. See also d'Argent, *supra* note 9, at 1808–1811.

25 *Certain Expenses Opinion, supra* note 22.

26 Frowein and Oellers-Frahm, *supra* note 9, at 1622; d'Argent, *supra* note 9, at 1810; see also: Roberto Ago, '"Binding" Advisory Opinions of the International Court of Justice', (1991) 85 AJIL 439; cf.: *Difference relating to Immunity from Legal Process of a Special Rapporteur of the Commission on Human Rights, Advisory Opinion of 29 April 1999, ICJ Reports 1999*, 62.

27 Statute of the Administrative Tribunal of the International Labour Organization (adopted by the International Labour Conference on 9 October 1946 and last amended on 17 June 2019). Article XII was removed with the IX Resolution on 7 June 2016. For the text currently in force: https://www.ilo.org/tribunal/about-us/WCMS_249194/lang--en/index.htm (accessed 27 December 2020). See also *Judgment No. 2867 of the Administrative Tribunal of the International Labour Organization upon a Complaint Filed against the International Fund for Agricultural Development, Advisory Opinion of 1 February 2012, ICJ Reports 2012*, 10; Frowein and Oellers-Frahm, *supra* note 9, at 1622–1623; d'Argent, *supra* note 9, at 1810.

3 The Stance of the ICJ in Relation to Selected Advisory Opinions

This section briefly addresses three advisory opinions which considerably affected the international legal order, namely: the *Namibia*,[28] the *Wall*[29] and the *Kosovo*[30] opinions.

3.1 *The* Namibia Opinion

In the *Namibia Opinion*, the ICJ ascertained: the illegality of the continued presence of South Africa in Namibia and the obligation of South Africa to withdraw its administration immediately and put an end to its occupation;[31] the obligation of other UN member States to recognise the illegality of South Africa's presence in the Namibian territory and the invalidity of acts of South Africa on behalf of or concerning Namibia and the obligation of those States to refrain from any act recognizing or assisting such administration;[32] and that it was incumbent upon non-UN member States to assist the UN accordingly.[33]

When called upon to advise upon States' obligations, the ICJ determined the legality of a State's action towards another State within the international framework. While States cannot infer their legal obligations *sic et simpliciter* from the Court's advisory opinions, the Court's detailed analysis on the legal consequences of the illegality of a State's action shows that those opinions can have, at the very least, a justifying effect for international subjects acting in accordance with them.[34]

3.2 *The* Wall Opinion

In the *Wall Opinion*, the Court stated that: the construction of the Wall built by Israel on the Occupied Palestinian Territory infringed international law;[35] Israel was under an obligation to terminate those breaches[36] and to make reparation for the damage caused;[37] all States had an obligation not to recognise

---

28 *Namibia Opinion, supra* note 24.

29 *Legal Consequences of the Construction of a Wall in the Occupied Palestinian Territory, Advisory Opinion of 9 July 2004, ICJ Reports 2004*, 136.

30 *Accordance with international law of the unilateral declaration of independence in respect of Kosovo, Advisory Opinion of 22 July 2010 ICJ Reports 2010*, 403.

31 *Namibia Opinion, supra* note 24, para. 133 (1).

32 *Ibid.*, para. 133 (2).

33 *Ibid.*, para. 133 (3).

34 Frowein and Oellers-Frahm, *supra* note 9, at 1624.

35 *Wall Opinion, supra* note 29, para. 163 (3) (A).

36 *Ibid.*, para. 163 (3) (B).

37 *Ibid.*, para. 163 (3) (C).

the situation as legal and not to render aid or assistance in maintaining it; and States Parties to the Fourth Geneva Convention Relative to the Protection of Civilian Persons in Time of War[38] bore the additional obligation to ensure that Israel complied with international humanitarian law.[39]

While it has been argued that the ICJ ruling did not create legally effective obligations upon the State of Israel,[40] its stance had an impact on the subsequent posture of the Supreme Court of Israel, whose reasoning relied heavily on the ICJ Opinion.[41] As for other States, the Court explained in depth the legal consequences for States which contravened its assessment.[42] As noted by Judge Higgins, 'although it is found in the context of an advisory opinion rather than in a contentious case, the Court's position as the principal judicial organ of the United Nations suggests that the legal consequence for a finding that an act or situation is illegal is the same'.[43] The effect of this advisory opinion can be said to have, at least, reached the intensity of the *Namibia Opinion*: if it cannot be claimed that they *created* State obligations, their justifying effect of the merits has to be upheld.[44] Furthermore, this opinion also gave rise to the question of the lawfulness of countermeasures based on advisory opinions, particularly when the Court qualifies the original violation as having an *erga omnes* character.[45]

3.3 *The* Kosovo Opinion

In the *Kosovo Opinion*, faced with the question of the legality of the declaration of independence of Kosovo adopted on 17 February 2008, the Court opined that the declaration had not violated international law.[46]

In this instance, the ICJ confined itself to a formalistic appreciation of the declaration of independence, without scrutinising the legality of the acts

38 1949 Geneva Convention Relative to the Protection of Civilian Persons in Time of War (Fourth Geneva Convention) 75 UNTS 287.

39 *Wall Opinion*, *supra* note 29, para. 163 (3) (D).

40 Frowein and Oellers-Frahm, *supra* note 9, at 1624–1625 and 1629.

41 See: Israeli Supreme Court, HCJ 7957/04, *Zaharan Yunis Muhammad Mara'abe et al. v. The Prime Minister of Israel et al.*, 15 September 2005, para. 56: 'The opinion of the ICJ [...] is not *res judicata* [...]. However, [it] is an interpretation of international law, performed by the highest judicial body in international law [...] [and] should be given its full appropriate weight.' and paras. 37–74.

42 *Wall Opinion*, *supra* note 29, paras. 154–159; see also: Frowein, Oellers-Frahm, *supra* note 9, at 1625.

43 *Wall Opinion*, *supra* note 29, Separate Opinion of Judge Higgins, para. 38.

44 Frowein and Oellers-Frahm, *supra* note 9, at 1625–1626.

45 *Ibid.*, at 1627.

46 *Kosovo Opinion*, *supra* note 30, para. 123 (3).

which underlay it.[47] This has been explained by academics as an attempt of the Court to narrow down the scope of its advisory opinions, to prevent their extensive reading.[48] It has also been remarked on various fronts that the Court interpreted the question put to it 'merely [as] a question of prohibition',[49] somehow reiterating the application of the PCIJ *Lotus* principle.[50] As in the *Wall Opinion*, the *Kosovo Opinion* concerned the international relations of two States or other international entities.[51] This places the opinion onto a field which, in some respects, might appear to be closer to the settlement of legal disputes, rather than the exercise of an advisory function, whose purpose is not to resolve contentious cases.

4 The *Chagos Opinion* in Retrospect

On 22 June 2017, the UNGA adopted Res. 71/292[52] by which it requested the ICJ to deliver an advisory opinion on: a) whether '"the process of decolonization of Mauritius [was] lawfully completed when Mauritius was granted independence in 1968, [...] having regard to international law"'[53] and b) '"the consequences [...] arising from the continued administration by the United Kingdom [...] of the Chagos Archipelago"'.[54] Various international subjects submitted written statements, written comments, written replies to questions put by some judges and written comments to them and presented oral statements to the Court.[55]

47 Frowein and Oellers-Frahm, *supra* note 9, at 1626–1627.

48 *Ibid.*, at 1629; see also: R. Falk, 'The Kosovo Advisory Opinion: Conflict Resolution and Precedent', 105 *AJIL* (2011) 50 at 51.

49 Frowein and Oellers-Frahm, *supra* note 9, at 1626–1627; see: *Kosovo Opinion*, supra note 30, Declaration of Judge Simma, para. 2 and *Kosovo Opinion*, supra note 30, para. 84.

50 *The S.S. Lotus case* (*France v. Turkey*), PCIJ Publications, Series A No 10 (1927), especially at 18–20; Frowein and Oellers-Frahm, *supra* note 9, at 1626–1627.

51 Frowein and Oellers-Frahm, *supra* note 9, at 1628.

52 UNGA, Request for an advisory opinion of the International Court of Justice on the legal consequences of the separation of the Chagos Archipelago from Mauritius in 1965, Res. A/RES/71/292 (2017).

53 *Chagos Opinion*, *supra* note 1, para. 1.

54 *Ibid.*, para. 1.

55 For the written proceedings: https://www.icj-cij.org/en/case/169/written-proceedings; for the written replies to questions put by some judges and written comments to them: https://www.icj-cij.org/en/case/169/other-documents; for the oral statements: https://www.icj-cij.org/en/case/169/oral-proceedings (accessed 31 March 2021).

In the opinion, having established its jurisdiction,[56] the Court turned to the question of discretion[57] and concluded that it was entitled to deliver an advisory opinion.[58] The ICJ added that '[i]t [was] for the Court to state the law applicable to the factual situation [...] [without the] need for it to interpret restrictively the questions put to it by the [UNGA]'[59] As to the first question, the Court: 1) defined the relevant period of time as that elapsing between 'the separation of the Chagos Archipelago from its territory in 1965 and its independence in 1968';[60] and 2) circumscribed the applicable international law to the law on self-determination;[61] 3) qualified the action of the UNGA to invite the United Kingdom ("UK") to comply with its international obligations as being within its mandate and scope;[62] and 4) deemed the process of decolonisation of Mauritius as not lawfully completed when Mauritius acceded to independence in 1968.[63] As for the second question, the UK's continued administration of the Chagos Archipelago was qualified by the Court as a wrongful act entailing: the UK's international responsibility[64] and the UK's obligation to terminate its administration of the territory as soon as possible.[65] According to the ICJ, it was upon the entire international community to cooperate with the modalities chosen by the UNGA.[66]

The *Chagos Opinion* seems to corroborate the thesis that the ICJ takes the advisory function as an opportunity to clarify and possibly expand upon the form and substance of international law. Three arguments support this view. First, reasoning *a contrario*, it is highly unlikely that a pronouncement – even if advisory in nature – of the principal judicial organ of the UN does not produce effects on the international community. An ICJ product possesses a connotation of authoritativeness which its lack of binding force cannot deprive of. Second, and as highlighted by the declarations and a dissenting opinion appended by some judges,[67] there is a risk that advisory proceedings are

56 *Chagos Opinion, supra* note 1, paras 55–62.
57 *Ibid.*, paras. 63–68.
58 *Ibid.*, paras. 69–91.
59 *Ibid.*, para. 137.
60 *Ibid.*, paras. 140–143, particularly para. 140.
61 *Ibid.*, paras. 144–161, particularly para. 161.
62 *Ibid.*, paras. 163–169, particularly para. 167.
63 *Ibid.*, paras. 170–174, particularly para. 174.
64 *Ibid.*, para. 177.
65 *Ibid.*, para. 178.
66 *Ibid.*, paras. 175–182, particularly paras. 179–180.
67 *Ibid.*, Declaration of Vice-President Xue, para. 4; Declaration of Judge Tomka, para. 2; Dissenting Opinion of Judge Donoghue, paras. 1–3 and 21; Declaration of Judge Gevorgian, paras. 3–5.

triggered in order to bring contentious matters before the Court, circumventing States' consent.[68] To acknowledge this risk implies acceptance that, in practice, advisory opinions can impact international law. Third, even assuming that the *Chagos Opinion* did not concern a dispute pending between two States, the Court took a very precise position on several international legal issues, as did the judges individually, and a well-reasoned opinion might arguably unfold tangible effects.[69]

With 116 votes in favour, 6 against and 56 abstentions,[70] on 22 May 2019 the UNGA adopted Res. 73/295,[71] by which it welcomed the ICJ opinion, reiterated its core statements and also embraced a proactive approach urging the UK, *inter alia*, to withdraw its colonial administration within six months[72] and to cooperate with Mauritius in facilitating the resettlement of Mauritian nationals in the Chagos Archipelago.[73] This resolution voiced a precise stance of the UNGA, suggesting legal effects triggered by the advisory opinion. The robust opposition to the adoption of this resolution manifested by the UK[74] also seems to weigh in favour of the law-making effect of the ICJ advisory opinions. In fact, when the UK called for an international resistance to the passing of the

---

68 R. Higgins, 'A comment on the current health of Advisory Opinions', in V. Lowe and M. Fitzmaurice (eds)., *Fifty Years of the International Court of Justice. Essays in Honour of Sir Robert Jennings* (CUP, 1996), 567 at 571. For a discussion on the absence of State consent in ICJ advisory opinions: M. M. Aljaghoub, 'The Absence of State Consent to Advisory Opinions of the International Court of Justice: Judicial and Political Restraints' 24 *Arab LQ* (2010) 191.

69 *Chagos Opinion, supra* note 1, Declaration of Vice-President Xue; Declarations of Judges Tomka and Abraham; Separate Opinion of Judge Cançado Trindade; Joint Declaration of Judges Cançado Trindade and Robinson; Dissenting Opinion of Judge Donoghue; Separate Opinions of Judges Gaja, Sebutinde and Robinson; Declarations of Judges Gevorgian, Salam and Iwasawa.

70 UNGA, Request for an advisory opinion of the International Court of Justice on the legal consequences of the separation of the Chagos Archipelago from Mauritius in 1965, Official Records, Seventy-third session, A/73/PV.83 (2019), at 25.

71 UNGA, Advisory opinion of the International Court of Justice on the legal consequences of the separation of the Chagos Archipelago from Mauritius in 1965, Res. A/Res/73/295 (2019).

72 *Ibid.*, para. 3.

73 *Ibid.*, para. 4.

74 UNGA Official Records, A/73/PV.83, *supra* note 70, United Kingdom, at 9–11 and at 25. For an analysis of the UK's response to the *Chagos Opinion*, see also: T. Burri, 'In the Wake of the ICJ's Opinion in Chagos: Britannia Waives the Rules', *Völkerrechtsblog*, 9 July 2019: https://voelkerrechtsblog.org/articles/in-the-wake-of-the-icjs-opinion-in-chagos-britannia-waives-the-rules/ (accessed 21 December 2020).

resolution and downplayed the legal effects of advisory opinions,[75] it gave the impression to have acknowledged and echoed their reach.

5 The *Chagos Opinion* in Prospect

More than two years have elapsed since the ICJ delivered its *Chagos Opinion.* Not just the States involved in the advisory proceedings, but the whole international legal community, have had time to distil the opinion in granular detail. Academics recognised that this opinion played a significant role in the advancement of issues such as self-determination[76] and territorial integrity.[77] In practice, however, the UK has not withdrawn from the Chagos Archipelago within the six-month time-limit as instead requested by the UNGA.[78]

On 15 October 2019, delegates in the UNGA Fourth Committee (especially Mauritius and South Africa) called upon the UK to comply with the advisory opinion by the deadline of 22 November 2019.[79]

On 18 May 2020, the UN Secretary-General published a report on the implementation of the *Chagos Opinion*[80] whereby Mauritius complained about the UK's failure to comply with the advisory opinion and the UNGA resolution,[81] also upheld by Argentina,[82] and the UK reiterated its previous

75 UNGA Official Records, A/73/PV.83, *supra* note 70, United Kingdom, at 11.

76 S. Allen, 'Self-Determination, the *Chagos Advisory Opinion* and the Chagossians', 69 *ICLQ* (2020) 203; P. Weismann, 'Peoples' Right to Self-Determination. The Case of the Chagos Archipelago', 21 *International Community Law Review* (2019) 463.

77 R. McCorquodale, J. Robinson and N. Peart, 'Territorial Integrity and Consent in the Chagos Advisory Opinion', 69 *ICLQ* (2020), 221.

78 UNGA Res. A/Res/73/295, *supra* note 71, paras. 3 and 4.

79 UNGA, 'Delegates Call upon United Kingdom to Comply with Ruling by International Court of Justice that Chagos Archipelago's Decolonization Was Never Lawfully Completed', Meetings Coverage, Fourth Committee, Seventy-fourth session, GA/SPD/696 (2019): https://www.un.org/press/en/2019/gaspd696.doc.htm (accessed 27 December 2020).

80 UNGA, Report of the Secretary-General, Advisory opinion of the International Court of Justice on the legal consequences of the separation of the Chagos Archipelago from Mauritius in 1965, A/74/834 (2020).

81 *Ibid.*, at 5–14 and particularly at 12, para. v.

82 *Ibid.*, at 3–5. See also Argentina's point on the pivotal role of the UNGA and its advisory committees in the decolonization processes: UNGA, 'Delegates Urge Administering Powers to Fulfil Obligations Under Decolonization Declaration, as Fourth Committee Continues Joint General Debate', Meetings Coverage, Fourth Committee, Seventy-fifth session, GA/SPD/721 (2020): https://www.un.org/press/en/2020/gaspd721.doc.htm (accessed 27 December 2020).

stance,[83] with the 'unequivocal support' of the United States.[84]

On 30 July 2020, the Court of Appeal of England and Wales dismissed the appeal of some Chagossians concerning their resettlement to the Chagos Islands[85] and delivered a judgment which allegedly did 'not enter the debate which arises at the international level'[86] but at the same time observed that '[w]hilst it is accordingly correct to say that [the advisory opinion] sets out the view of the ICJ upon the law it is not intended to have binding effect. It is for the requesting organ of the UN, here the General Assembly, to set out what it considers to be the consequences of the law as expressed in the Advisory Opinion, assuming of course that the General Assembly accepts that opinion.'[87] Two points stem from these remarks: i) it is somewhat hard to understand why the very body which requests the advisory opinion would not accept it once it is rendered by the Court; and ii) in the present case, the UNGA had indeed taken action to align with the *Chagos Opinion* and the UK has not conformed with such action.

On 15 October 2020, again in the UNGA Fourth Committee, the UK emphasised that it 'would cede sovereignty over the Chagos Archipelago to Mauritius when that Territory is no longer required for defence purposes'.[88] The *Chagos Opinion* has already attracted much attention from the international legal scholarship and will unsurprisingly inspire a wealth of literature.[89] For the many interests at stake, the matter is quite naturally prone to politicisation.[90]

---

83 UNGA, Report of the Secretary-General, A/74/834, *supra* note 80, at 14–17 particularly at 14–15.

84 *Ibid.*, at 17–18.

85 *R (Hoareau and Bancoult (No. 5)) v. Secretary of State for Foreign & Commonwealth Affairs* [2020] EWCA Civ 1010, para. 184. For a thorough analysis: P. Webb, 'The United Kingdom and The Chagos Archipelago Advisory Opinion: Engagement and Resistance' (forthcoming 2021) *Melbourne Journal of International Law*.

86 *R (Hoareau and Bancoult (No. 5)) v. Secretary of State for Foreign & Commonwealth Affairs* [2020] EWCA Civ 1010, para. 139.

87 *Ibid.*, para. 113.

88 UNGA, 'Speakers Urge Fulfilment of Decolonization Agenda, End to Israel's Impunity in Occupied Palestinian Territories, as Fourth Committee Continues Debate', Meetings Coverage, Fourth Committee, Seventy-fifth session, GA/SPD/718 (2020): https://www.un.org/press/en/2020/gaspd718.doc.htm (accessed 27 December 2020). On Mauritius' reaction: BBC news, 'Chagos Islands dispute: Mauritius calls US and UK 'hypocrites'', 19 October 2020: https://www.bbc.com/news/world-africa-54598084 (accessed 21 December 2020).

89 E.g. T. Burri and J. Trinidad (eds.), *The International Court of Justice and Decolonisation. New Directions from the Chagos Advisory Opinion* (CUP, 2021).

90 For a discussion from the perspective of transnational legal theory: S. Minas, 'Why the ICJ's Chagos Archipelago advisory opinion matters for global justice – and for 'Global Britain'', 10 *Transnational Legal Theory* (2019) 123.

The advisory opinion has affected the bilateral relations between Mauritius and the UK and, in a more far-reaching fashion, other multilateral relations across the globe. However, this chapter reflects on the consequences prompted by the opinion from a strictly legalistic perspective.

International scholars have discussed the UK's non-compliance with the ICJ Opinion and the UNGA legal advice[91] and some suggested that forceful States, especially those with veto power in the UN Security Council like the UK, will somehow find ways to avoid their legal obligations.[92] Issues such as States' responsibility and compliance remain focal and salient questions of contemporary international law. They go down to the roots of the whole system, its very mandate and essence. But these issues concern obligations of *all* kinds and arise from a more general discourse on the effectiveness of the international legal standards. As to ICJ advisory opinions, the *Chagos Opinion* example can lead to reflections as to whether, despite not being *per se* legally binding, they can produce legal effects and urge States to adopt certain measures in practice. Whether or not States conform to such legal effects remains a distinct issue.

Indeed, the effects of advisory opinions cannot be assessed only *a posteriori* in light of States' compliance with them. In theory, State's deference to an ICJ advisory opinion shows that the opinion can produce effects on the legal plane. But a State's disinclination, let alone its defiance, to abide by an ICJ advisory opinion cannot deprive it of its legal reach. In other words, both from a chronological and a logical perspective, the legal consequences produced by an advisory opinion remain independent from the State's (non-)observance of those very consequences. Additionally, advisory opinions' impact should be appraised not only with a view to international actors directly concerned by the opinion as such, rather with regard to the whole of the international community.[93]

On 28 January 2021, the International Tribunal for the Law of the Sea ("ITLOS" or "the Tribunal") delivered a judgment in the preliminary objections phase of the Mauritius/Maldives dispute,[94] by which it affirmed its jurisdiction

---

91 *Ex multis*: Webb, *supra* note 85; Allen, *supra* note 76; Weismann, *supra* note 76; McCorquodale, Robinson and Peart, *supra* note 77.

92 G. Lythgoe, 'Asymmetrical international law and its role in constituting empires: the ICJ Chagos Advisory Opinion', 71 *NILQ* (2020) 305 at 315. See also G.J. Naldi, 'Self-Determination in Light of the International Court of Justice's Opinion in the Chagos Case', 7 *Groningen Journal of International Law* (2020) 216, at 232–235, discussing possible developments at the UK's end.

93 See Webb, *supra* note 85, discussing, *inter alia*, the consequences which unfolded from the *Chagos Opinion* in international, regional and domestic courts.

94 *Dispute concerning delimitation of the maritime boundary between Mauritius and Maldives in the Indian Ocean (Mauritius/Maldives)*, Preliminary Objections, Judgment of 28

over the delimitation of the maritime boundary.[95] Whilst acknowledging that advisory opinions do not bind the requesting entities in the same way as judgments compel parties to disputes, the Tribunal held that 'judicial determinations made in advisory opinions carry no less weight and authority than those in judgments because they are made with the same rigour and scrutiny by the "principal judicial organ" of the United Nations with competence in matters of international law'[96] and 'consider[ed] that those determinations do have legal effect'.[97] This is also supported by the ITLOS' reading of the UNGA Res. 73/295, which emphasized the fundamental role the UNGA had been 'entrusted'[98] with by the ICJ within Mauritius' process of decolonisation and determined its relevance for the assessment of the legal status of the Chagos Archipelago.[99] Accordingly, the ITLOS found that the ICJ had clarified the status of the Chagos Archipelago in its advisory opinion and did not uphold the Maldives' argument on the existence of a sovereignty dispute.[100] Judge *ad hoc* Oxman's Separate and Dissenting Opinion rejected the ITLOS' jurisdiction, detailing the distinction between the authoritative nature of an ICJ advisory opinion and binding legal effects and differentiating between the UNGA's competence and the legal effects of its resolutions.[101]

Mauritius urged the UK to comply with the ITLOS judgment's findings[102] while, in line with its previous position,[103] the UK rejected the ruling on the basis that it was not a party to the contentious proceedings.[104]

January 2021, ITLOS, List of Cases No. 28. For the developments: https://www.itlos.org/en/main/cases/list-of-cases/dispute-concerning-delimitation-of-the-maritime-boundary-between-mauritius-and-maldives-in-the-indian-ocean-mauritius/maldives/ (accessed 21 March 2021).

95 *Ibid.*, para. 354 (6).

96 *Ibid.*, para. 203.

97 *Ibid.*, para. 205 and, similarly, paras. 202, 204.

98 *Ibid.*, para. 227.

99 *Ibid.*, paras. 224–230.

100 *Ibid.*, paras. 242–245.

101 *Ibid.*, Separate and Dissenting Opinion of Judge *ad hoc* Oxman, paras. 27–33, particularly para. 27. Judges *ad hoc* Oxman and Schrijver also appended a Joint Declaration.

102 P. Wintour, 'UN court rejects UK claim to Chagos Islands in favour of Mauritius', 28 January 2021, The Guardian: https://www.theguardian.com/world/2021/jan/28/un-court-rejects-uk-claim-to-chagos-islands-in-favour-of-mauritius, (accessed 22 March 2021).

103 For a recollection: UK Parliament, House of Commons Library, C. Mills, Briefing Paper Number 9134, 'Disputes over the British Indian Ocean Territory: February 2021 update', 8 February 2021, at 5, 15–23: https://commonslibrary.parliament.uk/research-briefings/cbp-9134/ (accessed 22 March 2021).

104 *Ibid.*, at 5, 14 and 24–27.

In any event, the ITLOS statements that '[t]he [ICJ's] determinations [in the *Chagos Opinion*] have legal effect and clear implications for the legal status of the Chagos Archipelago', that 'Mauritius' sovereignty [...] can be inferred from' them and that the UK's non-compliance with the UNGA resolution 'is contrary to the authoritative determinations made in the advisory opinion'[105] seem to support the law-making effects of ICJ advisory opinions.[106]

6 Conclusions

For the general public, law might be conceived as *a given* imposed from the above, an unintelligible technicality, a formalistic superstructure which burdens all but remains a prerogative of very few. In fact, law – and public international law especially – is the result of a process:[107] it evolves through some sort of metamorphosis, precisely because it is affected by historical and social changes. It is the practice of international actors which creates international law, rather than international law being established before – and without – them.

A court – any court, but the ICJ in particular – remains a judicial body even when it performs advisory functions.[108] Its opinions might not produce immediate binding effects upon States and other international subjects; they do, however, play an active part in the administration of international justice and in the development of international law.[109] This is so for two main reasons: i) they remain an expression, a legal determination of the very *forum*, the ICJ, which is entitled to render judgments on international legal matters;[110] and ii) they must be considered, at the very least, subsidiary means of international law under Article 38 (1) (d) of the ICJ Statute.[111]

---

105 *ITLOS judgment*, *supra* note 94, para. 246.

106 For a critique: S. Thin, 'The Curious Case of the 'Legal Effect' of ICJ Advisory Opinions in the Mauritius/Maldives Maritime Boundary Dispute', 5 February 2021, *EJIL:Talk!*: https://www.ejiltalk.org/the-curious-case-of-the-legal-effect-of-icj-advisory-opinions-in-the-mauritius-maldives-maritime-boundary-dispute/ (accessed 21 March 2021). For a further analysis: N. Klein, 'Chagos: A boundary dispute tips over a sovereignty ruling', 8 February 2021, *The Interpreter*: https://www.lowyinstitute.org/the-interpreter/chagos-boundary-dispute-tips-over-sovereignty-ruling (accessed 28 March 2021).

107 R. Higgins, *Problems and Process: International Law and How we use it* (OUP, 1994), 2–12; P. Webb, *International Judicial Integration and Fragmentation* (OUP, 2013), 4.

108 Pellet and Müller, *supra* note 10, at 839.

109 Aljaghoub, *supra* note 20, 155–200.

110 See Oellers-Frahm, supra note 2, at 1046.

111 ICJ Statute, *supra* note 16, Article 38 (1) (d); see also: Oellers-Frahm, *supra* note 2, at 1046; Pellet and Müller, *supra* note 10, at 837–839.

In a fictional world, where only formal sources could contribute to international law,[112] advisory opinions would be, at best, entrusted with an unspecified, limited role in a legal *vacuum*. In the real world, those opinions influence the trajectory of international law from the inside. They can impact international law in principle but, more importantly, they are capable of doing so in practice.

112 Cf. Oellers-Frahm, *supra* note 2, at 1054, 1055.

CHAPTER 9

"Know Thyself"

Racial Discrimination before the ICJ – Recent Jurisprudential Developments

Ioannis Konstantinidis

1 Introduction

Being the oldest United Nations human rights treaty and enjoying widespread participation, the International Convention on the Elimination of All Forms of Racial Discrimination (CERD or "the Convention") was adopted in 1965 and entered into force in 1969.[1] The Convention sets forth an overarching goal: the elimination of all forms of racial discrimination. In pursuit of this goal, the Convention requires States Parties to respect and protect fundamental human rights and the dignity of human beings against racial discrimination.

Article 22 of the Convention grants jurisdiction to the International Court of Justice (ICJ or "the Court") over any dispute regarding the interpretation or application of CERD "which is not settled by negotiation or by the procedures expressly provided for in this Convention."

Having fallen into oblivion for almost four decades, Article 22 has preoccupied the judges of the ICJ since 2008. After granting provisional measures in *Georgia v. Russian Federation*, the Court subsequently dismissed the case for want of jurisdiction.[2] Later, in 2017 and 2018 respectively, the ICJ granted provisional measures in *Ukraine v. Russian Federation*[3] and *Qatar v. United Arab Emirates*.[4] In June 2019, it rejected the request for the indication of provisional

1 International Convention on the Elimination of All Forms of Racial Discrimination (CERD), United Nations, Treaty Series, vol. 660, p. 195.

2 *Application of the International Convention on the Elimination of All Forms of Racial Discrimination (Georgia v. Russian Federation), Preliminary Objections, Judgment, ICJ Reports 2011*, p. 70.

3 *Application of the International Convention for the Suppression of the Financing of Terrorism and of the International Convention on the Elimination of All Forms of Racial Discrimination (Ukraine v. Russian Federation), Provisional Measures, Order of 19 April 2017, ICJ Reports 2017*, p. 104

4 *Application of the International Convention on the Elimination of All Forms of Racial Discrimination (Qatar v. United Arab Emirates), Provisional Measures Order of 23 July 2018.*

© KONINKLIJKE BRILL NV, LEIDEN, 2022 | DOI:10.1163/9789004467668_013

measures submitted by the respondent in the latter case.[5] In November 2019, the ICJ found that it has jurisdiction in *Ukraine v. Russian Federation* (*Preliminary Objections*).[6] The above-mentioned cases are still pending before the Court.

In the aforementioned instances, the ICJ has had the opportunity to deal with novel issues of law and partially elucidate certain abstruse aspects of CERD, thus contributing to the development of international human rights law. In light of its recent jurisprudence, this article sets out to present and assess the Court's contribution to the decipherment of the Convention. In particular, it focuses only on a limited number of topical issues as they have emerged in the aforementioned cases: the scope *ratione materiae* of the Convention and the concept of 'national origin', the alternative or cumulative character of Article 22 preconditions for the seisin of the Court and the exhaustion of local remedies as precondition for admissibility of inter-State claims of breach of CERD.

2 The Scope *Ratione Materiae* of CERD and the Meaning of *National Origin*

The present section aims at introducing the complex issue of the scope *ratione materiae* of CERD. The analysis focuses on a specific issue that arose in the context of *Qatar v. United Arab Emirates* (*Provisional Measures and Preliminary Objections*). In its Order on Provisional Measures in the present case, the Court summarized the parties' diverging interpretations of the scope of CERD *ratione materiae* as follows:

> The Court considers that, while the Parties differ on the question whether the expression 'national origin' mentioned in Article 1, paragraph 1, of CERD, encompasses discrimination based on the 'present nationality' of the individual, the Court need not decide at this stage of the proceedings, in view of what is stated above, which of these diverging interpretations of the Convention is the correct one.[7]

---

5 *Application of the International Convention on the Elimination of All Forms of Racial Discrimination* (*Qatar v. United Arab Emirates*), *Provisional Measures Order of 14 June 2019*.

6 *Application of the International Convention for the Suppression of the Financing of Terrorism and of the International Convention on the Elimination of All Forms of Racial Discrimination* (*Ukraine v. Russian Federation*), *Preliminary Objections, Judgment, 8 November 2019*.

7 See *supra* note 4, para. 27. It is worth noting that the differing views on this point are underlined in several of the separate and dissenting opinions appended to the Provisional

Whether discrimination on the basis of a person's present nationality (as Qatar seems to have argued) is in breach of CERD certainly depends on the meaning and scope of the words 'national ... origin'.[8] Article 1 (1) of CERD defines racial discrimination as follows:

> ... the term 'racial discrimination' shall mean any distinction, exclusion, restriction or preference based on race, colour, descent, or *national* or ethnic *origin* which has the purpose or effect of nullifying or impairing the recognition, enjoyment or exercise, on an equal footing, of human rights and fundamental freedoms in the political, economic, social, cultural or any other field of public life.[9]

In other words, racial discrimination requires that the action or omission be based on certain grounds and have a certain purpose or effect with respect to the enjoyment of human rights and fundamental freedoms.[10]

Article 1 (2) and (3) present certain actions and omissions that would not be 'racial discrimination' for the purposes of CERD. Article 1 (2 and 3) states:

> 2. This Convention shall not apply to distinctions, exclusions, restrictions or preferences made by a State Party to this Convention between citizens and non-citizens.
>
> 3. Nothing in this Convention may be interpreted as affecting in any way the legal provisions of States Parties concerning *nationality*, citizenship or naturalization, provided that such provisions do not discriminate against *any particular nationality*.

The terms 'national origin' and 'nationality' have ignited interpretative debates during, and as well as since, the drafting of the Convention. As noted by P. Thornberry, the "fundamental ambiguity in 'national origin' and 'nationality'

Measures Order. See the joint declaration of Judges Tomka, Gaja and Gevorgian. See also the dissenting opinions of Judge Salam (paras. 3(a) and 5) and of Judge Crawford (para. 1).

8 The phrase 'present nationality' is not found in Convention. That said, the concept of 'present nationality' emerged as CERD's negotiators made proposals in order to clarify what kinds of discrimination the Convention would prohibit and what would remain outside the scope of the Convention entirely or addressed in exceptions to the general prohibition.

9 CERD, Article 1 (emphasis added).

10 Article 1(2) and (3) set out certain actions and omissions that – while otherwise falling within the definition in Article 1(1) – would not be 'racial discrimination' for the purposes of CERD. See CERD, Article 1(2 and 3).

is that the terms refer not only to legal nationality or citizenship but also to a concept of community in a spectrum that includes ethnicity."[11]

In order to clarify the meaning of the term 'national origin', recourse to the interpretation rules of the Vienna Convention on the Law of Treaties (VCLT) of 1969 is indispensable.[12] The following exploratory analysis proceeds in a manner likely to be followed by the ICJ in its pursuit to interpret the meaning of 'national origin' in the subsequent Preliminary Objections phase of *Qatar v. United Arab Emirates.*[13]

The following elements of treaty interpretation, in accordance with Articles 31–33 of the VCLT, are to be considered for purposes of this preliminary inquiry into the meaning of 'national origin' and 'nationality', in order to determine the material scope of 'racial discrimination' under Article 1 of CERD: a) ordinary meaning to be given to the Convention's terms 'national origin' as used in Article 1 (1); b) context, including the CERD's preamble; c) object and purpose of CERD; and d) supplementary means.[14]

2.1 *National Origin under the General Rule of Treaty Interpretation*

Ordinary meaning of 'national origin' and 'nationality': The terms 'national origin' and 'nationality' both have several meanings, some of which overlap. It would be simplistic to argue that "[t]he term 'national origin' is different in scope and has a different meaning than 'nationality'."[15] Neither of these terms has an 'ordinary meaning' distinguishing it from the other. In addition, an etymological analysis of the two terms is likely to cause a plethora of interpretive complexities. Furthermore, 'nationality' (in the politico-legal and/or

11 P. Thornberry, *The International Convention on the Elimination of All Forms of Racial Discrimination: A Commentary* (OUP, 2016), p. 125.

12 Vienna Convention on the Law of Treaties (VCLT), United Nations, Treaty Series, vol. 1155, p. 331.

13 The United Arab Emirates filed preliminary objections to the jurisdiction of the Court and the admissibility of Qatar's application on 29 April 2019. Indeed, the first objection focuses on the nationality/national origin issue.

14 According to CERD Article 25, the Chinese, English, French, Russian and Spanish texts are equally authentic. In accordance with Article 33(3) of the VCLT, it is presumed that the relevant terms have the same meaning in each authentic text.

15 Application of the International Convention on the Elimination of All Forms of Racial Discrimination (*Qatar v. United Arab Emirates*), Provisional Measures, Verbatim Record, 28 June 2018, p. 40. See also E. Schwelb, "The International Convention on the Elimination of Racial Discrimination," *International and Comparative Law Quarterly*, 1966, vol. 15, p. 1003. To illustrate from the treaty terms, CERD's French text uses 'ressortissants' in Article 1(2) where the English text has 'citizens', but 'citoyenneté' in Article 1(3) where the English text has 'citizenship'.

ethnographical sense) interprets slightly differently across language groups. Because of the ambiguities surrounding the terms 'national origin' and 'nationality', the Court will find it necessary to consider the other VCLT elements, beginning with the context.

Context: No clear conclusions about the meaning of 'national origin' emerge from the context as evidenced by the preamble of CERD, and the term 'nationality' is not found there. The preamble provides two apparently non-exclusive illustrations of prohibited discrimination to be covered by the Convention, namely distinctions on the basis of "race, colour or national origin" (para. 2) and discrimination on the grounds of "race, colour or ethnic origin" (para. 7). CERD's preamble is also inspired by a series of pre-existing international instruments, including *inter alia* the Charter of the United Nations (Charter) and the Universal Declaration of Human Rights (Universal Declaration). The Charter's human rights provisions do not clarify the present issue: Articles 1 (3) and 55 (c) of the Charter affirm the objective of promoting respect for human rights "without distinction as to race, sex, language, or religion"; but the term 'race' is not defined and the terms 'national origin' or 'nationality' do not figure in the Charter's human rights clauses. CERD's preambular reference to the Universal Declaration selects only three grounds – "race, colour, or national origin" – from among the Declaration's longer list; again, the selection appears to be illustrative of racial discrimination rather than supportive of a limitative interpretation of 'national origin'. The preambular references to other United Nations declarations just reaffirm political commitments, without shedding light on the meaning of the terms the Convention uses to translate those political pledges into legally binding obligations.

Object and purpose: The ICJ is likely to pay particular attention to CERD's object and purpose, which on the one hand focuses on a certain type of discrimination – *racial* discrimination – rather than the multiple varieties enumerated in the Charter and Universal Declaration, yet on the other hand employs four specific terms supplementary to race – colour, descent, national and ethnic – in delineating the scope of a treaty to eliminate *all* forms of racial discrimination. The object and purpose of eliminating racial discrimination should be discernible from the common thread among the five listed terms.

Certainly, CERD was concluded at the height of the decolonization period. This does not dictate, however, the manner in which racial discrimination might arise. One could argue that CERD is one of those treaties that is of a humanitarian and civilizing character. Its overall object and purpose is to improve the rights of individuals as against invidious racial discrimination.[16]

16 It is worth looking at the interpretative approach the ICJ adopted with regards to Convention on the Prevention and Punishment of Genocide. *Reservations to the*

Such discrimination can arise in the context of discrimination based upon a person's nationality.

2.2 *National Origin and Supplementary Means of Interpretation*

Travaux préparatoires: Beginning with the *travaux préparatoires,* they highlight that there was "no clear agreement whether the term 'national origin' was to be understood in the politico-legal or in the ethnographical sense."[17] The strong support for the word 'national' to remain in the Convention, and the course of negotiations between State Party Representatives, corroborate a broad interpretation of 'national origin' (i.e. including the politico-legal meaning of the term). At the very least, the *travaux préparatoires* do not exclude the possibility of national origin including present nationality.[18]

In addition to the *travaux préparatoires,* it is perfectly possible to regard the pronouncements of the treaty body established by the Convention, the Committee on the Elimination of Racial Discrimination (CERD Committee or Committee) as a supplementary means of interpretation under Article 32 of the VCLT. In its General Recommendation XXX, the Committee is of the view that differential treatment on the basis of citizenship or immigration status can constitute discrimination under the Convention. It recognizes that the different treatment of a given citizenship can only be lawful, if it is applied pursuant to a legitimate aim, and it is proportional to the achievement of this aim.[19] This is likely to suggest that the Committee considers that national origin comprises a person's 'present nationality', or alternatively that the Committee can entertain nationality based disputes in certain circumstances.[20] The Committee itself has recently confirmed the above in its first inter-State communication.

In March 2018, prior to submitting a case before the ICJ, Qatar decided to submit an inter-State communication against the United Arab Emirates

---

Convention on Genocide, Advisory Opinion: ICJ Reports 1951, p. 15, at p. 23.

17 E. Schwelb, *op. cit,*, p. 1006; P. Thornberry, *op. cit.*, p. 143: "The inconclusive discussions of 'national origin' in the *travaux préparatoires* allow comparatively little room for precise comment on the position of non-citizens in the emerging ICERD framework."

18 Authors concur that the negotiating history does not provide clear answers to the ambiguities inherent in the treaty's text. See Schwelb, *op. cit.*, pp. 1003–1007, and P. Thornberry, *op. cit.*, p. 143.

19 CERD Committee General Recommendation XXX ('Discrimination Against Non-Citizens'), at I.4.

20 General Recommendation XXX has considerably influenced the Committee's approach to individual complaints under CERD, in a manner that could confirm its view that nationality is encompassed within national origin. See DR *v. Australia*, Communication No. 42/2008, CERD/C/75/D/42/2008, paras. 6.3 (2009). See also *DF v. Australia*, Communication No. 39/2006, CERD/C/72/D/39/2006 (2008).

before the CERD Committee. Having examined the positions of the Parties, the Committee issued in August 2019 its decisions on jurisdiction and admissibility. Relying on Article 1 (3) of CERD and its own practice, including General Recommendation XXX, the Committee observed that it might examine whether a distinction based on citizenship constitutes prohibited discrimination by reference to the standards of legitimate aim and proportionality.[21] The Committee concluded that it has competence to examine whether the difference in treatment of Qatari citizens (i) pursues a legitimate aim, (ii) is proportional to the achievement of this aim, and (iii) does not result in a denial of fundamental human rights.[22] On the basis of the above brief analysis, it could be argued that present nationality is encompassed within national origin and that a given nationality cannot be discriminated against unreasonably, namely without a legitimate aim and in a disproportionate manner. That said, the exact status of pronouncements of the CERD Committee is open to debate. Indeed, the CERD Convention does not accord to the Committee any express power to interpret the Convention in a manner that is binding upon States Parties and, as a general matter, States Parties do not regard such pronouncements as legally binding. Even so, they tend to be highly influential for international and national courts and tribunals.[23]

3 The Thorny Question: Article 22 Preconditions

Article 22 of CERD provides that:

> Any dispute between two or more States Parties with respect to the interpretation or application of this Convention, which is not settled by negotiation or by the procedures expressly provided for in this Convention, shall, at the request of any of the parties to the dispute, be referred to the International Court of Justice for decision, unless the disputants agree to another mode of settlement.

21 See CERD/C/99/04, paras. 53–62.

22 *Ibid.*, para. 63.

23 *Ahmadou Sadio Diallo (Republic of Guinea v. Democratic Republic of the Congo), Merits, Judgment, ICJ Reports 2010*, p. 639, at p. 663–664, para. 66; see also *Legal Consequences of the Construction of a Wall in the Occupied Palestinian Territory, Advisory Opinion, ICJ Reports 2004*, p. 136, at p. 179–181, paras. 109–110 and 112, and at 192–193, para. 136 (in which the Court referred to various pronouncements of the Human Rights Committee and the Committee on Economic, Social and Cultural Rights).

In other words, States Parties to the Convention consent to the jurisdiction of the ICJ to hear any dispute regarding the interpretation or application of the Convention "which is not settled by negotiation *or* by the procedures expressly provided for in this Convention". One could argue that the wording of Article 22 introduces the following idea: a previous action (an attempt to settle the dispute) must have taken place prior to the referral of any dispute to the Court. By 'procedures', Article 22 refers to Article 11 of CERD, which establishes a different procedure allowing a State Party to inform the CERD Committee of its concerns regarding the acts or omissions of another State Party and defines the procedure that is to be followed. Hence, the Committee plays a key role in the resolution of disputes between States Parties, including through the conciliation commission mechanism set forth in Articles 11, 12 and 13 of the Convention.

The question of whether Article 22 preconditions are alternative or cumulative was clearly left open at the provisional measures phases of *Georgia v. Russian Federation,*[24] *Ukraine v. Russian Federation*[25] and *Qatar v. United Arab Emirates.*[26] The issue was raised again by the United Arab Emirates in March 2019, when it unsuccessfully requested the Court to indicate provisional measures in *Qatar v. United Arab Emirates.*[27]

In *Georgia v. Russian Federation* (*Preliminary Objections*), the Court was of the view that Georgia had not made sufficient attempts to negotiate matters falling under CERD. For that reason, in addition to the fact that Georgia did not claim to have resorted to the CERD Committee procedures (inter-State communication), the Court found that it did not need to examine whether the two preconditions are cumulative or alternative. The case was dismissed.[28]

It is worth noting that six members of the Court dissented on this point. Five of those, in a joint dissent, would have actually found neither negotiation nor resort to the CERD Committee to be a precondition; and even if Article 22 established preconditions, those would not be cumulative.[29]

---

24 See *supra* note 2, p. 70, at p. 140, para. 183.

25 See *supra* note 3, p. 104, pp. 125–126, para. 60.

26 *Application of the International Convention on the Elimination of All Forms of Racial Discrimination (Qatar v. United Arab Emirates), Provisional Measures Order of 23 July 2019*, para. 39.

27 *Ibid.*, para. 25.

28 See *supra* note 2, p. 70., p. 139, paras. 182–184.

29 *Joint dissenting opinion of President Owada, Judges Simma, Abraham and Donoghue and Judge ad hoc Gaja, ICJ Reports, 2011*, p. 104, at p. 142, 145, para.12 and paras. 155–157; See also Separate opinion of Judge Abraham, *ICJ Reports*, 2011, p. 104, at p. 224 and 231, para. 23. See also *Dissenting opinion of Judge Cançado Trindade, ICJ Reports, 2011*, p. 239, at 290, para.

Subsequently, in *Ukraine v. Russian Federation* (*Provisional Measures*), after observing that the matter had not been resolved by negotiations (and that Ukraine acknowledged not having invoked the mechanism before the CERD Committee, which in Ukraine's view was merely an alternative precondition), the Court stated that "it need not make a pronouncement on the issue at this stage of the proceedings."[30] In June 2019, the ICJ held oral hearings in *Ukraine v. Russian Federation* (*Preliminary Objections*), where the *unfathomable* question was debated again. Having reminded the Court that it is responsible for the fact that this question is still unresolved,[31] the Russian Federation argued, for the third time, that Article 22 preconditions are cumulative.[32] The United Arab Emirates raised the same issue in its preliminary objections to the jurisdiction of the Court and to the admissibility of Qatar's application submitted on 29 April 2019.[33] It is worth reminding that the case involving Qatar and the United Arab Emirates might be more appealing to the curiosity of international law experts. Contrary to Georgia and Ukraine, Qatar submitted an inter-State communication against the United Arab Emirates to the CERD Committee in March 2018, one month prior to filing a case under CERD against the same State before the ICJ.

Are the applicants in the three above-mentioned CERD cases correct in maintaining that the Article 22 preconditions are alternative and not cumulative? In November 2019, the Court unravelled the mystery in its judgment in *Ukraine v. Russian Federation* (*Preliminary Objections*). A good faith interpretation of Article 22 in accordance with the ordinary meaning to be given to the terms of CERD in their context and in the light of its object and purpose, pursuant to Article 31 (1) of VCLT, indicates that an alternative interpretation of the two criteria seems more plausible and reasonable.

Having stated that that " 'or' may have either disjunctive or conjunctive meaning",[34] the Court interpreted Article 22 in its context and in light of the object and purpose of CERD.

---

116. Of the dissenting Judges, Judges Abraham, Donoghue and Cançado Trindade remain on the Court at the present time.

30 See *supra* note 3, p. 104, para. 60.

31 *Application of the International Convention for the Suppression of the Financing of Terrorism and of the International Convention on the Elimination of All Forms of Racial Discrimination* (*Ukraine v. Russian Federation*), *Preliminary Objections*, Verbatim Record, 3 June 2019, p. 55.

32 *Ibid.*, pp. 52–63.

33 See Preliminary Objections submitted by the United Arab Emirates, 29 April 2019, p. 77, para. 145.

34 See *supra* note 6, para. 107.

If it were necessary to follow both procedures cumulatively, extensive delays would be required before the ICJ could be seized of a dispute under the Convention. According to Articles 11–13 of the Convention, applicable between all States Parties, the following steps and time periods would be of relevance:

- A State Party may bring the matter to the attention of the Committee.
- 3-month period for receiving State to submit its written explanations.
- The right to return to the Committee, which is subject to necessary conditions, namely: the right must be exercised within six months from the receipt by the receiving State of the initial communication to the CERD Committee; and the Committee must have ascertained that the matter has not been adjusted to the satisfaction of both parties, whether by bilateral negotiations or by any other procedure open to them.
- The Committee shall ascertain exhaustion of all available domestic remedies, unless their application is unreasonably prolonged.
- 3-month period for attempt to reach agreement on appointment of an *ad hoc* Conciliation Commission, after which the Committee may elect the Commission's members not yet agreed upon.
- Period (length unspecified) for the Commission to have fully considered the matter and to prepare its report.
- 3-month period for States to inform the Committee whether or not they accept the recommendations in the report.

In light of the above-mentioned procedure, it would be an unreasonable interpretation of Article 22 of CERD to require pursuit of both negotiations and the non-binding CERD procedure, as cumulative preconditions for referral of a dispute to the ICJ for a binding decision. The provision "which is not settled by negotiation or by the procedures expressly provided for in the Convention" is more naturally read as allowing resort to the ICJ for a binding resolution of the dispute, provided that the applicant shows that it has pursued one alternative without success. In the words of the Court, "the context of Article 22 rather indicates that it would not be reasonable to require States parties which have already failed to reach an agreed settlement through negotiations to engage in an additional set of negotiations in accordance with the modalities set out in Articles 11 to 13 of CERD."[35]

In order to further support its view, the Court underlined that the CERD's substantive articles entail obligations of various kinds – some involving pursuit of long-range and far-reaching objectives and others involving results to be attained either immediately or in any event promptly. If this is read in

---

35 See *supra* note 6, para. 110.

conjunction with the extensive period of time required for the procedure before the Committee – the result of which is a non-binding recommendation by an *ad hoc* Conciliation Commission – one could reasonably argue that, with regards to the Committee procedures, the drafters explicitly made negotiations a precondition to the exercise of any procedural right. It is the Court's view that "the achievement of such aims could be rendered more difficult if the procedural preconditions under Article 22 were cumulative."[36]

Finally, yet importantly, although the ICJ decided not to examine the *travaux préparatoires* of Article 22,[37] those corroborate the fact that the drafters of the Convention did not envisage both prior negotiations and the conciliation mechanism under CERD as cumulative requirements under Article 22. Rather, the *travaux préparatoires* show that the distinction and separation between the CERD conciliation mechanisms and the ICJ procedure were intended by the drafters, as the two are not dependent upon each other.[38] Furthermore, it was stressed that unilateral recourse was important for effective enforcement, and that there were also many opportunities for alternative dispute resolution open to the parties.[39]

4 Exhaustion of Local Remedies and Admissibility of Breach of Claims of CERD

Following the jurisdictional perplexities of Article 22, this section briefly focuses on the admissibility of an inter-State claim pursuant to CERD. In particular, it attempts to shed light on whether such a claim is barred by the local remedies rule. The issue has been raised in both *Ukraine v. Russian Federation* (*Preliminary Objections*) and *Qatar v. United Arab Emirates* (*Provisional Measures*). While in the latter case, the Court's Order of 23 July 2018 noted that the issue had been raised by the United Arab Emirates, but ultimately concluded that "the issue of exhaustion of local remedies need not be addressed by the Court",[40] the question was debated in detail in the oral hearings in the former case (*Preliminary Objections*).

36 *Ibid,* para. 111.

37 *Ibid,* para. 112.

38 This contribution does not intend to present a detailed overview of the *travaux préparatoires*. For more information, see https://hr-travaux.law.virginia.edu/racial-discrimination.

39 United Nations General Assembly, Official Record of the Third Committee, 1367th Meeting, A/C.3/SR.1367 (7 December 1965), p. 454, para. 39 (delegate of Italy) and para. 40 (delegate of Belgium).

40 See *supra* note 4, p. 15, para. 42.

The arguments put forward by the parties illustrate the key issues raised by the local remedies rule in these cases. Qatar, for example, argued in the first instance that the issue relating to local remedies was not a matter to be resolved during the hearing for provisional measures. Nevertheless, it contended that the requirement to exhaust local remedies does not apply to claims submitted by a State Party both on its own behalf and on behalf of its nationals (a mixed claim). Conversely, the United Arab Emirates argued that Qatar's claim was in fact one of diplomatic protection, not one brought by Qatar in its own right. In *Ukraine v. Russian Federation (Preliminary Objections)*, the Russian Federation claimed that the exhaustion of local remedies rule applies, since, as noted by the Court, CERD is "intended to protect individuals from racial discrimination."[41] The Russian Federation was of the view that Ukraine failed to prove that the exhaustion requirement had been met.[42] In response to the Russia Federation' arguments, Ukraine contented that local remedies rule does apply in the case, since Ukraine did not bring the case before the Court on behalf of specific individuals. Conversely, Ukraine's claims "relate to a broad pattern of conduct by the Russian Federation in Crimea and Ukraine is asserting claims in its own right."[43] In its judgment dated 8 November 2019, without entering into a detailed analysis, the Court confirmed Ukraine's view and stated that "Ukraine does not adopt the cause of one or more of its nationals, but challenges, on the basis of CERD, the alleged pattern of conduct of the Russian Federation with regard to the treatment of the Crimean Tatar and Ukrainian communities in Crimea."[44]

In order to examine this issue, our preliminary analysis will focus mainly on the relevant CERD provisions and the jurisprudence of the Court.

4.1 *CERD Provisions*

CERD's implementation measures include the following procedure: (1) a Committee procedure for inter-State communications, (2) an optional Committee procedure for individual communications, and (3) an ICJ procedure for inter-State claims. Strictly speaking, Article 22 of CERD does not explicitly require States Parties to exhaust local remedies before instituting

41 See Preliminary Objections submitted by the Russian Federation, 12 September 2018, p. 223, para. 446.

42 *Ibid.*

43 See Written Statement of Observations and Submissions on the Preliminary Objections of the Russian Federation submitted by Ukraine, 14 January 2019, p. 199, para 373.

44 See *supra* note 6, para. 130.

proceedings before the Court. On the other hand, Article 11 of the Convention does require exhaustion of local remedies.[45]

The haunting silence in Article 22 on the issue of exhaustion of local remedies may give rise to the argument that it is not a precondition for inter-State claims before the ICJ. After all, if the drafters had wanted to impose such a precondition, they would have put this in clear language, following the examples of Articles 11 (3) and 14 (7) (a) of the Convention. In addition, one could argue that Article 11 is contained in Part II of CERD, whereas Article 22 which regulates recourse to the ICJ in inter-State disputes regarding the interpretation and application of this Convention is contained in Part III. As indicated above, these are different ways to obtain remedy for alleged violations of the Convention.

4.2 *Non-Application of the Exhaustion Requirement in Inter-State Claims under CERD*

In light of the pending CERD cases before the Court, it is appropriate to explore whether there are circumstances where the exhaustion of local remedies is not required for State-to-State claims under CERD. There are, indeed, a series of well-established circumstances where the local remedies rule does not apply. For the purposes of this contribution, our analysis will focus on the general position on the non-application of the exhaustion of local remedies, as it appears to be of relevance to both *Ukraine v. Russian Federation* and *Qatar v. United Arab Emirates*.

Nowadays, it is recognized in international law that exhaustion of local remedies is not required for claims initiated by a State in its own right. The same logic applies to a claim, if mixed (i.e. on behalf of direct and indirect injury to a State), is *preponderantly* a direct injury to the State.[46]

Article 14 (3) of the ILC Draft Articles on Diplomatic Protection sheds light on this issue by articulating the test of preponderance: "Local remedies shall be exhausted where an international claim, or request for a declaratory judgement related to the claim, is brought preponderantly on the basis of an injury to a national or other person referred to in draft article 8." In the same vein,

---

45 CERD Article 11(3).

46 For an analysis on the types of injury, see H. Abtani, 'Types of Injury in Inter-States Claims: Direct Injury to the State', in J. Crawford *et al.* (eds.), *The International Legal Order: Current Needs and Possible Responses: Essays in Honour of Djamchid Momtaz* (Brill, 2017), p. 199. See also A.A. Cançado Trindade, *The Application of the Rule of Exhaustion of Local Remedies in International Law: Its Rationale in the International Protection of Individual Rights* (CUP, 1983), pp. 172–86.

as pointed out by J. Crawford and T. Grant, "[b]y implication, a claim brought preponderantly on the basis of a direct injury to the State is not subject to the requirement of exhaustion."[47] Principal factors to be considered in making this assessment are the following: the subject of the dispute, the nature of the claim and the remedy claimed.[48]

The categorization of a claim is therefore essential to determining whether exhaustion of local remedies is a requirement prior to the seisin of the ICJ. An inter-State claim under CERD will normally be based either on an indirect injury to a State Party or a mix of a direct/indirect injury arising from the discriminatory action or omission suffered by an individual or group of individuals. J. Dugard has noted that, "[i]n practice it is difficult to decide whether the claim is 'direct' or 'indirect' where it is 'mixed', in the sense that it contains elements of both injury to the State and injury to the nationals of the State."[49] This notwithstanding, the case law is instructive.

The cases of *Interhandel* and *ELSI* both centred on the injury sustained by the respective companies on whose behalf the companies were exercising diplomatic protection. In the former case, Switzerland sought the restoration of the assets of *Interhandel* to that company or a finding by the ICJ that the dispute was fit for submission for judicial settlement, arbitration or conciliation. Switzerland contended that the claim was brought on the basis of a direct injury to itself resulting from a treaty breach, and an indirect wrong to itself arising from the injury sustained by a national corporation – thus it was a mixed claim. The Court decided, however, that the State's claims could not be segregated from the claims of the individuals injured.[50] Accordingly, it was the Court's view that the injury was primarily indirect. The Court came to a similar conclusion in the latter case. In *ELSI*, the United States sought compensation "equal to the full amount of the damage suffered by Raytheon and Machlett."[51] Having had recourse to "the applicants claim and particularly referred to the form of reparation sought",[52] the Court noted that it was not in a position to identify a direct injury to the United Stated that was "both distinct from, and

47 J. Crawford and T. Grant, "Local Remedies, Exhaustion of" (2007), in A. Peters (2021–) and R. Wolfrum (2004–2020) (eds.), *Max Planck Encyclopedia of Public International Law* (Oxford University Press, 2008–), available at http://www.mpepil.com/, para. 28.

48 J.R. Dugard, "Draft Articles on Diplomatic Protection with commentaries", *Yearbook of the International Law Commission*, 2006, Vol II, Pt 2, p. 76.

49 *Ibid.*, p. 74.

50 *Interhandel Case (Switzerland v. United States of America)*, *ICJ Reports 1959*, p. 6, p. 28.

51 *Elettronica Sicula S.p.A. (ELSI) (United States of America v. Italy)*, *ICJ Reports 1989*, p. 15, p. 21.

52 S. Wittich, 'Direct Injury and the Incidence of the Local Remedies Rule', 12 *Austrian Review of International and European Law* (2002) p. 161.

independent of, the dispute over the alleged violation in respect of Raytheon and Machlett."[53]

On the other hand, a particular reference to the *United States of America v. Iran* (*Merits*) must be made. In this case, the Court considered that the claim related primarily to a direct injury to the State. This was relatively straightforward given that the claim was related to the United States diplomatic and consular staff in Tehran.[54] More relevant to the pending cases before the Court, however, is *Avena and Other Mexican Nationals*. This case could be classified as a mixed claim, in the sense that there is direct injury to the interests of the State and to the State's nationals, provided the latter is not preponderant. In this case, the ICJ also considered that the claim primarily related to a direct injury to the State – though it was a mixed claim.[55]

While Mexico identified 54 Mexican nationals who were entitled to diplomatic protection, it characterized the claim as being made both "in its own right and in the exercise of its right of consular protection of its nationals."[56] Consistent with this, Mexico sought remedies specific to the 54 Mexican nationals, along with a finding that the U.S. Government was obliged to take all the necessary steps to ensure that the regular and continuous violations of the rights of Mexico and its nationals under the Vienna Convention stopped.[57]

One could argue that the pending CERD cases before the Court are analogous to the *Avena* situation. In its Application, Ukraine asks the Court to hold the Russian Federation accountable "for its unlawful actions under the Terrorism Financing Convention and CERD, and to redress the harm caused to *Ukraine and its people* by the Russian Federation's illegal violations of their rights."[58] The claims under CERD refer to alleged discriminatory measures against Crimean Tatar and ethnic Ukrainian communities in Crimea. In a similar fashion, Qatar's application instituting proceedings in the ICJ refers to the "severe and irreparable harm *to Qatar and Qataris*" caused by various "discriminatory measures" of the United Arab Emirates.[59] Nevertheless, specific individuals are not the subject of the claims. Rather, the claims analyse

---

53 See *supra* note 51, p. 15, para. 51.

54 *United States Diplomatic and Consular Staff in Tehran* (*United States of America v. Iran*), ICJ *Reports 1980*, p. 3.

55 In relation to Article 36(1) of the Vienna Convention on Consular Relations, see *Avena and Other Mexican Nationals* (*Mexico v. United States of America*), ICJ *Reports 2004*, p. 12, p. 36, para. 40.

56 See *supra* note 51, p. 15, para. 12.

57 *Ibid.*, para.13.

58 Ukraine's Application Instituting Proceedings in the ICJ, 16 January 2017, para. 16.

59 Qatar's Application Instituting Proceedings in the ICJ, 11 June 2018, para. 2.

the impact of discriminatory measures on people more broadly. In light of the applications, it transpires that in both cases claims are based on harm to a large class of unspecified persons. In both *ELSI* and *Diallo*, there were identifiable persons who could be expected on their own to exhaust local remedies. In the context of harm to thousands of persons, it is doubtful that a State seeking to address mass harm must satisfy the local remedies rule prior to instituting an inter-State claim. It may be argued that, in case of a mass claim, the focus of claim is direct to the State by means of massive harm to the State's nationals.

5 Conclusions

This contribution began by highlighting three controversial jurisdictional and admissibility issues under CERD, as evidenced by recent cases brought before the ICJ pursuant to this multilateral instrument. These issues are a) the definition of 'national origin' and whether it encompasses 'present nationality"'; b) the preconditions of Article 22 prior to the seisin of the Court; and c) the applicability of the local remedies rule in cases under CERD. All three legal questions raise highly complicated issues of public international law, and are not, therefore, capable of definitive answers. The Court has recently elucidated the second and the third question in *Ukraine v. Russian Federation* (*Preliminary Objections*). This judgment will inevitably have an impact on the pending case between Qatar and the United Arab Emirates.

Does 'national origin' encompass 'present nationality'? Given the imprecise language of the Convention, the answer cannot be definitive. In the same vein, the term 'nationality' itself is not devoid of ambiguity. Following a brief analysis based on the interpretative tools of the VCLT, including General Recommendation XXX and the recent decisions of the CERD Committee in the inter-State communication submitted by Qatar, it can be argued that discrimination on the basis of present nationality can fall within the scope of discrimination on the basis of 'national origin'. It remains to be seen whether the ICJ will reach the same conclusion in light of the particular facts in *Qatar v. United Arab Emirates*.

Are Article 22 preconditions cumulative or alternative? Although the drafting history and the limited practice do not categorically exclude a cumulative reading of the preconditions, in the Court's view, logic dictates that the preconditions shall be viewed as alternative. If States were not able to negotiate and find a solution to their dispute, it would seem unreasonable to expect a State to then initiate CERD procedures that do not lead to a binding decision, given that the resolution of the dispute would still require the parties to reach an agreement before the dispute could be fully resolved.

Last but not least, following an overview of the relevant CERD provisions and the Court's jurisprudence, we concluded that exhaustion of local remedies is not likely to be required when a State invokes the jurisdiction of the ICJ pursuant to Article 22 of the Convention. To date, the Court has not required exhaustion of local remedies in cases where a State brings in its own right as well as on behalf of its nationals under a treaty for the protection of individual rights. This has been confirmed by its recent judgment in *Ukraine v. Russian Federation* (*Preliminary Objections*).

Acknowledgements

This research was made possible by NPRP grant NPRP11S-1212-170090 from the Qatar National Research Fund (a member of Qatar Foundation). The findings achieved herein are solely the responsibility of the author.

CHAPTER 10

Reparation for Injuries and beyond – the Design of the Personality and Powers of International Organizations by International Courts

Rita Guerreiro Teixeira

1 Introduction

Hundreds of international organizations populate the international system today, their mandates covering a wide range of issues and many having widespread or near universal membership. They are recognised as autonomous subjects of international law, possessing international legal personality and, with it, certain powers and obligations. However, the path to establishing a legal position for these actors was nothing short of sinuous over the last century and a half.

Since the emergence of the first international bodies in the 19th century, the debate on their legal status and the extent of their powers has occupied both practitioners and academics. After their creation, the Permanent Court of International Justice ('PCIJ', 'Permanent Court') and, later, the International Court of Justice ('ICJ', 'Court') have weighed in and played an important role in the discussion. This chapter traces back the conceptualisation of the legal status and scope of powers of international organizations since the beginning of the 20th century, focusing on the contribution of the advisory opinions of those international courts.

The first part of this contribution briefly overviews the doctrinal discussions in the first half of the 20th century, the development of the doctrine of functionalism, and the early findings of the PCIJ. The second part analyses the advisory opinions of the ICJ concerning the legal status of international organizations and their powers, departing from the 1949 *Advisory Opinion on Reparation for Injuries Suffered in the Service of the United Nations*.[1] It analyses the reasoning of the Court in its different advisory opinions together with the international context in which they were issued. The third and final part

1 *Reparation for Injuries Suffered in the Service of the United Nations, Advisory Opinion, 11 April 1949, ICJ Reports 1949 ("Reparation for Injuries").*

© KONINKLIJKE BRILL NV, LEIDEN, 2022 | DOI:10.1163/9789004467668_014

discusses the long-lasting effects of the jurisprudence of the world courts on the study and theorisation of international organizations, even as criticism of the functionalist approach becomes more frequent.

2 A New Discipline in the Turn of the Century

The emergence of the first international bodies created by States is usually dated back to the establishment of the river commissions in Europe in the early 19th century, namely the Central Rhine Commission of 1804 and the European Danube Commission of 1856. In the second half of the century, several international public administrative unions were established – such as the Universal Telegraphic Union, in 1865, and the General Postal Union, in 1874 –, which would later become open international organizations.[2] However, it took several more decades for international organizations to be considered as a topic worthy of systematic study in legal research. In the turn of the century, the constitutive instruments of international organizations were still being studied as treaties establishing mechanisms for cooperation between States, with no attention being paid to their special institutional features. A large number of authors was still sustaining "*in categorical and uncompromising terms*" that States were the only subjects of international law.[3]

A first impetus to the study of the discipline was given by Kazansky, who conducted an exhaustive study of the law of international organizations in the last years of the 19th century. He described a developing international administration, constituted by international organs created by treaty, that imposed restrictions on the sovereignty of States for the pursuit of social interests, such as the development of communications, the progress of education, the increase of prosperity, and security.[4]

Most decisive for the development of a new discipline were the writings of Reinsch, who, in the beginning of the 20th century, undertook to systematically study the international organizations existing at the time and grouped them according to their fields of activity. Reinsch's work describes "*public*

2 Cf. J. E. Alvarez, *International Organizations as Law-Makers* (Oxford University Press, 2005), at 18. C. F. Amerasinghe, *Principles of the Institutional Law of International Organizations* (Cambridge University Press, 2005), at 67.

3 D. Bederman, 'The Souls of International Organizations: Legal Personality and the Lighthouse at Cape Spartel', 36 *Virginia Journal of International Law* (1996), 275 at 334.

4 P. Kazansky, 'Théorie de l'Administration Internationale', 9 *Revue Générale de Droit International Public* (1902) 353 at 361–363.

international unions" as institutions that revolve around specific functions, which were delegated by their member States in order to pursue their common goals more effectively.[5] States retained all the decision-making power.[6] The Unions were apolitical, since they were built around a single, identifiable function, and aimed at the "*betterment of civilization in all its aspects*."[7] Reinsch has been credited with the early development of the doctrine of functionalism.[8]

In 1920, the creation of the League of Nations brought significant developments to the field. The League was the first universal organization, and it was awarded with a mandate to protect international peace and security and with much broader competences than those organizations studied by Reinsch and Kazansky.[9] Soon, a number of authors started to favour granting it legal personality – among them Oppenheim, Lawrence, and Corbett. While Oppenheim highlighted the *sui generis* character of the League[10] and Lawrence agreed that it was "*an anomalous international person*",[11] Corbett advocated bringing it into an existing category of international persons.[12] By the mid-1920's, the idea that other subjects of international law besides States could exist was starting to gain traction in doctrinal writings.[13]

---

5 P. S. Reinsch, *Public International Unions, Their Work and Organization: A Study in International Administrative Law* (McGinn & Co Boston, 1911), at 4–5, 136–138. See, for an analysis, J. Klabbers, 'The EJIL Foreword: The Transformation of International Organizations Law', 26 *European Journal of International Law* (2015) 9 at 39–42.

6 Reinsch (1911), at 4, 102.

7 *Ibid.*, at 11.

8 Klabbers (2015 "EJIL Foreword"), at 13. However, see G. F. Sinclair, 'The Original Sin (and Salvation) of Functionalism', 26 *European Journal of International Law* (2015) 965 at 969, advising caution in reading present-day concepts back into the writings of earlier historical figures. See also, generally, D. Howland, 'An Alternative Mode of International Order: The International Administrative Union in the Nineteenth Century', 41 *Review of International Studies* (2015) 161.

9 Covenant of the League of Nations, adopted on 28 April 1919, Preamble. See Bederman (1996) 275, at 349. C. Brölmann, *The Institutional Veil in Public International Law: International Organisations and the Law of Treaties* (Hart Publishing, 2007), at 48–49.

10 L. Oppenheim, 'Le caractère essentiel de la Société des Nations', 26 *Revue Générale de Droit International Public* (1919) 234.

11 T.J. Lawrence, *The Principles of International Law* (7th ed. rev. by P. H. Winfield, Macmillan & Co, 1937), at 77–80.

12 P. E. Corbett, 'What is the League of Nations?', 5 *British Yearbook of International Law* (1924), 119 at 120, 147–148, claiming that there was a mere difference in the degree of authority attributed to the League when compared with existing confederations.

13 Bederman (1996), 335.

In 1929, the Legal Advisor of the International Zone of Tangier, charged with an examination of the legal status of the Cape Spartel Lighthouse Commission, found that it was an international organization with a separate legal personality. He seemingly based his conclusion on the legal capacities that the Commission was exercising in practice, inferred from its conduct, even if they were not expressly enshrined in the 1865 Convention Concerning the Administration and Upholding of the Lighthouse at Cape Spartel.[14]

The PCIJ, established in 1921, would soon be confronted with questions concerning international organizations. In 1922, the PCIJ was faced with a request concerning the competence of the International Labour Organization (ILO) to deal with questions of agricultural labour. In its *Advisory Opinion on the Competence of the ILO as to Agricultural Labour*, the Permanent Court addressed the issue as a matter of interpretation of the treaty that established the organization. It focused on determining "*what the terms of the Treaty actually mean[t]*"[15] and concluded that there was no real ambiguity as to the fact that these included agricultural labour.[16] Nothing in the reasoning of the Court seems to have been affected by the fact that this was a particular type of treaty, establishing a "*permanent labour organization*".[17]

Despite this dismissive start, later that decade the PCIJ would put forward the idea that an international organization could be considered as an autonomous actor, possessing a number of powers attributed by its member States. In its *Advisory Opinion on the Danube Commission* (1927), the Permanent Court characterised the European Commission of the Danube as an "*international institution with a special purpose*", having "*the functions bestowed upon it by the Definitive Statute with a view to the fulfilment of that purpose.*"[18] This is largely identified as the adoption of the language of functionalism by the PCIJ and the formulation of the doctrine of attributed powers.[19]

---

14 Giuseppe Marchegiano, 'The Juristic Character of the International Commission of the Cape Spartel Lighthouse', 25 *American Journal of International Law* (1931) 339. Cf. Brölmann (2007 "Institutional Veil"), at 59. Bederman (1996), at 362–363.

15 *Competence of the ILO in regard to International Regulation of the Conditions of the Labour of Persons Employed in Agriculture* (Advisory Opinion, 12 August 1922), PCIJ Publications 1922, Series B, no. 2 ("*Competence of the ILO as to Agricultural Labour*"), at 23.

16 *Competence of the ILO as to Agricultural Labour*, at 39.

17 *Ibid*, at 23. Cf. J. Klabbers, 'The Life and Times of the Law of International Organizations', 70 *Nordic Journal of International Law* (2001) 287, at 295.

18 *Jurisdiction of the European Commission of the Danube between Galatz and Braila* (Advisory Opinion, 8 December 1927), PCIJ Publications 1927, Series B, no. 14, at 64.

19 V. Engström, *Constructing the Powers of International Institutions* (Martinus Nijhoff Publishers, 2012), at 32. Klabbers (2001), at 296. Bederman (1996), at 366.

A year later, in the *Advisory Opinion on the Interpretation of the Greco-Turkish Agreement* (1928), the PCIJ would build on this reasoning and broaden it, admitting that organizations could have powers beyond those expressly stated in their constitutions.[20] In this case, since the Mixed Commission established by Greece and Turkey had powers to settle disputes, the Permanent Court found that it must also have had the powers to submit disputes on questions of principle to an arbitral tribunal, which was better placed to decide them.[21] The PCIJ equally noted that the Mixed Commission established between the two States was "*constituted as a corporate body*" and, as such, possessed certain exclusive functions that its member States could not individually perform.[22]

With these findings, the PCIJ laid down the first steppingstones for the establishment of the theory of implied powers, which would be consolidated two decades later by the ICJ.

3 Reparation for Injuries and Beyond

3.1 *Recognition of a New Legal Actor*

By mid-century, the political mood was of determination in furthering institutionalised international cooperation and enthusiasm towards the role it could play in ensuring lasting peace after the World Wars.[23] This led to the well-known "*move to institutions*" that characterised the 20th century.[24]

It was in this environment that a request for an advisory opinion concerning the capacity of the UN to bring a claim for compensation against a State for injuries suffered by one of its agents was submitted to the ICJ. In the *Reparation Opinion*, issued in 1949, the ICJ found that the UN had international legal personality, putting an end to the discussion on whether international law recognised subjects other than States. The ICJ was of the view that the functions and attributions that member States had conferred on the UN could only be pursued if the organization enjoyed "*a large measure of legal personality*".[25] It

20 *Interpretation of the Greco-Turkish Agreement of December 1st, 1926*, PCIJ Publications 1928, Series B, no. 16 ("*Interpretation of the Greco-Turkish Agreement*").

21 *Interpretation of the Greco-Turkish Agreement*, at 20–21. See also, Engström (2012), at 339. Klabbers (2001), at 296.

22 *Interpretation of the Greco-Turkish Agreement*, at 25. See E. Lauterpacht, 'The Development of the Law of International Organization by the Decisions of International Tribunals', 152 *Recueil des Cours de l'Académie de Droit International* (1980) 379, at 404–405.

23 Engström (2012), at 40. Alvarez (2005), at 23.

24 D. Kennedy, 'The Move to Institutions', 8(5) *Cardozo Law Review* (1987) 841–988.

25 *Reparation for Injuries*, at 9.

further established that this personality was objective and opposable vis-à-vis non-member States.[26]

While the *Reparation Opinion* rendered the discussion on the possibility of international organizations enjoying international legal personality essentially mute,[27] the same cannot be said about the debate on the process and criteria for acquisition of that personality.

In this respect, the ICJ based the recognition of the legal personality of the UN on the fact that the organization

> was *intended to exercise and enjoy* and is *in fact exercising and enjoying* functions and rights which can only be explained on the basis of the possession of [...] international personality.[28]

The ambiguity of this statement, however, left space for proponents of both the 'will theory' and the 'objective theory' to continue their debate.[29] While, according to the former, the ICJ confirmed that acquisition of personality is the result of the *intention* of its founder States, expressly established in the constituent instrument or inferred from it,[30] the latter argue that the legal personality of organizations is, like that of States, original and arises from the objective fact that the organization exists and meets certain criteria established in general international law.[31]

This advisory opinion continues to fuel the debate in literature in the 21st century. Recently, it has been proposed that the appropriate interpretation of the above statement is that a combination of the two elements is required – *i.e.*, according to the Court, the acquisition of international legal personality is "*a process ignited by the intention of the contracting parties to create a new subject of international law*" that is completed only with the "*concrete exercise*"

26 *Ibid.*, at 15.

27 Brölmann referred to this opinion as having created "*instant doctrine, if not instant custom*". Catherine Brölmann, 'The International Court of Justice and International Organisations', 9 *International Community Law Review* (2007) 181, at 184.

28 *Reparation for Injuries*, at 9 (emphasis added).

29 See, for more development on the contours of this debate, T. Gazzini, 'Personality of international organizations', in J. Klabbers, Å. Wallendahl (eds.), *Research Handbook on the Law of International Organisations* (Edward Elgar, 2011), at 34–35. J. Klabbers, *An Introduction to International Organizations Law* (3rd ed., Cambridge University Press, 2015), at 46–50.

30 P. Sands, P. Klein, *Bowett's The Law of International Institutions* (6th ed., Sweet & Maxwell, 2009), paras. 15-005, 15-006. Amerasinghe (2005), at 80–81.

31 J. Brownlie, *Principles of Public International Law* (5th ed., Oxford University Press, 1998), at 678–680. M. Rama-Montaldo, 'International Legal Personality and Implied Powers of International Organizations', 44 *British Yearbook of International Law* (1970) 111 at 124–126.

of the powers conferred to it.[32] Still another interpretation put forward is that the Court established a regime of presumptive personality of organizations: if an organization performs acts that can only be explained on the basis of international legal personality, it is presumed to possess it.[33]

Finally, the Court's findings in the *Reparation Opinion* resonate also in new contexts today. An example is the debate on the legal status of new institutional arrangements established by States for cooperation that are distinct from the traditional international organizations. The question has been recently posed with some notoriety in relation to the Conferences of the Parties and Meetings of the Parties that have been established by multilateral environmental agreements for implementation, development and review of such agreements.[34] A number of authors argue that such institutions are, in fact, international organizations, "*albeit of a less formal, more ad hoc nature*" than traditional ones.[35]

The most in-depth study on this matter was conducted by Churchill and Ulfstein and they use the reasoning of the Court and the argument of "*necessary implication*"[36] to sustain that the powers that are conferred upon these institutional arrangements and the manner in which they are exercised may be interpreted to necessarily include legal personality and treaty-making capacity.[37] The authors point out that, just as is the case with traditional international organizations, the fact that the founders do not expressly provide for their legal personality should not prevent them from having it, making an

---

32 Gazzini (2011), at 36–37.

33 J. Klabbers, 'Presumptive Personality: The European Union in International Law', *in* M. Koskenniemi (ed.), *International Law Aspects of the European Union* (Kluwer, 1998), at 243 *et seq.*

34 *E.g*, the Conference of the Parties to the UN Framework Convention on Climate Change, the Meeting of the Parties to the Montreal Protocol on Substances that Deplete the Ozone Layer, the Conference of the Parties to the Convention on International Trade in Endangered Species of Wild Fauna and Flora.

35 R. R. Churchill and G. Ulfstein, 'Autonomous Institutional Arrangements in Multilateral Environmental Agreements: A Little-Noticed Phenomenon in International Law', 94(4) *American Journal of International Law* (2000) 623 at 659. See also, P. Sands, *Principles of International Environmental Law* (2nd ed., Cambridge University Press, 2003), at 108–109. However, the argument remains controversial – cf. Alvarez (2005), at 7. G. Loibl, 'The Proliferation of International Institutions Dealing with International Environmental Matters' in N. M. Blokker and Henry G Schermers (eds.), *Proliferation of International Organizations: Legal Issues* (Kluwer, 2001), at 166–168.

36 *Reparation for Injuries*, at 9, 12.

37 Churchill and Ulfstein (2000), at 655. The same arguments, albeit less developed are used in Sands (2003), at 109.

explicit reference to the *Reparation Opinion*.[38] Furthermore, they also give consideration to the intention of State Parties, arguing that there is no clear indication that, when deciding to establish conferences of the parties rather than traditional international organizations, they intend to establish an institutional framework that is less effective or dynamic internally or externally.[39]

3.2 *Powers of International Organizations*

Following up on early (and broad) references in the PCIJ case law, the ICJ formulated the doctrine of implied powers in clear terms, for the first time, in the *Reparation Opinion*:

> the Organization must be deemed to have those powers which, though not expressly provided in the Charter, are conferred upon it by necessary implication as being essential to the performance of its duties.[40]

With this language, the Court incorporated in its reasoning the tradition of functionalism that had been gaining ground since the beginning of the century – to the extent that this opinion has been referred to as the "*epitome of the functional approach to organizations*".[41]

Notably, the reasoning of the Court still grounded implied powers on the consent of members. In the case of the UN, the powers in questions arose "*by necessary intendment out of the Charter*", emphasising that they were equally conferred by member States, only implicitly, and thinning the dividing line between attributed and implied powers.[42]

The ICJ readdressed the extent of powers of organizations in later advisory opinions, two of which became landmarks in the debate. In the *Advisory Opinion on Certain Expenses of the United Nations*, the ICJ emphasised that the purposes and powers of international organizations are not unlimited and that they are conferred by member States.[43] However, it also formulated a presumption that, when an organization takes action to fulfil one of its stated purposes, it is not acting *ultra vires*. Moreover, even if the action would be undertaken by the wrong organ in the organization, this would not necessarily imply its

38 Churchill and Ulfstein (2000), at 649, 655.

39 *Ibid.*, at 633, 649.

40 *Reparation for Injuries*, at 12.

41 Engström (2012), at 42.

42 *Reparation for Injuries*, at 14. Cf. Klabbers (2001), at 303.

43 *Certain Expenses of the United Nations (Article 17, paragraph 2, of the Charter), Advisory Opinion of 20 July 1962, ICJ Reports 1962*, p. 151 ("*Certain Expenses*"), at 168.

invalidity because it could still be *intra vires* the powers of the organization as a whole.[44] These findings seemed to broaden the scope of implied powers compared to the *Reparation Opinion*: now they included all powers that could be related to the purposes of the organization, rather than only those that were *essential* to fulfilling those purposes.[45]

The Court reverted the apparent trend of broadening the scope of implied powers in the *Advisory Opinion of the Legality of the Use by a State of Nuclear Weapons in Armed Conflict*, requested by the World Health Organization ('WHO').[46] Here, the Court only admitted that organizations could have implied powers when they were the *"necessary implication of the Constitution of the Organization in the light of the purposes assigned to it by its member States."*[47] It found no connection between the purposes of the WHO and the competence to request this opinion. At the end of the century, the Court was going back to reiterating the principle of speciality and emphasising the functional limitation of the powers of international organizations.[48]

This shows that the ICJ has taken different views concerning the exact measure of powers enjoyed by international organizations throughout the years, both broadening and functionally limiting the scope of implied powers.[49] Surely, there are factual differences in each of the cases mentioned, as well as in the context of the requests, that can partially justify the different findings. There is, for instance, the difference between the broad mandate of the UN and the more limited mandate of a specialised organization; or the fact that the *Nuclear Weapons Opinion* concerned one of the most controversial questions of international politics at the time and the General Assembly had also requested an opinion on it.[50]

However, a correspondence can also be plausibly established between the Court's views and the contemporaneous international climate of either

---

44 *Ibidem.*

45 *See* Engström (2012), 48. Also, *Certain Expenses*, Dissenting Opinion by Judge Koretsky, at 268 – arguing in favour of a strict interpretation of the provisions of the UN Charter and fearing that the Court would turn to a method where *"the end justifies the means"*.

46 *Legality of the Use by a State of Nuclear Weapons in Armed Conflict, Advisory Opinion of 8 July 1996, ICJ Reports 1996*, p. 66 (*"Legality of Nuclear Weapons"*).

47 *Legality of Nuclear Weapons*, para. 25.

48 Brölmann (2007 "The ICJ"), at 185. Engström (2012), at 37, noting that this opinion was seen by many as a departure from earlier jurisprudence of the Court.

49 Cf. C. F. Amerasinghe, 'International Legal Personality Revisited', 47 *Austrian Journal of Public and International Law* (1995) 123 at 138, comparing the different formulations in the Court's advisory opinions.

50 In that case, the ICJ did give the requested opinion – see *Legality of the Threat or Use of Nuclear Weapons, Advisory Opinion, ICJ Reports 1996*, p. 226. Engström (2012), 61.

optimism or concern towards the development of international cooperation, the proliferation of organizations, and the erosion of State sovereignty. The *Reparation Opinion* was issued in the post-World War II period, amidst a climate of "*unbridled enthusiasm for international organizations*", which were "*inherently good*" and capable of providing peace and prosperity.[51] On the contrary, State sovereignty was looked at suspiciously and the prevailing idea was that States needed to be restrained in their actions by international standards. At the same time, the UN was affirming itself as a main actor in cooperation and maintenance of peace, while also broadening its field of action. Its action globally would be severely limited if it could not protect its agents against wrongdoings, which also required having the capacity to bring claims for compensation.

The *Certain Expenses Opinion*, issued in the 1960's, still benefited from a similar international environment, *"geared towards making organizations ever more effective."*[52] Furthermore, it was closely concerned with the budget of the UN, a fundamental element for the effectiveness of the organization's action.

It was towards the 1980's and 1990's that the faith in institutions started to fade and concerns re-emerged on the role of States in the international order.[53] The environment became hostile towards international organizations. They were being accused of politicisation and mismanagement, in some cases leading to withdrawal of member States.[54] The members of the European Union explicitly laid down the principle of attributed powers and the subsidiarity principle in the Maastricht Treaty.[55] The conception of organizations started to change, 'new institutionalism' emerged in political theory and concerns were expressed on avoiding "*competence creep*".[56] This was the context in which the *Nuclear Weapons Opinion* was issued.

These advisory opinions did not only seem to fit into the climate of their time but also decisively consolidated emerging trends in legal thought on

---

51 Klabbers (2001), at 299–300, 310.

52 Engström (2012), at 49.

53 *Id.*, at 57.

54 E.g. the UK and the US left UNESCO amidst claims of politicization of the organization. See Klabbers (2015, "EJIL Foreword"), at 51–55. The accusations of politicization started early in the century, already looming over the League of Nations and the ILO almost immediately after its creation. Sinclair (2015), at 970. However, they gained traction towards the later 80s and 90s.

55 Cf. Treaty on the European Union, signed in Maastricht on 7 February 1992, inserting article 3b into the Treaty establishing the European Economic Community. Klabbers (2015, "EJIL Foreword"), at 25–26.

56 Engström (2012), 57.

international organizations. Markedly, academic writings peaked between 1950 and 1970, a period that Klabbers identified as corresponding to a "*pragmatic idealism*" in legal thinking.[57] Since it was clear that international organizations existed and had international legal personality, particularly after the *Reparation Opinion*, the focus was on studying the practicalities of their functioning, such as treaty making-powers, financing, membership, responsibility.[58] After a period of quietude, a new wave of legal writings would start in the 1990's, this time refocusing on conceptualising international organizations, their powers and personality.[59] Again, authors were interested in theorising on the topic, precisely when the ICJ was reemphasizing functional limitations to the powers of organizations and refraining from expanding the scope of implied powers in the *Nuclear Weapons Opinion*.

4 New Perspectives on the Law of International Organizations

As several authors have pointed out, 60 years after the ICJ issued the *Reparation Opinion*, the concept of international legal personality remains a rather nebulous one, with no unanimous definition.[60] Even though there is agreement that some organizations are international legal subjects (although the identification of which ones remains under discussion),[61] questions persist about the extent of their powers, their obligations under international law and those of member States, and control by member States – to name just a few. In the past decades, there has been a move in theory and in practice in favour of strengthening control and accountability of international organizations and addressing rule of law and human rights concerns.[62] At the same time, there is

57 Klabbers (2001), at 289–290, 300 *et seq.*.

58 The exponent of this approach was probably the first edition of Henry G. Schermers, *International Institutional Law* (Martinus Nijhoff, 1972).

59 A third stage in the development of the law of international organisations, according with Klabbers. See Klabbers (2001), at 310 *et seq.*

60 Gazzini (2011), at 34. Nigel D. White, *The Law of International Organizations* (2nd ed., Manchester University Press, 2005), at 32.

61 See Klabbers (2015, "EJIL Foreword"), 29–31. See also the debate on the legal status of conferences of the parties. See *supra* note 35 and accompanying text.

62 Klabbers (2015, "EJIL Foreword"), at 76. A. Peters, 'The Constitutionalisation of International Organizations', in N. Walker, J. Shaw, S. Tierney (eds.), *Europe's Constitutional Mosaic* 253 (Hart Publishing, 2011), at 64–67. O.De Schutter, 'Human Rights and the Rise of International Organizations: The Logic of Sliding Scales in the Law of International Responsibility', in J. Wouters *et al.* (eds), *Accountability for Human Rights Violations by International Organizations* (Intersentia, 2010) 51. G. Ulfstein, 'Institutions

a renewed interest in the study of international organizations in a more theoretical and conceptual manner,[63] and the premises of functionalism have been more frequently questioned.

Critics of this doctrine suggest that it has, for the most part, remained unchanged since the early 20th century and, as such, cannot respond to the present challenges faced in the development of the law of international organizations.[64] Notably, they also make use of the advisory opinions of the ICJ to highlight the difficulties and shortcomings of functionalism.

For instance, the *Advisory Opinion on Interpretation of the Agreement between the WHO and Egypt* is presented as an example of the Court struggling with the difficulties of functionalism in accommodating the position of third parties – being a theory which focuses on the study of the relationship between member States and the organization, it has little to say about legal issues arising outside of it.[65] Confronted with a situation where Egypt was simultaneously a member State of the WHO and the counterpart in a treaty (the Host State agreement) the Court held that international organizations, as subjects of international law *"are bound by any obligations incumbent upon them under general rules of international law, under their constitutions or under international agreements to which they are parties."*[66] The novelty in this statement was the recognition that these obligations are owed to third parties outside the organization, even when they are also member States.

The *Certain Expenses Opinion* – in which the ICJ disregarded the division of functions among different organs of the UN, as long as the action performed

---

and Competences', in J. Klabbers, A.Peters, G. Ulfstein, *The Constitutionalization of International Law* (Oxford University Press, 2011), 45 at 55–67. J. M. Farrall, *United Nations Sanctions and the Rule of Law* (2007). B. Kingsbury, N. Krisch, R. B. Stewart, 'The Emergence of Global Administrative Law', 68 *Law and Contemporary Problems* (2005) 15 at 16–17

63 E.g. F. L. Bordin, *The Analogy between States and International Organizations* (Cambridge University Press, 2018). Engström (2012). Peters (2011). Brölmann (2007, "Institutional Veil"). J. Klabbers, 'Contending approaches to international organizations: Between functionalism and constitutionalism', in J. Klabbers, Å. Wallendahl (eds.), *Research Handbook on the Law of International Organizations* (Edward Elgar, 2011) 4. Alvarez (2005). See also the recent symposium on "Theorizing International Organizations Law" in issue 31(2) of the *European Journal of International Law*, February 2020.

64 Klabbers discusses the inappropriateness of applying Reinsch's theory to a *"new wave of international organisations"* in Klabbers (2015, "EJIL Foreword"), at 10, 21. See also Klabbers (2011), at 17.

65 Klabbers (2015, "EJIL Foreword"), at 10–11, 23, 62. See also Virally, 'La notion de fonction dans la théorie de l'organisation internationale', in S. Bastid *et al.* (eds.), *Mélanges offerts à Charles Rousseau: La communauté internationale* (A. Pedone, 1974), 277 at 280.

66 *Interpretation of the Agreement of 25 March 1951 between the WHO and Egypt, Advisory Opinion, ICJ Reports 1980*, p. 73, para 37.

was not *ultra vires* the powers of the UN – is pointed out as an example of the incapacity of functionalism to deal with yet another relevant relationship: the internal division of competences between the organs of an organization.[67]

Additionally, it has been argued that the different approaches taken by the ICJ in its advisory opinions pay testament to the struggles of functionalism in explaining implied powers and their exact scope.[68] The concept is difficult to reconcile with a strict notion of 'functional delegation'. Implied powers are always susceptible to the critique that there is a fine line between these powers and "*mission creep*".[69] The fact that the ICJ both expanded (in the *Reparation* and *Certain Expenses Opinions*) and limited (in the *Nuclear Weapons Opinion*) their scope at different moments adds to the uncertainty of implied powers and to the challenges of this theory.

The ICJ advisory opinions have equally been relied on to propose alternative approaches for theorising about the functioning of international organizations, such as constitutionalism. In this regard, it has been discussed that, in finding, in the *Reparations Opinion,* that the UN had objective international legal personality that was opposable to non-member States, the ICJ approached the UN Charter as a constitution, establishing a separate legal order existing beyond the circle of member States.[70] Moreover, the finding that organizations are subject, not only to the rules established in their constitutive instruments, but also to other rules of international law applicable to them, in the *WHO Opinion,* lends support to the constitutionalists' proposal of applying rule of law and human rights standards to international organizations.[71]

Finally, a marked feature of the international system today is that it is populated with hundreds of international organizations, often operating in similar domains and establishing complex inter-institutional relations of cooperation,

---

67 *Certain Expenses*, at 168. J. Klabbers, 'Theorizing International Organizations', in A. Orford, F. Hoffmann (eds.), *The Oxford Handbook of the Theory of International Law* (Oxford University Press, 2016), at 627.

68 Klabbers (2015, "EJIL Foreword"), at 27.

69 *Ibid.,* at 27–28.

70 Brölmann (2007, "Institutional Veil"), at 89. *Reparation for Injuries,* at 15. Although, as noted by Peters, "[t]he constitutionalist approach moves significantly beyond the older view that the founding acts of international organisations are constitutions" – Peters (2011), at 256.

71 V. Engström, 'Reasoning on powers of organizations', in J. Klabbers, Å. Wallendahl (eds.), *Research Handbook on the Law of International Organisations* (Edward Elgar, 2011), 56 at 66–68. Ulfstein (2011), at 79.

creating new challenges for the analysis of the personality and powers of each individual actor.[72]

The ICJ was already confronted with this question in the *Advisory Opinion on Judgment No. 2867 of the Administrative Tribunal of the International Labour Organization*,[73] where it struggled with the attribution of a conduct to an organization in the context of a "complex web of actors".[74] In this Opinion, the Court found that the Administrative Tribunal of the International Labour Organization was competent to hear a complaint introduced against the International Fund for Agricultural Development (IFAD) by an employee of the Global Mechanism of the UN Convention to Combat Desertification (UNCCD), an entity hosted by the IFAD.[75] The Court determined that the Global Mechanism did not have international legal personality nor capacity to enter into contracts or binding agreements because these were not conferred by any of the relevant instruments governing its functioning.[76] In its reasoning, the ICJ did not seem to consider whether such personality and capacity could necessarily follow from its functions – an argument put forward by the IFAD –, in deviation from the criteria established in the Reparations Opinion.[77] In addition, by focusing on analysing the relationship between the IFAD and the Global Mechanism, the Court failed to consider the relationship with the Conference of the Parties to the UNCCD and whether the latter possesses legal personality, missing the opportunity to clarify the legal status of this institution.[78]

It remains to be seen how the ICJ will deal with the aforementioned complexification of the international legal system and the novel focus on

72 See generally R. A. Wessel, 'Institutional Law Making: The Emergence of a Global Normative Web', in C. Brölmann and Y. Radi (eds.), *Research Handbook on the Theory and Practice of International Lawmaking* (Edward Elgar, 2016) 179. J. L. Dunoff, 'Mapping a Hidden World of International Regulatory Cooperation', 78 *Law & Contemporary Problems* (2015) 267.

73 Judgment No. 2867 of the Administrative Tribunal of the International Labour Organization upon a Complaint Filed against the International Fund for Agricultural Development, *Advisory Opinion, ICJ Reports 2012*, p. 10 ("Judgment No. 2867 of the ILOAT").

74 R. S. J. Martha, 'Attribution of Conduct after the Advisory Opinion on the Global Mechanism', in M. Ragazzi (ed.), *Responsibility of International Organizations: Essays in Memory of Sir Ian Brownlie* (Brill, 2013), 275 at 276–7, noting that "organizations set up subsidiary bodies and sister organizations or have become intertwined through resource sharing and other cooperative structures".

75 Judgment No. 2867 of the ILOAT, paras. 49–51.

76 *Ibid.*, paras. 57–61.

77 Reparation for Injuries, at 9. See Martha (2013), at 284

78 See Judgment No. 2867 of the ILOAT, paras. 67–68, 71–77. Martha (2013), at 283.

accountability and legitimacy of international institutions in its future jurisprudence, and whether it will continue to consolidate the role of international organizations as important actors in international law.

5 Conclusions

The long-lasting impact that the advisory opinions of both the PCIJ and the ICJ have had on the development of the law and theory of international organizations is noteworthy. Their findings have been invoked at all stages of development of the field: when recognizing the existence of an autonomous subject, different from States; when assuring that it enjoys the necessary powers to pursue its functions while also reinforcing the limitations of those powers; when consolidating the premises of functionalism and when proposing alternative approaches.

In particular, the broad statements made by the ICJ meant that its advisory opinions have merited different interpretations – a stellar example being the *Reparation Opinion*, which is used to sustain different positions in the debate. While, in part, contributing to the uncertainty surrounding certain aspects of the legal regime of international organizations, the openness of the Court's findings has also allowed the debate to evolve, as organizations themselves have changed significantly in their purposes and institutional structure over the last decades.

In 2015, J. Klabbers wrote that "*our understanding of the law of international organizations does not run very deep.*"[79] While that remains true by many accounts, a further assertion can equally be made: the shallow understanding we do have is vastly reliant on what the international courts, in particular the International Court of Justice, have told us.

---

79 Klabbers (2015 "EJIL Foreword"), at 9.

PART 4

The Contribution of the International Tribunal for the Law of the Sea (ITLOS) to the Developement of the Law of the Sea

Introduction

Fernando Loureiro Bastos

The Law of the Sea is a very dynamic and evolving area of international law. Although the United Nations Convention on the Law of the Sea (UNCLOS) of 10 December 1982 can be seen as a framework convention on the matter, the International Law of the Sea is not limited to its provisions. On the contrary, at present, the International Law of the Sea simultaneously includes rules of a customary nature settled over the centuries, a great number of treaties, both multilateral and bilateral, that have been multiplying during the most recent decades, and also secondary law created by a group of international intergovernmental organizations whose spatial application area is the sea (like the Food and Agriculture Organization of the United Nations, for fisheries, and the International Maritime Organization, for navigation). In addition, the subjects included in the scope of the Law of the Sea have been developing and diversifying in a very marked way since the end of the Second World War.

Accordingly, the International Law of the Sea can be understood as being composed of three major groups of matters. Firstly, it regulates the international legal regime of the various maritime spaces, whether these are subject to the sovereignty or jurisdiction of the coastal States (internal waters, territorial sea, contiguous zone, exclusive economic zone and continental shelf), are international common spaces (high seas) or internationalized maritime spaces (the Area). Secondly, it includes activities that can be pursued in maritime spaces, with an emphasis on economic activities, such as navigation, fishing, and the exploration of non-living natural resources, such as oil and natural gas. And, finally, it integrates conflict resolution mechanisms that occur in maritime spaces, with an emphasis on issues related to the delimitation of maritime borders and disputes involving ships engaged in activities of an economic nature.

The International Tribunal for the Law of the Sea (ITLOS) was created under the UNCLOS and was one of its main innovations. It is a permanent, universal, international court which specializes in the resolution of conflicts that occur in maritime spaces. ITLOS started working in August 1996 with the election of the first twenty-one judges. The Hamburg Tribunal can deal with disputes that are submitted to it by the States Parties to UNCLOS, by the European Union as a party to UNCLOS, under Annex IX of UNCLOS (as in the *Case concerning the Conservation and Sustainable Exploitation of Swordfish Stocks in the South-Eastern Pacific Ocean*), by States and by the various entities referred to in Part

© KONINKLIJKE BRILL NV, LEIDEN, 2022 | DOI:10.1163/9789004467668_015

XI UNCLOS (according to Article 187), and also by other States or international organizations that accept its jurisdiction. Pursuant to Article 20 of the Statute of ITLOS, the 'Tribunal shall be open to State Parties' (para. 1), and to 'entities other than States Parties in any case expressly provided for in part IX or in any case submitted pursuant to any other agreement concerning jurisdiction on the Tribunal which is accepted by all parties to that case' (para. 2).

The Seabed Disputes Chamber, provided for in Section 5 of Part XI of UNCLOS (Articles 186 to 191) and in Article 14 of the Statute of ITLOS, is part of ITLOS. In accordance with Article 15 of the Statute of ITLOS, special chambers, composed of three of more of its judges, can be established to deal 'with particular categories of disputes'. Under this provision, the following special chambers have been created: i) the Chamber of Summary Procedure, with five members; ii) the Chamber for Fisheries Disputes, with nine members; iii) the Chamber for Marine Environment Disputes, with nine members; iv) the Chamber for Maritime Delimitation Disputes, with eleven members; and v) the special chambers for a particular dispute, at a request of the parties, as happened, in 2000, for the *Case concerning the Conservation and Sustainable Exploitation of Swordfish Stocks in the South-Eastern Pacific Ocean,* in 2015, for the *Dispute concerning Delimitation of the Maritime Boundary between Ghana and Côte d'Ivoire in the Atlantic Ocean* and, in 2019, for the *Dispute concerning Delimitation of the Maritime Boundary between Mauritius and Maldives in the Indian Ocean.*

Since the beginning of the operation of ITLOS, almost three dozen cases have been submitted to it, nine of which related to provisional measures, eight to the prompt release of the vessels and crews, and three to the delimitation of maritime borders. Pursuant to Article 33 of the Statute of ITLOS, the Hamburg Tribunal decisions are final and must be enforced, with binding force, by all parties to the dispute.

The three chapters that are included in Part Four of this book are unmistakable proof of the dynamism of the International Law of the Sea and the importance of ITLOS for its development.

Firstly, *Nilüfer Oral*'s study, 'The Contribution of ITLOS to the Development of International Law for Protection of the Marine Environment and Conservation of Living Resources', aims to present the Hamburg Tribunal's contribution to the development of the conventional rules on the protection of the marine environment and the exploitation of fish stocks, in particular the legal framework contained in Part XII of UNCLOS, through a number of contentious cases (such as the *Southern Bluefin Tuna Cases*, the *MOX Plant Case,* the *Case concerning Land Reclamation by Singapore in and around the Straits of Johor,* the *Volga Case*, the *Hoshinmaru Case*, and the *M/V "Virginia G" Case*) and by two advisory opinions. On the one hand, the *Advisory Opinion on the Responsibilities and Obligations of States Sponsoring Persons and Entities with respect to Activities in the Area* – was concerned with the setting high standards of due diligence for sponsoring States and with establishing legal obligations to apply precaution and the best environmental practice and to conduct environmental impact assessments when conducting the exploitation of mineral resources in the Area. And, on the other hand, the *Advisory Opinion submitted the Sub-Regional Fisheries Commission*, was dedicated to the establishment of a ground-breaking international legal regime applicable to flag States whose fishing vessels engage in illegal, unreported and unregulated (IUU) fishing in the exclusive economic zone of other States.

Secondly, *Vasco Becker-Weinberg*'s text on the "Implications of the *M/V 'Norstar'* case (*Panama v. Italy*) and the *M/T 'San Padre Pio'* case (*Switzerland v. Nigeria*) for the Further Development of the Law of the Sea", concerns the content of the long-established freedom of the high seas, and, specifically, with the freedom of navigation, and the content of the principle of the exclusive flag State jurisdiction when confronted with bunkering activities in the high seas (and the exclusive economic zone) as well as the enforcement jurisdiction and prescriptive criminal jurisdiction of the coastal States.

Thirdly, with the study 'Limits on the Use of Force at Sea in the Jurisprudence of ITLOS: From *M/V Saiga* to *Ukraine/Russia*', *Maria Emilynda Jeddahlyn Pia V. Benosa* presents an overview of the character of, and limitations of, the use of force at sea by a variety of State actors, whether against their counterparts or when faced with non-State actors, taking into consideration the two *Saiga Cases*, the *M/V Virginia G Case*, the *Enrica Lexie Incident Case* and the *Case concerning the detention of three Ukrainian naval vessels*.

CHAPTER 11

The Contribution of ITLOS to the Development of International Law for Protection of the Marine Environment and Conservation of Living Resources

Nilüfer Oral

1 Introduction

The 1982 United Nations Convention on the Law of the Sea (hereinafter "LOSC")[1] stands out as one of the major achievements in international law for many reasons, amongst which is Part XII on protection and preservation of the marine environment and Part XV on the settlement of disputes. Chief among the innovations introduced by Part XV on settlement of disputes is the creation of the International Tribunal for the Law of the Sea (Annex VI). In addition, the Statute of the Tribunal provides for the establishment of special chambers composed of five of its elected members.[2] The LOSC also created the specialized Seabed Disputes Chamber for disputes arising in relation to Part XI for the Area. To date, the Seabed Chamber has issued only one advisory opinion. Overall, Part XV provides an unprecedented array of options for compulsory dispute settlement, including the option for States to select the constitution of an Annex VIII special tribunal specifically for disputes for fisheries, protection and preservation of the marine environment, marine scientific research and shipping, including pollution, which to date has not been invoked.

At the time it was adopted, Part XII on the protection and preservation of the marine environment broke important ground by providing the first overarching regime for the protection of the marine environment. In addition to the broad and unqualified obligation for States to protect and preserve the marine environment, Part XII introduced a number of clear obligations on all States to take measures against pollution of the marine environment from all sources, obligations to prevent transboundary harm, and a number of obligations of cooperation. Complementary to Part XII is Part IX on enclosed and semi-enclose seas that also provides a framework of regional cooperation in respect

1 United Nations Convention on the Law of the Sea (adopted 10 December 1982, entered into force 16 November 1994) 1833 UNTS 397 (hereinafter 1982 LOSC).

2 1982 LOSC, Annex VI, art 15.

© KONINKLIJKE BRILL NV, LEIDEN, 2022 | DOI:10.1163/9789004467668_016

of protection and preservation of the marine environment. In addition, the LOSC provides for rights and obligations related to the conservation and management of living resources of the sea including marine mammals. The 1995 Fish Stocks Agreement for Highly Migratory and Straddling Fish Stocks[3] provides a detailed set of rights and obligations, as well as applicable principles for the conservation and management of highly migratory and straddling fish stocks. Importantly, it adopted the settlement of provisions of Part XV *mutatis mutandis*.[4]

The LOSC was negotiated and adopted before the historical 1992 UN Rio 'Earth' Summit,[5] where new environmental principles, such as the precautionary approach and the use of environmental impact assessments, were adopted together with codification of new environmental concerns such as the protection of biodiversity and climate change. This 10-year time lag resulted in gaps in the LOSC. By contrast, the 1995 Fish Stocks Agreement having benefited from being negotiated after the 1992 Rio Conference addressed most of these new issues, except for climate change. Moreover, since the 1990s other new risks to the marine environment emerged, such as climate change (e.g., ocean acidification, sea-level rise) and marine plastics. The question is how the LOSC can adapt to these changes and what is the appropriate role for ITLOS in addressing these challenges.

The 21-member ITLOS was established in 1996 with its headquarters in Hamburg, Germany. At the time of writing this chapter, twenty-nine cases have been filed with ITLOS. Nine of the twenty-nine cases were for prompt release under Article 292, eight for provisional measures under Article 290, eight were brought for decisions on the merits[6] and two were advisory opinions. However, ITLOS has yet to decide any case on the merits involving protection of the marine environment or the conservation and management of marine living resources. Over the years, ITLOS has built up a limited jurisprudence touching upon these issues principally within the context of provisional measures and

3 Agreement for the Implementation of the Provisions of the United Nations Convention on the Law of the Sea of 10 December 1982 relating to the Conservation and Management of Straddling Fish Stocks and Highly Migratory Fish Stocks (adopted 4 August 1995, entered into force 11 December 2001) 2167 UNTS 3.

4 *Ibid.*, Art 30.

5 United Nations Conference on Environment and Development, 3 -14 June 1992, Rio de Janeiro; Rio Declaration on Environment and Development.

6 The *Case concerning the Conservation and Sustainable Exploitation of Swordfish Stocks in the South-Eastern Pacific Ocean* (*Chile v. European Union*) at the Parties' request was discontinued and removed from the Tribunal's list by order dated 17 December 2009.

prompt release cases. The few cases involving Part XII that reached the merits were decided by Annex VII arbitral tribunals.[7]

The present chapter will review the cases brought before ITLOS invoking obligations concerning protection and preservation of the marine environment and the conservation and management of marine living resources and assess the contribution of the Tribunal to the development of international law in this area.

2 ITLOS and Provisional Measures Cases Involving Part XII of the Convention

The *Southern Bluefin Tuna* case,[8] was the first request for provisional measures brought before the ITLOS under Article 290 of the LOS Convention and also the first application for compulsory dispute resolution by an Annex VII Arbitral Tribunal under Part XV. Australia and New Zealand requested ITLOS to prescribe provisional measures against Japan to refrain from undertaking a unilateral experimental fishing program in the southern Indian Ocean for the southern bluefin tuna. The core of the dispute concerned the conservation of the population of the southern bluefin tuna, which was a significantly overfished species with decreasing fish stock. The experimental fishing program would increase the catch limit of Japan in excess of what was agreed by the three countries under the 1993 Convention for the Conservation of Southern Bluefin Tuna (CCSBT).[9] According to the applicants, by undertaking the program, Japan would be in breach of Articles 64, 116–119 of the LOSC. In the request for provisional measures, the applicants requested ITLOS to require parties to act consistently with the precautionary principle pending final settlement of the dispute by the Annex VII Tribunal. In response, Japan challenged the jurisdiction of ITLOS, claiming it lacked *prima facie* jurisdiction under Article 288 (1) of the Convention, since the dispute concerned the interpretation or application of the CCSBT, rather than the LOSC. Japan also asserted that provisional measures would not be the appropriate course of action in the dispute given

7 *The South China Sea Arbitration* (*Republic of the Philippines v People's Republic of China*) PCA Case No. 2013-19, UNCLOS, Award, 12 July 2016; *Chagos Marine Protected Area Arbitration* (*Mauritius v United Kingdom*), PCA Case No. 2011-03, UNCLOS, Award, 18 March 2015.

8 *Southern Bluefin Tuna* (*New Zealand v. Japan; Australia v. Japan*) (*Provisional Measures, Order of 27 August 1999*) *ITLOS Reports 1999*, p. 280 (hereinafter *Southern Bluefin Tuna*).

9 Convention for the Conservation of Southern Bluefin Tuna, 1994 Austl. T.S. No. 16.

there was no risk of irreparable damage to the fish stock of southern bluefin tuna or no urgency of the application under Article 290(5) of the LOSC.

In its Order of 27 August 1999, ITLOS found that it had jurisdiction under Article 290(5) and ordered provisional measures. The Tribunal determined that provisional measures should be taken as a matter of urgency to preserve the rights of the parties and in order to prevent 'serious harm' and to 'avert further deterioration' of the southern bluefin tuna stock.[10] By doing this, the Tribunal provided for provisional measures despite its inability to 'conclusively assess the scientific evidence presented by the parties'.[11] This was the first time in international environmental law that an international tribunal issued an action in light of scientific uncertainties.[12] The Tribunal observed that 'the conservation of the living resources of the sea is an element in the protection and preservation of the marine environment'.[13] Significantly, given the lack of any reference to the precautionary principle in LOSC, the Tribunal ordered the parties to act with 'prudence and caution' to ensure that effective conservation measures were taken to prevent serious harm to the southern tuna stock.[14] While the Tribunal did not expressly mention the precautionary principle or approach, or clarify its standard or content in the order, it has been well accepted that the Tribunal implicitly applied this principle for the conservation of living resources.[15] For example, in this Separate Opinion, Judge Treves noted that each step in the deterioration of the southern bluefin tuna stock could be considered as 'a serious harm' due to its cumulative effect causing the collapse of the stock. It seems that the urgency of provisional measures was considered by taking into account a precautionary approach.[16] Considering that the Tribunal required the parties to resume negotiation, it can be said that the provisional measures played a valuable role in the conservation of marine living resources.[17] Unfortunately, the case did not reach a decision on the

10 *Southern Bluefin Tuna* (note 8), paras. 77 and 80.

11 *Ibid.*, para. 80.

12 S. Marr, 'The Southern Bluefin Tuna Cases: The Precautionary Approach a Conservation and Management of Fish Resources' 11(4) *EJIL* (2000) 815, 831.

13 *Southern Bluefin Tuna* (note 8), para. 70.

14 H. Tuerk, 'The Contribution of the International Tribunal for the Law of the Sea to International Law' 26(2) *Penn State International Law Review* (2007) 289, 300.

15 Separate Opinion of Judge Treves, 8.

16 S. Marr, 'The Southern Bluefin Tuna Cases: The Precautionary Approach a Conservation and Management of Fish Resources' 11(4) *EJIL* (2000) 815, 831, 819; Judge Treves, Separate Opinion, para. 9.

17 Y. Tanaka, 'Provisional Measures Prescribed by ITLOS and Marine Environmental Protection' 108 *Proceedings of the Annual Meeting* (2014) 365, 366.

merits as the arbitral tribunal instituted under Annex VII of the Convention ruled against its jurisdiction and revoked the provisional measures previously issued by ITLOS.[18]

The *Mox Plant* case,[19] brought by Ireland against the United Kingdom presented the first opportunity for international adjudication of provisions under Part XII and also Part IX of the LOSC on enclosed and semi-enclosed seas. The dispute concerned the potentially harmful impact on the marine environment of the operation of a MOX plant situated in the United Kingdom on the coast of the Irish Sea, a plant which recycled radioactive material from nuclear reactors into a new fuel. Ireland requested provisional measures to the effect that the United Kingdom halt the operation of the MOX Plant and stop the movement of any radioactive material on Irish waters, pending the final settlement of the dispute by a tribunal established under Annex VII. Ireland asserted that by authorizing the MOX plant, the UK had breached its obligations under Articles 192–194, 207, 211 and 213 of the LOSC, including by failing to take the necessary measures to prevent, reduce and control pollution of the marine environment of the Irish Sea. Ireland also claimed the UK had breached its obligations under Article 123. According to Ireland, the MOX plant would contribute to the pollution in the marine environment of the Irish Sea through discharges of radioactive materials or wastes from the plant and further noted the potential risks associated with the transportation of radioactive material used in the plant on marine environment. In response, the United Kingdom invited ITLOS to dismiss Ireland's request for provisional measures.

In its Order of 3 December 2001, ITLOS found that the prescription of provisional measures to stop the operation of the plant was not required by the urgency of the situation.[20] However, the Tribunal prescribed measures which, in essence, required the parties to cooperate pending the decision by the arbitral tribunal. By giving substance to the meaning of the term 'cooperation', the Tribunal asked the parties to enter into consultations, exchange further information about the potential impact and risks of the operation of the plant and devise appropriate measures to prevent pollution of the Irish Sea.[21] Significantly, ITLOS clearly affirmed the duty to cooperate as 'a fundamental

---

18 *Southern Bluefin Tuna Case between Australia and Japan and between New Zealand and Japan*, Award on Jurisdiction and Admissibility, Decision of 4 August 2000, XXIII RIAA pp 1–57.

19 *MOX Plant (Ireland v. United Kingdom), Provisional Measures, Order of 3 December 2001, ITLOS Reports 2001*, p. 95 (hereinafter *MOX Plant*)

20 *MOX Plant* (note 19), para. 81.

21 *Ibid.*, para. 84.

principle in the prevention of pollution of the marine environment under Part XII of the Convention and general international law'.[22] In his separate opinion, Judge Rüdiger Wolfrum identified the obligation to cooperate with other States whose interests may be affected as not only under Part XII of the LOSC but also a norm of international customary law for the protection of the environment and an overriding one especially when the interests of neighbouring States are at stake.[23] Similar to the *Southern Bluefin Tuna case*, the order in the *MOX Plant case* impliedly applied the precautionary principle without making any express reference to it, apart from noting that Ireland had argued for its application.[24] Helmut Tuerk, a former ITLOS judge, explained that the reason may be that the Tribunal considered 'provisional measures should not anticipate a judgment on the merits'.[25]

Unfortunately, the *Mox Plant case* never reached the merits phase suffering the similar fate of the *Southern Bluefin Tuna* case on jurisdiction.[26]

The third request for provisional measures made to ITLOS invoking Part XII was presented in the *Case concerning Land Reclamation by Singapore in and around the Straits of Johor*[27] related to the land reclamation activities carried out by Singapore. Malaysia considered that Singapore, by undertaking such activities breached its obligations under Articles 123, 192, 194, 198, 200, 204, 205, 206 and 210 of the LOSC, and the precautionary principle. In bringing a request for provisional measures, Malaysia sought an order requiring Singapore to suspend all land reclamation activities carried out

---

22 *Ibid.*, para. 82.

23 Separate Opinion of Judge Rüdiger Wolfrum.

24 *MOX Plant* (note 19), para. 71: "Considering that Ireland argues that the precautionary principle places the burden on the United Kingdom to demonstrate that no harm would arise from discharges and other consequences of the operation of the MOX plant, should it proceed, and that this principle might usefully inform the assessment by the Tribunal of the urgency of the measures it is required to take in respect of the operation of the MOX plant".

25 H. Tuerk, 'The Contribution of the International Tribunal for the Law of the Sea to International Law' 26(2) *Penn State International Law Review* (2007) 289, 302.

26 The case on the merits of the MOX Plant dispute was submitted to an Annex VII tribunal. In face of the potential exclusive competence of the European Community and the pre-emptive jurisdiction of the European Court of Justice, the Tribunal decided to suspend proceedings in the case. The European Court of Justice was seized of the case and rendered a judgment against Ireland ruling that by bringing the case before ITLOS and the Arbitral VII Tribunal Ireland had violated the provisions on the exclusive jurisdiction of the European Commission of the *European Communities v. Ireland*, C-459/03, *Judgment* (30 May 2006).

27 *Land Reclamation in and around the Straits of Johor (Malaysia v. Singapore), Provisional Measures, Order of 8 October 2003, ITLOS Reports 2003*, p. 10 (hereinafter *Land Reclamation*).

by Singapore near the Straits, exchange information with Malaysian on current and future projects, and undertake negotiations if any unresolved issues remain. Singapore sought the dismissal of the request for provisional measures by Malaysia.

In its Order of 8 October 2013, ITLOS did not find the requisite environmental urgency necessary to grant Malaysia's requests. The Tribunal did find, on the other hand, that there had been inadequate cooperation between the two parties and in a unanimous decision it issued provisional measures that *inter alia* directed the parties to cooperate. The prescribed provisional measures for cooperation included for consultations to begin and for the establishment of an independent expert group to study the effects of the reclamation activities, pending the final decision by the Annex VII tribunal.[28] Moreover, ITLOS ordered Singapore to refrain from undertaking any activity that may cause serious harm to the marine environment or irreparable prejudice to the rights of Malaysia. The Tribunal, once again, without making reference to the precautionary principle, noted that 'prudence and caution', require the parties to establish mechanisms and engage in cooperative behaviour involving exchange of information and assessment of risks of reclamation activities.[29] The Tribunal also reiterated its pronouncement in the *Mox Plant* provisional orders case that the duty to cooperate is a fundamental principle in the prevention of pollution of the marine environment under Part XII of the Convention and general international law and that rights arise therefrom which the Tribunal may consider appropriate to preserve under Article 290 of the Convention.[30] The parties eventually settled their dispute on 26 April 2005, which was reflected in the Award of 1 September 2005.[31] Provisional measures in this case played an important role in facilitating the cooperation of the parties and thereby providing the successful resolution of the dispute through diplomatic means.[32] The case also shows that the duty to cooperate is fundamental not as an abstract principle of international law, but as concrete measures to contribute to the resolution of disputes.

28 *Ibid.*, para. 27.

29 *Ibid.*, paras. 99 and 106.

30 *Land Reclamation* (note 26), 92 citing *MOX Plant* case (note 19), para. 82.

31 *Land Reclamation by Singapore in and around the Straits of Johor* (*Malaysia v. Singapore*), PCA Case 2004-05, Award on Agreed Terms, 1 September 2005, Annex (Settlement Agreement of 26 April 2005).

32 H. Tuerk, 'The Contribution of the International Tribunal for the Law of the Sea to International Law' 26(2) *Penn State International Law Review* (2007) 289, 304.

While ITLOS did not have the opportunity to rule on these disputes in the merits stage, the *Southern Bluefin Tuna* case, the *MOX Plant* case and the *Case concerning Land Reclamation by Singapore in and around the Straits of Johor*, nonetheless, did provide a limited opportunity for ITLOS to contribute to the development of international environmental law, particularly through underscoring the duty to cooperate as part of the obligation to protect and preserve the marine environment and recognizing implicitly an precautionary approach with 'prudence and caution' as elements of environmental obligations.[33] While ITLOS refrained from analyzing or applying the precautionary principle or approach, it nevertheless adopted a pragmatic approach aimed at greater cooperation and the timely resolution of the disputes even where the evidence begged the question of scientific uncertainty. The measures undertaken in the *MOX Plant* and *Land Reclamation* cases appear to demonstrate that prescription of provisional measures can be employed as 'a judicial tool' to enforce the obligations to carry out environmental impact assessment or joint monitoring, which are, in a sense, prerequisites for the protection of the marine environment.[34] While provisional measures have also contributed to enforcement of the community interests in marine environmental protection, it is important to acknowledge its limitation due to lacking enforceability.[35]

3 Prompt Release and Cases Concerning the Conservation of Living Resources

The Tribunal has addressed the conservation of living resources in the *M/V "Virginia G" Case*.[36] The dispute arose from Guinea-Bissau's arrest and later confiscation of a Panamanian-flagged oil tanker *M/V Virginia G* and the gas oil on board. The case concerned the coastal State's regulation of the selling of fuel to fishing vessels in the EEZ and the legality of confiscation of a vessel and its cargo for violating the coastal State's fisheries regulations in the EEZ. Guinea-Bissau asserted that the arrest and confiscation were made on the ground that *M/V Virginia G* unlawfully refuelled other foreign vessels that were

33 *Ibidem*.

34 Y. Tanaka, 'Provisional Measures Prescribed by ITLOS and Marine Environmental Protection', 108 *Proceedings of the Annual Meeting* (2014) 365, 366.

35 *Idem*, 367.

36 *M/V "Virginia G" (Panama v. Guinea-Bissau), Judgment, ITLOS Reports 2014*, p. 4 (hereinafter *M/V "Virginia G"*). See also, B. H. Oxman and V. P. Cogliati-Bantz, 'The M/V "Virginia G" (Panama/Guinea-Bissau)', 108(4) *AJIL* (2014) 769–775.

fishing in Guinea-Bissau's EEZ. The dispute was submitted to ITLOS by the way of a special agreement concluded between the parties.

A key issue before the Tribunal was the regulation of foreign vessels fishing in the EEZ. Specifically, the Tribunal was asked whether *M/V Virginia G*'s bunkering activity in support of other fishing vessels in Guinea-Bissau's EEZ was protected under the freedom of navigation and other internationally lawful uses of the sea under Article 58 of the LOSC, as claimed Panama[37] or whether the activity bore a closer connection to the coastal state's right to regulate fishing in the EEZ under Article 56 of the LOSC as asserted by Guinea-Bissau.[38]

In its Judgment of 14 April 2014, ITLOS concluded that the bunkering of foreign vessels engaged fishing in the EEZ is subject to regulation by the coastal State. The Tribunal took a holistic approach in reading Part V (EEZ) and in particular Article 56 of the Convention together with the provisions on living resources in Articles 61 to 68 of the Convention.[39] A key issue was whether the regulation of bunkering activities could be read into Article 62(4) activities. Rather than adopting a narrow interpretation, the Tribunal, taking into account other relevant instruments for guidance in defining 'fishing' and 'fishing-related activities', concluded the bunkering of foreign vessels fishing in the exclusive economic zone to have a direct connection to fishing activities as this enabled them to continue their activities without interruption at sea.[40] However, the majority declined to address whether this competence of the coastal State extended to the protection of the marine environment in general, as the laws of Guinea-Bissau had regulated bunkering within its fishing laws.[41] There was nonetheless support in the Joint Declaration of Judges Attard and Kelly that bunkering in general should fall under the jurisdiction of the Coastal State pursuant to Article 56(1)(b)(iii) of LOSC on the protection and preservation of the marine environment.[42]

The *Volga* (*Russian Federation v. Australia*) prompt release case was brought by Russia against Australia for the release of its fishing vessel and crew over alleged illegal fishing in the EEZ of Australian Territory of Heard Island and the McDonald Islands in the Southern Ocean.[43] At the time of its arrest, the

---

37 *Ibid.*, para. 165.
38 *Ibid.*, para. 193.
39 *Ibid.*, para. 209.
40 *Ibid.*, paras. 215–217.
41 M/V "Virginia G" (note 36), para. 224.
42 Joint Declaration of Judges Kelly and Attard, 14 April 2014.
43 *"Volga"(Russian Federation v. Australia), Prompt Release, Judgment,* ITLOS *Reports* 2002, p. 10

vessel was holding over 130 tonnes of Patagonian toothfish, a species that, described by Australia, as "seriously depleted" and a "matter of international concern", further protected under the Conservation of Antarctic Marine Living Resources ("CCAMLR").[44] In its determination of the criterion for assessing the gravity of the offense in regard to the reasonableness of the bond to be posted, Australia invited the Tribunal to take into account "the serious problem of continuing illegal fishing in the Southern Ocean" and the dangers this poses to the conservation of fisheries resources and the maintenance of the ecological balance of the environment."[45] The Tribunal merely took note of this and proceeded to treat the matter within the narrow lens of Article 292. Australia has requested a bond in the amount of AU$ 3,332,500 and also with additional two conditions: that the vessel carry a VMS, and that information concerning particulars about the owner and ultimate beneficial owners of the ship be submitted to its authorities. Australia pointed out that these were important tools to allow for the monitoring of illegal fishing activities.[46]

The Tribunal limited the bond only to the full value of the vessel, fuel, lubricants and fishing equipment in the amount of AU$ 1,920,000.[47] Moreover, the Tribunal denied granting the additional conditions requested by Australia claiming these fell outside the financial scope of setting a reasonable bond or security under Article 73(2).[48] The Tribunal's narrow reading of Article 73(2) limited only to "financial" bonds or security is debatable given the purpose of the two conditions requested by Australia could be seen as "reasonable" in light of the underlying offense of illegal fishing. The Tribunal had an opportunity to contribute to strengthening conservation interests of a depleted fish stock and the protection and preservation of the marine environment by including such additional conditions.

Judge Cot, in his separate opinion, highlighted at some length the gravity of illegal, unreported and unregulated fishing pointing to "CCAMLR's verdict on the devastation caused by illegal fishing in the region is damning."[49] He was of the view that "[t]he measures taken by Australia, both in terms of prevention and enforcement, clearly fall within the scope of the efforts made by international organizations to combat illegal, unreported and unregulated fishing", and moreover fell well within the exercise of its sovereign rights."[50]

44 *Ibid.*, para. 67.
45 *Ibid.*, para. 68–69.
46 *Ibid.*, para. 75.
47 *Ibid.*, para. 73.
48 *Ibid.*, paras. 76–77.
49 Separate Opinion of Judge Cot, 6.
50 *Ibid.*, 11.

The *Hoshinmaru* prompt release case[51] concerned the arrest and confiscation of a Japanese flagged fishing vessel and its crew by the Russian authorities on the ground that the vessel infringed national fisheries legislation in its EEZ and amounted to IUU fishing. The issue before the Tribunal concerned the reasonableness of the bond fixed by the Russian authorities. In its Judgment of 6 August 2007, ITLOS held that the amount of the bond was not reasonable and ordered the prompt release of the Japanese flagged fishing vessel, Hoshinmaru, and its crew without any conditions.[52] The Tribunal, in assessing the reasonableness of the bond, acknowledged the serious problem of illegal fishing in stating that the offence committed by the Master of the Hoshinmaru should not be considered as a minor offence or an offence of a purely technical nature. Monitoring of catches, which requires accurate reporting, is one of the most essential means of managing marine living resources. Not only is it the right of the Russian Federation to apply and implement such measures but the provisions of Article 61, paragraph 2, of the Convention should also be taken into consideration to ensure through proper conservation and management measures that the maintenance of the living resources in the exclusive economic zone is not endangered by over-exploitation.[53] Unfortunately, the Tribunal failed to reflect the severity of illegal fishing as an offense by reducing the bond from approximately 980,000 US Dollars to approximately 390,000 US Dollars.

The Tribunal demonstrated its willingness to adopt a holistic interpretation in the case of *M/V Virginia G*, by reading conservation and management rights of the coastal State to include regulation of bunkering activities. This is an important contribution for conservation as the Tribunal could have deemed these to be part of the freedom of navigation activities under Article 58 of the LOSC. By contrast, the Tribunal's decisions in the cases involving bonds posted vessels that have engaged in IUU fishing cases have failed to ascribe the necessary level of seriousness of IUU fishing by reducing the value and the ability to impose additional conditions.

4 Advisory Opinions

The *Advisory Opinion on the Responsibilities and Obligations of States Sponsoring Persons and Entities with respect to Activities in the Area* (Seabed Disputes

51 *Hoshinmaru (Japan v. Russian Federation), Prompt Release, Judgment of 6 August 2007, ITLOS Reports 2005–2007*, p. 18 (hereinafter *Hoshinmaru*).

52 *Ibid.*, para. 102.

53 *Hoshinmaru* (note 51), para. 99.

Chambers Advisory Opinion)[54] adopted by the Seabed Disputes Chamber is a historic opinion with importance for protection of the marine environment. The Opinion can be traced back to the request of the government of Nauru to the International Seabed Authority (ISA) seeking legal clarification on the responsibility and liability of a State sponsoring activities in the Area.[55] Previously, Nauru had submitted an application for approval of a project for seabed mining exploration activities but was concerned about the potential liabilities or costs of its potential sponsorship of a mining entity. Nauru was of the view that such exposure to financial risk would prevent developing States that do not possess the financial and technical capacities from effective participation in such exploration activities in the Area and would undermine the obligations and principles under Article 148 and Part XI of the LOSC.[56]

Based on this communication, ISA requested ITLOS pursuant to Article 191 of the LOSC and Article 131 of the Rules of the Tribunal to render an Advisory Opinion on three questions: the legal responsibilities and obligations of the LOSC States Parties regarding the sponsorship of activities in the Area, the extent of liability of a State Party for any failure to comply with the provisions of the LOSC, and the necessary measures that a sponsoring State must take in order to fulfil its responsibility under the Convention.[57] The first question is of particular relevance for international environmental law. While this advisory opinion was based on obligations from Part XI of the LOSC concerning seabed mining activities, the Seabed Disputes Chambers made certain pronouncements that have a broader impact on the interpretation of obligations contained in other parts of the Convention and notably Part XII.

In its Advisory Opinion of 1 February 2011, the Chamber, on the central issue of the meaning of 'responsibility to ensure' under Article 139 (1) of Part XI of the Convention, stated that the 'obligation to ensure' requires the sponsoring State to 'take measures within its legal system and that measures must be "reasonably appropriate"'.[58] The Chamber further characterized the obligation of a

54 *Responsibilities and obligations of States with respect to activities in the Area, Advisory Opinion, 1 February 2011*, *ITLOS Reports 2011*, p. 10 (hereinafter *Seabed Disputes Chambers Advisory Opinion*).

55 Republic of Nauru, Statement to Council Meeting – International Seabed Authority, 3 May 2010 (available on ITLOS website under the heading 'Dossier submitted on behalf of the Secretary-General of the International Seabed Authority pursuant to Article 131 of the Rules of the Tribunal').

56 *Ibid.*

57 *Seabed Disputes Chambers Advisory Opinion* (note 54) *Request for Advisory Opinion*, 11 May 2010.

58 *Seabed Disputes Chambers Advisory Opinion* (note 54), para. 120.

sponsoring State 'to ensure' as an obligation of due diligence and as an obligation of conduct and not of result.[59] Quoting from the ICJ in the *Pulp Mills* case and relying on the ILC's 2001 Articles on Prevention of Transboundary Harm from Hazardous Activities, the Chamber described due diligence as 'an obligation which entails not only the adoption of appropriate rules and measures, but also a certain level of vigilance in their enforcement and the exercise of administrative control applicable to public and private operators'.[60] By doing this, Chamber's recognition that the responsibility to ensure is an obligation of conduct rather than result can be linked directly to the ICJ's reasoning in the *Pulp Mills* case.[61]

The Chamber accepted that in riskier activities in relation to the environment, due diligence may impose more rigorous and severe requirements,[62] and discussed the precautionary approach as formulated in principle 15 of the Rio Declaration. The Chamber noted that the approach is a legal obligation under the Nodules Regulations and Sulphides Regulations,[63] and went further by emphasizing the intrinsic link between due diligence and the precautionary approach as 'an integral part of the general obligation of due diligence of sponsoring States'.[64] Most significantly, the Chamber recognized 'a trend towards making this [precautionary] approach part of customary international law' based on the fact that the approach has been incorporated into a growing number of international treaties and other instruments in its formulation under Principle 15 of the Rio Declaration.[65]

Interestingly, the Chamber also noted that the obligations relating to the preservation of the environment of the high seas and in the Area may be considered to have the *erga omnes* character.[66] While dicta, the express characterization of obligations in the high seas to be one that is owed to all States (*erga omnes*) is a significant contribution to the development of the regime of the high seas, where no State enjoys sovereignty. The Opinion also touched on 'direct obligations' of States, which are relevant to fulfilling the due diligence

59 *Ibid.*, para. 110.

60 *Ibid.*, para. 115, quoting *Pulp Mills on the River Uruguay* (*Argentina v Uruguay*), Judgment, *ICJ Reports 2010*, 14, para. 197.

61 D. Freestone, 'Responsibilities and Obligations of States Sponsoring Persons and Entities with Respect to Activities in the Area' 105(4) *AJIL* (2011) 755, 760.

62 *Seabed Disputes Chambers Advisory Opinion* (note 54), para. 117.

63 *Ibid.*, para. 125.

64 *Ibid.*, para. 131.

65 *Ibid.*, para. 135.

66 *Ibid.*, para. 180.

obligation to ensure. 'Best environmental practices' and 'environmental impact assessments' were included among the list of direct obligations.[67]

The *Seabed Disputes Chambers Advisory Opinion* is the first time the Seabed Disputes Chamber has been called upon to issue an advisory opinion. It is noteworthy that the opinion sets high standards of due diligence for sponsoring States for the protection of the marine environment and establishes a legal obligation to apply precaution and best environmental practices, and to conduct environmental impact assessments.[68]

The next advisory opinion was the *Request for an Advisory Opinion Submitted by the Sub-Regional Fisheries Commission* (SRFC Advisory Opinion).[69] The Sub-Regional Fisheries Commission, a fishing commission comprised of seven West African States, requested an opinion from ITLOS concerning the IUU fishing taking place in the EEZ of SRFC members pursuant to Article 33 of the Convention of the SRFC (CMAC),[70] which expressly authorized the Permanent Secretary of the Commission to seek Advisory opinions, and Article 138 of the Rules of the Tribunal. This was the first such request to the full Tribunal. The jurisdiction of the Tribunal to issue advisory opinion was one of the most contested issues in this case, as unlike in the case of the Seabed Chamber, the LOSC does not expressly grant ITLOS a competence to issue advisory opinions. However, such competence is provided for in the Rules of the Tribunal.[71]

The SRFC presented the Tribunal with four questions concerning the obligations of foreign vessels engaged in IUU fishing in the EEZ of another State, including the liability of such vessels, the liability of the State or international agency issuing fishing licenses and the rights and obligations of the coastal State in ensuring the sustainable management of shared stocks and stocks of common interest.[72]

---

67 *Seabed Disputes Chambers Advisory Opinion* (note 54), paras. 145 and 148.

68 D. Freestone, 'Responsibilities and Obligations of States Sponsoring Persons and Entities with Respect to Activities in the Area' 105(4) *AJIL* (2011) 755, 760.

69 *Request for Advisory Opinion submitted by the Sub-Regional Fisheries Commission, Advisory Opinion of 2 April 2015, ITLOS Reports 2015* p. 4 (hereinafter *SRFC Advisory Opinion*).

70 Convention on the Determination of the Minimal Conditions for Access and Exploitation of Marine Resources within the maritime areas under the jurisdiction of the SRFC's Member States (adopted on 8 June 2012, entered into force 16 September 2012).

71 ITLOS, Rules of the Tribunal (adopted on 28 October 1997, amended on 15 March 2001, 21 September 2001, 17 March 2009, 25 September 2018 and 25 September 2020), art 138(1): The Tribunal may give an advisory opinion on a legal question if an international agreement related to the purposes of the Convention specifically provides for the submission to the Tribunal of a request for such an opinion.

72 *SRFC Advisory Opinion* (note 69), para. 64

The Advisory Opinion of 2 April 2015 of the Tribunal is ground-breaking. First, the Tribunal opened the jurisdictional gateway to advisory opinions when such jurisdiction is conferred by another agreement.[73] Moreover, the Tribunal also recognized its role in facilitating the implementation of LOSC in stating it was 'mindful of the fact that by answering the questions it will assist the SRFC in the performance of its activities and contribute to the implementation of the Convention.'[74] In answering the questions, the Tribunal, through its interpretive powers, provided an evolutive interpretation of the LOSC. On the question of flag State obligation for IUU fishing, recognizing that IUU fishing was not 'directly addressed in the Convention',[75] the Tribunal interpreted Article 94 of the LOSC, which establishes the obligation for the flag State to exercise 'effective jurisdiction and control' over vessels flying its flag on administrative, technical and social matters, to apply to fishing activities.[76] Referring to its order in the *Southern Bluefin Tuna* case, the Tribunal restated that the conservation measures concerning living resources was 'an integral element in the obligation to protect and preserve the marine environment', and that Article 192 applied to 'all maritime areas', including EEZ.[77] This meant that the flag State has 'an obligation to ensure compliance by vessels flying its flag with the relevant conservation measures concerning living resources enacted by the coastal State for its exclusive economic zone.'[78] Referring to the *Seabed Disputes Chambers Advisory Opinion*, the Tribunal clarified the obligation to ensure compliance as one of due diligence that entailed 'an obligation "to deploy adequate means, to exercise best possible efforts, to do the utmost" to prevent IUU fishing by ships flying its flag.'[79] The failure of the flag State 'to comply with its 'due diligence' obligations concerning IUU fishing activities conducted by vessels flying its flag in the exclusive economic zones of the SRFC States', would be a violation of the international law of State responsibility and give rise to liability.[80]

The *SRFC Advisory Opinion* by the Tribunal should be considered as one of its most important outputs by demonstrating how gaps in the LOSC can be addressed through careful interpretation, thereby ensuring the Convention's

---

73 *SRFC Advisory Opinion* (note 69), para. 67–69.
74 *Ibid.*, para. 77.
75 *Ibid.*, para. 110.
76 *Ibid.*, para. 119.
77 *Ibid.*, para. 120.
78 *Ibid.*
79 *Ibid.*, para. 129.
80 *Ibid.*, paras. 146 and 216.

longevity and relevance as well as contributing to protection of the marine environment and conservation of marine living resources. The advisory opinion will be a significant tool for the SRFC members as well as other States affected by IUU fishing to pressure flag States to comply with their due diligence obligations under the LOSC. Finally, the opinion is also significant for demonstrating the dual role of ITLOS for both handling contentious disputes and for providing guidance on the interpretation and application of the LOSC and other agreements.

5 Conclusions

The 1982 LOSC provides a full legal arsenal of codified rights and obligations for the protection and preservation of the marine environment and for the conservation of marine living resources that includes a landmark part providing multiple compulsory dispute settlement resolution options. When ITLOS first opened its doors in 1996 with 21 elected judges, it was reasonable to have anticipated that States would utilize Part XV to further individual and collective interests for the protection and preservation of the marine environment and its living resources. After some twenty-five years, the final tally is somewhat disappointing especially given the continued and expanded threats to the marine environment.

Despite these limitations, the Tribunal made efforts to contemporize the interpretation and application of the LOSC in its jurisprudence to match the evolving standards of international environmental law. This was first seen in the early provisional measures' cases, where the Tribunal employed the 'prudence and caution' approach implicitly referring to the precautionary principle. Ideally, the Tribunal could have been bolder, but it's cautious approach may be understood in the background of the nascent period of the development of its jurisprudence. Over time, the Tribunal has given more teeth to Part XII and to the provisions on the conservation and management of marine living resources. The reluctance of the Tribunal to address IUU fishing in its cases was subsequently remedied by its historic advisory opinion on IUU fishing. The Tribunal provided a very clear set of obligations for flag States whose vessels engage in IUU fishing in the EEZ of other States, even though the LOSC does not address IUU fishing or the obligations of fishing vessels. This opinion should have inspired States to bring cases on the merits before the Tribunal, but to date it has not been the case.

Threats to the marine environment have evolved and increased since the adoption of the LOSC, including climate change and the very serious problem of IUU fishing. The provisions on protection of the marine environment and the conservation and management of marine living resources and the creation of a specialized permanent tribunal provided States with an important tool to enforce the obligations that would contribute significantly to ensuring a healthy and sustainable marine environment. This tool has not been sufficiently utilized by States. As seen from cases decided thus far, judicial intervention is not limited to determining violations of international law responsibilities and concomitant reparations, but also promotes cooperation, settlement of disputes and, as was seen in particular in advisory opinions, clarification of and guidance on the rights and obligations of States in line with the developments in international law.

Acknowledgements

The author extends her sincerest appreciation to the valuable assistance of Ms. Tutku Bektas (LLB Oxford University, LL.M NYU Law).

CHAPTER 12

Implications of the *M/V "Norstar"* Case (*Panama v. Italy*) and the *M/T "San Padre Pio"* Case (*Switzerland v. Nigeria*) for the Further Development of the Law of the Sea

Vasco Becker-Weinberg

1 Introduction

The development of the concept of the freedom of the high seas can be traced back to Roman ages and most prominently to Hugo Grotius and the notion of *Mare Liberum*, up to the codification efforts of the law of the sea in the last century. These efforts culminated with the high seas provisions in the *United Nations Convention on the Law of the Sea* (UNCLOS),[1] namely Articles 87[2] and 92,[3] which are similar to those enshrined in the 1958 *Geneva Convention on the High Seas*.[4]

1 *United Nations Convention on the Law of the Sea*, done at Montego Bay on 10 December 1982 and entered into force on 16 November 1994, published at 1833 UNTS 3.

2 "1. The high seas are open to all States, whether coastal or land-locked. Freedom of the high seas is exercised under the conditions laid down by this Convention and by other rules of international law. It comprises, inter alia, both for coastal and land-locked States: (a) freedom of navigation; (b) freedom of overflight; (c) freedom to lay submarine cables and pipelines, subject to Part VI; (d) freedom to construct artificial islands and other installations permitted under international law, subject to Part VI; (e) freedom of fishing, subject to the conditions laid down in section 2; (f) freedom of scientific research, subject to Parts VI and XIII. 2. These freedoms shall be exercised by all States with due regard for the interests of other States in their exercise of the freedom of the high seas, and also with due regard for the rights under this Convention with respect to activities in the Area."

3 "1. Ships shall sail under the flag of one State only and, save in exceptional cases expressly provided for in international treaties or in this Convention, shall be subject to its exclusive jurisdiction on the high seas. A ship may not change its flag during a voyage or while in a port of call, save in the case of a real transfer of ownership or change of registry. 2. A ship which sails under the flags of two or more States, using them according to convenience, may not claim any of the nationalities in question with respect to any other State, and may be assimilated to a ship without nationality."

4 Articles 2, 5 and 6 of the *Convention on the High Seas*, done at Geneva on 29 April 1958 and entered into force on 30 September 1962, published at 450 UNTS 11

© KONINKLIJKE BRILL NV, LEIDEN, 2022 | DOI:10.1163/9789004467668_017

Yet, despite the long-established principle of the freedom of the high seas and specifically that of navigation, the scope and the extent of the principle of exclusive flag State jurisdiction can still be the source of controversy between flag and non-flag States.

The Judgement of the International Tribunal for the Law of the Sea (ITLOS) on the *M/V "Norstar"* case,[5] found that the bunkering on the high seas of leisure boats carried out by the Panamanian flagged ship, the *M/V "Norstar"*, was within the freedom of navigation and that, consequently, the Decree of Seizure issued by Italy extending to such activities the latter's prescriptive criminal jurisdiction constituted an interference with that freedom.[6]

Despite both States recognizing that bunkering activities in the high seas are part of the freedom of the high seas and subject to the exclusive jurisdiction of the flag State,[7] Italy believed to be exercising criminal jurisdiction with respect to crimes of tax evasion and smuggling committed on Italian territory.

Italian authorities were of the view that the fuel was bought in Italian territory on false pretences to avoid payment of taxes, with the intention to be sold at a reduced price to mega yachts outside the territorial waters of Italy using the *M/V "Norstar"*, knowing that, after its sale, the fuel would be reintroduced undeclared into Italian territory.

Contrary to the Judgment of the Tribunal, the Joint Dissenting Opinion (JDO) by seven judges, including an *ad hoc* judge,[8] underlined a distinctive view of the possible interference with the freedom of navigation regarding bunkering in the high seas.

The main question raised by the *M/V "Norstar"* case is whether, or not, the principle of exclusive flag State jurisdiction prohibits the exercise of prescriptive jurisdiction on the high seas by non-flag States. The case also deals with other important aspects, such as the possible breach by Italy of its obligations to act in good faith and in a manner that does not constitute an abuse of right, as provided in Article 300 of UNCLOS[9] and the request for payment of

---

5 *The M/V "Norstar" case* (*Panama v. Italy*), *Judgment*, 10 April 2019, *ITLOS* Case No. 25, [online: https://www.itlos.org/fileadmin/itlos/documents/cases/case_no.25/Judgment/C25_Judgment_10.04.pdf (accessed September 2019)]

6 *Ibid.*, paras. 68–70.

7 *Ibid.*, para. 219.

8 *Joint Dissenting Opinion of Judges Cot, Pawlak, Yanai, Hoffmann, Kolodkin and Lijnzaad and Judge ad hoc Treves* [online: https://www.itlos.org/fileadmin/itlos/documents/cases/case_no.25/Judgment/C25_DO_joint.pdf (accessed September 2019)].

9 *"States Parties shall fulfil in good faith the obligations assumed under this Convention and shall exercise the rights, jurisdiction and freedoms recognized in this Convention in a manner which would not constitute an abuse of right."*

a compensation for damages suffered by Panama as a consequence of Italy's conduct.[10]

Although Article 92 of the Convention was not mentioned specifically by Panama, there is a connection between the latter and said Article 87, as the principle of exclusive flag State jurisdiction is an integral part of the freedom of navigation. The Tribunal, therefore, pursuant to Article 293 of UNCLOS, considered that in order to assess what the freedom of navigation entailed, it should have recourse to other provisions of UNCLOS, namely Article 92.[11]

This contribution attempts to highlight the different views of the Judgment and the JDO in the *M/V "Norstar"* case regarding the interpretation of the freedom of navigation and the principle of exclusive flag State jurisdiction, as provided in Articles 87 and 92 of UNCLOS

Moreover, the findings of *M/V "Norstar"* case concerning the freedom of navigation and the principle of exclusive flag State jurisdiction will again be put to test in the *M/T "San Padre Pio"* case,[12] which is still pending before ITLOS. Therefore, the outcome of both cases can play a significant role for the further development of the law of the sea.

2 Background

On 16 November 2015, Panama instituted proceedings against Italy concerning the arrest and detention of the *M/V "Norstar"*, with respect to the interpretation and application of Article 87(1) lit. a) of UNCLOS, namely the exercise of the freedom of navigation.

During the period 1994–1998, the *M/V "Norstar"* was engaged in supplying gas oil to mega yachts, off the coast of Italy, which would return to an Italian port without declaring it.[13]

---

10 *The M/V "Norstar"* case, para. 68.

11 *Ibid*, p.aras. 136–138, 216–218, 225. Article 293 of UNCLOS reads: "1. A court or tribunal having jurisdiction under this section shall apply this Convention and other rules of international law not incompatible with this Convention. 2. Paragraph l does not prejudice the power of the court or tribunal having jurisdiction under this section to decide a case *ex aequo et bono*, if the parties so agree."

12 *The M/T "San Padre Pio" case* (*Switzerland v. Nigeria*), *Provisional Measures, ITLOS Case No. 27* [online: https://www.itlos.org/cases/list-of-cases/case-no-27/ (accessed September 2019)].

13 *Ibid.*, paras. 69–70.

In 1997, the Italian fiscal police initiated an investigation on suspicion that the ship was involved in selling fuel purchased in Italy in the high seas, exempt of tax duties, to Italian and other European Union leisure boats. In 1998, criminal proceedings were instituted and on 11 August 1998 a Decree of Seizure was issued against the ship and the seizure of the oil was ordered. This Decree was carried out on 25 September with the judicial assistance of the Spanish authorities, as the ship was calling into the port of Palma de Mallorca.[14]

On 18 January 1999, the request by the shipowner for release of ship was denied. Only on 11 March of that year the possibility of its release upon the payment of bail was accepted but did not occur.[15]

On 14 March 2003, the accused were acquitted, the seizure revoked, and the ship was to be returned. Yet, the shipowner did not take possession of the ship,[16] and on 25 March 2015, the Port Authority of the Balearic Islands announced the public auction of the ship.[17]

Considering the aforementioned facts, only the bunkering activities by the *M/V "Norstar"* took place in the high seas, outside the territory of Italy and the internal waters of Spain.[18]

While Panama considered Italy's exercise of extraterritorial prescriptive jurisdiction a breach of its freedom of navigation and its exclusive jurisdiction,[19] Italy submitted that the Decree of Seizure was not in the context of criminal proceedings concerning bunkering on the high seas, but crimes that occurred in Italy. It also underlined that the Decree of Seizure was enforced in Spanish internal waters and not on the high seas.[20] As a result, Italy considered that Article 87 of UNCLOS was not applicable, and consequently could not have been breached.[21]

---

14 *Ibid.*, paras. 70–75.

15 *Ibid.*, paras. 76–78.

16 *Ibid.*, para. 80.

17 *Ibid.*, para. 86.

18 ITLOS considered that it was necessary for Spain to be a party to the proceedings, *The M/V "Norstar" case (Panama v. Italy), Judgment, Preliminary Objections, 4 November 2016, ITLOS Case No. 25*, paras. 173–175, https://www.itlos.org/fileadmin/itlos/documents/cases/case_no.25/Preliminary_Objections/Judgment/C25_Judgment_04.11.16_orig.pdf (accessed September 2019).

19 *The M/V "Norstar"* case, note 5, paras. 166, 177, 186.

20 *Ibid.*, para. 203.

21 *Ibid.*, para. 187.

3 The Judgment

The dispute between Panama and Italy included the Decree of Seizure, the request for its execution and the arrest and detention of the *M/V "Norstar"*.

In order to assess the possible breach of the freedom of navigation by the Decree of Seizure and the request for its execution, it was necessary for the Tribunal to assess the location where the alleged crimes took place, whether in the high seas or in the territory of a non-flag State, and if the prescriptive jurisdiction by a non-flag State constitutes a breach of the freedom of navigation of the flag State.

Regarding the former, the Tribunal noted that although the location of enforcement is relevant for the purpose of assessing the applicability and breach of Article 87 of UNCLOS, it is not the sole criterion that should be considered. ITLOS observed that even when in internal waters, this provision may be applicable and breached if a non-flag State extends its laws extraterritorially to activities of foreign ships on the high seas and criminalize them.[22]

On 10 April 2019, ITLOS rendered its Judgment on the case and found that there was a breach of the freedom of navigation.[23] ITLOS also found that the due regard obligation provided in Article 87(2) of UNCLOS was not breached,[24] or for that matter the obligation to act in good faith included in Article 300 of the Convention.[25]

The Tribunal considered that the ordering and requesting by Italy of the arrest of the *M/V "Norstar"* in the exercise of its criminal jurisdiction and application of its customs laws to bunkering activities carried out in the high seas, prevented the ability of the ship to navigate and conduct legitimate commercial activities in the high seas. As a result, Italy breached the freedom of navigation and other lawful uses of the sea related to the latter, as provided in Articles 87 (1) (2) and 92 of UNCLOS.

ITLOS found that the prescriptive jurisdiction was a breach of the principle of exclusive flag State jurisdiction. The Tribunal noted that a breach would not depend on the enforcement by a non-flag State, evidently with the exception of those situations where there is a valid legal basis for enforcement by a non-flag State, namely the previous agreement from the flag State and those "*cases expressly provided in* [UNCLOS] *or in other international treaties*."[26]

22 *Ibid.*, paras. 226–227.
23 *Ibid.*, paras. 224–225.
24 *Ibid.*, para. 231.
25 *Ibid.*, para. 303.
26 *Ibid.*, para. 224

4 The Joint Dissenting Opinion

The JDO found that Italy did not violate Article 87 (1) of UNCLOS and consequently, no compensation was due for the loss of the *M/V "Norstar"*. The JDO considered that in order for this provision to be violated, it must first be applicable to the conduct, i.e. the issuing of the Decree of Seizure and the request for its execution.[27]

Despite finding that Article 87 of UNCLOS was relevant to establish the Tribunal's jurisdiction, the JDO considered that this was not enough to determine that this provision applies to the conduct in question.[28]

The JDO was of the view that Italy exercised criminal jurisdiction for acts considered under Italian law to have been committed on Italian territory and not in the high seas, specifically the crimes of tax evasion and smuggling of fuel. The JDO found that "[s]*ince the alleged crime was initiated and completed in Italian territory, there is no doubt that its location was Italy and not the high seas*."[29] It also considered that the ship was used as part of an apparent criminal scheme concerning the commission of the said crimes.[30] Therefore, despite the conduct on the high sea being an element of the alleged crime, Italy was entitled to investigate these crimes and exercise its prescriptive criminal jurisdiction, particularly as Articles 87 and 92 of UNCLOS do not exclude the right of non-flag States to exercise their prescriptive criminal jurisdiction with respect to high seas activities.[31]

The JDO concluded that:

> It is widely recognized that a State may extend its prescriptive criminal jurisdiction to conduct beyond its territory when a constituent element of an alleged crime has occurred in its territory or where there is a sufficient connection to it. It may do so, in particular, if the alleged crime, of which the conduct is a part, originated in its territory, or if it was completed in its territory and, at least in some cases, when the alleged crime produces harmful effects in the State's territory. ...[32]
>
> ... a State may exercise its prescriptive criminal jurisdiction with respect to conduct on the high seas where such conduct is integral to an

27 *Joint Dissenting Opinion*, note 8, para. 14.
28 *Ibid.* See also para. 27.
29 *Ibid.*, para. 32.
30 *Ibid.*, paras. 20, 33, 35.
31 *Ibid.*, paras. 19, 30.
32 *Ibid.*, para. 31.

alleged crime committed in the State's territory, not when it is justified or allowed by international law to do so, but when it is not prohibited by international law to do so. Article 87 of the Convention does not contain such a prohibition. Therefore, even if, quod non, Italy through the Decree of Seizure and the Request for its execution exercised its prescriptive criminal jurisdiction with respect to the supplying of mega yachts on the high seas with fuel for the purchase of which taxes were allegedly not paid in its territory and which was subsequently allegedly smuggled into its territory, it did so in conformity with international law.[33]

5 The M/T "San Padre Pio"

The present review of the *M/V "Norstar"* case sought to point out some of the complexities of the Judgment and the JDO, as well as underline the main aspects where these could have further elaborated on the respective grounds.

In this regard, the *M/T "San Padre Pio"* case, submitted to ITLOS after the *M/V "Norstar"* case, constitutes an opportunity for clarification on some of the key matters addressed in the Judgment and the JDO, in addition to other aspects concerning the interpretation of Articles 87 and 92 regarding the freedom of navigation and the principle of exclusive flag State jurisdiction.

The dispute between Switzerland and Nigeria relates to the interception by Nigeria, on 23 January 2018, of the *M/T "San Padre Pio"* in the exclusive economic zone (EEZ) of Nigeria, when the ship was engaged in ship-to-ship transfers of gas oil. The interception was followed by the arrest and detention of the vessel, crew and cargo.

Switzerland submitted the dispute to arbitration under Annex VII of UNCLOS, by a Notification and Statement of Claim, conveyed to Nigeria by diplomatic Note dated 6 May 2019.[34] In the Notification, amongst others, Switzerland requests the arbitral tribunal to recognize that Nigeria breached Switzerland's rights under UNCLOS, namely the freedom of navigation[35] and the exclusive flag State jurisdiction.[36] Switzerland seeks reparation in respect of the alleged violations of its rights in connection with Article 58 of UNCLOS.[37]

33 *Ibid.*, para. 36.

34 A copy of the Notification is annexed to Switzerland's request for the prescription of provisional measures under Article 290(5) of UNCLOS [online: (accessed September 2019)].

35 Article 58 in conjunction with Article 87 of UNCLOS.

36 Article 58 in conjunction with Article 92 of UNCLOS.

37 Article 58 of UNCLOS reads: "1. In the exclusive economic zone, all States, whether coastal or land-locked, enjoy, subject to the relevant provisions of this Convention, the freedoms

Switzerland considers that these violations resulted in damages to the *M/T "San Padre Pio"*, the crew and cargo, "*as well as all persons involved or interested in the operation of the "San Padre Pio"*."[38] Switzerland claims that the actions of Nigeria are prohibited under the Convention, and that any exceptions to this prohibition must be explicit and cannot be implied.[39]

Nigeria does not accept the connection made by Switzerland between Articles 87 and 92 of UNCLOS and the EEZ regime. Firstly, it considers that Switzerland "*completely ignores the major qualification on those rights in the EEZ under Article 58*," as they must be compatible with the other provisions of UNCLOS, specifically "*Nigeria's sovereign rights for the purpose of exploring and exploiting, conserving and managing living and non-living natural resources in (...) the EEZ established in Article 56*". Secondly, Switzerland fails to recognize the rights of Nigeria "*to enforce laws and regulations concerning the prevention, reduction and control of pollution arising from or in connection with seabed activities*," pursuant to Articles 208 and 214 of UNCLOS. Thirdly, the *M/T "San Padre Pio"* was operating as a supply ship to one of Nigeria's most important oil and gas production facilities. This ship was doing so in the middle of the night, in direct violation of the conditions imposed by Nigeria, among other breaches of Nigerian law.[40] Nigeria further states that the ship "*had been under*

---

referred to in article 87 of navigation and overflight and of the laying of submarine cables and pipelines, and other internationally lawful uses of the sea related to these freedoms, such as those associated with the operation of ships, aircraft and submarine cables and pipelines, and compatible with the other provisions of this Convention. 2. Articles 88 to 115 and other pertinent rules of international law apply to the exclusive economic zone in so far as they are not incompatible with this Part. 3. In exercising their rights and performing their duties under this Convention in the exclusive economic zone, States shall have due regard to the rights and duties of the coastal State and shall comply with the laws and regulations adopted by the coastal State in accordance with the provisions of this Convention and other rules of international law in so far as they are not incompatible with this Part." On this provision, see A. Proelss, 'Article 58', in A. Proelß (ed.), *United Nations Convention on the Law of the Sea* (UNCLOS) *Commentary* (Verlag C. H. Beck, 2017) pp. 445–446, 455.

38 *Request for the prescription of provisional measures of the Swiss Confederation, under Article 290, paragraph 5, of the United Nations Convention on the Law of the Sea, 21 May 2019*, para. 25 [online: https://www.itlos.org/fileadmin/itlos/documents/cases/case_no_27/2019-05-21_Request_of_Switzerland_for_provisional_measures_PART_I.pdf (accessed September 2019)].

39 *Ibid.*, paras. 28 and 30.

40 *Statement in response of the Federal Republic of Nigeria to the request for the prescription of provisional measures of the Swiss Confederation, 17 June 2019*, para. 1.5 [online: https://www.itlos.org/fileadmin/itlos/documents/cases/case_no_27/Volume_I_-_Statement_in_Response_of_Nigeria.pdf (accessed September 2019)].

surveillance due to clear indications that it was likely involved in the illegal theft, refinement and bunkering of oil from Nigeria's EEZ and was, in fact, bunkering illegally in the dead of night." Fourthly, Switzerland is attempting to use the provisions of the Convention to prevent Nigeria from trying accused criminals before its national courts, thus hindering Nigeria's right and duty to exercise its criminal jurisdiction.[41]

In light of this brief outline of the positions of both States in the *M/T "San Padre Pio"* case, several questions may be raised and examined by ITLOS. In particular, whether Nigeria could have exercised enforcement jurisdiction against the ship, her crew and cargo in respect of Nigeria's domestic laws in its EEZ and outside any safety zone established in accordance with international law. In addition, the Tribunal may examine if Article 56 of UNCLOS is the basis for the exercise of Nigeria's jurisdiction regarding both living and non-living marine natural resources in its EEZ, as well as, if Articles 208 and 214 of the Convention provide the grounds for Nigeria to exercise its enforcement jurisdiction actions the *M/T "San Padre Pio"* and its crew.

Likewise, ITLOS may need to consider if the principle of exclusive flag State jurisdiction applies in the present case and, if so, what limits does it impose on the rights of Nigeria in the EEZ, specifically concerning the possibility to enforce domestic laws against foreign flagged vessels without the consent of the flag State.

The *M/V "Norstar"* case is bound to be referenced and considered in the *M/T "San Padre Pio"* case. It will be interesting to examine how the Tribunal will decide and if it will provide some additional clarity to its interpretation and application of the freedom of navigation and the exercise of prescriptive and enforcement jurisdiction in the *M/V "Norstar"* case.

6 Conclusions

In the M/V "Norstar" case, ITLOS took the view that the prescriptive jurisdiction by Italy was a breach of the principle of exclusive flag State jurisdiction. However, it could have elaborated further on the grounds for that assessment and what would be the scope to consider that a breach has occurred.[42]

Indeed, this interpretation of the Tribunal may be very narrow in cases where the freedom of navigation and the principle of exclusive flag State jurisdiction

41 *Ibid.*, para. 1.6.
42 *The M/V "Norstar"* case, note 5, paras. 216–217.

result in excluding the possibility of a non-flag State exercising jurisdiction in its own territory regarding acts committed onboard a foreign ship on the high seas and where a link with the non-flag State may be established.

Lacking further elaboration, UNCLOS would not be able to prevent a State from legislating on the exercise of extraterritorial jurisdiction, for example, in the case of acts committed by its nationals on board a foreign ship that breach international human rights law.[43]

Moreover, although it is an essential element in the public order of the oceans that ships are subject exclusively to the jurisdiction of the flag State,[44] it is long established that States' may exercise extraterritorial jurisdiction over their nationals on board a foreign ship on the high seas.[45] UNCLOS also recognizes certain cases of universal jurisdiction, such as the transport of slaves and piracy,[46] and also provides enforcement provisions, namely concerning the right of hot pursuit and the right of visit.[47] The freedom of navigation is not an absolute freedom.[48]

In the case of the JDO, although maintaining that the *MV/ "Norstar"* was only part of a criminal scheme and that the crimes were not committed in the high seas, it questions the notion that the freedom of navigation can be invoked to prohibit the extraterritorial application of criminal and customs laws of a non-flag State to the high seas. This would imply interpreting Articles 87 and 92 of UNCLOS as excluding the prescriptive jurisdiction from the protection of enforcement by non-flag States set out in these provisions.

However, similarly to the Judgment, the JDO could have elaborated further on the grounds for this assessment and its support in the provisions of

43 V. Becker-Weinberg, "Flag States' liability for wrongful acts by Private Military and Security Companies on board ships", in H. N. Scheiber, J. Kraska *et al.* (eds.), *Ocean Law and Policy: Twenty Years of Development under the UNCLOS Regime* (Brill, 2016), pp. 220–248. Also see D. Guilfoyle, "Article 92", in A.Proelß (ed.), *United Nations Convention on the Law of the Sea (UNCLOS) Commentary* (Beck/Hart, 2017), p. 702.

44 This is consistent with the general principle enshrined in Article 92(1) of UNCLOS, which provides that ships shall only sail under the flag of one State and shall be subject to its exclusive jurisdiction on the high seas.

45 For an historical outline, see C. J. Colombos, *The International Law of the Sea* (David McKay Company Inc., 1967), pp. 47–69, 285–315. Also see *S.S. Lotus (France v. Turkey)*, PCIJ Publications, Series A No 10 (1927), at 25JI, paras. 64–65.

46 Articles 99 and 100 of UNCLOS.

47 Articles 109(4), 110 and 111 of UNCLOS.

48 Article 87(2) reads: "*These freedoms shall be exercised by all States with due regard for the interests of other States in their exercise of the freedom of the high seas, and also with due regard for the rights under this Convention with respect to activities in the Area.*"

UNCLOS. It could also have provided more insight as to where the line should be drawn on the admissibility of non-flag States prescriptive jurisdiction.

Notwithstanding, in the *M/T "San Padre Pio"*, ITLOS will have the opportunity to further elaborate on its findings expressed in the different views of the Judgment and the JDO in the *M/V "Norstar"* regarding the interpretation of the freedom of navigation and the principle of exclusive flag State jurisdiction, as provided in Articles 87 and 92 of UNCLOS. Currently pending before ITLOS, the *M/T "San Padre Pio"* offers the prospect for further clarification of the Tribunal's interpretation and application of the freedom of navigation and the exercise of prescriptive and enforcement jurisdiction in the *M/V "Norstar"* case. The outcome of both cases can play a significant role for the further development of the law of the sea.

Acknowledgements

This article is a revised and extended version of a first version published in *Il Diritto Maritimo* (2019), pp. 760–766.

CHAPTER 13

Limits on the Use of Force at Sea in the Jurisprudence of ITLOS

From M/V Saiga *to* Ukraine/Russia

Maria Emilynda Jeddahlyn Pia V. Benosa

1 Introduction

The lack of variety in the types of cases brought to the International Tribunal for the Law of the Sea (ITLOS) in the early years of its constitution echoed doubts raised during the negotiations of the Third United Nations Conference on the Law of the Sea, on the wisdom, economy, and legitimacy of introducing additional specialized bodies and modes for peaceful settlement of maritime disputes, to those that then existed under international law. More than twenty years later, however, the growing majority of cases seeking prompt release of arrested vessels and/or detained crew, and those requesting prescription of provisional measures pending the constitution of a proper tribunal vested with jurisdiction under Annex VII of the Law of the Sea Convention,[1] have provided valuable insights on the character of, and limitations on, the use of force at sea by a variety of state actors, whether against their counterparts or when faced with non-state actors. For one, the second judgment on the very first case brought before ITLOS by Saint Vincent and the Grenadines following Guinean authorities' arrest of the vessel M/V Saiga, has yielded oft-cited guidelines on what constitutes excessive force in the conduct of law enforcement operations at sea. This contribution surveys, thus, the wealth of ITLOS jurisprudence for guidance not only on the aforementioned limitations on the use of force at sea, but also regarding insights on what the court interprets the legal bases thereof to be. Finally, such jurisprudence shall be examined vis-à-vis those of other international courts and tribunals, particularly those to which disputes can be brought under Part XV of the LOSC, on the subject of the use of force.

1 United Nations Convention on the Law of the Sea (adopted 10 December 1982, entered into force 16 November 1994) 1833 UNTS 3, 1834 UNTS 3, 1835 UNTS 3 (hereinafter LOSC).

© KONINKLIJKE BRILL NV, LEIDEN, 2022 | DOI:10.1163/9789004467668_018

2 The Use of Force

The quintessential statement prohibiting force lies at the cornerstone of modern international law itself, the UN Charter, which may be violated by "the threat or use of force "against the territorial integrity or political independence of any state".[2] States, however, are not precluded from exercising their inherent right of individual or collective self-defence, in case of an armed attack,[3] and force may likewise be authorized or implied in resolutions of the Security Council under Chapter VII of the UN Charter. In addition to distinguishing between most grave forms of use of force which constitute an armed attack, and less grave forms thereof, the International Court of Justice explained in *Nicaragua v. United States*,[4] that States are bound by the law on the use of force arising both from treaty and customary international law. On a more practical level, such use of force contemplated under the Charter is also understood to be more in tune with force of a military nature, in relation to which questions on the existence of an armed conflict and liability for acts of aggression may be raised, and rules of engagement prescribed. This is to be distinguished from the use of force in law enforcement contexts, which state actors are generally empowered to employ, subject to guidance that deadly force can only be exerted as a last resort.[5] The possibility exists, however, for such permissible use of force in a law enforcement context to be plotted on one end of a conflict continuum, with the threat or use of force that violates Article 2 (4) of the UN Charter on another. This is especially true in the case of "gray zone" campaigns and strategies to counter tactics employed thereunder, where both state and non-state actors alike undertake acts "short of war",[6] allowing them to specifically operate below the threshold in Article 2 (4), while achieving long-term, culminating effects similar thereto.

2 UN Charter, Article 2 (4).

3 *Id.*, Article 51.

4 *Military and Paramilitary Activities in and against Nicaragua (Nicaragua v. United States of America)*, *ICJ Reports 1986*, 14 (*Merits Judgment of June 27*).

5 See UN Code of Conduct for Law Enforcement Officials (UN GA Res. 34/169, 1979); UN Basic Principles on the Use of Force and Firearms by Law Enforcement Officials (UN Congress on the Prevention of Crime and the Treatment of Offenders, 1990).

6 L. J. Morris *et al.*, *Gaining Competitive Advantage in the Gray Zone: Response Options for Coercive Aggression Below the Threshold of Major War* (Rand Corporation, 2019), p. 17.

While there is substantial similarity in the respective texts, Article 301[7] of the LOSC "echoes, but is not quite identical with"[8] Article 2 (4) of the Charter. Article 301 does not employ a preceding "the", but instead the language "*any* threat or use of force" and refers to such force in any other manner inconsistent, not only with the purposes of the UN, but more broadly "with the principles of international law" as embodied in the Charter. Besides Article 301, the LOSC does not specifically delineate other parameters for the use of force, save for the related duty to avoid adverse consequences in the exercise of enforcement powers, such as endangering the safety of navigation, creating any hazard to a vessel, bringing it to an unsafe port or anchorage, or exposing the marine environment to an unreasonable risk.[9]

3 The Use of Force in ITLOS Jurisprudence

3.1 *The* Saiga *Standard*

Not only a notable decision given its precedence in the growing case list of the ITLOS, the *M/V Saiga* cases[10] presented the Tribunal with a first opportunity to assert its stature within the international judicial community, soon after the entry into force of the LOSC only a few years earlier in 1994. *M/V Saiga* involved the arrest by Guinean authorities in its exclusive economic zone (EEZ) of a Vincentian flagged oil tanker allegedly engaged in the bunkering of fishing vessels. Guinean authorities claimed the arrest to have been a valid conduct of hot pursuit commencing from its contiguous zone, and that in any case, it had a right to regulate bunkering within a customs radius extending to its EEZ. Saint Vincent and the Grenadines challenged Guinea's authority to regulate bunkering in the EEZ, claiming that the subject activity was guaranteed to it by the LOSC as part of its enjoyment of the freedom of navigation and/or other internationally lawful uses of the sea. The Tribunal, finding itself competent to determine the compatibility of coastal States' laws and regulations with the LOSC,[11] concluded that coastal States are not empowered to apply their

7 LOSC, Article 301: "In exercising their rights and performing their duties under this Convention, States Parties shall refrain from any threat or use of force against the territorial integrity or political independence of any State, or in any other manner inconsistent with the principles of international law embodied in the Charter of the United Nations."

8 J. Norton Moore and M. Nordquist, *United Nations Convention on the Law of the Sea, 1982: A Commentary*, Vol. V, p. 154. (1989).

9 LOSC, Article 225.

10 *M/V Saiga* (No. 1) (*Saint Vincent and the Grenadines v. Guinea*), 1997 ITLOS. 16 (Prompt Release Judgment of December 4) [hereinafter *Saiga 1*]; *M/V Saiga* (No. 2) (*Saint Vincent and the Grenadines v. Guinea*), *1999 ITLOS* 10 (Judgment of July 1) [hereinafter *Saiga* 2].

11 *Saiga* 2, para. 121.

customs laws in parts of the EEZ, other than in artificial islands, installations and structures.[12]

Besides the primary issue on the exercise of rights and jurisdiction in the EEZ, the Tribunal likewise had the opportunity of shedding light on issues and standards relating to flag state jurisdiction vis-à-vis nationality jurisdiction, the establishment of a genuine link between a ship and flag state,[13] exhaustion of domestic legal remedies, and the doctrine of necessity. One of the most important findings of the *Saiga* case, however, related to its examination of facts surrounding the arrest of the fated vessel, ultimately addressing questions of whether the exercise of hot pursuit[14] was lawful, and whether Guinean authorities used excessive and unreasonable force in stopping and arresting the *Saiga*. Saint Vincent and the Grenadines claimed that the *Saiga* was first detected by radar while it was either outside Guinea's EEZ or about to leave it,[15] but that, in any case, any pursuit was interrupted.[16] *Saiga* was then unarmed, fully laden with gas oil, and coursing at a maximum speed of 10 knots.[17] Furthermore, no visual and auditory signals were given to it prior to the commencement of the pursuit,[18] contrary to Guinea's claims that the patrol boat sent to search for the *Saiga* "sounded its siren and turned on its blue revolving light signals when it came within visual and hearing range."[19] Saint Vincent and the Grenadines also claimed that Guinean authorities fired at the *Saiga* with live ammunition, using solid shots from large-calibre automatic guns.[20] While denying that it had employed large-calibre ammunition, Guinea maintained that its authorities only used gunfire as a last resort.[21]

The Tribunal largely agreed with St. Vincent and the Grenadines, finding that besides a lack of signals, hot pursuit was interrupted when the patrol boat was recalled acting on information that *Saiga* was changing its course,[22] although the lack of a legal basis to extend its customs jurisdiction to parts of its EEZ also readily lent support to the invalidity of the hot pursuit. In finding that Guinea had used excessive (or unreasonable) force, the Tribunal took

12 LOSC, Article 33 (1) and Article 60 (2).
13 *Saiga 2*, para. 83.
14 LOSC, Article 111.
15 *Saiga 2*, para. 140.
16 *Saiga 2*, para. 141.
17 *Saiga 2*, para. 153.
18 *Ibidem.*
19 *Saiga 2*, para. 148.
20 *Saiga 2*, para. 153.
21 *Saiga 2*, para. 154.
22 *Saiga 2*, para. 147.

into account the circumstances of the arrest, in the context of the applicable rules of international law, mindful that the Convention does not contain express provisions on the use of force in the arrest of ships. The Tribunal then referred to Article 293 of the LOSC, by virtue of which other rules of international law not incompatible with the same Convention are held applicable for deciding a case. The Tribunal thus delimited the scope of such "other rules of international law" as follows: that the use of force must be avoided as far as possible, and where force is unavoidable, it must not go beyond what is reasonable and necessary in the circumstances.[23] Further, considerations of humanity must apply in the law of the sea, as they do in other areas of international law.[24]

In supporting this formulation of the scope of international law rules for the conduct of law enforcement at sea, the Tribunal also referred to earlier iterations of the reasonableness and necessity standards in the reports of joint commissions in the pre-LOSC arbitral proceedings *SS I'm Alone* and *Red Crusader*. The Final Report of the Commission in *SS I'm Alone* concluded that not only was the sinking by a US revenue cutter of a Canadian-registered British vessel on suspicion of smuggling of intoxicating liquors in the high seas of the Gulf of Mexico not justified by anything in the Prohibition Era US-UK Convention,[25] it could also not be justified by any principle of international law.[26] An earlier interim report likewise underscored the need for using only necessary and reasonable force, even though the same could incidentally lead to the sinking of a vessel. On the other hand, the Commission in *Red Crusader* found that the Commanding Officer of the "Niels Ebbesen", a Danish vessel in charge of fisheries inspection around the Faroe Islands,[27] exceeded legitimate use of force over a 31-minute interval during which it sought the compliance of the Skipper of the British trawler with an earlier

---

23 *Saiga 2*, para. 156.

24 *Ibidem.*

25 Special Agreement: Convention to Aid in the Prevention of the Smuggling of Intoxicating Liquors into the United States, January 23, 1924, U.S.-United Kingdom, U.S.T. 685.

26 As explained in the Interim Report of the Commission: "[While] the United States might, consistently with the Convention, use necessary and reasonable force for the purpose of effecting the objects of boarding, searching, seizing and bringing into port the suspected vessel; and if sinking should occur incidentally, as a result of the exercise of necessary and reasonable force for such purpose, the pursuing vessel might be entirely blameless. But the Commissioners think that, in the circumstances stated ... the admittedly intentional sinking of the suspected vessel was not justified by anything in the Convention."

27 Investigation of certain incidents affecting the British trawler Red Crusader (*UK v. Denmark*), R.I.A.A. (1961), [hereinafter *Red Crusader*], p. 526.

boarding and arrest procedure. Such excessive use of force was found, on the basis of its having fired without warning of a solid gunshot and creating danger to human life without proven necessity following the lapse of 18 minutes after its first firing.[28] The Commission further found that the escape of the Red Crusader did not justify the violent action received,[29] and that other means should have been attempted.[30]

But ITLOS also went beyond just relying on general international law notions of reasonableness and necessity in *Saiga*. It also imported into its jurisprudence, principles that have been "followed over the years in law enforcement operations at sea" – that is, the normal practice for stopping a ship at sea, which the Tribunal summed up as follows:

> [First], to give an auditory or visual signal to stop, using internationally recognized signals. Where this does not succeed, a variety of actions may be taken, including the firing of shots across the bows of the ship. It is only after the appropriate actions fail that the pursuing vessel may, as a last resort, use force.[31]

Consistent with the *I'm Alone* and the *Red Crusader* cases, the Tribunal added that even in employing force "appropriate warning must be issued to the ship and all efforts should be made to ensure that life is not endangered".[32] To fill the lack of guidance in conventional rules, the Tribunal likewise referred, prior to its entry into force, to the UN Fish Stocks Agreement's reaffirming of the basic principle on the use of force when arresting ships at sea – thus, the use of force must be avoided "except when and to the degree necessary to ensure the safety of the inspectors and where the inspectors are obstructed in the

28 *Red Crusader*, p. 538.

29 From *Red Crusader*, p. 536: (*b*) *The facts concerning the firing are as follows:* At 03.22 hours one round of 127 mm. gun-shot was fired astern and to the right of the trawler, at a distance estimated at 2.100 meters with the elevation 24/r25; At 03.23 hours the first stop-signals were given by steam whistle – signal K; At 03.25 hours one round of 127 mm. gun-shot was fired ahead and to the left, at the same estimated distance with the elevation 24/ 1 20; At 03.26 hours the signal K was repeated by steam whistle; It is established that no signal by radio, steam whistle, blank shot or otherwise was attempted earlier than 03.23 hours and it is also clear that these two shots, as well as the first two machine-gun shots astern, fired at 03.40 hours.

30 *Ibidem.*

31 *Saiga 2*, para. 148.

32 *Saiga 2*, para. 156.

execution of their duties".[33] Furthermore, "the degree of force used shall not exceed that reasonably required in the circumstances."[34]

3.2 *Developments after* Saiga

While the Tribunal may have engaged in judicial legislation by providing guidelines on the normal procedures for boarding and inspection of vessels where the LOSC is silent, it still left much to be clarified in respect of the variety of actions that may be taken. Given the narrow set of facts it contended with in *Saiga,* the Tribunal did not have an opportunity to draw distinctions as to the character of force to be employed, depending, for example, on who the action is directed against (ex. pirate, illegal fisher, other non-State actors under the effective control of a State, etc.), or which maritime zone the enforcement action is being conducted in. As noted by other scholars on the issue, the use of force examined by the respective tribunals in the cases of the *Saiga,* the *I'm Alone* and the *Red Crusader,* is such constabulary use of force employed for maritime law enforcement only, which does not, however, exceed the threshold of the use of force prohibited by Article 2 (4) of the UN Charter.[35] This is in contrast to other recognized legal bases for interception operations at sea, such as flag State consent, agreed pre-authorization, UN Security Council resolutions, and the right of visit (whether at peacetime on the basis of Article 110 of the LOSC, or under the law of naval warfare),[36] or the customary international law rules on countermeasures[37] – which may be imbued with both law enforcement and military characteristics, as varying responsibilities begin to fill gaps left by the shifting of the traditional role of navies in war fighting. Over time, however, the same Tribunal, or others constituted under Part XV and Annex VII of the LOSC would evaluate the same issues differently.

After *M/V Saiga*, similar disputes arising from law enforcement action taken by coastal States in respect of activities within their EEZ have been brought to the Tribunal. However, issues on the legality or excessiveness of the force employed have not been specifically resolved, due in part to the fact that most of these disputes have been brought as prompt release proceedings, limiting

33 Agreement for the Implementation of the Provisions of the UN Convention on the Law of the Sea of 10 December 1982 Relating to the Conservation and Management of Straddling Fish Stocks and Highly Migratory Fish Stocks, August 4, 1995, 2167 UNTS 3.

34 *Ibidem.*

35 M. Fink, *Maritime Interception and the Law of Naval Operations* (Springer, 2018), p. 196.

36 R. McLaughlin, 'Authorizations for Maritime Law Enforcement Operations', 98 (2) *International Review of the Red Cross* (2016), 465–491.

37 C. Allen, 'Limits on the Use of Force in Maritime Operations in Support of WMD Counter-Proliferation Initiatives', 81 *INT'L. L. STUD. SER.* (2006) 77.

the Tribunal's jurisdiction to issues relating to compliance with the provisions of Article 73 of the LOSC.[38] Questions on the permissible use of force in maritime law enforcement operations could have arisen in the case of the *Juno Trader*, for example, another Vincentian flagged vessel which, prior to its boarding and arrest, was allegedly shot at by a zodiac that later turned out to be a complement of Guinea-Bissau's navy vessel *Cacine*, resulting in injuries to one of the former's crewmen.[39]

In 2014, the Tribunal decided another case involving the bunkering of fishing vessels, this time by the Panamanian flagged M/V Virginia G, in the EEZ of Guinea-Bissau.[40] In this case, the Tribunal finally had an opportunity to shed light on an issue that has divided the bench since its first decision in *Saiga*, on the right of coastal States to regulate bunkering in the EEZ.[41] The Tribunal, in giving a holistic reading to Articles 56, 61 and 68 of the LOSC, as supported by State practice, found that bunkering is among those activities that coastal States may regulate in the EEZ in view of its close connection with fishing and support activities – which fall under such sovereign rights of coastal States in the conservation and management of its natural resources.[42] Like in *M/V Saiga*, the applicant State claimed that the respondent coastal State "used excessive force in boarding and arresting the M/V Virginia G", but this time, in violation of Arts. 110, 224, 225, and 300 of the Convention, and relevant international law, including the Convention for the Suppression of Unlawful Acts Against the Safety of Maritime Navigation, and fundamental principles of safety of life at sea and collision prevention.[43] Panama contended that Guinea-Bissau's

38 *The "Camouco" Case (Panama v. France), 2000 ITLOS 10 (Prompt Release Judgment of Feb 7); The "Monte Confurco" Case (Seychelles v. France), 2000 ITLOS 86 (Prompt Release Judgment of December 18); The "Grand Prince" Case (Belize v. France), 2001 ITLOS 17 (Prompt Release Judgment of April 20); The "Chaisiri Reefer 2" Case (Panama v. Yemen), 2001 ITLOS 82 (Order of Jul 13); The "Hoshinmaru" Case (Japan v. Russian* Federation), 2007 ITLOS 18 (*Prompt Release Judgment of August 6*); The "Tomimaru" Case (Japan v. Russian Federation) 2007 ITLOS 74 (*Prompt Release Judgment of August 6*).

39 *"Juno Trader" (Saint Vincent and the Grenadines v. Guinea-Bissau)*, 2004 ITLOS 17 (Judgment of December 18).

40 *M/V "Virginia G" (Panama v. Guinea-Bissau)*, 2014 ITLOS 4 (Judgment of April 14), [hereinafter *Virginia G*].

41 The Dissenting Opinions in *Saiga 1* underscored that the main decision's finding on the right of Guinea to regulate bunkering in its EEZ merely amounted to *obiter dictum*, for being outside the scope of prompt release proceedings, and since the Respondent Coastal State sought to enforce customs laws in the EEZ, and not fisheries laws that directly related to its sovereign rights under Article 56 of the LOSC.

42 *Virginia G*, para. 217.

43 *Idem*, para. 329.

FISCAP officers boarded the vessel without identifying themselves, and brandished weapons and confined the crew at gunpoint despite a lack of resistance from the crew of the Panamanian vessel.[44]

Besides citing differing findings of fact,[45] the Tribunal, in rejecting the claims of Panama, strictly applied the invoked provisions and Conventions, without drawing therefrom, general international legal principles that could be of potential application when deciding the legality or proportionality of the use of force, as Panama had urged.[46] According to the Tribunal, and consistent with its earlier finding in *M/V Saiga*, "the use of force in enforcement activities at sea is not generally prohibited."[47] The Tribunal likewise narrowly construed the applicability of Arts. 110 and 224 of the Convention which are made applicable to the EEZ by virtue of Article 58 (2), and which provisions Panama cite as having been violated since the "[M/V Virginia G] was boarded unannounced, by men who bore no identification".[48] Article 110 is thus considered to apply only to the list of cases provided thereunder, where the ships subject of enforcement activities are engaged in piracy, slave trade, unauthorized broadcasting, or are without nationality, or of the same nationality as the visiting flag State. On the other hand, Article 224 remains under the purview of Part XII of the Convention, on the Protection and Preservation of the Marine Environment. The Tribunal thus explained that while "some of [the] requirements of general international law are incorporated in Articles 110 and 224 of the Convention, [this] does not imply that [they] set out their own principles applicable to enforcement activities undertaken pursuant to Article 73, paragraph 1".[49] Unlike Article 224, the Tribunal held that Article 225 on the duty to avoid adverse consequences in the exercise of enforcement powers, is of general application and thus covers enforcement under Article 73 (1). However it concluded that it was not presented with sufficient evidence[50] on either Guinea-Bissau's endangerment of the safety of navigation or creation of any hazard to a vessel, or its bringing of the same to an unsafe port or anchorage, or exposing the marine environment to an unreasonable risk.[51] The SUA Convention was held inapplicable because the facts arose outside the context

44 *Id.*, para. 351.
45 *Id.*, para. 361.
46 *Id.*, para. 340.
47 *Id.*, para. 360.
48 *Id.*, para. 335.
49 *Id.*, para. 342.
50 *Id.*, para. 374.
51 LOSC, Article 225.

of terrorism, and has been expressly excepted by Article 2 of the same.[52] On the basis of these findings, the Tribunal unanimously ruled that Guinea-Bissau did not use excessive force "leading to *physical injuries* or *endangering human life* during the boarding and sailing of the M/V Virginia G",[53] possibly implicitly adding yet another, higher dimension to the applicable standard for the determination of the limits on the use of force.

3.3 Guyana *v.* Suriname

Earlier, in 2007, an LOSC Annex VII Arbitral Tribunal in a dispute between Guyana and Suriname arrived at a nuanced conclusion on the employment of excessive force in maritime law enforcement operations.[54] In deciding whether the action taken by the Suriname Navy in respect of the activities of holders of oil concessions granted by Guyana in the maritime area claimed by both countries, the Annex VII Tribunal affirmed that indeed, "force may be used in law enforcement activities, provided that such force is unavoidable, reasonable, and necessary."[55] Despite this, the Annex VII Tribunal ultimately held that the order given to the rig constituted an explicit threat that force might be used if the order was not complied with.[56] However, the same Tribunal took the analysis further and found that the action mounted by Suriname "seemed more akin to a threat of military action rather than a mere law enforcement activity [and] therefore constituted a threat of the use of force in contravention of the Convention, the UN Charter and general international law."[57] In one fell swoop, the Annex VII Tribunal in *Guyana v. Suriname* seemed to have bridged a gap on the conflict continuum between individual instances of maritime law enforcement action under which reasonable, necessary and unavoidable use of force is permissible, to such action conducted by military agents that may have a bearing upon "political independence" and "territorial integrity", and which breaches the prohibition on the use of force under Article 2 (4) of the UN Charter. Such reasoning has faced similar criticism as would later be directed by Italy against Panama in *M/V Norstar*, where the latter attempted to plead breaches of human rights violations before the Tribunal, thus "[confusing] the law that the Tribunal can apply to disputes under the Convention by

---

52 *Virginia G*, para. 376.
53 *Idem*, p. 125.
54 *Guyana v. Suriname*, Perm. Ct. Arb. (LOSC Annex VII Tribunal), Case No. 2004-04 (Award of Sep. 17, 2007).
55 *Id.*, para. 445.
56 *Id.*, para. 440.
57 *Id.*, para. 588.

virtue of Article 293, and the extent of the jurisdiction of the Tribunal under Article 288, paragraph 1".[58]

ITLOS, however, has not thus far made (or had the opportunity to make) similar findings in those cases subsequently brought before it, as the tribunal had in *Guyana v. Suriname* with regard to maritime law enforcement action conducted by naval forces and their complements, as was the case in *Camouco,*[59] *Monte Confurco,*[60] *Grand Prince,*[61] *Volga*[62] and *Virginia G.*[63] After all, even if it upheld the narrow application of Article 110 of the LOSC, the Tribunal explained in *Virginia G* that by the same Article, the Convention leaves it for coastal States to decide which authorities under its national law will be responsible for exercising law enforcement activities[64] – that is, whether to use warships[65] or military aircraft,[66] or any other ships or aircraft duly authorized or clearly marked and identifiable as being on government service.[67] Neither has the Tribunal made similar pronouncements on other actions that are ostensibly military in character and have a greater likelihood of being characterized as challenges to political independence or territorial integrity. The *Ara Libertad*[68] and the *Enrica Lexie Incident*[69] concerned the arrest of vessels or persons claimed to be imbued with sovereign immunity by their State counterparts, yet there is a dearth in analysis based on breaches of Article 2 (4) of the UN Charter in ITLOS.

Interestingly, however, in the Annex VII Tribunal proceedings in *Enrica Lexie,*[70] India raised precisely the argument that Italy violated Article 88 of the

---

58 *M/V "Norstar" (Panama v. Italy)*, 2019 ITLOS Case No. 25 (Judgment of April 10), para. 144.

59 French surveillance frigate *Floreal* observed Camouco's violations by employing a helicopter carried on board the same. It was arrested, rerouted and escorted under the supervision of the French navy to Reunion Island.

60 Also boarded by the Floreal; both were engaged in illegal fishing within the exclusive economic zones of French territories.

61 Boarded by the French surveillance frigate *Nivose* in the EEZ of the Kerguelen Islands.

62 Boarded by Australian military personnel from an Australian military helicopter from the Royal Australian Navy frigate HMAS Canberra, at a point beyond the limits of the EEZ of Australian Territory in Heard and McDonald Islands.

63 Officials from three different entities took part in the enforcement operation: maritime fishing inspectors, sailing crew, and a protection squad (armed forces personnel and navy infantry).

64 *Virginia G*, para. 345.

65 LOSC, Article 110 (1).

66 LOSC, Article 110 (4).

67 LOSC, Article 110 (5).

68 *"ARA Libertad" (Argentina v. Ghana)*, 2012 ITLOS Case No. 20 (Order of December 15).

69 *"Enrica Lexie" Incident (Italy v. India)*, 2015 ITLOS Case No. 24 (Order of August 24).

70 *Italy v. India*, Perm. Ct. Arb. (LOSC Annex VII Tribunal), Case No. 2015-28 (Award of May 21, 2020), [hereinafter *Enrica Lexie*].

LOSC enjoining States Parties to reserve the use of the high seas for peaceful purposes, in relation to Article 301. India underscored the fact that the Italian Marines' conduct which resulted to two deaths is contrary to the *Saiga* standard[71] and even in excess of the benchmark in *Guyana v. Suriname* for a violation of Article 2 (4) of the UN Charter.[72] On the other hand, Italy contended that India's position would actually hold that "any use of force by a State is inconsistent with [peaceful uses of the high seas]".[73] However, despite the fact that both States' arguments revealed the gaps in the law on the use of force at sea, with Italy claiming that India's position essentially amounts to a dilution of the *jus ad bellum* by lowering the threshold for armed attack,[74] the Tribunal quickly resolved that Italy did not breach Article 88 because the Italian Marines merely acted under the apprehension that the Enrica Lexie was under a pirate attack.[75]

4 Military Activities at Sea: *Ukraine v. Russia*

To date, the conclusion in *Guyana v. Suriname* appears to be the exception rather than the rule. Prior to the disposition of the issue in *Enrica Lexie*, the Annex VII Tribunal in the *Arctic Sunrise Arbitration* concluded that the Russian Federation breached its obligations to the Netherlands not on the basis of a finding of excessive force used – though the facts could have very well led to such a finding – but instead mainly on the lack of legal basis for law enforcement action against alleged violations committed by the Greenpeace-chartered Netherlands-flagged vessel.[76] In the *South China Sea Arbitration,* the operation by China's Coast Guard of its law enforcement vessels in a dangerous manner was adjudged irreconcilable with an obligation of responsible navigation,[77] though the concerned Tribunal did not make an overt finding on the use of

71 *Id.*, para. 1049–1050.
72 *Id.*, para. 1051.
73 *Id.*, para. 1061.
74 *Id.*, para. 1059.
75 *Id.*, para. 1077.
76 *Netherlands v. The Russian Federation*, Perm. Ct. Arb. (*LOSC Annex VII Tribunal*), *Case No. 2014-02* (*Award on the Merits of August. 14, 2015*), paras. 241, 275, 278, 285.
77 *Philippines v. China*, Perm. Ct. Arb. (*LOSC Annex VII Tribunal*), *Case No. 2013-19* (*Award of July 12, 2016*), [hereinafter *South China Sea*], para. 1094–1108. The acts of China's vessels were considered to be in total disregard of good seamanship and neglect of any precaution, including maneuvers that created an immediate danger, and which were not undertaken in response to a pre-existing threat. The Tribunal also emphasized that where the operational requirements of law enforcement ships stand in tension with the COLREGS,

force. Two possibilities exist: tribunals may be less willing to indulge in the same line of argument as the Tribunal in *Guyana v. Suriname* and appear to overstep their jurisdiction by arriving at a finding of a State's violation of the UN Charter and general international law; on the other hand, applicant States may likely want to proceed with caution when raising the issue, as any court or tribunal's finding on the same may ultimately weigh on and restrict its own activities that straddle the thin line between a law enforcement and military character.

Yet, it is in fact perhaps this *law enforcement-military activities* dichotomy that is of most interest in contemporary discussions on the use of force, in the light of great power competition for sea control in key maritime thoroughfares. Most recently, and almost two decades since *M/V Saiga*, the very jurisdiction of ITLOS to prescribe provisional measures[78] hinged, in *Ukraine v. Russia*, on the determination of whether the action taken by Russian authorities against three Ukrainian Navy vessels had the character of maritime law enforcement or military activities.[79] In this case, Russian Coast Guard vessels blocked the entry of three Ukrainian vessels upon their entry into the Kerch Strait.[80] During the pursuit, one Coast Guard vessel fired at the *Berdyansk*, wounding three members of its crew and causing damage to the vessel.[81] Both States have availed themselves of the right, under Article 298 of the LOSC to declare such military activities as excepted from jurisdiction under Part XV compulsory procedures entailing binding decisions.[82] The Tribunal would then have jurisdiction only if Ukraine is able to prove that the actions of the Russian Coast Guard were undertaken in the context of law enforcement.

In arriving at its finding of *prima facie* jurisdiction and the inapplicability of exceptions under Article 298 of the LOSC, the Tribunal emphasized that the distinction between military activities and law enforcement activities cannot be solely based on whether the vessels involved are engaged in that particular type of activity.[83] The traditional distinction between naval vessels and law

---

the latter must prevail. In this case, the actions of Chinese vessels were found to not be mere occasional negligence, but a conscious disregard of the regulations. The Tribunal also took note of the disparity in size of the Chinese and Philippine vessels, the shallow waters in which the incidents took place, and the creation of a two-meter-high wake causing additional risk to the Philippines' crews.

78 LOSC, Article 290 (5).

79 *M/V "Norstar" (Panama v. Italy)*, 2019 ITLOS Case No. 25 (Judgment of April 10), para. 144. *Case Concerning the Detention of Three Ukrainian Vessels, (Ukraine v. Russia)*, 2019 ITLOS Case No. 26 (Order of Provisional Measures of May 25), [hereinafter *Ukraine v. Russia*].

80 *Ukraine v. Russia*, para. 31.

81 *Ibid.*

82 *Id.*, para. 47–49.

83 *Id.*, para. 64.

enforcement vessels in terms of their roles has become considerably blurred.[84] Further, it is not uncommon today for States to employ the two types of vessels collaboratively for diverse maritime tasks.[85] Rather, the distinction should be based on the nature of the activities that actually took place.[86] In such a case, the relevant tribunal would have to conduct an objective evaluation and consider the events prior to the arrest and detention.[87] In doing so, the Tribunal found that the dispute was primarily about the regime of passage[88] through the Kerch Strait[89] (though domestic charges filed in Russia against the 24 Ukrainian servicemen is based on their commission of a crime of aggravated illegal crossing of Russia's state border),[90] and one that is not military in nature.[91] As regards the use of force, the Tribunal held that Russia undisputedly used force, when it chased the Ukrainian vessels after their decision to retreat from passing through the strait eight hours after their initial attempt, and when Russian forces fired warning shots first, then targeted shots at the Ukrainian vessels leading to damage to one of the vessels and injury to some of the servicemen.[92] Given these facts, the Tribunal then characterized Russia's use of force in the context of law enforcement rather than military action,[93] consistent with subsequent proceedings and charges against the servicemen.[94]

5 Conclusions

In so far as Russia claims that the mission of one of the Ukrainian vessels was actually to commit a non-permitted secret incursion, and in consideration of the notoriety[95] of the conflict between the two States,[96] it does not seem

84 *Ibid.*
85 *Ibid.*
86 *Id.*, para. 66.
87 *Ibidem.*
88 Ukraine relied on the 2003 Treaty between the Russian Federation and Ukraine on Cooperation in the Use of the Sea of Azov and the Kerch Strait.
89 *Ukraine v. Russia*, paras. 68, 71, 72.
90 *Idem*, para. 32.
91 *Id.*, para. 72.
92 *Id.*, para. 73.
93 *Ibidem.*
94 *Idem*, para. 76.
95 *Id.*, para. 69.
96 See General Assembly resolution 75/192, *Situation of human rights in the Autonomous Republic of Crimea and the city of Sevastopol, Ukraine*, A/RES/75/192 (16 December 2020), available from https://undocs.org/en/A/RES/75/192. See *also* A/73/L.47 (2018), *The problem of militarization of the Autonomous Republic of Crimea and the city of Sevastopol,*

far-fetched for a competent tribunal to later make a finding in a fully-fledged case, where the issue is properly submitted before it, that force employed even in the context of maritime law enforcement may have breached standards under Article 2 (4) of the UN Charter, or be justified under certain notions of self-defence, however anticipatory. After all, questions on the passage regime in the Sea of Azov simmer above underlying disputes on its legal status (i.e. claims of status as inland waters), and failure to fulfil undertakings of maritime boundary delimitation[97] – issues that may have a direct bearing on a State's territorial integrity. This is also possible, despite Ukraine's claim that military activities and law enforcement activities are "distinct, mutually exclusive categories".[98] After all, the emphasis of the Tribunal in its order of provisional measures appears to be on a post-fact determination of the character of the operations undertaken, paying no particular significance to the character of units involved (the Russian Coast Guard against the Ukrainian Navy), and acknowledging the blurring of boundaries[99] between maritime law enforcement and naval operations. While underscoring that the dispute primarily bears on passage, the Tribunal in the same Order seems to be in better agreement with Ukraine's view that the involvement of warships does not automatically connote military activities, in view of the fact that "many countries use their navies and coast guards for law enforcement at sea".[100]

The findings of ITLOS in *Ukraine v. Russia* figures greatly in related proceedings involving the same parties pending before two Annex VII Tribunals. In 2016, prior to the events involved in the ITLOS proceedings, Ukraine had initiated arbitration against Russia concerning coastal States rights in disputed maritime areas following Russia's annexation of Crimea.[101] Ukraine likewise instituted Annex VII Arbitration contemporaneously with its Request for

---

Ukraine, as well as parts of the Black Sea and the Sea of Azov, available from https://undocs.org/A/73/L.47.

97 D. Koval, and V. J. Schatz, *Ukraine v. Russia: Passage through Kerch Strait and the Sea of Azov: Part I: The Legal Status of Kerch Strait and the Sea of Azov*, *Völkerrechtsblog*, at https://voelkerrechtsblog.org/ukraine-v-russia-passage-through-kerch-strait-and-the-sea-of-azov/ (January 10, 2018).

98 *Ukraine v. Russia*, para. 55.

99 *Idem*, para. 64.

100 *Id.*, para. 58.

101 *Dispute Concerning Coastal State Rights in the Black Sea, Sea of Azov, and K. Strait, Ukraine v. the Russian Federation, Perm Ct. Arb. (LOSC Annex VII Tribunal), Case No. 2017-06,* [hereinafter *Coastal State Rights*].

Provisional Measures before the ITLOS.[102] In 2020, the Tribunal in *Coastal State Rights* rendered an Award on Preliminary Objections,[103] rejecting Russia's claims that it is devoid of jurisdiction because of the military and law enforcement activities exceptions under Article 298. The Tribunal held that for the exception to apply said military activities must be the subject of the dispute itself[104] – that is, neither the mere presence of military vessels or aircraft[105] nor the existence of a background of armed conflict would automatically trigger the application of the exception.[106] Referring to the findings of ITLOS in *Ukraine v. Russia,* it also acknowledged growing State practice of "[relying on military forces] for non-military functions such as disaster relief, evacuations, or the reestablishment of public order."[107] The similar disposition of this Tribunal and ITLOS on the application of the military activities' exception may possibly indicate how the *Detention* Tribunal would later rule on Russia's preliminary objection invoking the same exception.[108]

Such observations obtain particular relevance given the increasing employment of non-State actors of uncertain linkage or doubtful attribution to State sponsors, as part of strategies for gray zone campaigns which are "characterized by intense political, economic, informational, and military competition more fervent in nature than normal steady-State diplomacy, yet short of conventional war".[109] Tactics used under these campaigns include the employment of maritime militia,[110] which as seen in the practice of China in the East and South China Seas is essentially "an armed mass organization primarily comprising mariners working in the civilian economy who are trained and can be mobilized to defend and advance ... maritime territorial claims, protect 'maritime rights and interests', and support the PLA Navy in wartime".[111] There can be

---

102 *Dispute Concerning the Detention of Ukrainian Naval Vessels and Servicemen, Ukraine v. the Russian Federation, Perm Ct. Arb. (LOSC Annex VII Tribunal), Case No. 2019-28,* [hereinafter *Detention*].

103 *Coastal State Rights, Award on Preliminary Objections of February 21, 2020.*

104 *Idem,* para. 330.

105 *Id.,* para. 334.

106 *Id.,* para. 331.

107 *Id.,* para. 335.

108 *Detention,* Press Release of December 2, 2019.

109 J. L. Votel *et al.*, *Unconventional Warfare in the Gray Zone,* 80 Joint Force Quarterly 1 (2016), 101–109, available at https://ndupress.ndu.edu/Portals/68/Documents/jfq/jfq-80/jfq-80_101-109_Votel-et-al.pdf.

110 J. Holmes, *Five Shades of Chinese Gray-Zone Strategy, The National Interest,* https://nationalinterest.org/feature/five-shades-chinese-gray-zone-strategy-20450 (May 2, 2017).

111 Conor Kennedy and Andrew Erickson, *China's Third Sea Force, The People's Armed Forces Maritime Militia: Tethered to the PLA* (China Maritime Report No. 1, March 2017) *China*

two approaches to the character of such non-state groups: first, as relied upon by Russia before ITLOS, the Tribunal in *South China Sea* found that despite the fact that vessels engaged in a stand-off with the Philippine armed forces were not all military vessels and even included paramilitary vessels, the situation still presented a quintessentially military situation.[112] Such a finding may not only lead to a finding of a violation of Article 2 (4) of the UN Charter, but also that the situation amounts to an inter-State conflict to which the rules of naval warfare or the provisions of international humanitarian law would apply.[113] On the other hand, such militia vessels may very well be considered complements of Navy and Coast Guard vessels engaged in maritime law enforcement action, which in any case would be subject to the *Saiga* standards for the use of force.

As for States aiming to enhance strategies in countering gray zone tactics, ITLOS' order prescribing provisional measures in *Ukraine v. Russia* and the Annex VII Tribunal's Award in *Coastal State Rights* afford some leeway in the deployment of naval resources for essentially policing purposes, unburdened by notions and connotations of war-like posturing when grey-hull ships are employed instead of white-hull vessels. At the same time, with sufficient training, such naval personnel who presumably already receive more specialized instruction in terms of preparing for the possible breakout of conflict at sea, may be better equipped and qualified to make the immediate operational shift from maritime law enforcement rules on the use of force, to rules of engagement for military actions, and back, depending on the exigencies of the situation at sea.

Maritime Studies Institute, at http://www.andrewerickson.com/wp-content/uploads/2017/03/Naval-War-College_CMSI_China-Maritime-Report_No-1_People's-Armed-Forces-Maritime-Militia-Tethered-to-the-PLA_Kennedy-Erickson_201703.pdf.

112 *South China* Sea, para. 1161.

113 Common Article 2, 1949 Geneva Conventions, 75 UNTS 31, 75 UNTS. 85, 75 UNTS. 135, 75 UNTS. 287.

PART 5

Investor-State Dispute Settlement and Its Impact on International Investment Law

Introduction

Catherine Kessedjian

ISDS (acronym for Investor-State Dispute Settlement) is, for some time now, at the forefront of controversies. States who have signed BITs (Bilateral Investment Treaties) with broad terms in favour of investors and with consent to arbitration, as a matter of principle, now realize that these proceedings are lengthy, costly and may not lead to consistent and predictable solutions. How could it be, since arbitral tribunals are appointed for one case at a time and there is no mechanism to ensure a kind of "*jurisprudence constante*" or a form of precedent?

In addition, civil society organizations have voiced concerns that private judges are not the proper adjudicator when public goods and interest of a society at large is at stake in the dispute between a State and an investor. Indeed, very often environmental issues, or water resources and management thereof are at the centre of the dispute, to name only a few of the issues that fall outside the parties' strictly defined scope of the dispute.

This is why voices have been heard to the effect that a reform is needed or even that the current system as a whole should be replaced. The replacement of the present system is advocated by the European Union (EU), followed by Canada and a number of Latin American countries, among others. At the same time, other countries continue to back the present system while recognizing that some reform may be needed, such as the selection of adjudicators, a stricter control of conflict of interests, the question of double-hating and the like.

UNCITRAL was alerted to these controversies in 2015. The Secretariat conducted a study on whether the United Nations Convention on Transparency in Treaty-based Investor-State Arbitration ("Mauritius Convention") could provide a useful model for possible reforms. At its forty-ninth session, in 2016, the Commission requested the Secretariat to conduct broad consultations, take into consideration the views of all States and other stakeholders, including on how this project might interact with other initiatives in this area and on the format and processes that could be used. Informed by the work done by the Secretariat, the Commission decided that Working Group III would be working on the reform of ISDS.

The first meeting of WG III took place in November 2017. Since then, the work went on at a slow pace considering the difficulties inherent to the topic. First, the group decided that the process would be "government led". This

© KONINKLIJKE BRILL NV, LEIDEN, 2022 | DOI:10.1163/9789004467668_019

decision raised several concerns from civil society organizations. Indeed, UNCITRAL has always been very liberal in admitting observers from many different kinds of NGOs, think tanks, lobby groups and the like. Consequently, these groups wondered whether they would have the same influence as before. The Secretariat assured them that UNCITRAL tradition would be kept. It is true that many organizations have been accredited to Working Group III. However, it remains to be seen how the process will develop when time constraints and limited resources will impact the process. Indeed, the covid pandemic already limits the number of hours devoted to plenaries and, as we write, working methods will evolve into more informal meetings that will be difficult to follow for many NGOs who may have only one or two persons that follow the negotiations.

The second decision dealt with the work plan. Three stages were defined. The Group would first hear concerns about the present system and issues that were up for reform. Then, delegates would have to give some kind of hierarchy to these issues and explore whether a replacement was warranted or whether the issues identified could be solved by incremental reform. Inevitably, many redundancies occurred between phase 1 and 2. At the end of phase 2 it was clear that the room was divided in three groups: those (a minority) who thought that the present system could survive with very minor changes; those who thought that the present system needed reforms but that arbitration should be retained, perhaps with an appellate body or other specific improvement of the system; finally a group, approximately of equal number as the second one, advocated for a complete departure from the present system and the creation of a permanent body, be it a court or tribunal or other system closer to the WTO dispute resolution mechanism. Because these three groups could not be reconciled at that stage of the discussion, the decision was taken to continue work in parallel with two tracks: incremental reform and a permanent body.

This is the phase in which we stand. Each issue is discussed, with all options still open. When the discussion has been exhausted to the satisfaction of the delegates as understood by the Chair and the Rapporteur, the Secretariat is asked to propose language for the next round of negotiation. It is very difficult to predict when the process will come to a conclusion (probably not before 2025) and what will be the outcome. Indeed, the idea is that the Group will draft texts for the different options and States will have to decide, in the end, which option they prefer when seeing the exact language adopted. It may very well be that both texts (with sub options) could be adopted, and each State would choose in practice which one it prefers to adopt. This would hardly be ideal in our view, for it will increase fragmentation and complicate the resolution of disputes between States and investors. But, at this stage, flexibility is considered an added value for the future system to be designed when no common ground may be found among States. Hopefully, the next rounds of discussions will permit narrowing the disagreements to allow for fewer, coherent, options to emerge.

Against this background, in Part 5 of the present book, dedicated to Investor-State Dispute Settlement and its Impact on International Investment Law, *Somesh Dutta* addresses the issue of the inconsistencies in interpretation that arise in international investment arbitrations, discussing whether these inconsistencies may be considered the logical outcome of the fragmentation in international investment protection and of the obligation of "objective interpretation" under Article 31 of the Vienna Convention of the Law of Treaties, coupled with the absence of *stare decisis*. The author discusses also if substituting the existing ISDS mechanism with a "WTO styled" dispute resolution mechanism may be the most suitable solution and sustains that it would be preferable restraining the role of a Multilateral Investment Court to complementing investor-state arbitrations for ensuring a consistent international investment jurisprudence.

And, to conclude, *Łukasz Dawid Dąbrowski* comments on the recent interactions of the investment arbitration system with the Court of Justice of the European Union and with national courts. He addresses the role of arbitral awards in the formulation of an international law that may be universally accepted and applicable, at least until the creation of a common arbitral tribunal or of an appeal instance, questioning whether, on the other hand, the creation of such an institution could deprive investment arbitration of its characteristic features of flexibility and individuality.

Acknowledgements

The author discloses that she is an observer to the UNCITRAL Working Group III discussions, representing the ILA, together with Professors Andrea Bjorklund and August Reinisch, respectively rapporteur and chair of the ILA Committee of the Rule of Law and Investment International Law.

CHAPTER 14

The Quest for "Consistency" in International Investment Jurisprudence and the Idea of a Multilateral Investment Court

Somesh Dutta

1 Introduction

The international investment protection regime is supported by a 'unique'[1] dispute resolution system, called the investor-State dispute settlement ('ISDS') mechanism. However, in the recent past, such a 'hybrid'[2] mechanism faced severe criticism from stakeholders, *inter alia*, for lack of consistency in international investment jurisprudence. As the European Commission ('Commission') puts it, in the context of the backlash against the ISDS mechanism, the 'main concern is the complexity and the lack of predictability of ISDS decisions'.[3] In response to the said backlash against the ISDS mechanism, the United Nations Commission on International Trade Law ('UNCITRAL'), at its fiftieth annual session in July 2017, decided to entrust the Working Group III ('Working Group') with a broad mandate to begin deliberations on possible reforms.[4]

While it remains challenging to predict the future of international investment adjudication, in a sense that the popular 'investor-State arbitration' would remain the preferred mechanism for settling investor-State disputes or not, the approach adopted by the European Union ('EU') deserves special attention as it proposes radical reforms in the form of the Multilateral Investment Court

1 As it allows individuals and entities to bring claims directly against the host State at the international level.

2 J. E. Alvarez, 'Is Investor-State Arbitration "Public"?', 6 *IILJ Working Paper* (2016) https://www.iilj.org/wp-content/uploads/2016/09/Alvarez-Is-Invest-State-Arbitration-Public-IILJ-WP-2016_6-GAL.pdf (accessed 29 October 2020).

3 European Parliament Legislative Train Schedule, https://www.europarl.europa.eu/legislative-train/theme-a-stronger-europe-in-the-world/file-multilateral-investment-court-(mic) (accessed 19 October 2019).

4 Official Records of the General Assembly, Seventy-second Session, Supplement No. 17 (A/72/17), paras. 263 and 264.

© KONINKLIJKE BRILL NV, LEIDEN, 2022 | DOI:10.1163/9789004467668_020

('MIC'). It proposes that a World Trade Organization ('WTO') styled two-tier system should replace the existing ISDS mechanism.[5]

In light of the norms of international investment protection which remain fragmented, as they are contained in around 2,666 differently drafted international investment agreements ('IIAs'),[6] this contribution aims to address several questions such as how 'consistency' should be understood? Should it be differentiated from 'uniformity' in interpretation? What impact the rules of interpretation contained in the Vienna Convention on the Law of Treaties ('VCLT')[7] will have in shaping the understanding of 'consistency'?

Furthermore, in the context of the ongoing reform at the UNCITRAL level, the present chapter aims at exploring the potential impact of purely procedural reforms like the establishment of the MIC, on the question of 'inconsistency', which falls on the substantive side of law. More specifically, it will explore the feasibility of balancing the existing ISDS mechanism, i.e., *ad hoc* arbitrations, with the idea of the MIC, and whether a 'consistent jurisprudence' could still evolve if such a balance is sought.

2 The Issue of Inconsistency in International Investment Jurisprudence

Instances of judicial inconsistencies occur frequently, not only in the interpretation of recurring legal issues related to substantive standards of international investment protection, but also while applying customary international law. To highlight such inconsistencies, case-law examples relating to the Most Favoured Nation ('MFN') standard, and the defence of 'necessity' will be discussed below.[8]

5 European Commission President Jean-Claude Juncker, State of the Union Address, 13 September 2017, https://trade.ec.europa.eu/doclib/docs/2017/september/tradoc_156042.pdf (accessed 29 January 2021).

6 UNCTAD, International Investment Agreements Navigator https://investmentpolicy.unctad.org/international-investment-agreements (accessed 16 May 2020).

7 Vienna Convention on the Law of Treaties, 1155 UNTS 331, January 27 1980.

8 Inconsistencies exist while applying other standards also including national treatment, fair and equitable treatment standards.

2.1 *Varying Interpretation of Investment Protection Norms and Other Principles of Customary International Law*

2.1.1 MFN Standard

In *Maffezini v. Spain*,[9] the question that arose, in relation to the interpretation of the MFN clause, was whether the protection accorded under such a clause can be extended to 'jurisdictional or procedural' questions or not. The claimant argued that the MFN clause contained in the Argentina-Spain BIT[10] allows for a more favourable 'exhaustion of local remedies' requirement provided by a third/third-party treaty, which foresaw a waiting period of six months, as opposed to eighteen months, before referring a claim to an ICSID arbitral tribunal.[11] On the other hand, Spain contended that such an expansive interpretation would go against the *ejusdem generis*[12] principle, which foresaw that that MFN clauses can only operate in respect of the same matter, and cannot be extended to matters different from those envisaged by the basic treaty, i.e., not to jurisdictional or procedural questions.[13]

The arbitral tribunal accepted the arguments made by the claimant. It found that, although the MFN clause in hand does not expressly cover 'dispute settlement', there are good reasons to conclude that in present times, dispute settlement arrangements are inextricably related to the protection of foreign investments/investors, and as a consequence, dispute settlement provisions contained in a third-party/third treaty that are more favourable as compared to the basic treaty, may be extended to the beneficiary of the MFN Clause.[14] The arbitral tribunal finally affirmed its jurisdiction taking into consideration the broad and inclusive intention of the treaty parties and 'object and purpose' of the treaty.[15] However, it added that MFN-based jurisdiction may be subject to limitations placed by public policy considerations.[16] In its reasoning, it relied on the *Ambatielos* case[17] where it was decided that the extension of the MFN clause to issues concerning 'administration of justice' was compatible with the

---

9 *Emilio Augustin Maffezini v Kingdom of Spain*, ICSID Case No. ARB/97/7, Decision on Jurisdiction 25 January 2000.

10 Agreement between the Argentine Republic and the Kingdom of Spain on the Reciprocal Promotion and Protection of Investments, 3 October 1991 (entry into force 28 September 1992) 1699 UNTS 202 (1992).

11 Note 9, para. 40.

12 Note 9.

13 Note 9, para. 41.

14 Note 9, paras. 54–56.

15 Note 9, paras. 62–64.

16 *Ibid.*

17 *Ambatielos Claim (Greece v UK)*, *ICJ Reports 1953*, p. 10.

ejusdem generis principle, since dispute settlement provisions relating to the protection of commercial rights guaranteed under a treaty formed part of the 'protected subject-matter'.[18]

This 'expansive' teleological approach to treaty interpretation, established in the *Maffezini* case, was further followed by various arbitral tribunals (some interpreting a similar clause as found under the Argentina-Spain BIT, and some differently worded narrower clauses).[19] The approach adopted by the arbitral tribunal in the *Maffezini* case has been labelled as 'provisional' or 'plausible' as they would allow MFN-based jurisdiction unless persuaded that the contracting States Parties to the BIT actively intended to exclude it.[20]

A different view was adopted by an arbitral tribunal in *Salini v. Jordan.*[21] In the 'request for arbitration', the claimant relied on the MFN clause contained in the Italy-Jordan BIT[22] and made a similar argument as in the *Maffezini* case encouraging the tribunal to allow the application of a more favourable dispute settlement provision contained in a third/third-party treaty.[23] Italy, on the other side, argued that the said MFN clause does not allow for an interpretation where the claimants can avail themselves of more advantageous dispute settlement provision contained in any other IIA.[24]

The arbitral tribunal decided that the MFN clause contained in the said BIT does not apply to its dispute settlement provisions, and ultimately denied jurisdiction for the contract-based dispute.[25] The arbitral tribunal, in its reasoning, referred to both, the *Ambatielos* case, and the *Maffezini* case. With regard to the *Ambatielos* case, the tribunal held that the ruling cannot be applied to the

---

18 Note 9.

19 In *Maffezini v Spain,* the MFN clause referred to 'all matters subject to this Agreement' (Article 4(2) of the Argentina – Spain BIT). On the other hand, the MFN clause discussed in *Siemens v Argentina* (Decision on Jurisdiction) and *Hochtief v Argentina* (Decision on Jurisdiction) applied only to 'treatment of investments and 'activity in connection with investments'.

20 See J. Maupin, 'MFN-Based Jurisdiction in Investor-State Arbitration: Is There Any Hope for a Consistent Approach?' 2(2) *JIEL* (2011) 157, 179–80.

21 *Salini Costruttori SpA and Italstrade SpA v Jordan*, Decision on Jurisdiction, *ICSID* Case No ARB/02/13.

22 Agreement between the Government of Hashemite Kingdom of Jordan and the Government of the Italian Republic on the Promotion and Protection of Investments, 21 July 1996 https://investmentpolicy.unctad.org/international-investment-agreements/treaty-files/3379/download (accessed 2 December 2020).

23 Note 21, para. 21; See also K. Diel-Gligor, *Towards Consistency in International Investment Jurisprudence: A Preliminary Ruling System for ICSID Arbitration* (Brill Nijhoff, 2017).

24 Note 21, para. 23.

25 Note 21, para. 119.

present case because in that case, the claimant had invoked substantive provisions like 'treatment in accordance with justice, right and equity', and not jurisdictional provisions. It also noted the dissenting opinions in the judgment of the International Court of Justice ('ICJ') (which had initially ruled in the *Ambatielos* case on the issue of the obligation to arbitrate the case) where it was held that the MFN clause promises such 'MFN treatment' only in matters of commerce and navigation, and not with respect to 'the administration of justice'.[26] With respect to the *Maffezini* decision, it held that the two situations in both cases are not comparable as the MFN clauses were differently drafted (one narrower than the other).[27]

This 'restrictive' approach was adopted in *Salini* because there was no indication that the contracting States intended that the said MFN clause would apply to jurisdictional issues, and also because it found that the claimant did not provide evidence of any practice between the contracting States that would support their arguments regarding an expansive interpretation of the MFN clause in question.[28] The threshold was set higher in this finding as it required a clear expression of the application of MFN clauses to dispute settlement provisions. This interpretive approach is termed as 'affirmative' or 'definitive'.[29] This approach was further adopted in various other decisions by subsequent ICSID arbitral tribunals.[30]

2.1.2 'Necessity' under Customary International Law

In customary international law, several circumstances may be invoked by a State to preclude the wrongfulness of their conduct, which is otherwise a breach of its international obligation. Such circumstances have also been codified in the Draft Articles on Responsibility of States for Internationally Wrongful Acts, prepared by the International Law Commission ('ILC Draft Articles'), and includes, *inter alia*, the defence of 'necessity'.[31] In general, the

26 See also *Ambatielos Claim* (*Greece v UK*), Joint Dissenting Opinion of Judges Mc Nair, Basdevant, Klaestad, Read, *ICJ Reports 1953*, 25.

27 Note 21, paras. 117–18.

28 *Ibid.*

29 J. Maupin (note 20), 157, 179–80.

30 *Plama Consortium v Bulgaria,* Decision on Jurisdiction, *ICSID Case No. ARB/03/24*, 8 February 2005; See also Telenor *v Hungary*, Award, *ICSID Case No. ARB/04/15*, 13 September 2006.

31 International Law Commission, Draft Articles on Responsibility of States for Internationally Wrongful Acts, UN Doc. A/RES/56/83 (2001), Arts. 20–25. Other circumstances are 'consent', 'self-defence', '*force majeure*', 'distress', 'counter-measures'.

defence of 'necessity' remains a widely recognized principle under customary international law, both in scholarly works and jurisprudentially.[32]

In international investment adjudication context, the defence of 'necessity' frequently interacts with 'security exception clauses'.[33] In the aftermath of the politico-economic crisis in Argentina at the turn of the 21st century, a series of investment decisions gave rise to conflicting decisions regarding the interplay between the defence of 'necessity' and 'security exception clauses'. In response to a series of investment claims brought by US investors, Argentina invoked, on the one hand, the 'security exception clause' contained in Article XI of the Argentina-US BIT, and on the other hand, relied on the defence of 'necessity' under customary international law as codified under the above-mentioned ILC Draft Articles.[34] In the context of the 'necessity' defence, it argued that the impugned regulatory actions were taken to safeguard 'essential security interests', i.e., the Argentine fiscal and economic system, against 'grave and imminent peril', and thus, their wrongfulness as well as any consequential responsibility must be precluded.[35] However, the relationship between such defences remains somewhat unclear.

In *CMS Gas Transmission Company* case,[36] the arbitral tribunal did not explicitly analyse the interplay between 'necessity' and the 'security exceptions'. It confined itself to the question of whether the requirements set out in the ILC Draft Articles with regard to 'necessity'[37] have been met and answered in the negative. It further took a separate review of the conditions set out in the 'security exception clause' of the Argentina-US BIT but followed the same approach it used while examining the necessity defence under the ILC Draft

32 *Gabcikovo-Nagymaros Project (Hungary v Slovakia), Judgment, ICJ Reports 1997*, 7, para. 51; See also B. G. Rodick, *The Doctrine of Necessity in International Law* (Columbia University Press, 2020).

33 Such clauses are categorized as 'non-precluded measures clauses' and are frequently used in IIA treaty practice to carve out measures for safeguarding essential security interests from an IIA's prospective scope. The difference between the defense of 'necessity' and 'non-precluded measures clauses' is that the latter is invoked to defend the alleged breach of a treaty obligation, whereas 'necessity' precludes international responsibility once it is established that there has been a breach of a treaty obligation; See Newcombe and Paradell, *Law and Practice of Investment Treaties* (Kluwer Law International, 2009) at pp. 488–91.

34 Treaty Concerning the Reciprocal Encouragement and Protection of Investment, Argentine-US, Washington, DC, 14 November 1991 (entry into force 20 October 1994) 31 ILM 124 (1992).

35 K. Diel-Gligor (note 23), at p. 321.

36 *CMS v Argentina*, Award, *ICSID Case No. ARB/01/8*, 12 May 2005.

37 Note 31, Article 25.

Articles. Thus, it 'conflated' the prerequisites of the treaty exception with those of the customary international law defence.[38] This approach was further adopted in *Enron v. Argentina*[39] and *Sempara v. Argentina*,[40] where the arbitral tribunals held that, in practice, inasmuch as the conditions for its exercise is concerned, treaty exception is inseparable from customary law standard of 'necessity' as codified under the ILC Draft Articles. However, the tribunals agreed that, in theory, the treaty regime is *lex specialis,* and is separate from the customary law standard.

The above-discussed interpretive approach, however, has been opposed in the findings of several other arbitral awards. In *LG & E v. Argentina,* the tribunal considered the 'security exception clause' independently from the defence of 'necessity' under customary international law.[41] It engaged in an independent analysis of the different prerequisites of the defence of 'necessity' as codified under the ILC Draft Articles.[42] Thus, it treated, both in theory and in practice, the 'security exception clause' as *lex specialis*[43] to the defence of 'necessity' under customary international law. Several other tribunals followed this 'differentiating' approach,[44] and agreed with the position that the two necessity related defences invoked by Argentina entail different conditions of application, and thus need to be treated distinctly.[45] Moreover, in *Mitchell v. Congo,*[46] the ICSID *ad hoc* committee held that any defence under customary international law comes into play only if the 'primary-ranked' treaty-based defence was found to be unsuccessful.

The above case-laws clearly highlight the inconsistency in decision-making regarding the interpretation and application of both, substantive investment

38 This approach has been described as methodology of 'confluence'; See Jurgen, Kurtz, 'Adjudging the Exceptional at International Investment Law: Security, Public Order and Financial Crisis', 59 *ICLQ* (2010) 325, 341–51. See also Note 23, at p. 322.

39 *Enron v Argentina,* Award, *ICSID Case No. ARB/01/3,* 22 May 200).

40 *Sempara v Argentina,* Award, *ICSID Case No. ARB/02/16,* 28 September 2007.

41 *LG & E v. Argentina,* Award, *ICSID Case No. ARB/02/1,* 25 July 2007, paras. 229–44.

42 *Idem,* paras. 246–58.

43 K. Diel-Gligor (note 23), at p. 324.

44 This approach has been described as the 'methodology of treaty exception as *lex specialis*': See R. Dolzer, 'Emergency Clauses in Investment Treaties: Four Versions' in M. H. Arsanjani, J. Cogan, *et al.* (eds.), *Looking to the Future – Essays on International Law in Honor of W. Michael Reisman* (Brill Nijhoff, 2011) 705–18.

45 *El Paso v Argentina,* Award, ICSID Case No. ARB/03/15 (31 October 2011), para. 588; *Total v Argentina,* Decision on Liability, *ICSID Case No. ARB/04/1,* 27 December 2010, para. 219.

46 *Mitchell v Congo,* Decision on Annulment, *ICSID Case No. ARB/99/7,* 1 November 2006, para. 55.

protection standards such as the MFN clauses and principles of customary international law. In particular, the split of opinion on the relationship between the 'security exception clauses' and the defence of 'necessity' under customary international law is interesting to note because all cases involved the exact same legal basis, i.e., the Argentina-US BIT and customary international law, and also related to the same factual background, i.e., the losses foreign investors suffered due to the Argentine politico-economic crisis.

2.2 *Reasons for Variations in Interpretation*

One view is that 'lack of public international law expertise', on part of the arbitrators, is a major contributing factor for inconsistent interpretation leading to the overall legitimacy crisis in investment treaty arbitration.[47] While sufficient importance must be attached to the subject-matter expertise of adjudicators, considering the specifics in which the existing ISDS mechanism works, it needs to be explored which other factors shape the decision-making in international investment adjudication.

2.2.1 The Obligation of 'Objective Interpretation of Standards of Protection'

Article 31 of the VCLT provides that 'a treaty shall be interpreted in good faith in accordance with the **ordinary meaning to be given to the terms of the treaty** in their context and in the light of its object and purpose'. From this rule regarding treaty interpretation, it is clear that the 'wording' of a provision is the starting point of treaty interpretation. The said rule is based on the view that the 'text' must be presumed to be the authentic expression of the intention of the parties, and treaty interpretation must start with the elucidation of the meaning of the text, and not by an independent investigation into the intention of the parties from other sources such as *travaux préparatoires*, or any predilections based on presumed intention.[48]

The above-discussed rule of treaty interpretation contained in the VCLT is termed as the 'obligation of objective interpretation'.[49] Let us now approach

---

47 S. D. Franck, 'The Legitimacy Crisis in Investment Treaty Arbitration: Privatizing Public International Law Through Inconsistent Decisions' 73 *Fordham Law Review* (2005) 1521.

48 See *Wintershall v Argentina, ICSID Case No. ARB/04/14*, Award, para. 78, 8 December 2008; See also *Methanex v USA*, UNCITRAL (NAFTA), Final Award, para. 22, 3 August 2005.

49 See M. Bungenberg and A. Reinisch, *From Bilateral Arbitral Tribunals and Investment Courts to a Multilateral Investment Court: Option Regarding the Institutionalization of Investor-State Dispute Settlement* (Springer, 2019).

the inconsistencies/varying interpretations relating to the MFN standards of investment protection (above-discussed), from the perspective of the said rule.

In the *Maffezini* case, Article IV, paragraph 2 of the above-mentioned Argentina-Spain BIT was invoked by Spain. This article provides that '**in all matters governed by this Agreement**, such **treatment** shall be no less favourable than that accorded by each Party to investments made in its territory by investors of a third country'.

Further, in the *Salini* case, the impugned provision, i.e., Article 3, paragraph 1 of the above-mentioned Italy-Jordan BIT provided that 'both Contracting Parties, within the bounds of their own territory, shall grant investments effected by, and the income accruing to, investors of the other Contracting Party **no less favourable treatment than that accorded to investments** effected by, and income accruing to, its own nationals or investors of Third States'.

These examples show how the same investment protection standard, i.e., the MFN principle, can be formulated differently in different IIAs. From the formulation of such treaty standards, it is understandable that a certain degree of 'interpretive liberty' can be exercised by the arbitral tribunals in ISDS proceedings. It can be inferred that the two opposing schools of thoughts, 'expansive' and 'restrictive' established in the *Maffezini* and in the *Salini* cases, respectively, find their justification from the 'distinct language' of the MFN clause in both cases. However, it must be noted that in *Maffezini,* the tribunal's decision was not solely motivated from the linguistic differences; rather it also relied, more generally, on the overall object and purpose of modern MFN clauses.[50] Though the fundamental differences, on part of the adjudicators, in the interpretation of a particular treaty standard or a principle of public international law cannot be denied as one of the strong reasons behind varying interpretations leading to inconsistency, it remains possible that linguistic difference primarily, coupled with the peculiarity of the treaty in hand (its overall object and purpose), may also be a sufficient justification for varying interpretations of the same investment protection standard. This seems plausible, especially when approached in the context of rules of interpretation recognized in public international law (Article 31 of the VCLT).

2.2.3 The Absence of *Stare Decisis*

In international adjudication (in the context of investor-State adjudication), the role of precedent[51] remains an interesting aspect. As there is no legal

50 Note 9, Decision on Jurisdiction, paras. 54–55.

51 The doctrine of *stare decisis* obligates adjudicatory bodies to follow previous cases when making a ruling on a similar issue.

obligation to follow the rulings of a previous decision, irrespective of the fact that similar legal issues are in question, arbitral tribunals often tend to neglect such rulings while deciding a case.

This can be seen in the *LG&E* case where the tribunal throughout its legal reasoning on the interplay between the 'security exception clauses' and customary law of 'necessity' did not refer a single time to the *CMS v. Argentina* Award, which ruled previously on a similar interpretive issue. This is coupled with another fact, that one of the arbitrators adjudicated both cases (as a member of both the tribunals), which indicates that such a previous ruling was ignored consciously. The omission of reference to any relevant ruling, not only breaks-off any link to potentially established lines of jurisprudence, but further complicates the handling of precedents for future adjudicatory bodies dealing with similar issues.[52]

3 The Desirable Level of Consistency in International Investment Jurisprudence

After discussing a few examples of inconsistent decisions on similar legal issues, and the probable reasons for such variations in the interpretive exercise, the question remains if such variations in interpretation are a natural outcome? And, if so, what should be the desirable level of 'consistency' in the context of international investment jurisprudence?

Fragmentation exists in the international investment regime, i.e., in the standards of international investment protection that are contained in a large number of IIAs. Past attempts to multilateralize the norms of international investment protection could not garner sufficient support in the global community, and it remains highly likely that the standards of international investment protection would continue to evolve in a fragmented manner. Considering the said fragmentation and taking into account the rules of public international law on treaty interpretation as contained in the VCLT, 'inconsistency' in international investment jurisprudence (in a sense that there are different outcomes by various arbitral tribunals while interpreting the same standard of protection under similar circumstances) may be considered as a logical outcome. Thus, a logical way to ensure 'consistency', or the 'desirable level of consistency', in international investment jurisprudence context, would be to establish a system ensuring a 'coherent

52 K. Diel-Gligor (note 23), at pp. 326–29.

interpretation of international investment protection standards in accordance with the rules of treaty interpretation as recognized under public international law'.

In the legal context, the notions of 'consistency' and 'coherence' have been used in a similar manner. 'Consistency' is defined as requiring that a rule must be interpreted and applied uniformly in every similar or applicable instance,[53] while 'coherence' is described as the interpretation and application of legal rules in a manner that treats like cases alike in order to enhance the perception of justice and fairness within a legal regime.[54] It must be noted here that the 'desirable level of consistency', highlighted in this chapter, aims to deviate from the (interchangeable) understanding of the terms 'consistency' and 'coherence' as considered in legal context, and is inspired more from the understanding of the said notions, in an abstract sense, where 'consistency' is considered as 'always behaving or happening'[55] and 'coherence' is understood as reasons/ideas/opinions which are clear and carefully considered, and each part of it connects or follows in a natural or reasonable way.[56]

Further, the understanding of 'consistency' as 'a coherent interpretation of international investment protection standards in accordance with the rules of treaty interpretation as recognized under public international law' has the potential to counterbalance the void created by the absence of *stare decisis* in international investment adjudication. The said understanding of 'consistency' would also allow the application of the doctrine of *jurisprudence constante*.[57] According to this doctrine, though the interpretive exercise by investment arbitration tribunals would be guided primarily by the 'codified sources of law', in this context IIAs, they may also acknowledge previous rulings on similar legal issues to foster legal development through reference to a body of consistent line of cases.[58]

---

53 T. M. Franck, *Fairness in International Law and Institutions* (Clarendon Press, 1995) 38.

54 *Id.*, at pp. 38–41.

55 See Cambridge University Press, Cambridge Dictionaries Online http://dictionary.cambridge.org/dictionary/english/consistent (accessed 27 July 2020).

56 *Ibid.*

57 As opposed to *stare decisis*, *jurisprudence constante* does not bound adjudicating bodies to follow a previous ruling on a similar legal issue. However, the persuasive value of such rulings is identified.

58 A K. Bjorklund, 'Investment Treaty Arbitral Decisions as Jurisprudence Constante', 1 *TDM* (2010).

4 The Role of MIC in Ensuring a Consistent International Investment Jurisprudence

What role the proposed MIC could play in removing unjustified inconsistencies in international investment jurisprudence will depend on what understanding of 'consistency' is adopted for the purposes of ISDS reform, and subsequent interpretive practice. Two possible roles may be identified for MIC: 'substitutive' or 'complementary'. A 'substitutive' role would replace the existing ISDS mechanism altogether with a permanent mechanism/standing body inclusive of an appellate mechanism, which appears to be the case from the EU policy standpoint. However, it would be interesting to analyse, especially if the 'the desirable level of consistency' is – 'a coherent interpretation of international investment protection standards in accordance with the rules of treaty interpretation as recognized under public international law', whether there exists a possibility to avoid radical reform like 'substitution', and to envisage a more 'complementary' role for the MIC where it acts as a standing appellate mechanism complementing the existing ISDS mechanism. In such a case, it would be an opportunity to retain the advantages of the existing ISDS mechanism along with increasing its legitimacy with a system of review.

4.1 *The Position of the European Union on the ISDS Reform*

The Negotiating Directives for a Convention establishing a Multilateral Court for the Settlement of Investment Disputes' ('Negotiating Directives')[59] issued by the Council of the European Union in March 2018 clarifies that the 'multilateral court 'should' be composed of a tribunal of first instance and an appeal tribunal'.[60]

Further, recent IIA treaty practice of the EU, in particular under the EU-Canada Comprehensive Economic and Trade Agreement (CETA)[61] and the EU-Vietnam Investment Protection Agreement,[62] affirms that it is in favour of a WTO styled mechanism[63] and encourages other States to make a move

59 http://data.consilium.europa.eu/doc/document/ST-12981-2017-ADD-1-DCL-1/en/pdf (accessed 15 January 2021).

60 *Ibid.*

61 http://ec.europa.eu/trade/policy/in-focus/ceta/ceta-chapter-by-chapter/ (accessed 27 July 2019).

62 http://trade.ec.europa.eu/doclib/press/index.cfm?id=1437 (accessed 27 July 2019).

63 The section on 'what is the multilateral investment court' mentions that 'the multilateral investment court should be for investment dispute settlement what the World Trade Organization is for trade dispute settlement, thus upholding a multilateral rules-based system'.

towards a multilateral investment court. This approach is reflected in Article 8 (29) of CETA, which provides that 'the Contracting Parties shall pursue with other trading partners the establishment of a multilateral investment tribunal and appellate mechanism for the resolution of investment disputes', and 'upon establishment of such a multilateral mechanism, the CETA Joint Committee shall adopt a decision providing that investment disputes under this section will be decided pursuant to the multilateral mechanism and make appropriate transitional arrangements'.

As regards the 'first instance' mechanism, the CETA Joint Committee will appoint fifteen members of the tribunal with five members each from Canada and the member States of the EU. The remaining five members shall be nationals of third countries.[64] Their appointment will be for a five-year term, renewable once.[65] As far as the constitution of the tribunal of first instance is concerned, cases will be heard in divisions consisting three members of the tribunal, of whom one shall be a national of a member State of the EU, one a national of Canada and, one a national of a third country who shall act as the chair of the division.[66] Depending on the agreement of the disputing parties, especially when the claimant is a small or a medium-sized enterprise or if the compensation or damages claimed are relatively low, there is also a possibility for deciding cases by a sole member appointed randomly from the third country nationals. In relation to this, CETA further clarifies that a request for the resolution of the dispute through a sole member shall receive a 'sympathetic consideration' from the respondent. However, such a request must be made before the constitution of the division.

Regarding the appellate body established under the CETA, it has powers to uphold, modify or reverse a decision based on; (i) errors in the application or interpretation of applicable law, (ii) manifest errors in the appreciation of the facts, including appreciation of relevant domestic law, or (iii) other shortcomings as provided under Article 52 (1)[67] of the ICSID

64 Article 8.27 (2) of CETA.

65 Article 8.27 (5) of CETA.

66 Article 8.27 (6) of CETA.

67 Convention on the Settlement of Investment Disputes between States and Nationals of Other States 575 UNTS 159 (opened for signature 18 March 1965, entered into force 14 October 1966) ('ICSID Convention'). See Article 52 (1) – Either party may request annulment of the award by an application in writing addressed to the Secretary-General on one or more of the following grounds:

(a) that the Tribunal was not properly constituted;
(b) that the Tribunal has manifestly exceeded its powers;
(c) that there was corruption on the part of a member of the Tribunal;
(d) that there has been a serious departure from a fundamental rule of procedure; or
(e) that the award has failed to state the reasons on which it is based.

Convention.[68] Similar provisions can be found in relation to an appellate mechanism also in the EU – Vietnam Investment Protection Agreement.[69]

4.2 *'Complementarity' to Avoid Radical Reform*

The above discussions highlight the 'substitutive' role for the MIC, where the idea is to introduce radical reform by replacing the existing ISDS mechanism with a system allowing States to have greater influence in selecting the members of such a standing body. To support a more 'complementary' role for the MIC, where the idea is to support the existing ISDS mechanism through a standing appellate body only, a closer look at the functioning of the existing dispute resolution institutions dealing with investor-State disputes is inevitable.

In the context of ISDS proceedings, it is the PCA and the ICSID which are dealing with the majority of known investor-State disputes arising out of various IIAs.[70] In particular, the ICSID has firmly established itself as the facility of choice for investor-State dispute settlement, having administered more than 70% of all known cases.[71] Demand for the Centre's services continues to increase, demonstrating the importance of its role. For example, in the Financial Year 2018 ICSID registered 57 new cases, the highest number in ICSID's history.[72]

Furthermore, in response to the ongoing backlash against the existing ISDS mechanism, the ICSID is in the process of amending its procedural (arbitration) rules for the settlement of international investment disputes.[73] Procedural concerns relating to 'transparency' in arbitral proceedings, 'non-disputing party submissions', 'independence and impartiality' of arbitrators, 'duration and costs' of the proceedings are being addressed in this process.

Irrespective of several shortcomings in the existing ISDS mechanism which need to be addressed with adequate modifications in the system, investor-State 'arbitration' continues to work and remains an effective mechanism for the

68 Article 8.28 of CETA.

69 Article 3.54 of the EU-Vietnam Investment Protection Agreement https://trade.ec.europa.eu/doclib/docs/2018/september/tradoc_157394.pdf (accessed 30 December 2020).

70 https://www.iisd.org/pdf/2014/investment_treaty_arbitration.pdf (accessed 30 December 2020).

71 https://icsid.worldbank.org/en/Documents/resources/2018ICSIDAnnualReport.ENG.pdf (accessed 31 July 2019).

72 *Idem.*

73 ICSID Rules and Regulations Amendment: Working Papers https://icsid.worldbank.org/resources/rules-and-regulations/icsid-rules-and-regulations-amendment-working-papers (accessed 27 January 2020).

resolution of international investment disputes. Moreover, according to the survey conducted by ICSID concerning compliance with awards of costs[74]: (i) most awards in favour of States are paid, (ii) States generally comply with awards in favour of claimants, and (iii) States do not always seek to enforce awards in their favour that have not been complied with.

From the above analysis, it appears that there is a strong possibility of balancing the functioning of the existing ISDS mechanism, provided it exists with necessary procedural reform as to the satisfaction of the stakeholders, with a standing appellate body. Though it cannot be denied that from a 'consistency' perspective, the lack of a mechanism for an 'effective review' of arbitral awards rendered by '*ad hoc*'[75] tribunals are considered to be one of the major shortcomings; a 'substitutive' role for the MIC creates a far-reaching impact with a potential to gradually diminish the relevance of existing dispute resolution institutions. An 'effective review', based on specified grounds (for example under the CETA), can also be ensured through a standing body, acting as an appellate mechanism only, thus supporting the 'complementary' role of the MIC.[76]

5 Conclusions

Inconsistencies exist not only in the interpretation of recurring legal issues related to substantive standards of international investment protection, but also while applying customary international law. However, considering the fragmentation in international investment protection regime and the obligation of 'objective interpretation' under Article 31 of the VCLT, coupled with the absence of *stare decisis*, interpretive variations may be considered as a logical outcome. Accordingly, as far as consistency in international investment jurisprudence is concerned, interpretive exercise needs to be done in a manner

74 https://icsid.worldbank.org/en/Documents/about/Report%20on%20ICSID%20Survey.pdf (accessed 30 July 2019).

75 *Ad hoc* in a sense that though the institutions discussed here have a permanent character, there is no standing body with a developed practice for resolving international investor-State disputes. Arbitral tribunals dealing with such disputes are constituted (depending on the specificities of arbitration agreement) for resolving a particular dispute.

76 https://undocs.org/A/CN.9/WG.III/WP.185 (accessed 25 March 2021), p. 10; States like China and South Africa have already supported the idea of complementing the existing ISDS mechanism with a standalone appellate body, complementing the current arbitration regime https://uncitral.un.org/en/working_groups/3/investor-state (accessed 25 March 2021).

ensuring 'a coherent interpretation of international investment protection standards in accordance with the rules of treaty interpretation as recognized under public international law'.

Furthermore, to remove 'unjustifiable inconsistencies' in investor-State adjudication arising out of a large pool of IIAs, substituting the existing ISDS mechanism with a 'WTO styled' dispute resolution mechanism may not be the most suitable solution. Unlike codified multilateral rules on the basis of which inter-State trade disputes are resolved under the WTO framework, the 'rules' of international investment protection remain fragmented, thus promoting the adoption of an understanding of 'consistency' different from that under the WTO jurisprudence.

Finally, taking into account the functioning of the dispute resolution institutions facilitating the existing ISDS mechanism, in specific the ICSID and its ongoing revision of the Arbitration Rules, the role of the MIC could be limited to complementing investor-State arbitrations. It may not be necessary to substitute the existing ISDS mechanism altogether for ensuring a consistent international investment jurisprudence. Also, from the perspective of 'effective review of decisions', the status of the MIC as a 'complementing' appellate body would appear more suitable.

CHAPTER 15

Arbitration Procedure in Bilateral Investment Treaties – Interactions between National, European and International Courts

Łukasz Dawid Dąbrowski

1 Introduction

The term bilateral investment treaties refers to bilateral agreements for the promotion and reciprocal (mutual) protection of investments. Investment law on has been one of the fastest growing fields of international economic law over the last decades. Historically, developed and developing countries have sought to secure a stable legal environment for international investment.[1] More recently, the ideological and political background has evolved and the emphasis in BITs has changed from protection to treatment issues. In the age of globalization, which resulted in developments of transnational and multinational corporations, whose economic and political power is growing increasingly, this kind of agreements may still play an important role in different kinds of relations between companies and States. This means that rules of BITs in respect of investor-state dispute settlement also play an important role in the international commercial relations. In that respect, a significant question for the purposes of the present contribution is not the scope of rights and/or obligations of investors or States according to BITs, but the interactions between arbitration procedure and different kinds of national and international courts. This article aims at trying to find answers to several questions. Whether there is a strong connection with national courts, leading to review of the validity of the arbitral award made by national courts? And if so, to what extent such judicial review can be exercised by those courts? On the other hand, is there a possibility of parallel commercial arbitration proceedings and courts trials? And how can those interactions impact on the (uniform) interpretation of international law? The main method we propose to use is formal-dogmatic.

1 P. Juillard, *Bilateral Investment Treaties in the Context of Investment Law*, Investment Compact Regional Roundtable on Bilateral Investment Treaties for the Protection and Promotion of Foreign Investment in South East Europe, 28–29 May 2001, Dubrovnik, Croatia, p. 1, available at https://www.oecd.org/investment/internationalinvestmentagreements/1894794.pdf.

© KONINKLIJKE BRILL NV, LEIDEN, 2022 | DOI:10.1163/9789004467668_021

This contribution focuses mainly on an analysis of the provisions of selected BITs and international arbitrations rules. The paper focuses also on the judgments of the Court of Justice of the European Union and some selected cases in arbitration procedures.

2 Overview of Investments Treaties

The main goal of BITs is to create favourable and equitable conditions for investments by investors of one contracting party in the territory of the other contracting party.[2] In fact, each BIT constitutes a separate legal regulation, but these treaties have, as a rule, similar structure and scope of application.[3] BITs provide major benefits, including national treatment, "most-favoured nation" treatment, protection from expropriation, reparation of investments, protection against unlawful activities, as well as protection against legal changes leading to unjustified harm to investors. The investment treaties concluded between two governments protect the foreign investors concerned from specific behaviour and abuses by the host government.[4] In a general sense, BITs should reduce legal barriers to trade.[5] Apart from the above-mentioned rights, BITs give investors additional benefits, such as access to neutral investor-state dispute settlement (a neutral, third-party arbitrator) when a problem arises with the host government. Of course not all of BITs have provisions for investor-state arbitration, like the USA-Australia 2004 BIT.[6] Nevertheless, investor-state disputes are triggered by a wide range of State measures, and the majority of cases involve the cancellation of a project, agreement or license and the expropriation of a foreign investment.[7] Sometimes BITs provide for arbitration only

2 K. J. Vandevelde, 'A Unified Theory of Fair and Equitable Treatment', 43 *New York University Journal of International Law and Politics* (2010) 1, p. 43–106.

3 M. Perkowski, E. Gruszewska, 'Interpretation of Bilateral Treaties for the Promotion and Protection of foreign investments', *32 Studies in Logic, Grammar and Rhetoric* (2013) 45, p. 94.

4 OECD, "The impact of investment treaties on companies, shareholders and creditors", in *OECD Business and Finance Outlook 2016* (OECD Publishing, 2016) http://dx.doi.org/10.1787/9789264257573-13-en, p. 225.

5 K. J. Vandevelde, *The First Bilateral Investment Treaties: U.S. Postwar Friendship, Commerce, and Navigation Treaties* (2017), http://ssrn.com/abstract=2993300, p. 37.

6 K. J. Vandevelde, 'A Brief History of International Investment Agreements' 12 *U.C. Davis Journal of International Law & Policy* (2005) 1, p. 188.

7 Z. Ph. Williams, 'What, When, Where and Why? Patterns in Investor-State Arbitration' in K. Singh, B. Ilge (eds.), *Rethinking Bilateral Investment Treaties: Critical Issues and Policy Choices*, (SOMO, 2016), https://www.somo.nl/rethinking-bilateral-investment-treaties-critical-issues-and-policy-choices/, p. 35.

for a limited scope of claims, typically compensation for expropriation.[8] When a dispute between the contracting state and the investor of the other contracting state cannot be settled in an amicable way (which should be treated as a precondition to arbitration) international arbitration is usually the next step.[9] The Polish-Korea BIT, for instance, says that if within six months from the date either party requested amicable settlement, the dispute can be submitted to arbitration.[10] The period allowed to initiate arbitral proceedings can be shorter, and in the case of the Polish-Israel BIT it is three months.[11]

Some BITs list the rules which investors may use in arbitration proceedings.[12] Sometimes, like in the Polish-Iran[13] or Polish-Canada[14] BITs, agreements indicate only the Arbitration Rules of the United Nations Commission for The International Trade Law (UNCITRAL). However, the majority of BITs provide for several rules, besides the ones mentioned above: 1) International Centre for the Settlement of Investment Disputes (ICSID), 2) Institute of Arbitration at the Chamber of Commerce in Stockholm, 3) International Chamber of Commerce in Paris. Those are the most often mentioned rules, other rules like the Rules of the Singapore International Arbitration Centre, in case of the Polish-Singapore BIT, were mentioned less frequently.[15]

BITs may contain provisions regulating different aspects of the conduct of international arbitration such as: the composition of the tribunal and place of arbitration, qualification and impartiality of arbitrators, provisional and final remedies, regulating diplomatic support and invocation of State immunity, transparency, accountability and quality. Most often treaties which refer to internationally recognized mechanisms, do not contain a specific statement on the applicable arbitration rules, delegating the design of these rules entirely to the tribunals.[16] In some treaties, e.g. the Poland-Singapore[17] and

8 J. Pohl, K. Mashigo, A. Nohen, 'Dispute Settlement Provisions in International Investment Agreements: A Large Sample Survey', *OECD Working Papers on International Investment*, 2 *OECD Publishing* (2012), p. 16, available at http://dx.doi.org/10.1787/5k8xb71nf628-en.

9 *Investor-State Disputes Arising from Investment Treaties: A Review*, UNCTAD Series on International Investment Policies for Development (2005) p. 3.

10 Article 8 of the Poland-Korea BIT (1991).

11 Article 8 (2) of the Poland-Israel BIT (1991).

12 *Dispute settlement provisions in international investment agreements: A large sample survey*, Organization for Economic Co-operation and Development Investment Division, Directorate for Financial and Enterprise Affairs Paris (OECD, 2012) p. 8.

13 Poland-Iran BIT (1998).

14 Poland-Canada BIT (1990).

15 J. Pohl, K. Mashigo, A. Nohen (2012), *op. cit.*, p. 20.

16 *Ibidem*, p. 24.

17 Article 13(2) of the Polish-Singapore BIT (1993).

Poland-Arab Emirates[18] BITs, it is also indicated the grounds for the arbitration decision: 1) the investment treaty itself, 2) the national law of the contracting Party, 3) the rules relative to conflicts of law, 4) the rules and the universally accepted principles of international law. In the literature, there is also mention of: 5) a common interpretation that the States Parties to the BITs have agreed on and 6) other treaties that the States Parties to the BITs have concluded.[19] Sometimes the BITs provisions may indirectly indicate the grounds for a judgment, as it is the case of the Austria-Croatia BIT, according to which "The Contracting Parties are not bound by the present Agreement insofar as it is incompatible with the legal acquis of the European Union in force at any given time.[20] The indication of the grounds for the ruling may have a significant meaning in the context of recently adopted decisions by national courts[21] and arbitral tribunals.[22] The BITs do not mention jurisprudence (case-law), as it is not generally considered a primary source of law. However, case-law is a supportive instrument of interpretation of the legal regulations, which means that we cannot preclude this source from the arbitration process – particularly when the case-law is used to strengthen the arguments of the decision. Some BITs also contain statutes of limitation that bar access to arbitration if a claim has not been brought within a specified period of time. For instance, the USA-Uruguay[23] and USA-Rwanda[24] BITs provided for a 3-year limitation from when an investor has "acquired knowledge or should have acquired knowledge of the alleged breach".

3 Interactions with the European Court of Justice

In academic literature, Europe is described as the mother of the current international investment regime because bilateral investment treaties and

18 Article 9(3) of the Poland-Arab Emirates BIT (1993).

19 J. Pohl, K. Mashigo, A. Nohen, *op. cit.*, p. 29.

20 Article 11(2) of the Austria-Croatia BIT (1997).

21 See the Judgment of the Swedish Court of Appeal in Stockholm, 22 February 2019, *Republic of Poland v. PL Holdings S.á.r.l.*, relating to arbitral awards issued 28 June 2017 and 28 September 2017, and revised 24 November 2017 in Arbitration Institute of the Stockholm Chamber of Commerce (SCC) case no. V 2014/163.

22 See Decision in *Addiko Bank and Addiko Bank D.D. v. Republic of Croatia, ICSID Case No. ARB/17/37*, 12 June 2020.

23 USA-Uruguay BIT (2005).

24 USA-Rwanda BIT (2008).

investor-state dispute settlements are European inventions.[25] The question of whether Europe remains the main user of the wide network of international investments disputes is now an open one. The judgment of the Court of Justice of the European Union (CJEU) in *Achmea* case (C-284/16)[26] has undermined arbitration clauses in inter-related BITs.

Arbitration clauses were commonly used in around 200 BITs concluded within the EU and hundreds adopted between EU's Member States with non-EU countries.[27] On 6 March 2018, the CJEU ruled in the *Achmea* judgment that the BITs violated EU law because they allowed an arbitral tribunal to interpret provisions of EU law in a dispute between investors and Member States, while such interpretation could not be effectively challenged via the domestic court process. As such BITs are not compatible with EU law, those agreements have been terminated by many EU States. An example is the case of the BIT between Poland and Portugal of 11 March 1993, which was terminated and expired on 3 August 2019. However, according to this BIT, the provisions for arbitration procedures shall remain in force until 3 August 2029 for investments made prior to the effective date of termination, i.e. before August 3, 2019 (*survival clause*). Nevertheless, according to a statement of the Polish government because of the *Achmea* judgment, arbitral tribunals established under the BIT would not have jurisdiction to hear cases due to the lack of valid consent for arbitration. Therefore, it seems no longer possible for investors to undertake any actions against Polish or Portuguese governments, even though the agreement allows such action for next 10 years. An attempt to undertake a given action would be found as an abuse of process as incompatible with EU law. The Court's decision, which was in line with previous statements of the European Commission, argued that most of BITs provisions are superseded by EU law and applying them could lead to discrimination between EU States.[28]

In this respect, the CJEU, in Opinion 1/17 of 30 April 2019, decided that the CETA Tribunal and Appellate Tribunal are compatible with EU law. The fact

---

25 B. Ilge, 'An Account of the EU's Engagement with Bilateral Investment Treaties', in K. Singh, B. Ilge (eds.), *Rethinking Bilateral Investment Treaties: Critical Issues and Policy Choices* (SOMO, 2016), p. 155

26 Judgment of the Court of Justice of the European Union (Grand Chamber) of 6 March 2018, Slowakische Republik v Achmea BV, C-284/16, ECLI:EU:C:2018:158.

27 *Dispute settlement provisions in international investment agreements: A large sample survey*, OECD Investment Division, Directorate for Financial and Enterprise Affairs (OECD 2012) p. 45.

28 J. Rogers, S. Goodall and C. Dowling, 'Brexit and investor-state dispute settlement. What impact will Brexit have on foreign direct investment?' 8 *International Arbitration Report* (2017), p. 24–27.

that the envisaged ISDS mechanism stands outside the EU judicial system does not mean, in itself, that that mechanism adversely affects the autonomy of the EU legal order (paras. 114, 115). The principle of the autonomy of EU law would only be breached if the CETA Tribunal could interpret and apply EU rules other than the provisions of the CETA or issue decisions preventing EU institutions from acting in accordance with EU law. In the above opinion, the Court refers to Opinion 1/09 of March 2011 (regarding the European Patent Court) considering that, differently than in the CETA case, the patent court whose creation was envisaged would be called upon to interpret and apply not only the provisions of the agreement creating a unified patent litigation system, but also other instruments of European Union law (in particular regulations and directives in conjunction with which that regulation would have to be read). The Court refers also to the *Achmea* case and decided that the CETA must also be distinguished from the investment agreement at issue in the case that gave rise to the judgment of 6 March 2018. The Court noted the principle of mutual trust, which played a crucial role in *Achmea* judgment. That principle obliges each of the EU States to consider that all the other Member States comply with EU law, including fundamental rights, such as the right to an effective remedy before an independent tribunal. The Court pointed out that this principle is not applicable to the relations between the EU and third countries.

Notwithstanding the above, a Declaration of the Member States of 15 January 2019 on the legal consequences of the *Achmea* judgment and on investment protection[29] was adopted. In this Declaration, EU Member States made a commitment, *inter alia*, to terminate all bilateral investment treaties concluded between them. Additionally, on 25 May 2020, the Agreement for the termination of Bilateral Investment Treaties between the Member States of the European Union was signed.[30] In this way, the future of bilateral investments treaties' arbitration procedures in the EU was decided. Or, at least, it seemed that way. In *Addiko Bank AG and Addiko Bank d.d. v. Republic of Croatia* case,[31] the arbitral tribunal concluded that the CJEU, in the above judgment and opinions, did not suggest that EU Member States were barred from offering to arbitrate disputes under treaties that were not even partly governed by EU law, but only by the express treaty provisions and by general principles of international law. In this

29 Declaration of the Representatives of the Governments of the Member States, of 15 January 2019 on the Legal Consequences of the Judgment of the Court of Justice in Achmea and on Investment Protection in the European Union, https://ec.europa.eu/info/publications/190117-bilateral-investment-treaties_en.

30 OJ L 169, 29.5.2020, p. 1–41.

31 *ICSID Case No. ARB/17/37.*

way, the arbitral tribunal decided that arbitration under the Austria-Croatia BIT was not incompatible with the EU acquis (paras. 269 et seq.) as it does not contain a choice of law clause giving rise to concerns of interpretation EU law.

In this respect, the Judgment of the Swedish Court of Appeal in Stockholm, 22 February 2019, in the *Republic of Poland v. PL Holdings S.á.r.l.* case, is noteworthy. The Court considered that the conclusion from the *Achmea* ruling is that EU regulations would not, as such, preclude Poland and PL Holdings from entering into an arbitration agreement and participating in arbitral proceedings regarding an investment-related dispute. According to the Court, in BITs a Member State is obligated to accept subsequent arbitral proceedings with an investor. The Court noted that the *Achmea* judgment would not as such preclude from entering into an arbitration agreement and participating in arbitral proceedings regarding an investment-related dispute. According to EU law, Member States cannot conclude agreements where one Member State is obligated to accept arbitral proceedings with an investor. It is not allowed, because in this way Member States could establish a system where they have excluded disputes from the possibility of requesting a CJEU preliminary ruling. In turn, EU law does not preclude arbitration agreements between a Member State and an investor in a particular case. The participation in the proceedings is based on party autonomy. It means that the State is free to enter into an arbitration agreement with an investor regarding the same dispute at a later stage, e.g. when the investor has initiated arbitral proceedings.[32] This means that "an arbitration agreement and arbitral proceedings between an investor and a Member State is therefore as such not in violation of the EU law".[33]

The issue of investment arbitration in the EU is, therefore, not yet fully settled. Some additional light may be brought by the CJEU, as the Swedish Supreme Court on 12 December 2019 referred for a preliminary ruling, asking whether EU law, as interpreted in *Achmea*, precludes an arbitration agreement if an arbitration clause has been concluded between a Member State and an investor.[34]

4 Interactions with National Courts

In the relation between arbitration proceedings and domestic courts, four dimensions can be listed. First, the most important, are the relations allowing

32 The Judgment of the Swedish Court of Appeal in Stockholm, 22 February 2019, Republic of Poland v. PL Holdings S.á.r.l., Case No: T 8538-17 (T 12033-17), unofficial translation from www.italaw.com/cases/6209, p. 43

33 *Ibidem*, p. 44

34 Decision of Swedish Supreme Court on Referral to ECJ, 12.12.2019, https://www.italaw.com/cases/6209, p. 15.

for bringing a case for consideration. Second, the relations connected with interim measures or injunctive relief. Third, the regulations relating to enforcement of an award granted by an arbitral tribunal and fourth, the possibility of the review of an arbitral award by national courts.

In the first dimension, we can list three types of regulations: 1) where only the access to domestic courts was provided, 2) where only international arbitration was provided, and 3) where BITs provided for both international arbitration and domestic remedies.[35] In the last situation, investors have a right to make a choice concerning the forum where they want to bring the claim – to international arbitration or domestic courts. BITs specify that a choice, once made by the investor, is final and exclusive. When an investor decides to bring a case to a national court, the possibility of initiating arbitration procedures is closed (*fork in the road provision*).[36] This is not frequent, but sometimes investors may prefer to choose national courts.[37]

According to the USA-Argentina BIT, for instance, submission of a claim to local remedies would preclude investor arbitration of that claim.[38] In turn, according to the Poland-Iran BIT, a dispute primarily referred to the national courts, as long as it is pending, cannot be referred to arbitration save with the parties' agreement, and in the event that a final judgment is rendered it cannot be referred to arbitration at all.[39] Such clauses are specifically intended to prevent multiple forums for one set of facts, when the dispute and the parties before the domestic courts are identical to those in the arbitration.[40]

Generally, the conditions of BITs determine whether an investor may eventually bring its case to international arbitration.[41] In that respect, treaties allow an investor access to international arbitration, in some cases: 1) if domestic courts have failed to deliver a decision within a given period of time – e.g. within one year[42] or 18 months[43]; 2) when the decision which was made by domestic courts fails to fully settle the dispute[44]; 3) when the decision taken by

35 J. Pohl, K. Mashigo, A. Nohen, *op. cit.*, p. 10, 11.

36 T. Gazzini, *Bilateral investment treaties*, in T. Gazzini, E. De Brabandere (eds.), *International Investment Law: The Sources of Rights and Obligations* (Martinus Nijhoff, 2012), p. 28.

37 E. L. Trakman, 'Choosing Domestic Courts Over Investor-State Arbitration: Australia's Repudiation of the Status Quo', 35(3) *UNSW Law Journal* (2012), p. 979–112.

38 K. J. Vandevelde, 'Bilateral Investment Treaties: History, Policy and Interpretation' *Thomas Jefferson School of Law Research Paper* (2010) *No. 3022249*. Available at SSRN: https://ssrn.com/abstract=3022249, p. 370.

39 Article 11 of the Poland-Iran BIT (1998).

40 *Investor-State Disputes Arising, op. cit.*, p. 20,

41 J. Pohl, K. Mashigo, A. Nohen, *op. cit.*, p. 14.

42 Article 10 (1) of the Poland-China BIT (1988).

43 Article 10 (3) of the Argentina-Netherlands BIT (1992).

44 Argentina-Austria BIT (1993); Argentina-Italy BIT (1990); Austria-Philippines BIT (2002).

domestic courts is "manifestly unjust or violates the provisions of the international investment agreement"[45]; and 4) when the BIT required the submission of a claim to local remedies before the submission to investor-State arbitration (e.g. Poland-China BIT[46] or Germany-Argentina BIT).[47] In the latter case, the BITs require as a first step the presentation of the investors' dispute to domestic courts. After local remedies have been exhausted, an action may be brought to international arbitration. Even though the requirement to exhaust local remedies before international arbitration procedures is not frequent,[48] in China BITs investors are required to exhaust local remedies first (namely an Administrative Review Procedure), before being allowed to seek resort to transnational arbitration, as it is the case of the China-German BIT, China-Netherlands BIT,[49] Poland-China BIT,[50] but also in the Poland-Arab Emirates BIT.[51] This type of provision, however, does not involve court proceedings and has, therefore, only a very limited restrictive effect.[52] Additionally, some BITs (like China BITs or Poland-Arab Emirates BIT) restrict access to international arbitration "through" national courts or administrative institutions to claims concerning alleged breaches of specific treaty provisions, such as the amount of compensation for expropriation, provisions on compensation for losses, or free transfers.[53] In this regard, the Poland-China BIT stipulates that the investor may challenge only the amount of compensation for the expropriated investment assets.[54] In turn, the Poland-Arab Emirates BIT[55] provides that when a dispute concerns expropriation, nationalization and compensation or transfers may be submitted to an *ad hoc* international arbitral tribunal. In the event

45 United Kingdom-Uruguay BIT (1991), Germany-Ecuador BIT (1996), Belgium/Luxembourg-Uruguay BIT (1991), Italy-Uruguay BIT (1990).
46 Article 10 (1) of the Polish-China BIT (1988).
47 V. J. Kenneth, 'Bilateral Investment Treaties: History, Policy and Interpretation' *Thomas Jefferson School of Law Research Paper* (2010), No. 3022249, https://ssrn.com/abstract=3022249, p. 370.
48 Investment Policies and Bilateral Investment Treaties in Africa, *Implications for Regional Integration,* 2016 Economic Commission for Africa Addis Ababa, Ethiopia, https://www.uneca.org/sites/default/files/.../eng_investment_landscaping_study.pdf, p. 24.
49 T. Gazzini, *op. cit.*, p. 7.
50 Article 10(1) of the Poland-China BIT (1988).
51 Article 9(2) of the Poland-United Arab Emirates (1993).
52 A. Berger, 'China's new bilateral investment treaty programme: Substance, rational and implications for international investment law making', American Society of International Economic Law Interest Group 2008 Conference in Washington, DC, November, available at https://www.die-gdi.de/uploads/media/Berger_ChineseBITs.pdf, p. 9, 11.
53 J. Pohl, K. Mashigo, A. Nohen, *op. cit.*, p. 14.
54 Article 10 (1) of the Poland-China BIT (1988).
55 Article 9 (2) of the Poland- United Arab Emirates (1993).

of a dispute other than the mentioned above, it may be submitted also to the *ad hoc* international arbitral tribunal, but after exhausting all local remedies.

In practice, such conditions always concern certain procedural steps that must be exhausted before proceedings can be instituted. In this respect, it is worth mentioning Article 26 of the ICSID Convention, according to which a State may require the exhaustion of local administrative or judicial remedies as a condition of its consent to arbitration under the Convention. In the absence of such a provision, there is no requirement to exhaust local remedies. It means that the State waived the right to demand prior exhaustion of local remedies as a condition for obtaining access to an ICSID arbitral tribunal, if it does not make prior reservation under article 26 of the Convention (*Amco* v. *Indonesia* case).[56]

In the second dimension mentioned above, some BITs contain provisions on interim measures or injunctive relief,[57] which can be used prior to arbitral proceeding or sometimes during this process. Interim relief may rely on: 1) domestic court systems, 2) arbitral tribunals, 3) or both. Treaties that rely on domestic courts to provide interim relief may specify that investors that seek interim relief from national courts do not waive their rights to arbitration. Taking advantage of domestic court systems, will take precedence before the initiation of arbitration proceedings. In turn, during the arbitration process it is more likely that interim measures will be applied by arbitral tribunals. The ICSID and UNCITRAL Rules also contain provisions on this matter.[58] The ICSID Convention and ICSID Arbitration Rules allow tribunals to "recommend any provisional measures which should be taken to preserve the respective rights of either party". Article 26 of the UNCITRAL Arbitration Rules allows tribunals to grant interim measures at the request of a party.[59]

In the area of the third dimension, some treaties determine under which conditions and legal regime an arbitral award may be enforceable. In this respect, according to the Poland-Iran BIT, national courts should not have jurisdiction over any dispute referred to arbitration. However, the above provisions do not bar the winning party to seek for the enforcement of the arbitral award before national courts.[60]

---

56 *Dispute Settlement, 2.3. Consent to Arbitration, International Center for Settlement of Investment Disputes, New York and Geneva 2003,* https://unctad.org/en/Docs/edmmisc232add2_en.pdf, p. 31.

57 Canada-Ukraine (1994), United States-Georgia (1994), United States-Uzbekistan (1994).

58 Article 26 of the UNICITRAL Rules, rule 39 of the ICSID Rules.

59 J. Pohl, K. Mashigo, A. Nohen, *op. cit.*, p. 30,31.

60 Polis-Iran BIT (1988).

The last dimension is also essential in arbitration proceedings. In general, investment treaties do not provide any revision (appeal) mechanisms in response to decisions rendered in arbitration proceedings.[61] The possible revision of arbitral awards requires the consent of both contracting States Parties – through amendments to investment treaties, or consent of parties of the dispute – through an agreement concluded before or after the arbitral award. Awards rendered by an arbitral tribunal, like those established under the UNCITRAL Rules, are subject to review by the national courts of the place of the arbitration. Generally, it is possible only in very specific (special) circumstances, such as bias, lack of due process, and excess jurisdiction.[62] For example, according to the Polish Code of Civil Procedure, a judgment of an arbitration court issued in Poland may only be set aside by the court in a special motion if: 1) an arbitration clause is void, invalid or has expired according to relevant law, 2) a party was deprived of the possibility to defend his rights before an arbitration court, 3) a judgment of an arbitration court concerns a dispute which is not covered by an arbitration clause or falls beyond the scope of that clause, 4) requirements concerning the composition of an arbitration court or the basic principles of proceedings before that court were not met, 5) a judgment was achieved by means of an offence or on the basis of a false or falsified document, 6) when other judgment has been issued in the same case between the same parties.[63] Regulations which offer grounds for review of arbitration awards to national courts are limited in scope. This limitation is greater than in the case of an appeal mechanism, where appeals are usually based on arguments that there were any errors in the trial's procedure or any errors in the judge's interpretation of the law. In case of review of arbitral award there are very specific circumstances provided by law. In the general sense, grounds for review are similar to those providing for the annulment of the award under Article 52 of the ICSID. According to those regulations either party may request the annulment of the award if: 1) the Tribunal was not properly constituted, 2) the Tribunal has manifestly exceeded its powers, 3) there was corruption on the part of a member of the Tribunal, 4) there has been a serious departure from a fundamental rule of procedure, 5) the award has failed to state the reasons on which it is based. International arbitration

61 B. Kingsbury, S. Schill, 'Investor-State Arbitration as Governance: Fair and Equitable Treatment, Proportionality and the Emerging Global Administrative Law', *New York University Public Law and Legal Theory Working Papers* (2009) p. 39.

62 W. W. Park, *Arbitration of International Business Disputes* (Oxford University Press, 2006), p. 44.

63 Articles 1205, 1206 of Polish code of civil procedure of 17 November 1964.

has long been driven by an understandable need for greater autonomy from national court supervision.[64] Thus, an arbitral award is valid and final, unless exceptional circumstances appear, such as fundamental procedural errors or jurisdiction issues.

5 Interaction with International Courts

At the international level, many institutions[65] engage with dispute resolution,[66] besides *ad hoc* arbitral tribunals. For example, the Permanent Court of Arbitration is currently administering 107 investor-State arbitrations and 69 cases under contracts involving a State or other public entity.[67] Thus, it is quite possible to pursue parallel proceedings. Parallel proceedings mean parallel court and arbitration proceedings leading by the same party or related parties against the same State. It also means multiple arbitration proceedings by the same or related parties under different investment treaties against the same State. Such a situation may threaten: 1) the credibility, certainty and procedural fairness of investment arbitration, 2) cause inconsistency in investment arbitration adjudication, like in the *CME*, *Lauder* and *Ample*[68] cases, in particular when contradictory decisions are made, and a party tries to enforce the judgment or the award, 3) can lead to the double recovery where a company, shareholder or another company within the same group brings a treaty claim and a claim for breach of contract,[69] and in consequence it can be an abuse of right to process to pursue this kind of parallel proceeding.

Parallel proceedings may take place for various reasons. Shareholders may initiate an arbitration to protect its BIT rights, while the investment (the subsidiary) initiates other proceedings (also domestic) to protect its contract or other legal rights, including those stemming from the international investment

64 W. W. Park, *op. cit.*, p. 12.

65 Such as the Permanent Court of Arbitration, the Stockholm Chamber of Commerce, the London Court of International Arbitration or the International Chamber of Commerce.

66 S. M. Schwebel, *In Defence of Bilateral Investment Treaties*, 31 (2) *Arbitration International* (2015), p. 184.

67 See https://pca-cpa.org/en/cases/ [data from March 2021].

68 *Ampal-American Israel Corp & others v Arab Republic of Egypt*, Decision on Liability and Heads of Loss, 1 February 2016, ICSID Case No ARB/12/11, www.italaw.com/sites/default/files/case-documents/italaw7310.pdf.

69 *Consistency, efficiency and transparency in investment treaty arbitration*, A report by the IBA Arbitration Subcommittee on Investment Treaty Arbitration, 2018, https://uncitral.un.org/.../investment_treaty_report_2018_full.pdf, p. 17–18.

arbitration. Often, parallel proceedings are undertaken by investors whose parent companies have a different nationality. Each company may be considered an investor under the relevant BIT and, therefore, commence its own arbitration. To this end, the investor may use any of its subsidiaries and rely on the same or a different BIT.

Arbitration procedures interactions are more visible in connection with national courts. Nevertheless, correlation between international proceedings could be significant as well, especially when two different awards were passed. BITs do not regulate this situation that sometimes could lead to a quite complicated state of affairs. One of the solutions, which may be under consideration, is the mentioned above *fork-in-the-road clause* (or principle). This principle prevents the same entity from bringing claims in both litigation and arbitration, but its effect is limited to that specific party and to national court or arbitration proceedings. Nevertheless, this principle can be used in case of different international arbitration proceedings. Further key principles which could be taken into account are *res judicata* and *lis pendens,* depending on whether arbitration proceedings were already completed or are still pending. In turn, a principle which is already used in some BITs concluded by the USA, e.g. with Rwanda and Uruguay, is the *consolidation of arbitral proceedings*. Consolidation of arbitral proceedings means the joinder of two or more pending arbitrations into a single proceeding. Consolidation may be sought by the party of the BIT where two or more claims have been submitted separately to arbitration and the claims have a question of law or fact in common and arise out of the same events or circumstances.[70] All of those principles (*fork-in-the-road, res judicata, lis pendens* and *consolidation of arbitral proceedings*) aim to prevent conducting different court procedures.

All of the above principles have to fulfil the triple identity of object, cause and parties. In other words, when the dispute and the parties before one arbitration tribunal are identical to the dispute and the parties in the international proceedings.[71] Some commentators have suggested that this triple identity test should be relaxed.[72] This means when claims are brought separately by shareholders and/or locally incorporated companies and/or companies within the same chain of ownership,[73] should be treated as a one party. In this context, in the literature[74] there is also a mention to the denial *of benefits clause,* which is

70 Article 33 of the USA-Rwanda BIT, article 33 of the USA-Uruguay BIT.

71 *Investor-State Disputes Arising, op. cit.,* p. 20,

72 Ch. Schreuer, 'Shareholder Protection in International Investment Law' 3 *TDM* (2005) 1, 14.

73 *Consistency, efficiency and transparency op. cit.,* p. 19.

74 Ibidem, p. 19

the right of the State to reserve the right to deny benefits of a treaty to 'a company incorporated in a State, but with no economic connection to that State'.

6 Conclusions

Traditionally, foreign investors could rely only on the domestic courts of the host State or diplomatic protection.[75] The domestic courts system is sometimes perceived as immature, not well-established or just biased.[76] Using the diplomatic level to resolve investment disputes could damage the inter-State relationships. Investment arbitration is, therefore, a response to the unreliability of domestic courts,[77] and one also that allows investors to resolve disputes with the host State through a legal mechanism in which the investor's home State does not play any decisive role.[78] However, arbitration procedures are now a major political issue in a number of jurisdictions, and some have rejected investor-State arbitration,[79] not only at EU level but globally. In academic literature, it is deemed that this is caused by: first, a belief that investors always win their cases, second, that arbitration is only for the biggest and most powerful entities. In fact, none of them are true: States win in c.a. half of the cases, and, respectively, many small and medium sized companies and individuals also use arbitration proceedings.[80]

BITs provide for arbitration in the context of different arbitral institutions, with different rules, and each dispute is decided by different panel of arbitrators,[81] chosen by the parties, that have opposing views on the relevant

75 T. Gazzini, *op. cit.*, p. 25.

76 G. Harten, 'A Critique of Investment Treaties' in K. Singh and B. Ilge (eds.), *Rethinking Bilateral Investment Treaties: Critical Issues and Policy Choices* (SOMO, 2016) https://www.somo.nl/rethinking-bilateral-investment-treaties-critical-issues-and-policy-choices/, p. 44.

77 *Ibidem.*

78 J. Bonnitcha, *Assessing the Impacts of Investment Treaties: Overview of the evidence*, (The International Institute for Sustainable Development, 2017) available at www.iisd.org/library/assessing-impacts-investment-treaties-overview-evidence, p. 7.

79 OECD (2016), "The impact of investment treaties on companies, shareholders and creditors", in *OECD* Business and Finance Outlook 2016, OECD Publishing, Paris, http://dx.doi.org/10.1787/9789264257573-13-en, p. 227.

80 M. Baker, C. Dowling, 'Developments and reform of investor-state dispute settlement – Q&A with Meg Kinnear, Secretary General, ICSID', 8 *International Arbitration Report* (2017), p. 3.

81 P. Eberhardt, C. Olivet, 'Profiting from Injustice: Tracing the Rise of Investment Arbitration Industry', in *Rethinking Bilateral Investment Treaties*, *op. cit.*, p. 248.

matters.[82] This decentralization or diversity may cause inconsistency in international law. However, the possibility of discrepancies in case-law is nothing new at the international as well as the national level. The decentralization of international law is illustrated by the activities of the different institutions, methods and procedures that influence the final shape of the contemporary international legal order.[83] International arbitration tribunals play a similar role. International courts, including arbitral tribunals, take into account their own decisions – arbitral tribunals take into account the judgments of international courts and tribunals (e.g. the CJEU). The review of arbitration case-law is carried out in this process, which verifies the current position and develops new standards. Decisions of arbitral courts may have an impact on the doctrine and even an influence on the development of international legal standards.[84] Diversity also fosters innovation in legal rules.[85] In this way, arbitration tribunals, including those based on BITs, participate in the process of creation of international law. Such a situation should not be considered in negative terms, but rather as having a positive impact on development of arbitration standards and the formulation of international law that may be universally accepted and applicable. At least, until the creation of a common arbitral tribunal or one appeal instance. Nevertheless, diversity is a characteristic feature of arbitration, which makes it useful and popular. Action aimed at establishing one institution or appeal body or taking far-reaching unification may deprive this institution of its characteristic features – flexibility and individuality.

82 Ch. Schreuer, 'Coherence and Consistency in International Investment Law' in Robert Echandi and Pierre Sauvé (eds.), *World Trade Forum: Prospects in International Investment Law and Policy* (Cambridge, 2013), p. 9.

83 I. Gawłowicz, *Prawo dyplomatyczne w orzecznictwie Międzynarodowego Trybunału Sprawiedliwości,* Warsaw 2018, p. 10.

84 *Ibidem,* p. 10,13–15. See also G. G. Fitzmaurice, *Some Problems regarding the Formal Sources of International Law,* in M. Kosskeniemi (ed.), *Sources of International Law* (Routledge, 2000). E. Benvenisti and G.W. Downs, 'Prospects for the Increased Independence of International Tribunals', in A. von Bogdandy and I. Venzke (eds.) *International Judicial Lawmaking* (Springer, 2012). A. von Bogdandy and I. Venzke, 'On the Democratic Legitimation of International Judicial Lawmaking', in A. von Bogdandy and I. Venzke (eds.), *op.cit.,* D.J. Bederman, *The Spirit of International Law* (University of Georgia Press, 2002).

85 See Ch. R. Drahozal, 'Diversity and Uniformity in International Arbitration', 31 *Emory International Law Review* (2017), p. 410.

PART 6

General Conclusions

CHAPTER 16

The Future of the Contribution of International Justice to the Development of International Law – a Plea for (Some) Disorder

Pierre Bodeau-Livinec

What does it take to imagine the future when one feels entirely and desperately deprived of divinatory skills or of a properly functioning crystal ball? Listening to experts in the field, accepting to confront your own assessments and convictions to their views, acknowledging that, while the future of international law – as the grammar of the international society – remains unpredictable by essence, venturing into new ideas is not prohibited.

Such an opportunity for informed and collective exchanges on the future of international law through the lenses of international courts and tribunals is exactly what the International Law Association Regional Conference organized in September 2019 at the University of Minho (Braga) had to offer. With their variety of topics and diversity of approaches, all the contributions to this volume will hopefully help in assessing the very significant impact which the rising of international justice has had on the development of international law in the last century.

Scholars, lawyers, government officials and, more broadly, practitioners of international law – if they are keen properly to perform their functions – cannot ignore the case-law emanating from universal and regional bodies involved in the judicial (or quasi-judicial) settlement of disputes having an international dimension. Notwithstanding the (growingly fragile) limits of confidentiality, each decision, judgment, opinion is potentially subject to worldwide online dissemination, comment, and appraisal as soon as it is somewhere and somehow issued.

One can easily see the limits and dangers of this bulimic appetite for 'judicial food'. Overwhelmed by the amount of information received on almost an everyday basis, stunned by this deafening court uproar, the candid international lawyer may soon lose the path towards proper understanding, genuine analysis and well-thought assessment of the durable echo which may attach to any judicial pronouncement. As demonstrative as it is of the attractiveness of international courts, the profusion of decisions does not always sustain the secret charms of jurisprudence … If it ever was a pointillist masterpiece, the

© KONINKLIJKE BRILL NV, LEIDEN, 2022 | DOI:10.1163/9789004467668_022

international case-law sketch now resembles a monumental fresco, impressive in dimensions but lacking coherence and internal consistency.

In a famous statement delivered in 2000 within the Sixth Committee of the UN General Assembly, Judge Gilbert Guillaume – then President of the International Court of Justice – emphasized the "unfortunate consequences" associated with the "proliferation of judicial bodies"[1] in the international community, namely the risk of an increased competition in the choice of courts (known as "forum shopping"), and, more worryingly perhaps, the likelihood of conflicting judgments rendered by courts insufficiently constrained by *res judicata*. He went on to suggest two potential solutions: entrusting the ICJ "with the task of acting as a court of appeal or review from judgments rendered by other international courts" or developing mechanisms equivalent to preliminary rulings, by which other tribunals could seek the opinion of the World Court on issues of international law raised before them.

Be it because of the lack of political will or a lost sense of necessity, none of these solutions has materialized in the last twenty years and one may doubt that this may drastically change in the near future. So much for the Kelsenian dream of a pyramidal order! But, as a matter of fact, is it really the case that we have witnessed in the last two decades some form of judicial fragmentation leading to the competitive choices and contradictory decisions foreseen by Judge Guillaume?

In all fairness, 'not really' or, better perhaps, 'not dramatically' would seem to be the most appropriate answer. Of course, one may quite easily find examples of "forum shopping" tactics or, less openly, of instances of competition among international courts and tribunals. It would however be quite adventurous to draw conclusions or identify long-term trends of judicial destabilization on the mere basis of such unfortunate situations.

Practice relating to the Montego Bay Convention provides an interesting illustration of these potential tensions and of their avoidance or resolution, owing to the complex architecture retained in Part XV – based on a balance between the obligation to submit all disputes not otherwise resolved to an international court or tribunal, on the one hand, and the free choice of procedures, on the other. While Article 287 may legitimately be construed as paving the way to intense forum shopping, it has not given rise to some kind of systemic competition between ITLOS, the ICJ and arbitral tribunals. There have been (and will be) instances of tensions and discordance, as famously exemplified

1 https://www.icj-cij.org/public/files/press-releases/1/3001.pdf.

by the *Southern Bluefin Tuna* case;[2] but one may also easily perceive in these judicial interactions moves typical of a gentle *ballet*: in the *Enrica Lexie* case for example, the Hamburg Tribunal quite wisely resisted the temptation to prescribe provisional measures which could potentially affect the proceedings on the merits before the PCA tribunal.[3] In a similar vein, even if contradictory approaches to substantive legal issues may certainly exist, a careful assessment of relevant decisions taken by courts and tribunals in law of the sea disputes would quite likely lead to the conclusion that their views eventually converge in building up a quite consistent body of case-law.[4]

This collaborative – rather than competitive of conflicting – approach is less prompted by a common concern for the constraints of *res judicata*[5] than by a widely-shared understanding of international law as a living normative and institutional system, and not a strict legal order. Even if courts have sometimes exposed their diverging views as a kind of (unfortunate) schoolyard argument,[6] they appear in the long run to prefer the virtues of dialogue and, hopefully, the prospects of mutual enrichment. The absence of a judicial pyramid does not leave international courts and tribunals in a splendid isolation: beyond

2 See the conflicting visions on jurisdiction and the pronouncement of provisional measures by ITLOS (*Southern Bluefin Tuna* (*New Zealand v. Japan; Australia v. Iapan*) case, Order of Provisional Measures, 27 August 1999, *ITLOS Reports 1999*, pp. 294–295, paras. 55 and 62), and the arbitral tribunal (*Southern Bluefin Tuna Case*, sentence of 4 August 2000, *UNRIAA*, vol. XXIII, paras. 63 and 66).

3 See ITLOS, *"Enrica Lexie"* (*Italy v. India*), Provisional Measures, Order of 24 August 2015, *ITLOS Reports 2015*, p. 204, para. 132.

4 See for example, as far as the "three-stage approach" to maritime delimitation is concerned, the *Delimitation of the Maritime Boundary in the Bay of Bengal* (*Bangladesh/Myanmar*) case, Judgment of 14 March 2012, *ITLOS Reports 2012*, pp. 64–68, paras. 226–240.

5 Especially given the restrictive interpretation of *res judicata* retained by the ICJ: as put in its 2016 decision on jurisdiction in the case relating to the *Delimitation of the Continental Shelf between Nicaragua and Colombia*, "[i]t is not sufficient, for the application of *res judicata*, to identify the case at issue, characterized by the same parties, object and legal ground; **it is also necessary to ascertain the content of the decision, the finality of which is to be guaranteed.** The Court cannot be satisfied merely by an identity between requests successively submitted to it by the same parties; it must determine whether and to what extent the first claim has already been definitively settled" (see *Question of the Delimitation of the Continental Shelf between Nicaragua and Colombia beyond 200 Nautical Miles from the Nicaraguan Coast* (*Nicaragua v. Colombia*), *Preliminary Objections*, Judgment of 17 March 2016, *I.C.J. Reports 2016*, p. 100, at p. 126, para. 59 (emphasis added)).

6 See for example the famous divergence between the ICTY and the ICJ on the interpretation of the criterion of "control" as used in Article 8 of the 2001 Articles on the Responsibility of States for Internationally Wrongful Acts (*Application of the Convention on the Prevention and Punishment of the Crime of Genocide* (*Bosnia and Herzegovina v. Serbia and Montenegro*), Judgment of 26 February 2007, *ICJ Reports 2007*, pp. 209–211, paras. 402–407.

the walls of their respective jurisdictions, the men and (still too rarely) women who are performing the difficult function of judging keep notice of the activities of their counterparts and, even indirectly through the use of references in their decisions, 'talk' to each other.[7] This may not satisfy the proponents of an illusionary order by which one court could firmly guide the work done by others. Quite likely, it may even strengthen the image of international case-law as a kaleidoscopic fresco ... But the development of international law will certainly benefit from this constant whispering, as disorderly as it may seem.

While I am conscious that I may disappoint the hopes of the editors who kindly extended to me the invitation to conclude this edited volume, I feel quite unable to guess what the "future of the contribution of international justice to the development of international law" will bring! More modestly, I will merely formulate three wishes, with the hope that they may add a few stones along the path of our collective reflections.

First, one could certainly expect that, based on the firm foundations built in the last century, international courts and tribunals could be entitled to open their doors to new categories of litigants – international organizations, individuals, corporations, representatives of the "civil society", etc. – which still lack proper judicial standing despite their increased influence at the universal level.

Second, one could reasonably hope that, beyond the efforts already made better to define the incompatibilities between an ICJ mandate and the performance of other "extrajudicial activities",[8] international courts and tribunals will persevere in consolidating the bench. In that spirit, making progress in the selection of judges, paying greater attention to diversity concerns and reconsidering the – sensitive – issue of the renewal of mandates would surely help in nurturing a sense of common ownership in international justice.

Third, and finally, one could strongly wish that the international courtroom itself better resemble the world *as we know it*. Here, I can only, and humbly, join President Joan E. Donoghue in the reflections she recently offered on the occasion of the 75th anniversary of the Court:

---

7 For a recent example of such an indirect dialogue, see the question that Judge Tomka directed to both parties to the case concerning *Armed Activities on the Territory of the Congo*, relating "to the weight to be given to the approach adopted by Trial Chamber VI [of the International Criminal Court] in the Ntaganda case in relation to the valuation of the harm suffered" (ICJ, CR 2021/9, 23 April 2021, p. 54).

8 See the Speech by H.E. Mr. Abdulqawi A. Yusuf, President of the International Court of Justice, on the occasion of the Seventy-Third Session of the United Nations General Assembly, 25 October 2018, pp. 11–12, available at https://www.icj-cij.org/public/files/press-releases/0/000-20181025-PRE-02-00-EN.pdf.

> Each time that I gaze out at the delegations representing parties, [...] I am struck that their composition bears too much resemblance to the groups of persons who gathered in 1945 to draft the Charter of the United Nations and the Statute of the Court. Very few of the counsel are from developing countries and almost all, regardless of nationality, are men.
>
> This is an unsatisfactory situation. While there are many aspects of international law on which jurists of all stripes can be expected to agree, we must acknowledge that there is no single, homogenized answer to many legal questions that arise in international disputes. As much as each individual may aspire to a cosmopolitan perspective, we must all have the humility to appreciate that we are shaped by our respective experiences. We must actively seek differing perspectives and promote open exchanges of ideas, especially with those whose views differ from our own.[9]

This, of course, may bring even more apparent disorder in a system used to its habits and its *entre-soi*. But it can arguably be considered as one of the conditions for expanding further the contribution of international courts and tribunals to the development of international rules reaching far beyond the classical realm of inter-state-relations. If international law is truly to become our "common good", international justice must itself develop as an essential instrument in its preservation and further development.

9 Joan E. Donoghue, "Reflections on the 75th Anniversary of the International Court of Justice", 16 April 2021, available at https://www.un.org/en/un-chronicle/reflections-75th-anniversary-international-court-justice.

Index